Recovering Theological Hermeneutics

RECOVERING THEOLOGICAL HERMENEUTICS

An Incarnational-Trinitarian Theory of Interpretation

JENS ZIMMERMANN

Baker Academic
Grand Rapids, Michigan

Published by Baker Academic
a division of Baker Publishing Group
P.O. Box 6287, Grand Rapids, MI 49516-6287
www.bakeracademic.com

Printed in the United States of America

Library of Congress Cataloging-in-Publication Data
Zimmermann, Jens, 1965–
    Recovering theological hermeneutics : an incarnational-trinitarian theory of interpretation / Jens Zimmermann.
        p.   cm.
    Includes bibliographical references and index.
    ISBN 0-8010-2727-6 (cloth)
    1. Philosophical theology. 2. Hermeneutics—Religious aspects—Christianity.
3. Hermeneutics—Religious aspects—Christianity—History of doctrines. I. Title.
BT55.Z56 2004
230′.01—dc22   2004016942

CONTENTS

PREFACE

Hermeneutics is all about self-knowledge, and self-knowledge is impossible without knowledge of God. This, in short, is the main argument of this book, an argument clearly expressed in mainstream Christian theology. Modern hermeneutics, however, has become extremely squeamish about the knowledge of God. The notion of revelation and particular religion are viewed with suspicion, often for good reason. The suggested solution, religious pluralism based on the reduction of religious knowledge to apophasis, to radically negative theology, may seem attractive, given our generally vague and noncommittal cultural attitude toward ultimate meaning, but it suffers from an incurable inconsistency. The reduction of religion to a general and universally incontestable kernel, such as love and compassion, lacks any possible foundation for these values. If we cannot really know what we know when we love our God, to borrow a phrase from a recent book on religion, how can we still know that the character of this unknown divinity is love or compassion?

On a more philosophical level, the debate about religion becomes the debate about otherness. Introduced mainly by the philosophy of Emmanuel Levinas, the latest preoccupation of philosophy is ethical transcendence. I will explain this idea and its well-intended humanist origin in detail in a later chapter, but in terms of hermeneutics, ethical transcendence insists on difference in interpretation to the point of making interpretation impossible. On this view, transcendence so radically resists comprehension as to make meaning altogether impossible because interpretation always entails correlation and sameness, the enemies of difference. For advocates of this radical transcendence, even philosophical hermeneutics, with its insistence on the historicity of our

7

understanding, is not radically transcendent enough because it begins in correlation and strives for integration rather than difference.

The recovery of theological hermeneutics thus offends two current sensibilities. Hermeneutics itself has come to mean philosophical hermeneutics, a discipline arising from the work of Martin Heidegger and brought to prominence by his student Hans-Georg Gadamer. This discipline is explicitly atheistic and draws on the Greek rather than the Judeo-Christian Logos. In this light, the very term "theological hermeneutics" may seem to constitute a contradiction in terms. For philosophical hermeneutics, theology is too positive, too confident, associated with "revelation," absolute timeless truth, and interpretive arrogance. Theology becomes at best a subsidiary discipline to philosophical hermeneutics, which claims to be a universally valid ontology of human understanding.

Theological hermeneutics, however, also offends the prophets of difference, those thinkers who, following Levinas, see even philosophical hermeneutics as bartering too much in sameness. Guided by Socratic wisdom, philosophical hermeneutics claims, after all, that only same can understand same, thus beginning in correlation and sameness rather than in difference. On this account, the label "theological hermeneutics" is a double condemnation.

This book is written to address these concerns and to establish a theological hermeneutics that can maintain both theology and hermeneutics by advancing the claim that, indeed, difference can be recognized and understood by difference. This is possible only because of the doctrine of the incarnation. The central argument of this book is the argument already advanced by the pastor-theologian Dietrich Bonhoeffer (1906–45), who believed that the truth of faith is something we inhabit and that it is given to us from the outside as "revealed and donated truth, Jesus Christ himself." In this case, because God recognizes us and in doing so gives us identity and self-knowledge, the seemingly impossible becomes reality: Contrary to hermeneutic philosophy, self-knowledge depends not on sameness or correlation but on difference. Difference is known in difference ("Ungleiches wird durch Ungleiches erkannt" [AS, 132]). In terms of biblical revelation, this means that God's word does not affect us because it is meaningful, but it is meaningful because it is God's word, the address by the transcendent, wholly other God. And yet it becomes meaningful even though it is so much outside our capacity to understand (ibid., 133). Real transcendence means that we are completely torn away from ourselves and redirected to God. The recovery of theological hermeneutics is the application of this basic principle to the contemporary hermeneutical discussion and thus an attempt to respond to Charles Taylor's challenge that hope for authentic human existence and self-knowledge will come from a God who speaks and is not silent: "There is a large element of hope. It is a hope that I see implicit in Judeo-Christian theism (however terrible the record of its adherents in history), and in its central promise of a divine affirmation of the human, more total than humans can ever attain unaided" (*Sources of the Self*, 521).

Following Taylor's hint requires a theologically motivated account of hermeneutics. Martin Heidegger, the grandfather of philosophical hermeneutics, already taught that any recovery of past traditions is always guided by questions arising from our present concerns. In this sense, as his student Gadamer put it, to understand is always to understand differently. This does not mean, however, that we are relieved of the hard work required to understand the past on its own terms. Both Heidegger and Gadamer insist that our questions concerning our object of understanding should be shaped by the nature of this object in order to prevent reading our own opinions into past traditions. In the case of theological hermeneutics, this crucial hermeneutic principle has been sorely neglected. Accounts of hermeneutic developments given by Wilhelm Dilthey, Gadamer, or the best modern historian of hermeneutics, Jean Grondin, do not really grasp the central importance of the incarnation, the Christ event, for theological hermeneutics and its subsequent secularization. Later hermeneutic approaches that rejected their theological roots are best understood as secularized derivations from theological interpretation rather than something new and radically different.

This book thus accepts the history of hermeneutics as a process of progressive secularization that culminates in postmodern hermeneutics. While one does not have to agree with Gianni Vattimo's thesis that secularization is part of salvation history, every thinking Christian should agree with him that the current postmetaphysical climate is highly conducive to recovering Christian faith for philosophy and public discourse.[1] Only from this perspective is a recovery of theological hermeneutics possible. This book attempts such a recovery in its three divisions. The first part, "Communion with God," counterbalances the deficiency of Grondin's hermeneutical survey by examining the roots of modern hermeneutics to show that premodernist Reformation hermeneutics was as philosophical (in the widest sense of the word) and universal as philosophical hermeneutics. The first chapter begins with the introduction to Calvin's hermeneutical framework, because it is the most systematic foundational manual of Christian belief to shape the succeeding centuries of theological interpretation. Calvin's interpretive framework is

---

1. See Gianni Vattimo, *After Christianity*, trans. Luca D'Isanto (New York: Columbia University Press, 2002), 58–68.

contrasted with modern and postmodern horizons of interpretation to establish the hermeneutical prejudice of this book.

Chapter 2 focuses on the word theology of Martin Luther to demonstrate how closely ontology, ethics, and exegesis are intertwined in premodern hermeneutics. Chapter 3 continues to trace this trend in the hermeneutics of Calvin's and Luther's heirs. The main focus is the period of the seventeenth century, notably the phenomenon of Pietism in England and Germany.

The hermeneutics of Pietism is of special interest for several reasons. First, it exhibits a text-to-action model that is unrivaled in the history of the church except, perhaps, at its beginnings. As a continuation of the Reformation, the Pietist movements involved not, as is often supposed, a quiet, self-absorbed asceticism but rather a vital revival movement of great social impact and eschatological vision. Perhaps never before in Protestantism was textual application practiced so radically as among the English Puritans and the early German Pietists.

Second, a comparison between German Pietism and English Puritanism shows their common conviction that hermeneutics must be relational and universal rather than technical. Third, the practical theology exhibited by the Puritan and Pietist writers yields valid insights for present-day theology and philosophy, as both struggle with the loss of center, values, and tradition so characteristic of our postmodern Western culture.

The occupation with hermeneutic history and development by theorists such as Gadamer and Grondin has set an important precedent by bringing premodern hermeneuts like Illyricus Matthias Flacius and Johann Dannhauer to our attention again. Their accounts lack depth, however, when it comes to the early modern period of hermeneutical history, for they tend to ignore the theological context in which these earlier writers conducted their hermeneutics. Although I do not suggest that the modern reader could or even should adopt a sixteenth- and seventeenth-century worldview, those familiar with contemporary hermeneutical issues will find that the Reformers and their heirs had much to say about the nature of understanding, the nature of truth, the applicatory and ethical dimensions of interpretation, and the universality of hermeneutics.

It would be useful for modern hermeneutics to throw a backward glance at the Puritans and the Pietists to learn why they showed strength in areas where philosophical interpretive theory is weak. To understand and learn from one another through dialogue is, after all, a hallmark of the hermeneutical endeavor. Beside these concrete issues, the close examination of premodern hermeneutical sources from a theological perspective also sheds light on the extent to which later non-Christian hermeneutics still borrows from the older tradition, albeit in a secularized form.

The secularization of premodern hermeneutics is the focus of part 2, "The Silencing of the Word." Chapter 4 describes how the rejection of Pietism (Kant) and the effort to make Christianity palatable to Enlightenment culture (Schleiermacher) occasioned the redefinition of central premodern theological concepts in immanent terms to shelter belief from invasion by scientific principles of truth. Unfortunately this shoring up of religious values occurred at the loss of transcendence and ethics. Instead of raising a universal transcendent norm for meaning and what it means to be human, hermeneutics lost both transcendence and ethics. Moralism and duty ethics took the place of relational ethics. And yet, central elements of the emergent philosophical hermeneutics continue to depend on theological principles. Even in silencing the divine word, hermeneutics depends on the *verbum* for its very life.

Chapter 5 confirms this argument by showing the dependence of Gadamer's philosophical hermeneutics on theological premises. Gadamer's work is presented as the best hermeneutic alternative for our time, whose success, however, depends on theological insights gleaned from premodern hermeneutics. His concept of the inner word and the idea of word event both stem from theological sources that are fundamentally at odds with the Heideggerian ontology that forms the basis of Gadamer's philosophical hermeneutics. The lack of a transcendent ethical foundation in modern philosophical hermeneutics is exposed most clearly by Levinas's critique of Heideggerian ontology.

Chapter 6 relies on Levinas's critical analysis as the clearest call to transcendence in contemporary philosophy. His work, too, depends on theological premises. His "ethics as first philosophy" is inspired by Old Testament ethics, and yet this theological inspiration is assiduously avoided by those who secularize Levinas's work to champion the ethics of deconstruction. Chapter 7 examines this ethics and Jacques Derrida's and John Caputo's challenge to Gadamer's philosophical hermeneutics. I argue that both writers depend on Levinas but avoid his confessional stance and hence end up denying the two hallmarks of theological hermeneutics—self-knowledge and knowledge of God—in favor of transcendence for transcendence's sake. In this chapter, Levinas's critique of hermeneutics culminates in the central question: does understanding require correlation and sameness, and thus sacrifice transcendence, or is there a way to conceive of difference understanding difference?

Part 3, "Recovering Theological Hermeneutics: An Incarnational-Trinitarian Approach," outlines a possible answer to this question. The works of Dietrich Bonhoeffer and Hans Urs von Balthasar provide a transcendent basis for a theological hermeneutics in the incarnation that allows for correlation without compromising transcendence. The main argument of this last section is that in the crucial hermeneutical areas of subjectivity, ethics, self-knowledge, and knowledge of God, a theological hermeneutics offers the best perspective based on an incarnational-Trinitarian foundation.

One last point: recovery means not mere repetition but reappropriation. *Recovering Theological Hermeneutics* does not attempt to return to some previous period of interpretive glory but aims to develop a theological hermeneutics in light of current research. Recovery, however, also means retrieving past hermeneutical traditions in order to let them speak again.

A finished book always represents a concerted effort of many contributors. I am grateful for the assistance of the editorial staff at Baker Academic, particularly Jim Kinney and Brian Bolger, who believed in this undertaking and suggested the present layout of the work. I am also indebted to Dr. Dennis Danielson, whose encouragement and friendship have helped me stay the course and whose comments on the final manuscript have made this a better book. I must also mention my friend and colleague Hans Boersma, whose suggestion to cut large sections of the original manuscript felt heartless at the time but is surely beneficial to the book and its readers.

This book could not have been completed without the financial support of the Social Sciences and Humanities Research Council, nor could I have conducted the necessary research without Dr. Bepler and her staff at the Herzog August Bibliothek in Wolfenbüttel, Germany.

As anyone who has ever written a book will know, more important than funding and research are understanding and support from one's family. I could never have written this book without the selfless support from my wife Sabine. Finally, I will always be indebted to my parents for their support of my academic career, and I gratefully dedicate this book to my father, Dr. Peter Zimmermann, whose friendship and intellectual companionship have enriched my life beyond measure.

ABBREVIATIONS

AGP   *Arbeiten zur Geschichte des Pietismus*, by Kurt Aland, E. Peschke, and M. Schmidt, 20 vols. (Bielefeld, Ger.: Luther Verlag, 1975)

AS   *Akt und Sein*, by Dietrich Bonhoeffer, DBW 2 (München: Chr. Kaiser Verlag, 1988)

AT   *Alterity and Transcendence*, by Emmanuel Levinas (New York: Columbia University Press, 1999)

BW   *The Bondage of the Will*, by Martin Luther, trans. O. R. Johnston and J. I. Packer (Westwood, NJ: Revell, 1957)

CCL   *The Cambridge Companion to Levinas*, ed. Simon Critchley and Robert Bernasconi (Cambridge: Cambridge University Press, 2002)

DBW   Dietrich Bonhoeffer Werke

DSC   *Das schöne Confitemini*, by Martin Luther, Calwer Luther Ausgabe 7 (Stuttgart: Calwer, 1996)

ED   *The Ethics of Deconstruction*, by Simon Critchley (West Lafayette, IN: Purdue University Press, 1999)

EE   *Evangelische Evangelienauslegung: Eine Untersuchung zu Luthers Hermeneutik*, by Gerhard Ebeling, 3rd ed. (Tübingen: Mohr/Siebeck, 1991)

EPS   *Ethics, Politics, Subjectivity*, by Simon Critchley (New York: Verso, 1999)

FWA   *August Hermann Francke: Werke in Auswahl*, ed. Edward Peschke (Berlin: Luther-Verlag, 1969)

GM   *Of God Who Comes to Mind*, by Emmanuel Levinas (Stanford, CA: Stanford University Press, 1998)

GW   *Gesammelte Werke*, by Hans-Georg Gadamer, 10 vols. (Tübingen: Mohr/Siebeck, 1986–)

H   *Hermeneutics: The Handwritten Manuscripts*, by Friedrich Schleiermacher, ed. Heinz Kimmerle, trans. J. Forstman and James Duke (Missoula, MT: Scholars Press, 1977)

HM   *Der Humanismus des anderen Menschen*, by Emmanuel Levinas (Hamburg: Felix Meiner, 1989)

IPH   *Introduction to Philosophical Hermeneutics*, by Jean Grondin (New Haven, CT: Yale University Press, 1991)

KG   *Kommentar zum Galaterbrief*, by Martin Luther, Calwer Luther Ausgabe 10 (Stuttgart: Calwer, 1996)

LW   *Works*, by Martin Luther, American ed. (Saint Louis: Concordia, 1955–86)

MRH   *More Radical Hermeneutics*, by John D. Caputo (Bloomington: Indiana University Press, 2001)

OB   *Otherwise Than Being, or Beyond Essence*, by Emmanuel Levinas (Pittsburgh: Duquesne University Press, 1998)

OS   *Outside the Subject*, by Emmanuel Levinas (Stanford, CA: Stanford University Press, 1993)

PC   *Predigten über die Christusbotschaft*, by Martin Luther, Calwer Luther Ausgabe 5 (Stuttgart: Calwer, 1996)

PH   *Philosophical Hermeneutics*, by Hans-Georg Gadamer, ed. David E. Linge (Berkeley: University of California Press, 1976)

PK   *Predigten über den Weg der Kirche*, by Martin Luther, Calwer Luther Ausgabe 6 (Stuttgart: Calwer, 1996)

PN   *Proper Names*, by Emmanuel Levinas (Stanford, CA: Stanford University Press, 1976)

PWRB   *The Practical Works of Richard Baxter*, by Richard Baxter, 4 vols. (Ligonier, PA: Soli Deo Gloria, 1992)

RB   *Is It Righteous to Be?* by Emmanuel Levinas (Stanford, CA: Stanford University Press, 2001)

SC   *Sanctorum Communio*, by Dietrich Bonhoeffer, DBW 1 (München: Chr. Kaiser Verlag, 1989)

SGW   *Sermon von den guten Werken*, by Martin Luther, Calwer Luther Ausgabe 3 (Stuttgart: Calwer, 1996)

SP   *Speech and Phenomena*, by Jacques Derrida (Evanston, IL: Northwestern University Press, 1973)

SW   *Schleiermachers Werke*, by Friedrich Schleiermacher, ed. Johann Bauer and Otto Braun, 4 vols. (Leipzig: Fritz Eckhardt Verlag, 1910)

SZ   *Sein und Zeit*, by Martin Heidegger (Tübingen: Max Niemeyer, 1993)

TI   *Totality and Infinity*, by Emmanuel Levinas (1969; repr., Pittsburgh: Duquesne University Press, 1998)

TM   *Truth and Method*, by Hans-Georg Gadamer (New York: Continuum, 1994)

UD   *Der ununterbrochene Dialog: Zwischen zwei Unendlichkeiten, das Gedicht*, by Jacques Derrida, trans. Martin Gessmann, Christine Ott, and Felix Wiesler. Manuscript, 2003. Abridged Version in *Neue Zürcher Zeitung* 44 (22 February 2003): 69

VL   *Very Little—Almost Nothing*, by Simon Critchley (New York: Routledge, 1997)

WA   *Luthers Werke: Kritische Gesamtausgabe* (Weimar: H. Böhlau, 1883–)

WJO   *The Works of John Owen*, by John Owen, ed. William Goold, 16 vols. (London: Banner of Truth, 1967)

WM   *Wahrheit und Methode: Grundzüge einer philosophischen Hermeneutik*, by Hans-Georg Gadamer (Tübingen: Mohr/Siebeck, 1990)

WSC   *The Works of Steven Charnock*, by Steven Charnock, 4 vols. (Southampton, UK: Banner of Truth, 1986)

PART I

COMMUNION
WITH GOD

I

INTRODUCTION

Although we possess many survey books on the history of hermeneutics, the so-called precritical tradition, a catchall phrase coined
by Hans Frei[1] for the interpretive practices from the early church to the
Enlightenment, is still not given due credit for its richness and complexity—neither by philosophers nor by evangelical theology. In philosophy
the intellectual snobbery that regards pre-Enlightenment hermeneutics as
inferior to modern and postmodern approaches because of an outdated
worldview greatly influenced and continues to shape the formulation of
interpretive theories. Unfortunately Christian evangelical circles (both
academic and popular) seem equally unfamiliar with the hermeneutical legacy of the Protestant Reformation. That seems the only plausible
explanation for why evangelicals have been very slow to avail themselves
of the rich pre-Enlightenment theological heritage to critique modernity
and have instead vilified postmodern thought in a continuous attempt to
defend a modernist version of Christianity. How did it come to this?

The answer is that very few scholars who write on interpretation theory
today have grasped the nature of hermeneutics before the Enlightenment.
Following the largely unchallenged account of Wilhelm Dilthey and Hans-
Georg Gadamer, the standard version of hermeneutical history argues

1. Frei points to the seventeenth century (Spinoza, Hugo Grotius, Richard Simon) for
the beginning of modernist critical principles but explains that these early ideas did not
flourish until the second half of the eighteenth century with German biblical scholarship
and the school of higher criticism (*Eclipse of Biblical Narrative*, 17).

that the narrowly defined ground of theological hermeneutics prevented it from articulating universal concepts of understanding. Until the advent of Schleiermacher, so the argument goes, the theological theory of interpretation boiled down to a set of rules for understanding the Bible. Thankfully, it is said, modern scholarship has moved beyond such narrowly conceived bounds to admit the broader, fresher, and more dialogical spirit of philosophical hermeneutics, which begins to clear up the stuffy air of theological and, God forbid, puritanical concepts. This account of hermeneutical history offers philosophical hermeneutics as the most universal ontological account of the human interpretive experience.

This book is written to challenge such a view of hermeneutical history. Both theology and philosophy have forgotten that the main goal of interpretation before the Enlightenment was communion with God. In this context, writings on the interpretation of God's self-revelation to humankind explored ontological issues, questions of interpretive horizons, and the nature of the human self. Theological interpretation did indeed formulate rules for biblical interpretation, but it did so in the context of worldview thinking.

It is my contention that a clear delineation of this goal and its consequences for what it means to be human and to coexist in human society will provide the needed context for claims made by philosophical hermeneutics, on the one hand, and expose the limits of fundamentalist or liberal theological hermeneutics, on the other. For both read the history of hermeneutics as one of increasing secularization of a Christian worldview and then present their own hermeneutics as a reaction to this development. Both reactions are inadequate because neither group has a clear grasp of premodern hermeneutics.

Philosophical hermeneutics suffers from the illusion that secularization is a purely positive development because it does away with the premodern universe and allows for an interpretive approach that constructs human finitude, interpretive humility, the role of art, and the nature of understanding without reference to God. The work of the German philosopher Hans-Georg Gadamer (1900–2002) is the best example of this postmodern existential humanism, a term to be understood in its most positive sense, for Gadamer's account of the hermeneutical experience is arguably the best ontological analysis of the interpretive process written in the twentieth century.

The problem is that the claims of philosophical hermeneutics and its account of hermeneutic history as presented by Jean Grondin, a prominent interpreter of Gadamer's philosophical hermeneutics, are valid only if his reading of hermeneutic history is correct. The most commonly accepted version of interpretive history in the humanities divides hermeneutical development from early Greek thought to modern philosophical hermeneutics into premodern,[2] modern, and postmodern phases. I will briefly outline this narrative and then explain the need for some careful revision.

From Aristotle to the Enlightenment, hermeneutics was a rather technical affair, concerned mostly with exegesis to remove textual and contextual difficulties that stood in the way of understanding an otherwise clearly graspable single author's opinion.

Philosophers and theologians alike believed that one could access an author's mind and intention directly via the text. In the late nineteenth and the early twentieth century, historical and literary criticism in literary studies and theology shifted the emphasis from the author's mind to the text's meaning, but the notion of an objective meaning that may be uncovered through rules of interpretation remained largely intact.

According to this view, a major turning point in hermeneutic history occurred with the work of Friedrich Schleiermacher (1768–1834). Influenced by the Romantic philosophers Schlegel and Fichte, as well as by his dislike of the Kantian faith-science divide, Schleiermacher problematized methodical understanding in his attempt to articulate a general, universal hermeneutics. Schleiermacher's biographer, the eminent social historian Wilhelm Dilthey (1833–1911), wanted to apply Schleiermacher's universalizing definition of hermeneutics as the art of understanding to emancipate the human sciences from their subordination to the natural sciences and their methodology. Dilthey's maxim "we explain nature but we understand mental life" captures his attempt to found human sciences on an interpretive psychology whose starting point is the wholeness of a person's life context (*Lebenswelt*) as it is given in his or her experience. Dilthey envisioned the human sciences as a discipline in their own right, for which the triad of life (or experience), understanding, and expression of the human spirit in history, text, and art functions as the foundation. Dilthey thus made the emergence of an inner word into outward expression the basis for historical and literary hermeneutics (*IPH*, 88).

Finally, in the "postmodern phase," authorial and textual authority recede before the reader's privileged position as coproducer or even producer of the text. The more radical postmodern developments not only proclaim the death of the author (Foucault) but also of the reader. As Stanley Fish explains, "The entities that were once seen as competing for the right to constrain interpretation (text, reader, author) are now all seen to be products of interpretation" (*Is There a Text?* 16). Fish's interpretive community is the

---

2. The term "premodern" as used throughout this book refers to pre-Kantian theological hermeneutics. While this term tends to blur the distinctions between medieval Catholic and Reformation theological views on interpretation, it is still preferable to the label "precritical" hermeneutics (a term Hans Frei uses), for Calvin and Luther's hermeneutics show that a naive, ahistorical exegesis was not common practice among earlier, premodern exegetes.

hermeneutical life vest that keeps the reader from drowning in subjectivism. Whether an interpretation counts as normative is now determined by each interpretive community. There seems, however, little room for universal constraints in interpretation. This relativist model cannot account for the ethical stance of attending carefully to a text, which had governed earlier approaches, nor can it ensure that the interpretive community does not become a tyrannical institution that favors one received interpretation to the exclusion of other voices. Radical postmodern interpretation is thus left to struggle hopelessly with the dangers of subjectivism.

In contrast to such interpretive nihilism, the more challenging and promising hermeneutic models are those whose rootedness in theological sources, however remote, resists a facile dismissal of authority and meaning in interpretation and which try to escape the renewed danger of subjectivism. Moving further away from the auxiliary conception of hermeneutics as technical rules of exegesis and application, the German philosopher Martin Heidegger (1889–1976) posited hermeneutics as the very mode of being of human existence. While Heidegger turned from hermeneutics in his later writings, his student Hans-Georg Gadamer continued to develop philosophical hermeneutics, applying it to the interpretation not only of texts but also of art, history, indeed, of human existence itself. Gadamer's work strives to balance the objective-subjective elements of text and reader. Gadamer's idea of fusing horizons allows the text to speak while recognizing the importance of the reader as an involved and biased agent.

Gadamer's contribution to philosophy consists in his tireless advocacy of a truth concept that is commensurate with human experience. He resisted the idolization of mathematical certainty as the only valid way of knowing and upheld the limits of human knowledge and understanding. In the absence of a theological voice with the necessary broad academic appeal, Gadamer preached human finitude, the value of tradition, and the importance of reason. He, more than anyone else in the twentieth century, rejected the apotheosis of the human interpreter by insisting that we are not gods and cannot attain knowledge concerning our existence with the kind of verifiable and objectivist certainty scientific epistemology aspires to. All knowledge, he insisted, is interpretation. No unmediated access to reality is possible.

In its desire to understand the interpretive nature of human existence, philosophical hermeneutics thus shifts the debate from the "what" to the "how" of interpretation in order to recover an appropriate relation of the interpreter to the object of interpretation. Gerald Bruns in his work *Hermeneutics Ancient and Modern* describes the current task and scope of hermeneutics as follows: "Hermeneutics is a tradition of thinking or of philosophical reflection that tries to clarify the concept of understanding. What is it to make sense of anything, whether a poem, a legal text, a human action, a language, an alien culture, or oneself?" (1).

This broad and existential scope of hermeneutics, deriving from the work of Heidegger and Gadamer, may also be expressed in terms of a shift from philology to ontology. Rather than reading texts and other objects as detached entities that are to yield their secrets through the application of scientific method, interpretation takes account of the relationship between text and interpreter. The object to be interpreted, whether it be a text, a work of art, or one's own self, is interpreted in light of its as well as the reader's own ontological embeddedness in history, tradition, and culture. In other words, the subject-object relation between text and interpreter has been put into question. While Gadamer and other advocates of philosophical hermeneutics insist that the text still speaks with its own voice even while the interpreter's objectivism is held in critical abeyance, critics of philosophical hermeneutics such as E. D. Hirsch have argued that the demise of the reader's objectivity condemns interpretation to the quagmire of subjectivism and relativism.

In response Gadamer has correctly insisted that so-called objectivism in interpretation theory is an illegitimate import of scientific method into the humanities. In adopting this criterion, we not only make a category mistake but also invite exactly what we want to avoid, for this objectivism, based on an ahistorical, autonomous, and—most importantly—uncritical concept of the self is much more subjective than the alleged subjectivist position of philosophical hermeneutics (*WM*, 364). Gadamer wants to overcome the subjectivism of modernist interpretation and examine the authority that the object, such as a text or a piece of art, has over the interpreter. We are asked to listen to the text rather than dominate it. Philosophical hermeneutics thus claims to have arrived at an interpretive model that requires respect before the text while recognizing the historically, culturally, and linguistically determined prejudices from which we approach the text and which shape our understanding of it.

Thus far we have examined the generally accepted account of hermeneutical development. Much of this story is undeniably true, but it remains an interpretation of intellectual history based on a misunderstanding of premodern theological hermeneutics. This teleological account of hermeneutic history from its naive, provincial theological beginnings to the universal claim of philosophical hermeneutics suffers from interpretive myopia and requires a larger perspective. The recovery of theological hermeneutics undertaken in this work intends to show that philosophical hermeneutics is not the triumphant arrival of thought at universal interpretive principles after a liberating journey away from the province of theology and religion but is, in fact, a return to interpretation as worldview thinking that pre-Enlightenment theology already possessed to a great measure.

We may not, however, blame this oversight on philosophical hermeneutics alone. After all, Protestant theology itself has aided the secularization
of hermeneutics by reducing earlier hermeneutics to the very caricature
of naive biblicism that secular accounts of hermeneutic history invoke to
establish their claims of superiority and uniqueness. Much of the blame
lies no doubt with the school of higher criticism, or historical-critical
method;[3] this method's modernist conception of the self and its concomitant
Cartesian epistemology measured interpretation by a positivist-scientific
yardstick whose supposed objectivity postmodern criticism has ironically
identified as the height of subjectivism.

Modernist interpretation emphasized historical-critical reading of the
scriptures that modified or denied the Bible's own claim to be divine revelation and largely abandoned the biblical text as a unity. As a result, other
texts gained more importance, and hermeneutics came to be conceived
more broadly, comprising secular literature as well.[4] Historical criticism
is, of course, enormously important for any textual work. The historical-
critical *school*, with its application of scientific method and a positivistic
approach to the biblical text, however, forces texts into the Procrustean
bed of an Enlightenment framework and rationalist standards, lopping
off offending and bothersome textual elements and unenlightened statements with almost Puritan zeal.

Modern fundamentalists who react against this so-called liberal theology
unfortunately proceed from the same assumption as the "enemy," namely,
that a text can have only one normative meaning but many possible ap-
plications, which can never become normative. Premodern interpreters
by contrast possessed superior interpretive concepts, such as progressive
revelation and typology, and were more keenly aware of the multiple layers
of textual meanings. Their view of God's word as a vehicle of typological
exegesis, the idea of *sensus plenior*, and the analogy of faith renders fundamentalist notions of stable, unitary meanings highly problematic.[5] Yet
fundamentalist interpreters cheerfully continue to use modernist principles
in their defense of theology, a highly unhelpful strategy of entrenchment,

3. The term "historical-critical" describes the nineteenth-century school of exegesis
that combined the indispensable grammatico-historical reading with typically modernist
(and often naturalist) interpretation to demythologize the biblical account.

4. The beginnings of this trend can be seen in Spinoza's and Schleiermacher's writings,
but Johann Salomo Semler (1725–91) is usually cited as the father of the historical-critical
school (Harrisville and Sundberg, *The Bible in Modern Culture*, 68).

5. As David S. Dockery has pointed out, adopting E. D. Hirsch's distinction between
meaning and significance bars the reader from according normative status to any meaning beyond the author's original intent; this highly problematic (romantic) ideal of our
ability to enter the original author's mind implicitly denounces the interpretive practices
not only of Augustine and the Reformation tradition but also of Paul's own interpretive
practice. See *Biblical Interpretation Then and Now*, 173.

the zeal of whose practitioners does little to conceal the increasing irrelevance of their effort.

What mitigates this Protestant penchant for self-destruction somewhat is its inherent capacity for self-criticism and renewal. It is often overlooked that the first full-scale attack against modernist interpretive principles in the twentieth century was carried out by Protestant theologians and not, as is commonly supposed, by philosophers. While postmodern critics usually credit Martin Heidegger's hermeneutics of facticity with undermining Cartesian subjectivism, the first open attack against modernist hermeneutics was Karl Barth's *Commentary on Romans*, which first appeared in 1919, seven years prior to Heidegger's work *Sein und Zeit* (1926). Barth's commentary already contains a critique of objectivist interpretation from a theological perspective.

In his preface, Karl Barth (1886–1968) criticizes the historical-critical method of biblical interpretation for its failure to recognize that understanding is not detached from history: "The critical-historical method of biblical research has its validity. It points to the preparation for understanding that is never superfluous. But if I had to choose between it and the old doctrine of inspiration, I would decidedly lay hold of the latter. It has greater, deeper, more important validity, for it points to the actual work of understanding, without which all preparation is useless." After pointing out the central role that the problem of understanding occupied in premodern hermeneutics, Barth also points to the historicity of understanding: "But my whole attention was directed to looking through the historical to the spirit of the Bible, which is the eternal Spirit. . . . The understanding of history is a continuous, increasingly open and urgent discussion between the wisdom of yesterday and the wisdom of tomorrow, which are one and the same" (*Der Römerbrief*, iv).[6] Barth laments the obsession with method and argues that the text needs to be interpreted as authoritative: "Of course, it is my private opinion that practicing the repristination of a classic theological train of thought regarded as 'theology' in the medieval period or during Protestant scholasticism would probably be more instructive than the chaotic business of our faculties today, for whom the concept of an authoritative *object* has become foreign and uncomfortable over against the pervasive normativeness of *method*" (*Theologische Fragen und Antworten*, 74; emphasis in original).

Barth thus opposes a scientific fascination with method in interpretation as well as interpretive arrogance; his reversal of the traditional relation between subject and object, in which the human subject interrogates the textual object and, if he or she masters it, obtains from it the answer is meant as a direct affront to rationalism. Most importantly, however, Barth

---

6. Unless otherwise noted, all translations from the German are mine.

finds the impulse for his criticism in the premodern theologians because they have not lost sight of the subsidiary role of historical research to the greater goal of understanding. Barth learned from Reformation theology the need for an integrative hermeneutical framework that allowed interpretation according to the spirit of the text rather than its meaningless dismantling in a supposed quest for neutrality and objectivity.

Barth's sympathy for pre-Enlightenment hermeneutics is continued not only in biblical theologians such as Gerhard Maier, who has proclaimed the death of the historical-critical method, but also in the work of Reformation scholars such as David Steinmetz and Richard Muller. For example, Steinmetz's essay "The Superiority of Pre-critical Exegesis" attacks modernist presumptions concerning authorial intentions and unitary meaning by showing that the medieval model of a fourfold interpretation is superior. Steinmetz concludes that "the medieval theory of levels of meaning in the biblical text with all its undoubted defects, flourished because it is true, while the modern theory of a single meaning, with all its demonstrable virtues, is false" (37).

Richard Muller agrees and suggests that the label "precritical" is highly misleading in light of the actual exegetical practice of early modern theological hermeneutics, for "medieval and Reformation commentators are just as keen to consider the enduring problems of philology and context. *Where the two groups part company is not over critical method but over critical presuppositions, indeed, over the matter of who constitutes the community of interpretation and what comprises its ethos*" (*Post-Reformation Reformed Dogmatics*, 3:337; emphasis mine). Muller puts his finger on the crucial issues: critical presuppositions and their resulting ethos. Pre-Enlightenment hermeneutics was all about presuppositions, about psychological and philosophical anthropology, the nature of reality, and ontology. All these interests converged in the one overarching interest of what it means to be human. The Westminster divines summed up the entire striving of the Reformation period in the first question of their catechism: "What is the chief and highest end of man? To glorify God and fully to enjoy him for ever" (*Westminster Confession*, 129). Full humanity meant to glorify God *by* enjoying communion with him, a communion that would then shape participation in the community. Communion with God is the key to pre-Enlightenment hermeneutics, and it is this concern with the divine-human fellowship that contradicts common views of Reformation hermeneutics as technical or less universal than modern approaches.

To return to our argument: the present recovery of theological hermeneutics shows that the interpretive model of the Enlightenment with its emphasis on the author's intention, an uninvolved reader, and detached, objective truth is sandwiched between early modern hermeneutics and postmodern hermeneutics because *both* differ from the Enlightenment in their insistence on the integral role of one's prejudices, beliefs, and historical horizons in interpretation. In this sense, hermeneutical history has come full circle by emphasizing again the foundational issues of understanding, the role of reason, of our finitude, and of our ethical stance toward the text.

While theology rode the first attack against modernist interpretation, it does not seem to have won the war. The current hermeneutical scene is dominated not by theological hermeneutics but by Gadamer's systematic exposition of philosophical hermeneutics and its application in the humanities. Yet most questions regarding interpretation, the reader's role, and even the importance of language for interpretation were originally raised in a *theological* context, namely, in the context of God's creative word. As John Milbank has pointed out, for example, the linguistic turn in philosophy had theological rather than philosophical origins.[7] Recent work on Heidegger's influences by Theodore Kisiel and John van Buren corroborate Milbank's argument of theological influence on the development of postmodern philosophical trends by showing that Heidegger was heavily influenced by Paul, Augustine, Luther, and Kierkegaard.

Moreover, Hans-Georg Gadamer, student of Heidegger and eyewitness to the revolutionary impact of his teaching, insists on theological influences as responsible for the departure from positivism and neo-Kantian philosophy, which had hitherto shaped academic life. According to his description, under the influence of Kierkegaard, Dostoyevsky, and the lasting impression of the First World War, philosophy and theology alike turned from a self-assured and rather abstract positivistic objectivism to an existential inventory of its assumptions. Heidegger himself began his investigations from a theological perspective. In fact, Heidegger's original draft of *Sein und Zeit* was a lecture for the Marburg society of theology in 1924 (*GW*, 3:197). Gadamer tells us that from the beginning, Heidegger was driven by the problem of language and by theological questions (ibid., 3:199)[8] and that Gadamer himself was influenced by the cross-fertilization of theology and philosophy in the 1920s and 1930s (ibid.).

It is no surprise, then, that in his work, as in that of his teacher Heidegger, theological insights coexist in uneasy tension with Greek conceptuality and moral philosophy. A close reading of his work will show that while Gadamer explicitly rejects a theological framework of interpretation, his

7. John Milbank argues persuasively that Christian thinkers (such as Vico, Hamann, Herder, and Berkeley) first introduced a modern linguistic turn into Western thought and that "the postmodern embracing of a radical linguisticality, far from being a problem for traditional Christianity, has always been secretly promoted by it" (*Word Made Strange*, 85).

8. "Und es waren theologische Fragen, die von Anfang an in ihm [Heidegger] drängten."

notion of self-understanding set forth in *Truth and Method* clearly borrows from theology. Likewise, his justification of the word-object connection in the development of his language philosophy draws heavily on the theological explanation of the *verbum* doctrine of Augustine, Thomas Aquinas, and Nicolaus Cusanus (*TM*, 418–38).

The debt Heidegger and Gadamer owe to theological impulses is significant. Otto Pöggeler, Gadamer himself, Thomas Sheehan, Theodore Kisiel, and John van Buren have already traced the most important theological influences in Heidegger's work. And while Gadamer's own relation to theology remains largely unexplored, the scope of such an undertaking goes beyond the focus of this book and must remain a project for the future. Heidegger's and Gadamer's indebtedness to theology reminds one, however, that current Continental philosophy in general and philosophical hermeneutics in particular arose in dialogue with theology and draw important insights from this conversation.

Given this indebtedness, it is surprising that current accounts of hermeneutics make very little effort to understand the motivations of their theological heritage. The current version of hermeneutical history, as told by Gadamer and Grondin, fails to acknowledge the depth and richness of prephilosophical theological hermeneutics because it no longer recognizes its ultimate concerns. Only ignorance of pre-Enlightenment hermeneutics in general and Reformation hermeneutics in particular can give rise to "the idea that early hermeneutics resembled a technical theory, and as a rule such theory was of much less universal application than present-day philosophical hermeneutics" (*IPH*, 3).

The important theological influence and the controversial claim that prephilosophical hermeneutics, and particularly premodern theological hermeneutics, were less universal in application demand a fresh look at theological hermeneutics prior to and just after the so-called Enlightenment. Thus part 1 of *Recovering Theological Hermeneutics* readmits a group of thinkers into the hermeneutical discussion who have been unduly neglected in the accounts of hermeneutical theory so far. Such neglect is not surprising, since these accounts are written mostly by philosophers, whereas the neglected group consists of theologians. Not only are these thinkers theologians; they also belong to the sixteenth and seventeenth centuries, a further liability since the insights of this period are often viewed as antiquated and outmoded. Yet it is this very tradition from which philosophical hermeneutics eventually emerges.

If the eminent historian and theoretician of hermeneutics Hans-Georg Gadamer is correct in claiming that we need to understand the past in order to understand our own tradition (*TM*, 293), a recovery of Reformation hermeneutics in light of present concerns is crucial. However, neither Gadamer nor Jean Grondin, his interpreter and fellow proponent of philosophical hermeneutics, seems to acknowledge that the theologians of the sixteenth and seventeenth centuries thought a great deal about ontological problems in interpretation and wrestled with the problem of understanding. Although some of the questions raised by post-Kantian hermeneutics did not explicitly occur to the theologians of the sixteenth and seventeenth centuries, their hermeneutical framework sheds light on problem areas of current hermeneutical theory.

But is not a recovery of premodern hermeneutics completely irrelevant in light of the official end of metaphysics so loudly proclaimed by Friedrich Nietzsche, Martin Heidegger, and Jacques Derrida? This question is central to this book because any attempt at articulating a Christian theory of interpretation is conducted within its own temporal horizon and must engage rather than avoid philosophical claims concerning our human condition.

The end of metaphysics, however, does not prohibit the recovery of theological hermeneutics but rather assists it. For one, the concept of the "end of metaphysics" is often misunderstood. What Heidegger (who takes this term from Nietzsche) actually meant and what Derrida also describes with this term is the never-ending process of overcoming (i.e., Heidegger's notion of *Verwinden*) metaphysical ideals and language. Heidegger means not that we have left metaphysics behind, but merely that with Nietzsche all possible variations of metaphysical possibilities have been reached (*Nietzsche II*, 78).[9] Since Western language and ideas depend on a long metaphysical tradition, we cannot just command metaphysics to end but can only argue against it from within this tradition.

Second, much depends on how we define metaphysics. If the term stands for the modern idols of autonomous human reason, its demise may well be a good thing. In light of twentieth-century philosophy, the recovery of a Christian interpretation theory should also address the question of the relation between Christianity and metaphysics. In other words, is Christianity a metaphysics? As we will see, for a theologian concerned with the God of the Bible, the death of the abstract and impersonal constructs that pass as gods in philosophy (or so-called onto-theology) is certainly no loss.

If metaphysics is defined as transcendence, however, as that which truly and radically lies outside ourselves and cannot be mastered by human understanding, then one should defend it because metaphysics as transcendence is crucial for a healthy notion of the human self and for human interaction, that is, for ethics. It is with this in mind that recent

---

9. Heidegger defines the end of metaphysics as "the historical moment in which the essential possibilities of metaphysics [*Wesensmöglichkeiten*] are exhausted." In this climate the past variations of metaphysical constructs have merely "the economic role of providing building material for the reconstruction of the world of knowledge."

post-postmodern thought draws on deeply metaphysical thinkers such as Emmanuel Levinas, for example, to renew discussion about ethical demands for human society. Levinas's work calls hermeneutics back to radical transcendence and clears the ground for the recovery of theological hermeneutics based on ethics as transcendence. We will see how his call to ethics dovetails and yet contrasts with the work of Dietrich Bonhoeffer. Levinas and Bonhoeffer are united in their call for radical transcendence but differ on its origin and meaning.

Finally, recovering theological hermeneutics requires an adequate engagement with postmodern thought. It is imperative for the articulation of a theological hermeneutics for our time to reject any simplistic (and often paranoid) images of postmodernism as the enemy. After all, most intellectual disciplines are leaving postmodernity behind for more constructive projects that nonetheless utilize important insights from postmodern thinkers. Now in the receding wake of postmodernity, we can clearly perceive that postmodern criticism of modernity allows a fresh look at religious traditions: beginning with Nietzsche, postmodern thinkers have relentlessly unmasked the Enlightenment hypocrisy of undermining and rejecting the source of Christian values while enjoying their benefits, such as the notions of human dignity, social welfare, self-sacrificial love, and human rights. Unfortunately, however, postmodern thinkers often enough mistakenly equate theological hermeneutics with Enlightenment concepts of self, reason, and truth in order to summarily dismiss it as another version of onto-theology or logocentrism.

My reading of theological sources argues that theological hermeneutics at its best has always been based on a relationship to the Divine, a "walking and conversing with God," as the Puritans called it. Whenever it has retained this relational emphasis, theological hermeneutics has avoided the pitfalls of rationalism or idealism. As David Lyle Jeffrey has pointed out, the crucial difference between Hellenistic philosophy and biblical thought is the incarnation of the divine Word (*People of the Book*, 57). God's self-revelation, the becoming flesh of the same divine Word that created reality, gives theological hermeneutics its unique relational character. The embodied theology of the incarnation disallows abstract propositionalism and hence detached moralism.

In other words, the goal of theological hermeneutics was from the beginning practical and existential guidance to a meaningful life. Jesus's invitation to his disciples of fulfilling the Torah was not, "as a hellenized reader might expect, to some pacific state of enlightened self-consciousness, but rather to self-denial, self-sacrificing imitation of his own so starkly mortal praxis: 'take up your cross and follow me'" (Jeffrey, *People of the Book*, 57). Social activism was thus grounded not in propositional dogma but in Jesus's personal example of universal and, indeed, cosmic, significance. As the chapter on Luther and the other theologians will show, premodern interpretation at its best remained faithful to the Hebraic concept of dialoguing with the Divine through the text. Premodern theological hermeneutics stressed human historicity and finitude long before Heidegger's existential analytic of *Dasein*. The analysis of the theological treatises in this book aims to show that the detailed doctrines about humans, God, and history were essential to interpretation of texts and of human life.

Premodern hermeneutics recognized clearly that self-understanding requires a careful balance of self-knowledge with a transcendent source of knowledge. Without one eye on the interpreter's human nature and another on the transcendent structures that make interpretation possible, genuine reciprocity in interpretation soon collapses into subjectivism, no matter how much we insist on reason as a universal measure for truth. Ultimately, hermeneutic presuppositions boil down to two main interpretive frameworks. A good understanding of this division allows a clearer view of the current hermeneutical landscape.

The Two Frameworks: Calvin's Revelatory Hermeneutics and the Silent Universe of Modern Philosophy

Consequently we know the most perfect way of seeking God, and the most suitable order, is not for us to attempt with bold curiosity to penetrate to the investigation of his essence, which we ought more to adore than meticulously to search out, but for us to contemplate him in his works whereby he renders himself clear and familiar to us, and in some manner communicates himself. . . . The invisible deity is made manifest in such spectacles, but . . . we have not the eyes to see this unless they be illumined by the inner revelation of God through faith. (Calvin, *Institutes*, 1.5.9)[10]

At one moment we understand our situation as one of high tragedy, alone in a silent universe without intrinsic meaning, condemned to create value. But at a later moment, the same doctrine, by its own inherent bent, yields a flattened world, in which there aren't very meaningful choices because there aren't any crucial issues. (Taylor, *Malaise of Modernity*, 68)

These two quotations show the two basic presuppositions for the enterprise of hermeneutics: transcendence or immanence. We will deal with this problem in greater philosophical depth in later chapters. The present section seeks to recover the transcendence of premodern theological hermeneutics as expressed in its revelatory framework in stark contrast

10. See also *Institutes*, 1.5.1.

to the "silent" (nontranscendent) universe of modern philosophy. The older, pre-Enlightenment framework is represented by John Calvin, rather than Luther, because Calvin systematically laid out a hermeneutical circle of self-knowledge. Because of their systematic nature, Calvin's writings, besides the Bible itself, constitute the most powerful formative force of Reformed and Puritan theology. Calvin's interpretation of human existence was tied to two basic "texts," consisting of the "book" of nature and the supranatural[11] revelation of the scriptures. Both of these sources gave the reader access to knowledge about the divine without which true knowledge concerning human existence was impossible.

John Calvin begins his *Institutes* with the famous epistemological remark that the knowledge of God and that of ourselves are inseparably connected: "Without knowledge of the self there is no knowledge of God . . . [and] without knowledge of God there is no knowledge of self" (1.1.1–2).[12] By knowledge Calvin means not scientific, empirical knowledge but something that comes closer, in modern parlance, to "existential apprehension." According to Calvin, we cannot understand ourselves and the human situation without reference to the divine Other. This is the basic hermeneutic circle of the theological tradition under discussion. Understanding of existence grows out of this circle, whose two halves are inseparably intertwined: "But while joined by many bonds, which [knowledge] precedes and brings forth the other is not easy to discern" (ibid.).

The central concept that links Calvin's natural and revealed theology with his ontology, soteriology, and ethics is his formulation of *imago Dei*. Calvin employs this term in both a wider and a narrower sense. In its wider sense, God's image is reflected in his entire creation. Hence knowledge of God begins for Calvin with the observation of nature. Calvin argues that even a brief glance at the universe and its creatures demonstrates that the universe must have a designer. This notion is the entrance point, the whole, of the circle according to which the parts, the particulars of human existence and the divine nature, must be understood. Calvin even sees this hermeneutical circle reflected in the organization of the Bible, for "the intention of Moses, in beginning [Genesis] with the creation of the world, is to render God, as it were, visible to us in his works" (*Commentaries on the First Book of Moses*, 58). But natural revelation can only serve

11. The term "supranatural" conveys the sense of "additional to" or "going beyond" natural revelation rather than the irrational qualities commonly associated with the term "supernatural."

12. As John T. McNeill, the editor of Calvin's *Institutes* in the Library of Christian Classics edition, points out, this hermeneutical circle is not original with Calvin but is mentioned in Augustine and Thomas Aquinas (36n3). Augustine in his *Soliloquies* 1.2.7 states: "I desire to know God and the soul. Nothing more? Nothing whatever"; in 2.2.1, Augustine prays: "Let me know myself, let me know you."

as an insufficient source of knowledge about God because even though the "divine wisdom" is "displayed for all to see" (*Institutes*, 1.5.2), human interpretive ability not only suffers from natural creaturely limitations but also is severely damaged by the effects of sin. Thus the Word of God is the better and more exact source of revelation, through which "God bestows the actual knowledge of himself upon us" (ibid., 1.6.1).

Calvin also emphasizes the practical and relational nature of knowledge derived from the observation of nature. As awesome and wondrous as nature in its intricate workings and interrelated systems may be, its ultimate purpose is to inspire curiosity for a relationship with nature's designer. God's power is reflected in nature so that we may "contemplate by what means the Lord shows in us his life, wisdom, and power, and exercises in our behalf his righteousness, goodness and mercy" (*Institutes*, 1.5.10).

Calvin argues that, on the one hand, God's fingerprints on nature are congenial to the independent nature of human inquisitiveness. Greek political philosophy, for instance, wrongly suggested that each person should slavishly adopt the religion customary in his own *polis* that was passed on by tradition. Besides the problem that a humanly conceived and tribally limited religion hardly constitutes a trustworthy authority on the issue of religion since it "far surpasses the world," Calvin thinks that tribal cults passed on by tradition can never satisfy an independent mind. "Who would acquiesce," Calvin asks, "in decrees of his ancestors, or enactments of the people, as to receive without hesitation a god humanly taught him?" It is a common human characteristic, Calvin thinks, to "stand upon [one's] own judgment rather than subject [oneself] to another's decision" (*Institutes*, 1.6.13). Thus tradition alone cannot be an adequate guide to religion—"it remains for God himself to give witness of himself from heaven" (ibid., 1.6.14).

Yet, on the other hand, the problem with this independent judgment in religious matters lies in the spiritual "dullness," the postlapsarian cancer of sin that has infected every human being and prevents a proper existential knowledge of God. Every sublime moment in which we are struck by the wonder of God's creation is vitiated by "the fact that men soon corrupt the seed of the knowledge of God, sown in their minds out of the wonderful workmanship of nature" (*Institutes*, 1.6.14). Although Calvin often uses the term "sin" to refer to the direct violation of God's commandments, these actions are merely the consequence of humanity's being in a sinful (i.e., fallen) state. In other words, Calvin uses "sin" primarily to describe humanity's deviation from its original purpose of reflecting God's glory and communing with him. Calvin's conception of sin is thus not so much moralistic as ontological. Despite all our natural capabilities, humanity's loss of spiritual wholeness through its separation from God constitutes nothing less than the loss of our true being, of our true humanity. Calvin shares with Augustine and Luther the conviction, one that sets them apart from other theological orientations within the Christian paradigm, that human beings are spiritually dead to true spiritual life—not sick, but dead so that "until we are renewed by the gospel and by the faith that proceeds from it, we are but as dead men. There is not one drop of life in us that deserves the name of life . . . we are as if buried in the grave" (*Sermons on Ephesians*, 129).

According to Calvin, humanity's loss of spirituality results in the hermeneutic inability to "read" human existence correctly. Among philosophers and theologians, this blindness commonly produces two extremes. Philosophers who indulge in the exposition of natural phenomena without giving consideration to the designer of nature are "so occupied in the investigation of the secrets of nature, as never to turn the eyes to its creator." The second extreme position is taken by philosopher-theologians who seem to have forgotten their finitude and limited perspective on divine matters. These metaphysicians "proudly soar above the world to seek God in his unveiled essence" (*Commentaries on the First Book of Moses*, 60).

While the first group separates God from nature, the second group not only foolishly attempts to explore God's essence (something Calvin rejects as not revealed to human beings) but also does so without considering the book of nature as an index to God's attributes. These philosophers miss the fact that "God—by other means invisible—(as we have already said) clothes himself, so to speak with the image of the world, in which he would present himself to our contemplation" (*Commentaries on the First Book of Moses*, 60). Because of our spiritual "dullness," however, the book of nature is insufficient to direct us to a relationship with God. Sin, defined as ontological deficiency, blurs our reading of God's natural revelation, an interpretive myopia that requires corrective lenses in the form of God's written word, "for by the Scripture as our guide and teacher, he not only makes those things plain which would otherwise escape our notice, but almost compels us to behold them; as if he had assisted our dull sight with spectacles" (ibid., 62).

Calvin expresses what it means to be truly human in terms of the *imago Dei*. The main trope that helps Calvin to connect the various manifestations of God to humanity is that of the mirror (Torrance, *Calvin's Doctrine*, 36). Just as nature mirrors God's divine nature and eternal power, humans, as part of that creation, also reflect the image of God. Indeed, our constant exposure to fellow humans as witnesses to God's presence obviates any appeal to ignorance. For human beings reflect the *imago Dei* in a double sense. First is the wider, which includes anything in the universe created by God, and in this sense Calvin attributes the term *imago Dei* even to the physical person insofar as the wonders of the human body bear witness to God's grace (*Institutes*, 2.12.7; 3.20.31). Even mute or deaf people still declare God's existence (ibid., 1.6.15), even in disabled bodies rays of God's glory can be seen in human beings' natural gifts and faculties (ibid., 1.15.3–4).

This wider sense of God's image in creation, however, is grounded on the special relation of the human creature to the Word of God, which constitutes the narrower sense of *imago Dei* (Torrance, *Calvin's Doctrine*, 42). Calvin writes: "Though the divine glory is displayed in man's outward appearance, it cannot be doubted that the proper seat of the image is the soul. . . . Let it be understood that the image of God which is beheld or made conspicuous by these external marks is *spiritual*" (*Institutes*, 1.15.3). Calvin argues that human beings were made for communion with God and for each other. T. F. Torrance summarizes Calvin's teaching on the subject:

> [The human being] was created an intelligent being capable of response to and communication with God, and created such that his true life depends on the maintenance of that communication. At the same time such a creation meant that [human beings] are made for intercourse with one another. . . . To this end all [human beings] are bound together by the sacred bond of the imago dei, and must treat each other in a mutual society only as in the image of God. (*Calvin's Doctrine*, 45)

The centrality of the *imago Dei* in Calvin's work reveals the restorative role of interpretation. The whole purpose of reading scripture is the restoration of our humanity to the fullness of the image of God in us as individuals and in society as a whole. Ideally the human community should reflect the harmonious coexistence of the Trinity. When our relationship with God is broken, however, as happened in the Fall, we also become alienated from one another, and the world is thrown into confusion (*Commentaries on the First Book of Moses*, 147). Hence social interaction and justice are also founded on the image of God. Calvin argues, for example, that murder is such a heinous crime because violating those made in his image violates God himself (ibid., 295).[13] Calvin thus grounds human dignity in the fact that human beings are made in the image of God. Even the shattered image commands such respect, especially since it reminds us of our true humanity as designed for communion with God toward the restoration of which Jesus has paid the price of redemption (ibid., 296). Calvin's use of

---

13. "Men are indeed unworthy of God's care, if respect be had only to themselves; but since they bear the image of God engraven on them, He deems himself violated in their persons. . . . This doctrine is to be carefully observed that no one can be injurious to his brother without wounding God himself. Were this doctrine deeply fixed in our minds, we should be much more reluctant than we are to inflict injuries" (*Commentaries on the First Book of Moses*, 296).

the *imago Dei* is an important link to the Jewish philosopher Emmanuel Levinas. As we will see in a later chapter, like Calvin, Levinas desires the separation of human dignity from morality to ensure an irreducible human dignity independent of any particular moral code.

Calvin's use of the *imago Dei* in its narrower sense, that is, humans created for communion with God, is closely linked to the Word of God. What, however, does Calvin intend by this general term? Word of God, for Calvin, is not limited to the Bible and its written letters. It would be "the height of absurdity," he argues, to identify God's word with a written utterance. Rather, he contends, "Word means the everlasting Wisdom, residing with God, from which both all oracles and all prophecies go forth" (*Institutes*, 1.13.7). This primordial wisdom, the same word through which the world was created and is still upheld, became manifest in the incarnation (ibid.). It is in the historical figure of Jesus that God's word has become flesh and his image is reflected most purely. The divine Word spoken as and through Jesus the Christ is God's restorative word to humanity. God's Word, in this sense, then, attests to God's faithfulness and the trustworthiness of his promise to reestablish communion with fallen humanity. Those who believe in the incarnated Word are restored to true humanity through communion with God. Thus like Luther, Calvin defines religion as personal relation with and allegiance to God. Although Calvin emphasizes obedience to divine authority, he does so in terms of a filial relation with the Creator, and his writings are full of intimate terms that describe God as "dear friend" and "loving father."

Equally important, however, is Calvin's insistence on the *imago Dei*'s significance for social justice. Unquestionably Calvin's social theory, derived from his understanding that human dignity consists in the image of God, an image for whose restoration God sacrificed the incarnated Word, is weighted toward love and justice. Moreover, in contrast to modern individualism, Calvin's Trinitarian theology stresses the importance of community. It is, however, precisely Calvin's emphasis on love and justice that seems to sully the applicatory dimension of his hermeneutics.

Theoretically, Calvin's hermeneutics may sound very good, but the true value of any theory lies in its implementation. Did Calvin manage to implement the insights gained from the biblical text, and did he manage to change, even if just in Geneva, the social landscape of early modern Europe, where social injustice and harsh treatment of the poor and the sick were commonplace? The main problem in answering this question lies in the difficulty of obtaining a balanced account of Calvin's social impact. Max Weber has enshrined Calvin and Calvinism as the foundation of modern-day capitalism, and Stefan Zweig has depicted Calvin as the grand inquisitor who brought the inquisition to the Reformation to satisfy his "tyrannical nature." Although the burning of Miguel Servetus remains a lamentable and shameful part of Calvin's legacy, Zweig's novelistic imagination clearly gets the better of his judgment as a historian when he writes that Calvin's Geneva sends "theologians equipped with excellent theological armour as agitators and disseminators of Calvin's teaching into the world according to an exactly calculated battle plan. For Calvin [had] long given up on limiting his power and ideas to this small Swiss town; across countries and oceans [extended] his untamable will to rule in order to subdue all of Europe, in fact the whole world, to his totalitarian system" (*Castello gegen Calvin*, 221).

It is certainly true that Calvin sacrificed the individual's rights and privacy for the sake of a community he wished to be shaped in accordance with biblical principles of justice and religion. Fred Graham observes that "Calvin's instincts were for the good of the public, but too often the good of the individual—which must be protected if in the long run the public is to benefit—was not protected. If anything, Calvin himself was harder on the wrongdoer than others in the Genevan community" (*Constructive Revolutionary*, 168). Calvin and the Geneva Council also suffered from a tendency to overlegislate, a weakness that was common in medieval society and still exists in modern democratic states. Calvin's Geneva may also serve as a warning that any professed Christian institution must be safeguarded against overzealous community members by a solid understanding of the power relation between the secular and the sacred, the church and the state.

Calvin's failure to improve the traditional legal and punitive systems, however, is balanced by his stance against economic exploitation, his introduction of socialized medicine (doctors and nurses worked in hospitals at the state's expense), and his concern for the poor and refugees; these implementations show a charitable side of Calvin that is neglected in Weber's and Zweig's accounts. Even in William Bouwsma's recent sympathetic biography, which stresses Calvin's emphasis on community and his theological rationale for respecting the poor, the section dealing with Calvin's social programs fails to mention his important social improvements in medical care and education (*John Calvin*, 191ff.).

The reason for choosing Calvin as a representative of Reformation hermeneutics is his conception of self-knowledge as consisting of both a knowledge of self and a knowledge of God. In all his writings, Calvin stresses self-knowledge but does so always in the context of divine transcendence. Modern hermeneutics also stresses self-knowledge, but in a context bereft of the divine. Self-knowledge is clearly the key element of philosophical hermeneutics, for Gadamer writes that "in the final analysis, all understanding is self-understanding" (*PH*, 55). The main difference between Gadamer and Calvin, however, is the nature of transcendence. Both know the danger of subjectivism: self-knowledge requires transcendence to prevent subjective navel gazing. The real question is whether philosophical hermeneutics can offer the radical exteriority necessary to lift the self beyond its own horizon.

The Silent Universe

The second main interpretative framework in current hermeneutics is atheism, agnosticism, or immanence as represented by the quotation from Charles Taylor cited at the beginning of the preceding section. While philosophical hermeneutics understands itself as a critique of modernity, it nonetheless shares its fundamental rejection of positive religion. In contrast to the theological presuppositions I have just described, the "silent universe" of current philosophy and hermeneutical theory is a universe without the divine. It is silent because there is no referent outside the finite human horizon. Belief in a created world has been replaced by the silent universe of naturalism. Although spirituality is again on the rise in Western culture, much postmodern philosophical thought is still dominated by a naturalistic paradigm that shapes current views on interpretation. Not all modern thinkers work consistently from this position. Gadamer's humanism, for example, makes him naturally distrustful of scientific naturalism with its denigration of human rationality and aesthetics; at the same time, however, he does not explicitly reveal his cosmological beliefs.

Richard Rorty, by contrast, proclaims with typical frankness that "[p]ragmatism starts out from Darwinian naturalism—from a picture of human beings as chance products of evolution. . . . Naturalists have no use for what Derrida calls 'a full presence which is beyond play', and they distrust, as much as he does, the various God-surrogates which have been proposed for the role of such a full presence" ("Remarks on Deconstruction and Pragmatism," 15–16). There is, of course, something positive in Rorty's insistence on eliminating Platonist idealism and other God surrogates from our thoughts. That way, at least, philosophical discourse becomes strictly immanent and can no longer borrow from theology. Despite several attempts in theological history to combine onto-theological metaphysical constructs with the relational biblical concept of truth and right living, the divine Word and Greek philosophical abstractions do not mix well.

On the other hand, however, Rorty's insistence on a naturalist universe without the divine leaves the creation of ultimate meaning in the hands of human beings alone. Despite Rorty's admirable enthusiasm for achieving human solidarity in the absence of transcendence, this "silencing of the word" through the increasing secularization of theological hermeneutics destroys ultimate meaning and so eviscerates any ethical guidelines of real power to direct our moral impulses. We end up losing transcendent norms for human dignity and hermeneutical guidelines for ensuring their implementation.

Current philosophical hermeneutics is keenly aware of having lost, to a great degree, moral vocabulary and moral confidence. For example, in his *Malaise of Modernity*, Charles Taylor laments the loss of horizons of significance, his term for value structures that lend purpose to human life, which have disappeared with the divine word. He elaborates in *Sources of the Self* that in the disenchanted universe of modern philosophy, modern humanist views, those views that also inform philosophical hermeneutics,[14] "no longer have anything like a constitutive good external to man" (93). Yet modern social reform and liberation movements have, in many cases, drawn on biblical sources, even those movements that claim to have rejected the theological outlook that the original story proclaimed (ibid., 96). It is simply a fact, Taylor asserts, that even "where the theology is lost, the story marches on . . . even though one might be puzzled if asked to state what underlying doctrine about humans, God, or history one relies on to make sense of this" (ibid.). This renewed emphasis on ethics is shared by Gadamer. Gadamer even states that hermeneutics must be tied to practice in order to be true to itself (*TM*, 312). Accordingly Gadamer's later writings develop the practical aspect of his philosophical hermeneutics based on Aristotelian ethics and the notion of phronesis.

The silencing of the divine word radically changes our understanding of self-knowledge. Whereas premodern interpreters needed knowledge of the divine and a relation with it to understand existence, philosophical hermeneutics operates, according to Gadamer, "unsupported by revelation" ("On the Origins of Philosophical Hermeneutics," 183). Thus self-knowledge can be gained only from the flow and contingency of human insights and history. There is no question that self-knowledge is hermeneutical. Gadamer and theological hermeneutics quite agree on that. What is highly debatable, however, is the modern contention that knowledge as interpretation necessarily precludes divine revelation. Taylor identifies diverging views of subjectivity as the key difference between the two frameworks: "The modern subject is self-defining, where on previous views the subject is defined in relation to a cosmic order" (*Hegel*, 6). Taylor correctly defines Descartes's rationalism as the pivotal moment of this paradigm shift. With Descartes the human self becomes the measure of reliable knowledge.

Christian readers of hermeneutical history must be cautious, however, in equating postmodern hermeneutics with Enlightenment humanism. There is, as it were, a subdivision within the silent-universe camp. While

14. See Jean Grondin's article "Gadamer on Humanism," in *Sources of Hermeneutics*, 111ff.

current hermeneutics shares modernity's unbelief, it tries hard to break with its idealist heritage. Again, Charles Taylor has articulated this difference with typical clarity and warns modern hermeneutics against chronological snobbery.

Since secular humanism regards the move away from the relevance of theology for the interpretation of human existence as a process of emancipation from childhood to maturity, the grown-up child all too easily shows disregard for her (theological) parent. Taylor explains that

> understanding the world in categories of meaning, as existing to embody or express an order of Ideas or archetypes, as manifesting the rhythm of divine life, or the foundational acts of the gods, or the will of God; seeing the world as a text, or the universe as a book (a notion which Galileo still makes use of)—this kind of interpretive vision of things which in one form or another played such an important role in many pre-modern societies—may appear to us as the paradigm of anthropomorphic projection onto the world, suitable to an age in which man was not fully adult. (*Hegel*, 5)

In other words, modern consciousness has been so conditioned by the Enlightenment's narrative of emancipation that past traditions are *felt* to be less sophisticated. As a result, any attempts to recover pre-Enlightenment elements are perceived as regressions. This perception, however, is based not on fact but on a certain, conveniently oversimplified interpretation of the human story. Hans-Georg Gadamer also mistrusts such simplifications: "The customary Enlightenment formula, according to which the process of the demagicification of the world leads necessarily from myth to logos, seems to me to be a modern prejudice" ("On the Scope and Function of Hermeneutical Reflection," in *PH*, 51).

Yet it is the very Enlightenment notion of truth as reason free from mystery or emotion that has impoverished modern thought and largely denies us (or at least makes difficult) access to rich traditions of pre-Enlightenment thought. I want to join Gadamer and Taylor in their plea to move away from such an analysis of the past, because it is in itself an illusionary construct based on the premise that humanity is on an ever-progressing path to intellectual and moral maturity.

Taylor, whose work deals with the conceptions of the human self, asks for a correction of such a self-righteous attitude toward the past: "Instead of seeing the issue between Galileo and the Paduan philosophers, between modern science and medieval metaphysics, as a struggle between two tendencies in the self, one deploying comforting illusions, the other facing stern realities, we might see it as a revolution in the basic categories in which we understand self" (*Hegel*, 5). In principle the same caution is needed in comparing philosophical hermeneutics with theological interpretation. It is important to realize that the basic worldview of premoderns, based on a Judeo-Christian worldview, is not less plausible because it lies in the past. To judge it inferior on this ground alone would mean to follow uncritically the Enlightenment view of the past. Such chronological snobbery stifles our dialogue with the past, for in any genuine dialogue, it is important to let the other horizon present itself as a truly alternative viewpoint before judgment is passed.

After all, the framework of philosophical hermeneutics and modernist biblical criticism[15] has no more intrinsic claim to validity than do the basic principles outlined by the earlier theological hermeneutical framework. There is, of course, no doubt that much scientific data was unknown to the thinkers of the sixteenth and seventeenth centuries. Yet as we know, at least since Thomas Kuhn's and Michael Polanyi's work, scientific data themselves do not provide us with a worldview. Rather an interpretive paradigm, or worldview, is already in place before data are fitted into it.

Once science becomes the platform for a metaphysics, a total explanation of reality, it advances from method to belief and thus enters into competition with philosophy and theology. Gadamer has clearly shown the pitfalls of such scientism and its application to the human sciences. Yet much of our aversion to and rather condescending attitude toward theological formulations of existential questions derives from the Enlightenment intuition or belief, one that still has a strong hold on our current culture, that faith and belief are dangerous, unscientific, and hence irrational vestiges of the past. Reformation theologians who witnessed the rise of science did not regard the tension between science and faith as necessary. John Howe (1630–1705), for example, could not see why a greater understanding of the universe and its workings should cause one to abandon belief in a creator. On the contrary, it is the intelligible design of nature that makes research possible in the first place:

> But that some, in later days, whose more enlarged minds have by diligent search and artificial helps got clearer notices concerning the true frame and vastness of the universe . . . than the great part of learned men have ever dreamed of before: that, I say, any of these should have chosen it for the employment of their great intellects, to devise ways of excluding intellectual power from the contrivance of this frame of things, having so great advantages from the rest of mankind besides to contemplate and adore the great Author and Lord of all, is one of the greatest wonders that comes under our notice; and might tempt even a sober mind to prefer vulgar and popular ignorance before their learned, philosophical deliberation. (*Works*, 1:44)

15. Biblical criticism is here meant to denote not the grammatical-historical efforts necessary for exegesis and interpretation, but the assumed objective interpretative stance that approaches texts with the modernist attitude of superiority described by Taylor.

Howe is also critical of those scientists who simply replace God with nature as the intelligent designer of creation. According to Howe, such sleight of hand becomes especially problematic in the case of human physical and rational abilities. "It were to be wished," Howe contends, "some of them had told us, or could yet tell us, what they meant by nature. Is it any intelligent principle? Is it anything else than the course and inclination of conspiring atoms which singly are not pretended to bear [the impression of intelligence]?" (*Works*, 1:139). Howe's example shows that Puritan thinkers were well able to engage issues on the level of their underlying presuppositions.

Thus when it comes to theoretical reflection, including the interpretation of human existence and moral action, we must approach theological interpreters as equals. Premodern interpretive practices were tested in the crucible of premodern hardships, which are often foreign to modern academics. The Puritans and later Pietists worked in the trenches of human misery and doubt, facing civil war, the plague, and persecution. Premodern interpreters were convinced that only an existentially relevant interpretive practice could maintain hope and human dignity in this environment, which is why they often characterized atheism and its denial of God as a betrayal of society. Long before Dostoyevsky, Nietzsche, and Foucault the Puritans warned that the loss of God entailed the loss of our humanity. John Howe concludes that "by whatsoever steps someone should advance in the denial of a Deity, they should proceed by the same, to the abandoning of their humanity, and by saying there is *no God*, should proclaim themselves *no men*" (*Works*, 1:24). All this is to say that for premodern interpreters scriptural interpretation always occurred within a worldview context, within an existential concern for their humanity. Their effort to live and die for their hermeneutic ideal should at least merit their inclusion in the history of hermeneutics, despite our historical distance from them and their theistic worldview.

Correcting Our Interpretive Prejudices

Gadamer's entire work rests on the premise that hermeneutics is not subjective since the interpreter strives to align himself with the horizon of the interpreted object. While prejudices are essential for our engagement of texts from the past, understanding comes into its own when the prejudgments it employs are no longer arbitrary but dictated by the object of interpretation (*WM*, 271). Only when we correct our interpretive projections in light of the subject matter can we avoid a vicious hermeneutical circle. In engaging premodern theological hermeneutics, however, this necessity poses a particular problem because the gap between interpretive horizons consists of two deeply different worldviews. For a reader who is existentially wedded to the framework of the silent universe, it is very hard to enter into a worldview premised on God's existence and his presence in creation. Because the difference is one not merely of time and culture but of profoundly different religious convictions, interpreting the past becomes especially difficult.

This is why it is so important to reread hermeneutic history through a theological prejudice that recognizes the main interest of premodern hermeneutics as communion with God. Current accounts of hermeneutic history clearly demonstrate the need for theological bias. Jean Grondin, in the introduction to his hermeneutical survey, tries to show the uniqueness of philosophical hermeneutics. He states that until the end of the nineteenth century, "hermeneutics limited itself to giving methodological directions to the specifically interpretative sciences, with the end of avoiding arbitrariness in interpretation as far as possible" (*Introduction to Philosophical Hermeneutics*, 1). Grondin believes that the formulation of specific ancillary hermeneutics during the Renaissance such as *hermeneutica sacra, hermeneutica profana*, and *hermeneutica juris* shows the "auxiliary" nature of hermeneutics at that time.

Philosophical hermeneutics, by contrast, is universal. This universality means that, "hardly limited to such purely interpretative sciences as scriptural exegesis, classical philology, and law, the horizon of interpretation comprehends all the sciences and modes of orienting one's life" (*IPH*, 24). Grondin summarizes the contrast between philosophical hermeneutic theory and earlier theological approaches as follows:

> We will take interpretation as referring to what occurs when a really or apparently unfamiliar meaning is made intelligible. Hermeneutic theory concerns itself with just this process of interpretation. This seems unimportant enough if interpretation were taken to be merely a tiny fraction of human experience. It assumes universal relevance, however, as soon as we become aware that all human behaviour is based on making sense of things, even if only consciously; and ultimately this is the best evidence for the universal claim of hermeneutics. Beginning in the twentieth century this universality penetrated philosophical consciousness, whereas earlier, apart from a few exceptions, the process of interpretation was treated as a special and local problem, governed by auxiliary normative disciplines within the individual interpretative sciences. (ibid., 19)

Grondin's bias leads to the mistaken conviction that premodern hermeneutics was less universal because it did not embrace Heidegger's idea that truth is interpretive. Rather than there being "a few exceptions," the general outlook of the reading culture that involved biblical literature realized very well that human behavior must be based on understanding one's existence. In fact, as I pointed out earlier, Heidegger is indebted for this insight to the theological tradition.

As we have already seen, the practical piety of the Puritans depended on the ontological status of humans as images of God and directly connected knowledge of this truth with moral conduct. Likewise, Augustine made clear in his *Confessions* that the universal hermeneutical purpose of humankind is to find happiness and "true happiness is to rejoice in the truth" (X.23.229). Thus the realization that "all human behaviour is based on making sense of things" is not a new feature introduced by modern consciousness but has been the premise of theological thinking all along.

More specifically, biblical exegesis, at least in reformational theological hermeneutics, was never only a technical exercise in which a detached observer dissected the text without any considerations of his or her own bias. As we have already seen and will learn further from the works of Puritan and Pietist theologians, theological hermeneutics made as sweeping a claim to universality as did post-Heideggerian interpretation. All knowledge and understanding were predicated on the assumption of a created universe. But it was especially in the understanding of moral and spiritual things that understanding was regarded as a gift from God existing in a conversion or change of perspective. Since the whole human race was regarded as contaminated by sin, every human being required regenerating grace to gain access to God's perspective. And even then, knowledge was seen as a continuous growth universally dependent on God's grace. The Puritan theologian Richard Baxter put it this way: "Moreover, it is most certain that when God calls us at first to the knowledge of his truth, he findeth us in darkness; and though he bring us thence into a marvellous light (Acts xxvi. 18; 1 Pet. ii. 9) yet he doth this by degrees, and not into the fullest light or measure of knowledge at the first" (*PWRB*, 2:387).

Related to the misconception that premodern hermeneutics is less universal than philosophical hermeneutics is Grondin's distinction between theological and philosophical hermeneutics. He implies that the latter is more concerned with universality than the former: "What is correct in the classical representation of hermeneutic history, is the idea that early hermeneutics resembled a technical theory, and as a rule such theory was of much less universal application than present-day philosophical hermeneutics" (*IPH*, 3). Contrary to Grondin's claim, however, theological hermeneutics is not merely technical but clearly universal in application, since application is its primary motivation. If a revelation from the divine creator of all things exists, then its teachings are to be read because they concern the reader in every sphere of life. Certainly the rules for interpretation that were comprised under the category of hermeneutics prior to "philosophical hermeneutics" are technical, but only in the sense that prephilosophical hermeneutics recognized a certain written text as the source of God's revelation and therefore concentrated its efforts on the correct reading of that text. Yet this reading was, as Gadamer himself admits, always performed with an eye to application. And each reading affected the complete horizon of the reader (*TM*, 307–40).

The real difference between philosophical hermeneutics and prephilosophical approaches lies in their respective theistic and atheistic/agnostic presuppositions, not in their differing degree of universality. Grondin overlooks the theological background according to which his proto-universalists, such as Jacob Spener's teacher Johann Dannhauer (1603–66), must be understood. For example, Dannhauer's use of rhetoric and logic for interpreting scripture as well as other texts was not innovative (*IPH*, 19). The majority of academically trained theologians in both Germany and England also used this approach.[16] Moreover, Dannhauer's work can hardly be described as a forerunner of philosophical hermeneutics, but like many Lutheran and Reformed orthodox theologians, he opposed rationalism and unbelief by viewing God's word as the ultimate authority in matters of faith and salvation. As recent scholarship has shown, these men used philosophical terms to defend a biblical worldview (*AGP*, 13:48). Thus if Grondin detects early traces of universalism in their writings, these traces testify not to the disappearance but to the continuation of their theological worldview.

Another problem with Grondin's approach is that, on the one hand, he wants to draw a distinction between universal (philosophical) and local (prephilosophical, i.e., theological) hermeneutics, while, on the other hand, he takes the central element in his approach, the *verbum interius*, from Gadamer, who in turn claims to have learned this concept from Augustine, a theologian who based the inner word on the image of God in man (*De Trinitate* 14 §9). The problem becomes especially apparent when Grondin identifies the *verbum interius* as "reason" and calls it "the most basic theme of hermeneutics" (*IPH*, 144).

If the *verbum interius* is indeed to be equated with reason, and reason is what "liberates us for the possibility of being human; is the realm of free and measured reflection," then we not only have returned to the unfounded Enlightenment trust in human reason (despite its now recognized finite perspective) but also do violence to Augustine. Grondin overlooks the simple fact that the *logos*, or reason, of Gadamer is not that of Augustine, for whom reason is a divine gift. Augustine could claim that understanding was possible because God has endowed humans with a structure of rationality patterned after the divine ideas in his own mind so that we can

16. John Morgan, in his study on Puritan education, *Godly Learning*, provides evidence for this claim and quotes one Puritan Bernard as saying: "Rhetorick is an Art sanctified by God's Spirit, and may be lawfully used in the handling of God's word" (108).

know truth because God has made us like himself. A harmony or correlation exists, therefore, between the mind of God, the human mind, and
the rational structure of the word (Nash, *Word of God*, 81). Therefore, the
inner word exists for Augustine only because there is a creator God. At
the same time, however, it is utterly crucial to realize that the correlation
of our minds and reality in Augustine's theology does not rely on Platonic
or Cartesian absolutes. God made and makes himself known not through
ahistorical knowledge or absolute spirit but through the incarnation.

While Augustine held that natural reason is sufficient to orient ourselves in this world, he also believed that the effects of sin did not allow
the human intellect to attain intimate knowledge of God, without which
true self-knowledge is impossible. The effect of sin on humanity's rational
faculty prevents our recourse to that faculty for a better self-understanding and "possibility of being human." Any such attempt would, at least
in Augustine's view, lead to self-delusion, because the sin-affected human
mind is in need of illumination from the divine light to obtain knowledge
concerning its true meaning and purpose (*On the Position of the Pelagians*
3.7). There is no doubt that our current intellectual climate demands a
reformulation of reason, but it cannot be the recovery of Enlightenment
reason, for, as we shall see in our discussion of Levinas, Cartesian rationality tended to neglect the emotional and relational aspects of reason;
yet without these, reason becomes an ahistorical and inhuman entity that
cannot reflect adequately on human experience and thus cannot offer
genuine self-knowledge.

Thus when Gadamer and Grondin appropriate theological concepts for
their description of a hermeneutical consciousness, they desire something
they cannot have. While Augustine can explain natural reason as the anticipation of divine illumination, Gadamer's and Grondin's use of Augustinian
Logos doctrine in their approach to hermeneutics seriously stretches, if
not distorts, Augustine's teaching. Their use of Augustine's "inner word"
secularizes a concept that is firmly grounded in a theological hermeneutics and anthropology. Ironically, by secularizing Augustine's concept of
the Logos, philosophical hermeneutics deprives itself of the incarnation
as the only plausible foundation for a radically relational and dialogical
hermeneutics. Only when we ground interpretation in the divine Word
that has become flesh do we find the proper balance between historicity
and transhistorical reality, between immanence and transcendence.

Not only philosophy but also theology would do well to heed this balance;
otherwise, our attempt to articulate a theological hermeneutic framework
will inevitably fail for two reasons. First, theological reflection that tries to
circumvent philosophical hermeneutics with its emphasis on linguisticality
and historicality is not only anti-intellectual but also fails to understand

its very own theological heritage from which these notions stem in the first place.

Second, there is no pure past, either for those who follow the Enlightenment creed of human progress or for those who equate the golden age of Christianity with transcendental idealism and its nostalgia for absolutes. The word "absolute" comes from the Latin *absolvere*, meaning to free, loosen, or unfetter. If we desire absolutes that are detached from history, we are not following the model of the incarnation. God makes himself known to us in history, and any theological hermeneutics must begin here. In this sense, Protestant thinking is doubly challenged, for in its zeal to fulfill the second commandment, it has developed a healthy sensitivity to idolatry. Yet it seems also that this proper desire for keeping God pure from idolatrous human construct is easily perverted into a desire for a God who stands outside the flux of time. As a result, Reformation thought exhibits an interesting paradox. While its recovery of New Testament Christianity imbued it with a strong sense of history, its iconoclastic tendencies for the transcendence of God often result in ahistorical and anti-aesthetic strands within this tradition. The biblical God, however, while the creator of time itself, has also entered that time in the incarnation. The radical consequence of the incarnation is that human knowledge of God cannot be ahistorical. This means that our knowledge of God and hence our self-knowledge are crucially tied to God's self-revelation in the incarnation and its interpretation in the Bible as the word of God.

My short examination of the two interpretive frameworks shows that the perspective from which hermeneutics is described is very important. The secularization and transference of theological concepts into the non-theistic paradigm of philosophical hermeneutics is highly problematic. Grondin's assessment lacks the theological context within which ideas such as Augustine's "inner word" must be understood (Grondin, *Sources of Hermeneutics*, 109). The same is true for an assessment of premodern hermeneutics. Rather than proving the usefulness of separating theological from philosophical hermeneutics according to their degrees of universality, Grondin demonstrates the difficulty of such an approach.

Neither should we follow Grondin in his easy dismissal of premodern interpreters as neglecting universal and espousing merely technical hermeneutics. On close examination, we will find that not only did philological and narrative criticism play a role in their exegesis, but the exegetes of the Bible also dealt in great depth with the problem of understanding. Hermeneutics, even long before philosophical hermeneutics, has always been concerned with self-understanding. John Calvin summarized this position well when he stated that "without knowledge of self there is no knowledge of God" (*Institutes*, 1.1.1). Conversely, true self-knowledge can be derived only from reading the Bible: "We must come, I say, to the Word, where God is truly and vividly described to us from his works" (ibid., 1.6.4). Both the theologian and the philosopher, at least in hermeneutics, desire a universal application of their theory. They merely differ in their sources and assumptions.

Grondin is certainly correct in reading the history of hermeneutics as a process of progressive secularization. And while we cannot help but read history through contemporary lenses, we can certainly try to correct false prejudices. It is to this end that this part of *Recovering Theological Hermeneutics* attempts to counterbalance the deficiency of Grondin's hermeneutical survey by examining the roots of modern hermeneutics from Luther to English Puritanism to German Pietism.

Having delineated my main goal, I now begin my survey of hermeneutic history with Martin Luther, whose name is associated with the beginning of the Protestant Reformation and whose writings provide a good introduction to a theological hermeneutics, whose most fundamental characteristic is its understanding of reality as constituted by the divine word.

2

IN THE BEGINNING WAS THE WORD

The Incarnational Hermeneutics of Martin Luther
(1483–1546)

> When, however, the Word of God truly comes, it comes as the enemy of
> our thinking and desires. It does not allow our thinking to stand, even in
> those matters which are most sacred, but it destroys and eradicates and
> scatters everything.
>
> —Martin Luther, "Lectures on Romans"

Martin Luther and Protestant Hermeneutics

Hermeneutics begins with the assertion that to be human is to interpret.
Hermeneutics concerns itself with the interpretation and understanding
of human existence, with self-knowledge. We have learned from Calvin
that God's word as set out in the Bible provides us with the two elements
necessary for adequate knowledge about our existence: knowledge of
God and knowledge of what it means to be human. This hermeneutical
circle is the structural foundation of knowledge for pre-Enlightenment
hermeneutics. Martin Luther adds another important dimension to Protestant hermeneutics: the incarnational nature of knowledge. For Luther
all knowing begins and ends with Christ. Any knowledge of God apart

from Christ is for him mere speculation at best and heresy at worst, for God chose to make himself known in the incarnation; thus for Luther, any God talk is firmly rooted in history. In this chapter I explore the implications of this incarnational focus for our attempt to articulate a Protestant hermeneutics.

The Protestant Reformation, which Martin Luther spearheaded, was first and foremost a hermeneutical revolution, for it revolved around the dissemination, reading, interpretation, and application of the Bible. While Luther drew heavily on the patristic and medieval traditions, his work marks a decisive break with medieval hermeneutics. The reformer's reevaluation of the scholastic tradition with what he called its "Aristotelian aberrations" constitutes a decisive turn in hermeneutic history for the relation of philosophy and theology. Luther believed that the use of Greek concepts, particularly those of Aristotle, had clouded rather than aided our knowledge of God. Luther clearly distinguishes Hebrew from Hellenistic thought and argues that through Greek philosophical conceptuality, theology has been turned into an abstract theology of glory: "A theologian of glory (that is, someone who does not know along with the apostle the hidden and crucified God, but sees and speaks of God's glorious manifestation among the pagans, how his invisible nature can be known from things visible and how he is present and powerful in all things everywhere) learns from Aristotle that the object of the will is good. . . . He learns that God is the highest good" (WA, 31:227).[1]

Luther believed that such theoretical speculations miss the mark, for they assume a clear-cut epistemology that allows human beings to fathom the very nature of God. God becomes, so to speak, an object of intellectual inquiry, an abstract concept one should (and actually could) pursue as the highest good. Luther, in his commentary on Paul's thought, identifies such Greek wisdom and Aristotelian conceptuality with worldly wisdom and works. In its attempt to explain the inexplicable and probe the nature of God, scholasticism drains God and the incarnation of their mystery and power; even worse, such speculations of worldly wisdom create a glorious but distant God no one dares to approach. Instead, Luther argues, one must become a theologian of the cross, for the cross destroys (Lat. *destruere*) the wisdom of the wise and directs the faithful to the concrete reality of the cross, a reality that is foolishness to the Greeks.

---

1. See John van Buren's essay "Martin Heidegger, Martin Luther," 165 ff. Van Buren shows that other key concepts used by Heidegger in *Sein und Zeit* may well have been taken from Luther. For example, Luther's *cursus ad mortem* was translated by Heidegger as *Vorlauf zum Tode*, "the anticipatory running ahead towards death" (171).

For Luther, God reveals himself most clearly in the historical event of the incarnation. Luther rejected philosophical absolutes or abstract eternal values because he understood the paradoxical nature of knowledge presented to the theologian: only in radical historicity is transcendence found. Moreover, this transcendence is not a concept but a person and is accessible only in terms of a personal and existentially involved encounter with God through Christ. Luther thus introduced two crucial aspects into Reformation hermeneutics. The first is the category of the personal in our acquisition of knowledge. This important element in hermeneutics has often been overlooked in assessing pre-Enlightenment hermeneutics mainly because prejudice and emotions were considered hindrances rather than aids to knowing in the epistemological model of the Enlightenment. The influence of this model and its public versus personal (or fact versus value) split has been so pervasive that even though academia has corrected this dichotomy, it is still prevalent in popular conceptions of real knowledge as detached and impersonal.

By contrast, Luther's familiarity with the relational truth concept of the biblical world enabled him to see the limitations of Greek metaphysics for expressing biblical theology. In particular he recognized the inadequacy of ancient Greek thought for expressing the fusion of transcendence and immanence in the figure of Christ, because Greek thought tended to elevate mind over matter and value the eternally transcendent over history. Instead Luther followed the Augustinian model of epistemology in recognizing that true knowledge of self requires not only transcendence (i.e., something greater than ourselves) but transcendence of a personal quality in order to ensure both the objective *and* the human quality of knowledge.

The Luther scholar Gerhard Ebeling explains that Luther's antipathy to Aristotelian philosophy was less a traditionally induced reaction to the Ockham nominalist school, of which the young monk was part during his studies in Erfurt, than the result of Luther's careful exegetical and hermeneutical work, in other words, his attention to the text: "From the very first the main principle of his exegetical work was to understand the distinctive nature of biblical modes of speech and thought, by contrast to the traditional philosophical language of scholastic theology" (Ebeling, *Luther*, 87).

Ebeling shows that Luther recognized a fundamental difference between biblical and Greek terminology as it was found in scholastic theology. Luther, for example, observes that *intellectus*, instead of being understood as a human faculty, is used in the Bible in a sense that is defined by its object, so that the formal concept is replaced by a concern for the particular thing toward which the mind is oriented. Hence genuine *intellectus* in biblical terms is not the knowledge of an arbitrary object but something specifically biblical, namely, the wisdom of the cross of Christ. Consequently, Luther argued, the biblical concept of the human intellect should be translated *sensualitas,* which includes the human *ratio* since both are incapable of understanding spiritual things (Ebeling, *Luther,* 87). Luther, as a good theologian, scholar, and humanist, was thus very aware of the confluence of concept and word, or, to use different terminology, of the inseparability of form and content. Concepts derived from a worldview in which truth is an abstract, nonrelational, and purely rational affair cannot but distort biblical ideas of truth and reality as relational and personal. Luther's biblical understanding of truth as relational and of belief as personal trust rather than assent to an impersonal verity requires an ethical dimension of interpretation. This ethical dimension provides a direct link with the thought of Emmanuel Levinas and with the hermeneutics of Dietrich Bonhoeffer, which we will pursue in the final section of this book.

Luther's rejection of Greek thought as normative for theology results in a second defining element of Reformation hermeneutics: a theological anthropology based on the human being as fallen and thus as limited in his or her rational capacities. Luther saw that the use of Greek rationality tended not only to disregard the historical nature of truth but also to dissolve the noetic effects of sin. If the intellect, defined as pure reason, could figure out God, it also could figure out the ultimate meaning of human existence. For Luther, true self-understanding meant understanding oneself as either out of communion with God or as being in communion with God through the saving grace of Christ. Yet this understanding of ourselves as either in Adam or in Christ was a position only accessible to those already in Christ, who defined the ultimate good and meaning of life as communion with God, from which flows love of one's neighbor. Yet the biblical text kept reminding Luther that human reason is incapable of coming to this insight by itself, an attitude that explains the ever-present sense of dependency on God's grace in interpretation throughout Luther's writings.

Luther's distrust of reason, albeit without a balancing belief in God, has become a palpable force in academia and popular culture through the interpretation of Nietzsche's thought in German and French philosophy. Derrida's work, for example, represents a consistent criticism of Western rationality. Derrida's flaws notwithstanding, theologians should welcome any attempt to redefine human rationality in a richer manner than the model of scientific epistemology followed by much philosophy has hitherto allowed. Philosophers like to lump all theologians together with those whose inability to reflect on their finitude and historical situatedness makes them hanker after timeless absolutes. Unfortunately Christian misunderstanding of postmodern philosophy's emphasis on the linguisticality and historicality of human existence as relativistic seems to offer no other haven than Platonic ideals or eternal values, thus fulfilling Nietzsche's dictum that Christianity is Platonism for the people. Culturally shaped notions of God, human nature, and reality are then elevated to transhistorical creeds on which the Christian faith depends.

As a result, ethics is reduced to rules for the regulation of moral conduct. In a cultural context where a church split into countless denominations, each adding its own spoken or unspoken rules, this situation becomes quickly one of confusion. In this context, Luther provides a radically different outlook. His emphasis on the Word of God as incarnation is far removed from Christian Platonism and allows a full appreciation of the linguisticality of human existence, the relational nature of truth and ethics.

"In the Beginning Was the Word": The Linguistic Foundation of Reality

At the heart of Luther's work lies God's word. Luther "lived by the Word of God; he lived for the Word of God. It is no mistake then, when interpreters of Luther take his doctrine of the Word of God as one of the most important single keys to his theology" (Pelikan, *Luther the Expositor*, 48). It is important to realize fully how comprehensive the concept of God's word is for Luther. To begin an account of Luther's theology with his view on inspiration and inerrancy unjustly narrows the scope of Luther's thought. Luther's theology begins not with the letter of the Bible, with the written word, but with the claim that God *is* Word. Luther understood the Hebrew God to be first and foremost a God of speech. He believed that God's creative power and redeeming love proceed from him in the form of spoken words. For Luther the linguist, translator, and communicator, linguisticality is part of God's very nature, and his creative and redemptive actions occur as words of self-revelation.

Luther's sermon on John's Gospel illustrates well his concept that creation and redemption result from God's words. In this sermon, directed largely to a peasant audience, Luther likens God to a man who walks along the street holding a conversation with himself. Luther reminds his audience that everyone conducts such monologues, especially when one's heart is brimming with emotion. He calls such inner dialogues "the word of the heart" (*das Wort des Herzens*) or "the inner word."[2] According

2. Luther writes, "The word of the heart is larger than the external word of the mouth. The former is often so big and strong that it occupies the entire heart and is, at the same time, incapable of expressions. For it is impossible for a man to voice fully the thoughts either of an overjoyed or of a very wrathful heart" (*LW*, 22:10).

to Luther's interpretation of John's prologue, such a conversation took place within the Trinity before creation: "God too, in His majesty and nature, is pregnant with a Word or a conversation in which He engages with Himself in His divine essence and which reflects the thoughts of His heart. This is as complete and excellent and perfect as God Himself. No one but God alone sees, hears, or comprehends this conversation. . . . God is so absorbed in this His Word, thought, or conversation that He pays no attention to anything else" (*LW*, 22:9–10; see also *WA*, 46:544–45).

Luther then states that just as the man in this analogy stops and shouts so that his inner words suddenly become audible, God called creation into existence. Luther equates this inner Word with the Son of God through whom creation was spoken into existence and who later became the external Word as the Jewish Messiah, the Christ: "And then we read that everything was created through this speech or Word of God; . . . yes, He was in the Father's heart from all eternity. If that is true, it follows that this Word was greater and more sublime than anything created and made, that is, He [Christ] must be God Himself" (*LW*, 1:9). The linguistic nature of God thus shapes Luther's Christology. The Word of God, in the cosmic sense, is the second Person of the Trinity and became the incarnate Word of redemption to humanity. Luther's doctrine of Christ as the Logos[3] of God was meant to avoid a Platonic matter-spirit dualism by defining the Word of God as Trinitarian utterance expressed in the different roles of the father as creator and the son as mediator and redeemer. Although the creating Word preceded the redeeming incarnation, Luther wanted to avoid Manicheism, that is, the impression that "creation [was] beneath the dignity of the God who redeemed human beings through the Word that was in Christ; for the cosmic Word of God had become flesh in the historical figure Jesus of Nazareth" (Pelikan, *Luther the Expositor*, 52). Thus Luther's doctrine of creation remains faithful to the Hebrew idea that the world is not dualistic, divided into matter and spirit. This implicit rejection of Platonism in Luther's thought is important to an understanding of his distinction between the spirit and the letter, and spirit and flesh, none of which implies a Platonic dualism of mind and body.

Moreover, Luther believes that the cosmic Word not only created but also upholds the entire cosmos: "Everything was created and is preserved through the Word," and "God the Father initiated and executed the creation of all things through the Word; and now He continues to preserve His creation through the Word, and that forever and ever . . . hence,

---

3. Luther seems to have understood logos in terms of word, or discourse, not, however, in the sense of the preexisting Christ as a pattern for rationality conceived according to the universal reason of Enlightenment philosophy.

as heaven, earth, sun, moon, stars, human beings, and all living things were created in the beginning through the Word, so they are wonderfully governed and preserved through that Word" (*LW*, 22:26). Thus for Luther creation and its preservation are an ongoing speech act of God. Luther goes so far as to say that through Christ, "who is the Word and wisdom of the Fathers . . . the Father continually brings forth the invisible and the non-existent to be visible and existent. . . . Those who are to be born ten and twenty years hence are an invisible thing now . . . yet they are to become visible and reality when they are born" (ibid., 22:28). The future, in other words, also lies in the word of God in the sense that Christ and his creative power brings it about.

Once the concept of an inner word and its external manifestation is posited, hermeneutics (that is, exegesis, interpretation, and appropriation) becomes the foundational dynamic for meaning and communication. Luther argues that human language can never express the fullness of the inner word; even with constant effort, an approximation to its full meaning is the best we can do. Matters become even more complicated when the dialogue partner is God himself. God's thoughts, Luther says, are so different from those of his creatures that no one can understand their full meaning: "Now if it is true that I cannot fully express the thoughts of my heart, how many thousand times less will it be possible for me to understand or express the Word or conversation in which God engages within His divine being, which He harbours in the shrine of His heart!" (*LW*, 22:11; see also *WA*, 46:546).

Because God reveals himself in personal categories, divine revelation is analogous to human communication. The personal quality of divine-human relations affords both the possibility and the limits of understanding. Hence while Luther emphasizes God's incomprehensibility, this wholly other God is also personal and present, eager to communicate with his creation. Any other view is rejected as unbiblical (*LW*, 22:29). A distant God is the God of what Heidegger attacks as onto-theology and what Luther calls Aristotelian scholasticism. Luther stresses that God does not exist in self-contained isolation like the unmoved mover and highest principle of scholastic onto-theology but that he seeks communion with his creatures through speech: "The people of Israel did not have a God who was viewed 'absolutely,' to use the expression, the way the inexperienced monks rise into heaven and think about God as He is in Himself. . . . Let not one, therefore, interpret David as speaking with the absolute God. He is speaking with God as he is dressed and clothed in His Word and promises, so that from the name 'God' we cannot exclude Christ whom God promised to Adam and the other patriarchs" (*Commentary on Psalm 51*, in *LW*, 12:312; see also *WA*, 42:329).

For Luther, God's self-revelation to humanity does not come in the non-relational framework and naked[4] rational transparency of scholasticism, which misappropriated Aristotelian categories for theology. Rather God has a face, and he reveals himself climactically in the incarnation. His most important word is clothed in human words in the Old Testament, which contains God's promise of the Word clothed in flesh and blood, the incarnation through which the human-divine discourse would be renewed. God's inner word thus became first audible through its feeble incarnation in human language, but its most perfect utterance was Jesus the Christ, whose life, work, and final kingship over creation form the kerygma of both the Old and the New Testaments. The proclamation's motivation is love and its message redemption and life for fallen humankind, the creation of a new humanity. Luther's concept of the Word, then, progresses from the inner conversation of God with its creative power outward to the redemptive incarnated Word in which God converses in the flesh, face-to-face, as it were, with his creature.

Luther's preoccupation with the word of God and its redemptive and creative power allows a summation of his theology in terms of a human-divine dialogue: God, out of the loving abundance of his inner conversation, creates humanity. In the Fall, his creatures end the conversation through disobedience, thereby isolating themselves from the life-sustaining conversation with God. God, however, renews his address to humanity through his covenant with Abraham and later with the nation of Israel. Yet because of its fallen condition, the elect tribe is an ungrateful and irritating dialogue partner, who, abusing its privileged position, becomes forgetful of its sinful nature and falls prey to pride. Luther, in fact, reads the Old Testament as a story about Israel's forgetfulness of its vocation as God's people called by grace (*WA*, 42:551–52; *LW*, 3:4–5). Pride in its calling kept Israel from its original purpose: to commune with God so that through their resulting conversation (in the sense of the lifestyle marked out by the Torah), the Gentiles would also be drawn to God (*WA*, 42:616; *LW*, 3:95; see also *LW*, 22:40ff.). Ultimately God wants to bring both Israel and the rest of the world into the conversation. He achieves this through an incarnation of the cosmic Word in Jesus of Nazareth.

Jesus is a paradigm of the perfect divine-human dialogue because he trusted God even in the face of death. The resurrection is proof that God's incarnate Word carries the power of life and new creation. This Word overcomes death and holds the power to impart new life to every listening ear. This new life consists in a radical change of the human heart (by which Luther, following the Pauline and Augustinian tradi-

---

4. Luther actually refers to Christ as the Word that veils the glorious godhead from the arrogant eyes of scholastic speculation (*LW*, 1:13).

tion, means the human will, i.e., that which directs human desire and ambition). This change of the creature's being results in the beginnings of a new conversation with God, one that is free from fear, one in which selfishness may be overcome, one that drives the recipient to fulfill God's ultimate purpose for creation: to converse with God and one's fellow human beings in unadulterated love. Luther describes the ethics flowing from this renewed human-divine dialogue in his *Commentary on Galatians*: "Good works do not occur except they flow from a cheerful, willing, and joyful heart; that is, they are done in the spirit of freedom" (*KG*, 106). How such ethics is possible will be discussed later, but this much may be said already: for Luther, genuine ethics is possible only through communication with the Word and its power to restore God's image in human beings, and this restoration is brought about by the creative and life-giving power of the Word.

Luther's belief in the Word's effecting a radical ontological change, followed by a gradual restoration of the divine image in human beings, does not imply God's detachment from his fallen creatures. Like Augustine before and Calvin after him, Luther believes that even the paltry remains of human greatness are due to Christ's sustaining power and are therefore remarkable: "But man alone is endowed with the glorious light of reason and intellect. Human beings' ability to devise so many noble arts and skills, their wisdom, dexterity, and ingenuity, all are derived from this light, or from the Word who was the light of men" (*LW*, 22:30). Yet compared to the being that once enjoyed communion with God, what appears glorious is a mere shadow of its former ontological state. The Fall not only had severed the intimate relationship between God and human beings but had actually affected the ontological structure of the creature.[5] Luther claims that "all our faculties today are leprous, indeed dull and utterly dead" (ibid., 1:66). The selfishness resulting from the Fall makes us unfit for ethics, and the noetic effect of sin prevents the reader from understanding God's word. Thus mere historico-grammatical research will never completely lift the text's obscurity. The reader's fallen condition lies like a veil over the word of God, a veil to be lifted only by God's grace.[6]

Luther's conviction that human understanding is deaf to God's word is so strong that he uses this ontological deficiency as a touchstone for bibli-

5. "Therefore that image of God was something most excellent, in which were included eternal life, everlasting freedom from fear, and everything that is good. However, through sin this image was so obscured and corrupted that we cannot grasp it even with our intellect" (*LW*, 1:65).

6. "The veil still remains on their heart. . . . Therefore let wretched men cease to impute, with blasphemous perverseness, the darkness and obscurity of their own heart to the all-clear scriptures of God" (*BW*, 26–27).

cal hermeneutics. In a sentence whose pathos equals that of Nietzschean deconstruction, Luther declares: "But the fact is that if the Word of God comes, it comes contrary to our thinking and our will. It does not allow our thinking to stand, even in those matters which are most sacred, but it destroys and eradicates and scatters everything" (LW, 25:415; see also WA, 61:423). The word is "like a hammer which breaks the rock in pieces"; the rock signifies the self-centered human will, bent on autonomy. Thus readers of the word, no matter how theologically trained, who feel superior to the word, to whom "the Word does not come contrary to or above what they think but in accord with what they think," pursue the wrong hermeneutics. Luther warns interpreters who think they have mastered the word of God that they thereby implicitly consider themselves judges of the word rather than being under the word (ibid.).

How, then, should one read? Luther advocates a careful balance of historico-grammatical exegesis and a sensitive mind in communion with God (Ebeling, *Luther*, 119).[7] In the final analysis, neither understanding nor application (and they are really inseparable) is possible through methodologies and abstract principles. Instead these activities are dynamic and ever changing, and they depend on the operation of God, that is, on the Holy Spirit. Only through an ongoing discourse does one gain "that newness of life through which we are zealous to obey God as we are taught by the Word and aided by the Holy Spirit." Thus the gospel brings about the gradual restoration of God's image (LW, 1:24–25). Again it is not human effort but God's Spirit who "offers resistance in us to unbelief, envy and other vices that we may earnestly strive to glorify the name of the Lord and his Word" (ibid., 1:64). Luther sees both hermeneutics and ethics as grounded in God, grounded not in a theoretical sense but in the sense of what Heidegger might call *physis*, an ever-sustaining power that lifts the veil of fallenness and selfishness and that addresses the whole person rather than merely the intellect (*Introduction to Metaphysics*, 170–71).

Of course, this account of Luther's hermeneutics is open to many charges by Lutheran orthodoxy and New Testament scholarship. Is such a reading of Luther not an anachronistic eisegesis of current issues into the work of a sixteenth-century mind? What about Luther's opposition of law and gospel? Even more importantly, is not Luther's hermeneuti-

---

7. Ebeling makes it clear that Luther's appeal to conscience and hermeneutics is not a call for subjectivism: "But [Luther] is not following the idealist interpretation of conscience as an independent voice within man's own heart which gives him independence, and is thus the basis for man's autonomy. What he means is that man is ultimately a hearer, someone who is seized, claimed, and subject to judgment, and that for this reason his existential being depends upon which word reaches and touches his innermost being" (*Luther*, 119–20).

cal imposition of a law-gospel dichotomy on the scriptures misleading? Furthermore, can Luther's exegesis retain any validity in light of recent exegetical works that take the Jewish context much more seriously and vitiate many of Luther's particular readings? For example, what about Luther's misreading of the Jews as semi-Pelagians?[8]

All of these are valid and important questions. Most of them, however, miss the purpose of the preceding description of Luther's hermeneutics, and those that do pertain to our ethical focus are indeed answerable. The remainder of this chapter attempts to answer the most important of these questions while simultaneously sketching in greater detail the basis of Luther's hermeneutics and its consequent ethics. Let us turn first to the charge of anachronism.

Ever since the Hebrew Bible became part of Western theological and philosophical thought, its account of creation by the word of God has also become our intellectual heritage. Thus issues of language and the power of the word along with the related issue of interpretation are inextricably intertwined in our thinking. It is only lately, in the form of the so-called linguistic turn in philosophy, that the concern about language and words has been reawakened and isolated from the provenance of theology, where it originated and is truly at home. It is indeed ironic that theology uses works of secular philosophers, such as Gadamer, to reinitiate its own concern for language, which, at least according to Luther, lies at the very heart of Christian theology. Conversely, Gadamer's emphasis on dialogue and understanding through language is impotent without the theological anchoring of such dialogue, a referent he simply rejects. As I shall argue in the last section, philosophical hermeneutics cannot unfold its potential without the theological foundation from which it inherited some of its most important elements. In short, to restate Luther's theology in terms of contemporary hermeneutical issues based on his clearly expressed concern for the word of God and words is a thoroughly hermeneutical endeavor; if one charges such undertaking with anachronism, then most, if not all, of our readings of texts are anachronistic.

"And the Word Became Flesh": Luther's View of the Bible

Reading Luther's theology as a human-divine communication has two important consequences for a theological and philosophical assessment of Luther's hermeneutics. First, recognizing Luther's organic and univer-

8. For this argument, see N. T. Wright's *The Climax of the Covenant*, 173 ff., and *What St. Paul Really Said*, 19.

sal view of the word of God goes a long way to solving disputes about Luther's view of the Bible. There is some consensus that "inerrancy" and "plenary inspiration" are terms whose final rigid definitions were determined in the nineteenth and twentieth centuries. Nonetheless, it is an important issue whether Luther could comment, in an apparently carefree manner, on the boundaries and content of the biblical canon because he thought that the Bible was only substantially the word of God, or whether he believed every single word to be inspired and in need of the most careful exegesis. The answer is really quite simple: because God, the cosmic Word, reveals himself in spoken human language, which is then captured in writing, every utterance is inspired and demands very careful historico-grammatical exegesis. Luther's view of the text as a historically conditioned incarnation of God avoids both bibliolatry (worship of the letter) and a mere husk-and-kernel approach that reduces biblical content to a basic moral message or to an existential decision toward inner freedom.

For Luther, in other words, the Bible is the word of God in a derivative sense, derived from his basic concept that God's speech is a powerful, creative force. As the church historian Jaroslav Pelikan observes: "The scriptures were the 'Word of God' in a derivative sense for Luther—derivative from the historical sense of Word as deed and from the basic sense of Word as proclamation. As the record of the deeds of God, which were the Word of God, the scriptures participated in the nature of that which they recorded. As the written deposit of the preaching of the apostles, they could be termed the 'Word of God' also" (*Luther the Expositor*, 108). The word of God in the historical sense was a deed of God. Put differently, God's word of redemption, intended to bring his people into intimate communion with himself, manifested itself in concrete historical action. Following the model of the incarnation, Luther thus fuses history and revelation into an inseparable unit. According to Luther, biblical hermeneutics must recognize the incarnation as its guiding principle.

In what is still the best study on Luther's hermeneutics, Gerhard Ebeling explains that for Luther, "the Gospels are only understood and interpreted evangelically—in contrast to the interpretive models of Catholics and Enthusiasts—if interpretation receives its principles from the incarnation. Only this approach does justice to the subject matter" (*EE*, 360). Analogous to the incarnation's combining the eternal with the historical in that the eternal God became present to humankind in the figure of Jesus, God's eternal word is also present in the Gospels' testimony of the incarnation. Since they are reliable testimony, Luther argues, historical distance is no disadvantage. Even contemporaries of Jesus, including his own family, did not believe his divinity, for such recognition is a gift from God. Thus historical revelation only works in conjunction with what Ebeling terms "inverbation": "The *verbum incarnatum substantiale* must be joined with the *verbum prolatum efficax*. History can only be revelation in the coexistence of history and words. . . . The word alone provides access to Jesus, who otherwise remains hidden to both purely intellectual and mere bodily [historical] encounter" (ibid., 363).

It follows that the subject matter of the Bible, the good news of God's love for humanity shown in the incarnation, cannot be understood through historical research alone. Nor in contrast to the historical school of the nineteenth century is historical distance a problem. The historical distance is nullified (not bridged) by the Word, which first created history and then was spoken into history. Luther concludes that it is the role of the Holy Spirit to make the incarnate Word present to the reader. Thus for Luther, a hermeneutics adequate to interpret the subject matter of the Bible is based on the unity of "Christ, Word, and Spirit" (*EE*, 365). Luther's theory differed from a theory of verbal inspiration, for he insisted on a word behind the word that requires from the reader constant revisions in interpreting the written letter (ibid., 368).

The contemporaneity of history and revelation based on Luther's understanding of the word of God was later pried apart by Enlightenment rationalism, epitomized in Lessing's "ugly ditch" between history and necessary truths of reason, and is finally being reestablished in recent theological scholarship.[9] The view that God's word was spoken into history, in human language, and into a spatial-temporal continuum explains Luther's historically oriented exegesis (Pelikan, *Luther the Expositor*, 89). Luther could dispense with allegorical readings since the literal historical meaning had in itself spiritual significance. Thus Luther did not have to allegorize the Old Testament or reject it as unimportant. Nor did he view the New Testament simply as a repository of timeless moral truths. In his exposition of the Sermon on the Mount, for instance, Luther interpreted the word as the concrete action of God. The concrete things of the created world were all words of God, because each of them owed its existence to God's creating deed. The concrete events of human history were all words of God because, in the mystery of divine providence, each

9. Beginning with the so-called Sanders revolution, New Testament scholarship has left Bultmann's existential exegesis and tries to close the gap between belief and history by placing the Christ events firmly within Jewish history and eschatological beliefs. Perhaps the most impressive work in this area of biblical studies is being done by N. T. Wright (*The New Testament and the People of God*; *Jesus and the Victory of God*; and *The Climax of the Covenant* are his impressive scholarly efforts that place Christ in the Jewish prophetic and covenantal tradition). This is not to say, however, that the split between history and mythology has entirely subsided. Dominic Crossan and Marcus Borg (though from different perspectives) still represent a formidable force arguing for a split between the Jesus of history and the Jesus of faith.

of them was the deed of God (ibid., 54). The Bible, then, becomes the recorded history of and commentary on God's redemptive word-deed. Thus the hermeneutical focus should be the redemptive intent of its ultimate author, God (under whose guidance redactors worked), and the fulcrum of the word is the incarnation and the cross as the climax of God's fulfilled promise.

Luther's often cited hostility toward scholastic theologians in the Heidelberg Theses must be viewed in this context. Scholastic speculations about the invisible qualities of God revealed in nature are ultimately useless, because God's most direct word is revealed in Jesus. The invisible God reveals himself as a God of love and suffering through his incarnate, redemptive Word. And only those who proclaim this Word deserve the title theologian: "The man who deserves to be called a theologian is not the one who seeks to understand the invisible things of God through the things that are made (Rom. 1:22) but the one who understands that the visible things and the hind parts of God are seen through suffering and the cross" (*LW*, 22:157; see also *WA*, 1:361–63).

To sum up, for Luther "the Word of God in the cosmic sense was the eternal Christ, and as the Word of God in the Old Testament was finally the anticipated Christ, so the Word of God in the New Testament was essentially the historical Christ. Given his doctrine of the Word, it was logical for Luther to see Christ and the cross as the central theme of God's redemptive word" (Pelikan, *Luther the Expositor*, 60). Luther's systematic Christological hermeneutic principle does not mean, however, that he simply read his opinion into the text; the assiduous use of all philological aids available at his time in his sermon and lecture preparation demonstrates Luther's desire to develop theology from the text. That is not to say, of course, that sometimes his vivid imagination saw Christ in the text where modern scholarship does not. However, respected strands of contemporary scholarship have come to agree in principle with Luther's reading of Paul and the plausibility of the Pauline assertion that Jesus the Christ is the fulfillment of Torah and that the messianic promises in Isaiah pertain to his redemption and vindication of humanity:

> When, therefore, Paul tells us that the gospel he preaches is the one promised beforehand in holy scripture, and that its central figure is one who was from the seed of David and is now marked out as Son of God, we would have to imitate Lord Nelson, putting a blind eye to the telescope, to deny that Paul intends to evoke precisely this collocation of scriptural themes, which is about as well attested in Jewish literature as any collection of messianic ideas. . . . He is announcing that the messianic promises of salvation have come true in Jesus. Jesus is the King not only of Israel but of all the world. (Wright, *What St. Paul Really Said*, 53)

Second, if Luther's basic Christological hermeneutics (if not all his readings) is somewhat vindicated by recent scholarship, his view of the Bible as God's word directed toward humanity with the central message of love and redemption should also once and for all dispel clichés about Luther's opposition of law and gospel. This opposition does not mean, for example, that Luther rejected the Old Testament as outmoded because it preaches law rather than gospel. Luther, in fact, repudiated the legalism other interpreters had found in the Old Testament and opposed to the New Testament (*DSC*, 36). Since he did not identify the Old Testament with mere legal requirements, he was able to find the word of God, the word of redemption, in the Old and in the New Testaments: "All human beings who ever were, are now, and ever will be illumined receive their light from Him, who is the true eternal Light. Those who possess life and light must acquire it from Him. *And since the beginning, this Word has always spoken through the mouths of the patriarchs, prophets down to the time of John the Baptist*" (*LW*, 22:37; emphasis mine). Luther thus recognized, often in opposition to radical reformers, the continuity between the Testaments. His view of the Bible as history also allowed him to set New Testament writings, such as Jesus's parables, firmly into the matrix of Old Testament prophecy. While his opponents often made the Sermon on the Mount "a new morality of so-called evangelical counsels, . . . Luther's interpretation of the Sermon sounded the redemptive note in these chapters and could, therefore, apply them to the everyday needs of his hearers in Wittenberg" (Pelikan, *Luther the Expositor*, 61). Luther's sense of the scriptures as the historical word with Christ as their hermeneutical center allowed him to replace the hitherto dominant fourfold medieval exegetical method with his famous law-gospel dialectic.

Luther's mature understanding of law and gospel is rooted in the division of God's written word into letter and spirit found in Luther's early writings. Thus it is important to come to grips with this primary distinction before examining his use of law and gospel. Perhaps no other phrase has been so misunderstood in the history of hermeneutics. As Ebeling points out, "Luther did not regard the literal meaning as such as the 'letter that kills' and the allegorical . . . interpretations imposed upon it as the 'life-giving Spirit'" (*Luther*, 104). Luther is not a Neoplatonist: he does not discard the textual kernel for a spiritual experience of God-consciousness (Schleiermacher), for a timeless message of self-authentication (Bultmann), or even for a timeless moral code (Christian fundamentalism). Instead the entire text, the whole, can be either the letter that kills or the life-giving Spirit, depending on whether "the understanding is oriented towards Moses or towards Christ" (ibid.). Recent Lutheran scholarship confirms Ebeling's conclusion: "Luther's use of Spirit does not denote some deeper spiritual meaning hidden behind the letter, inaccessible to the untrained reader; rather Spirit means simply to understand scripture in light of Christ's work, suffering, death, and resurrection" (Reader, "Luther als Ausleger," 258). In his later writings, Luther clarifies this view by substituting the words "law" and "gospel" for "letter" and "spirit." Consistent with his concept of the word of God, Luther sees Christ as the basic literal-spiritual meaning of the biblical text. To begin with Jesus the Christ as "the fundamental meaning and utterance of the holy scripture became Luther's basic hermeneutic principle" (Ebeling, *Luther*, 105). Thus Luther can see both letter and spirit (or law and gospel) at work in the Old Testament. Whenever Old Testament figures apply the Mosaic law in the spirit of Christ, that is, in terms of redeeming love toward one's neighbor, the gospel is at work. For even the Old Testament ethics, based on ceremonial and legal precepts, derived its measure and validity from its approximation of faith and love:

> The laws count if their works do not contradict faith and love; if they do they should be abolished. Thus we read that David did not kill the murderer Joab, although he doubly deserved death, and in 2 Samuel 14:11 he swears to Theoka's wife that her son should not die, although he strangled his brother. From these stories we see that faith and love should be the master of all laws and have power over them. Since all laws urge one toward faith and love, none of them counts any longer if interpreted contrary to faith or love. (*DSC*, 41)

Even in the Old Testament, faith in God's promise of redemption and love enables his people to apply moral regulations properly. Luther's Christological hermeneutical principle thus has direct ethical consequences. In fact, we have now arrived at the heart of Luther's hermeneutics. God's word, if adequately understood, brings redemption from human error, from human moral norms, and empowers individuals to act in accordance with Christ's ethical principles of selflessness (Ebeling, *Luther*, 119). The function of the law is therefore not to oppose the gospel but to act as *Lehrmeister*, a teacher pointing to the gospel. The law-gospel dynamic, however, is not a mere abstract theological distinction. At the bottom of the entire law-gospel concept lies Luther's ontological claim that genuine ethics is possible only if moral action flows from a willing rather than a coerced heart. Luther identifies the law of the Spirit in Paul's statement "the law of the Spirit of life set me free from the law of sin and death" (Rom. 8:2 NIV) as that which the law of the letter demands, namely, willingness toward the law through a changed heart: "Consequently the law of the Spirit consists in what the law of the letter demands, namely, willingness toward the law." To put it differently, renewed communion with the

Word through a changed heart causes one to love God, his word, and one's fellow human beings. For Luther "love is the fulfillment of the law" (*KG*, 105).

It is wrong to interpret Luther's letter-spirit (law-gospel) opposition as a Pietistic or even Neoplatonic dualism of body and spirit. When Luther speaks of understanding the Old Testament and its Ten Commandments spiritually, he does not mean an inner, merely contemplative balm for the soul as opposed to carnal use; this Platonic division is irreconcilable with Luther's understanding of the incarnate Word. Luther's reading of Romans 7 demonstrates his holistic view: he does not oppose flesh and spirit as inner and outer factions of the human person but describes them as opposing principles that pervade the whole human being. Since there is no body-spirit dualism, Luther can claim that to read the Old Testament spiritually is to read it as a proclamation of God's mercy in Christ, which, once appropriated, leads to decisive ethical action.

Luther's grasp of the Bible's historicity and his Christocentric hermeneutics save his Old Testament readings from the moralizing tendency found in other Christian humanists. Erasmus, for example, blends the New Testament with Greek philosophy: Christ is the renewal of human nobility, damaged in the Fall, that is already found and predicted in ancient Hellenistic writings (Reader, "Luther als Ausleger," 255). By contrast Luther's doctrine of Christ as the incarnate cosmic Word that calls humanity back into communion with God prevents him from reducing Christ to a teacher of timeless moral principles, a portrait that dominated Jesus scholarship from the eighteenth to the twentieth century and that has been challenged seriously by the work of E. P. Sanders and N. T. Wright.

So far we have looked at the foundational concepts of Luther's ethics. It now remains to show how Luther's ethics differs in practice from the mere moralism he disliked so much.

From Word to Works: Luther's Relational Ethics

In a word, the whole kingdom of Satan in human beings, could not be defined in fewer or more expressive words than by saying—they are ignorant of and despise God! For where there is unbelief, there is disobedience, there is sacrilege, there is blasphemy against God, there is cruelty and want of mercy towards our neighbour, there is the love of self in all the things of God and humanity! Here you have a description of the glory and power of "Free-will!" (Luther [to Erasmus in 1525], *BW*, 337)

The free-will debate between Luther and Erasmus may strike the
reader as rather antiquated and useless, yet, as the quotation indicates,
it reminds us that ethics hinges on theological anthropology. Stated
differently, any discussion about ethics must include a view of human
nature. One might argue that Luther and Erasmus's disagreement merely
concerns the decidedly Christian issue of individual salvation, an in-house
debate whose outmoded metaphysical nature is suspect and unable to
contribute anything to a reconstruction of ethics in postmodern times.
After all, as Richard Rorty reminds us, in postmodernity ethics is no
longer connected to any absolute norms but consists in the prudent
assessment and selective choice from our collective past moral practices ("Do We Need Ethical Principles?" 13). Rorty's refusal to ground
his discussion of ethical problems ontologically is symptomatic of his
pragmatism. Rorty reacts principally to utilitarian and Kantian ethics,
to whose duty-bound masculinity he prefers a more feminine approach
to ethics based on developing the feminine qualities of trust and moral
growth. The mature moral person will "always have to alternate between
judging and trusting, just as we shall always have to alternate between
relying on our instinctive emotional response and relying on explicit
principles and laws [none of which] can give us clear guidance. But
moral maturity requires both societies and individuals to outgrow the
hope of ever getting such guidance" (ibid., 27).

Luther would have certainly agreed with Rorty that ethics has very
little to do with duty. Yet from Luther's point of view, Rorty's approach to
life is still naive because it omits an important question: what if human
judgment is impaired? Even more importantly, what if Rorty's implied
goodwill toward mature ethical behavior is opposed by a deep-seated
selfishness in the human psyche? The consideration of human nature
reveals a possible parallel to Erasmus's argument: Rorty's emphasis on
choice suggests something akin to Erasmus's free will, namely, that we
are willing to learn, judge, and choose what is good. Luther, however,
emphatically denies that we have the ability to do what is good until we
know God. No one makes a truly wise ethical choice because everyone's
will is inherently selfish. This egotism, which takes many forms, from
social action for selfish reasons to indifference to the plight of others,
also extends to religious behavior. In fact, Luther's scathing attack on
his own religion makes one wonder if the Christian community is not a
preferred breeding ground for moralism, that is, for humanly devised,
self-pleasing ethics.

For Luther, as for the remaining representatives of premodern hermeneutics discussed in this book, truly wise ethical choices require a proper
assessment of human character as fallen and selfish. This knowledge
comes only in an encounter with God and through the concrete ex-

ample of his love, the supreme ethical act, Christ's death on the cross. Only from the heart changed by this encounter flows the main ethical impulse to love one's neighbor. For Luther, our understanding of reality is mediated through God's spoken and written word, on the basis of which human conversation in the sense of living-together becomes possible and fruitful.

Luther's attack on Erasmus is thus not merely doctrinal. One must keep in mind that for Luther, godly living requires not legal obedience but a relationship with God. Erasmus inverts what Luther regards as the biblical foundation and superstructure for ethics: genuine freedom through belief in God and, flowing from that belief, works of righteousness. Luther understands Erasmus's refusal to recognize God's sovereignty over human beings as threatening the very foundation of ethics. Genuinely good actions are done out of trust in God, because only moral action out of complete trust is free from the stain of vainglory and human approval; and the basis of God's trustworthiness is his sovereignty, "for if you doubt, or disdain to know that God foreknows and wills all things, not contingently but necessarily and immutably, how can you believe, confidently trust to, and depend upon His promises?" (*BW*, 44).

For Luther ethics is a response to and flows from God's love. In other words, ethics has very little to do with duty and norms. Instead ethics is by definition *relational*. Luther believes that righteous acts must originate from a deeply personal relation to God. He expresses the quality of this relation in terms of adoption into God's family (*Kindschaft*). This family membership is nothing less than a re-creation, which results in the indwelling of each believer by Christ himself. Ethics, then, becomes a deeply ontological and relational affair. To be human is in effect the formation and transformation wrought by the Christian's participation in the Trinity: "Because the life of the Christian is not his own but that of Christ who lives in him" (*KG*, 193). For Luther the central concept of biblical ethics is the work of the Holy Spirit through whom Christ takes shape within the believer. While evangelical jargon often refers to this mystical indwelling as a changed heart, Luther cautions against an easy identification between feelings and ethics. Luther issues this warning because he knows well that even the Christian continues to share humanity's finitude and does not obtain full self-knowledge. Often, he argues, "a Christian doesn't know himself. Therefore don't orient yourself by what you feel and what your heart shows you. Rather you know that you are a Christian because you seize believingly the word which God has spoken" (*PK*, 115).

Without this reorientation of one's entire being ethics is impossible, even if one tried to emulate and imitate Christ as a great moral teacher. In his treatise *Little Lesson on What to Expect from the Gospels*, Luther writes that one should not turn Christ into a Moses, as if he were nothing but a teacher and an example like the other saints, as if the gospel were a legal or moral manual:

> Thus [to prevent this view] you should understand Christ's word, work, and suffering in two ways: yes, you do take Christ as an example. As he prays, fasts, and helps others so you should do and help your neighbor. But that is the least element of the gospel, because it makes Christ no more useful than any other holy man. His life remains restricted to himself and cannot aid you. The main element and foundation of the gospel is that before you take Christ as an example, you must accept him as a donation [*Gabe*] and a gift. (*KG*, 25)

Receiving Christ as a gift means to recognize God's love toward rebellious human beings. Luther thus recognizes that ethics begins with God's giving himself to human beings, binding himself to humanity in Christ. In each believer, the communion with the real person of Christ is the basis for good works. Luther explains enthusiastically, "To understand the gospel is to recognize the excessive [*überschwengliche*] goodness of God. This is the great fire of God's love to us; it makes heart and conscience glad, secure, and satisfied" (*KG*, 15). Genuine ethics is possible only after belief in Christ has fulfilled the first commandment, to love God. Following Augustine, Luther calls this the main work of faith. As the Christian communes with God through prayer and the word, Christ's image is impressed on him and becomes the source of good works: "Out of Christ's picture of grace in you must obtain [*schöpfen*] faith and trust that you are forgiven. Thus faith does not begin with works, nor do they produce it; rather faith flows from the blood, wounds, and death of Christ" (*SGW*, 132). The Christian depends on God's continual aid for ethical behavior: "Help, help, heavenly Father, so that just as the heart has begun to believe and to love you, so shall our mouth speak and our hands act. Thus we are to improve from the inside out, not the other way around. One should not pour water into the spring; on the contrary, water must come out of the spring. I have evil in my heart; it walks and sleeps with me and it will not be lessened by outward deeds" (*PK*, 49).

Luther teaches that only a change of the very core of our fallen humanity can bring us into a relationship with God. To be in communion with God is to be fully human, and to be fully human, at least for Luther, is to be ethical, for that is how God made human beings. The central issue that Luther saw in his debate with Erasmus (and with humanism in general) was that we cannot by our own will or agency enter into communion with God, but that the ontological change required for ethics must be effected by God. According to Luther, God demands that "we must become a different being [*ein anderes Wesen*]," "a different creature [*eine andere Kreatur*]," and "a different person [*eine andere Person*]." In a lengthy illustration, Luther depicts conversion as a new birth and concludes, "The child neither creates itself nor does it give birth to itself, but after it has been created, it creates works" (*PK*, 49; *WA*, 41:612).

Luther's view that biblical ethics cannot stem from our own efforts defines his view of the gospel as essentially the faithfulness of God to his creation. The good news is that God, who initiated the human-divine dialogue in the first place, does not relinquish his intent to restore fallen humanity to its fullness, and to be fully human means to converse and commune with God.

Luther is fully aware that ethics is possible without belief in Christ. In fact, non-Christians often seem more selfless than so-called followers of Christ. So why does one need a relation to the biblical God? Very simple, says Luther. The basic purpose of ethics in any culture (he really has only Western thought in mind) is to achieve the greatest amount of bliss and happiness: "The sages of the world have asked since the beginning of the world, how can one become righteous and blessed?" (*PK*, 24; *WA*, 41:608). Given the depravity of human nature, however, Christianity is the only religion that can even begin to achieve that goal. The problem of Greek metaphysics, Luther argues, is its reliance on human goodness as an "often hidden quality of the soul" that needs to be awakened and exercised (*WA*, 578). Luther agrees that pagans can do good deeds and even seemingly fulfill the requirements of the great commandment to love one's neighbor, but they will not do so out of free, genuine love for the other. Thus the problem of nontheological ethics lies in the requirement of love. Without the infusion of divine grace, says Luther, our self-centered nature does not truly love others. Because real love of one's neighbor must stand the test of the cross,

> human nature may imitate love but no further than up to the cross. From the cross, however, it turns away; indeed, here human nature feels the contradiction and resists grace with hostility. By the cross, however, I understand disgust; because human nature loves, praises, commits acts of charity, and blesses only as long as it doesn't get hurt. Whenever you hurt it or go against its will, it immediately shows its true face: its love disappears and turns into hate, clamoring, and evil. This is because [human nature] depends on deception, not on truth; it loves the appearance, not the thing itself; its [true] friendship does not belong to the neighbor but to his goods and possessions. (*KG*, 230)

The true measure of unconditional love for one's neighbor is Christ's death and resurrection. God reached out to mankind while fully knowing that humanity hated him. Such supernatural love, argues Luther, is the only legitimate ground of ethics, and the genuine token of having been touched by the power of the living word is the manifestation of divine love in human relations. Thus, Luther concludes, the cross is the touchstone of love. Here then is the final dynamic of self-knowledge and knowledge of God, which is also the foundation of Calvin's thought: biblical ethics requires self-knowledge, that is, recognition of one's self-centeredness. This happens in the encounter with the cross. Whoever embraces the cross has come to see that human nature is selfish to the core and needs God to overcome selfishness. Then ethics and love toward one's neighbor become possible. On the other hand, whoever misunderstands or hates the cross continues to wallow in self-deception and self-indulgence, and his or her good works will always be tainted by selfishness.

In light of present debates on ethics, a modern reader of Luther is compelled to ask, Even when we grant Luther's theistic universe, can—and, in fact, do—we not get along pretty well without relational ethics? In other words, how does Christian ethics really differ from other forms of moral discourse that also claim to be effective? Presumably, Luther would answer that Christian ethics differs from others in that it begins with trust in God, for "all other works a [non-Christian] can also do; but knowing with certainty to be loved by God, that is only possible for the Christian who has been illumined and matured by grace" (*SGW*, 115). Faith is, after all, "to trust [God] always and everywhere" (*Commentary on Romans*, 82). Thus, to paraphrase the common reformational dictum, faith comes before works. Luther argues that scholastic theology in its reliance on pagan wisdom (i.e., Aristotle) has inverted this relation by making faith into a virtue, when it actually precedes all "virtues." For, "in reality it [faith] alone makes all works good, pleasing and valuable because faith trusts God. . . . [The scholastics] have turned faith into a *habitus*, when throughout the holy scriptures a deed that comes from faith is called a godly deed" (ibid.). Faith, at least for Luther, can never be a habit because a habit is something we can develop and control by ourselves.

In contrast to habit, faith is given and sustained by God; it is the discourse with God that prompts genuine ethical behavior, because now ethics is founded on God's love—not on an abstract, theoretical concept (God, the highest good) but on the concrete relation with Jesus himself: "So when you listen or watch how Christ does something or suffers you should not doubt that he himself is yours in his work and suffering, and you can rest in him as if you had done it yourself, as if you yourself were Christ" (*KG*, 25). Having experienced God's love, the believer is free to love others. To our age, in which freedom has become a consumer's good, implicitly defined as the liberty to do as we please or to achieve a certain standard of living (Thielicke, *Freedom of the Christian Man*, 29),

Luther's definition of freedom is refreshingly different. As God expressed his freedom by binding himself to humanity, our freedom too lies in serving others: "Our freedom is a freedom for the servanthood of love: the apostle [Paul] says we should serve one another in love. Because that is freedom: to know no obligation but to love one's neighbor. Love teaches effortlessly how to live properly; however, if love is missing, one cannot have enough regulations" (*KG*, 233).

We can see now that Rorty's question "Can one not have ethics without faith in God?" misses the point because it defines ethics as what Luther calls works or moral deeds. For Luther, however, ethics (or virtue, as he calls it) is a state of being toward God and one's neighbor rather than moral behavior. This crucial distinction is important for our later discussion of John Caputo, Dietrich Bonhoeffer, and Emmanuel Levinas. Luther's concept of ethics as relation rather than moral behavior lays an important foundation for a theological theory of interpretation as an ethical enterprise. Ethics here becomes not so much a set of moral guidelines for interpretation but rather defines the heart of hermeneutics as ethical, as oriented, first of all, to the person of Christ and, second, to one's neighbor. Ethics is thus first of all an orientation to the transcendent other, an insight philosophy has rediscovered through the work of Emmanuel Levinas (1906–96). Moreover, Luther also clearly understands Christian ethics not as a moral code but as a state of being brought about by an ontological change from self-centeredness to an outward, other-oriented self. Dietrich Bonhoeffer has recovered this insight for philosophical theology; we will unpack this idea in the last section.

Luther does, however, anticipate the pragmatist's question: why is exteriority (i.e., transcendence) necessary? Why can we not live according to human-made moral norms rather than appeal to an "external" power? Luther's answer to this "pagan-morality," as he calls it, is that it, too, is based on faith, namely, faith in human goodness and teachability. The pragmatist's, and even the moralist's, problem is the human will. In Luther's biblically informed worldview, ever since the Fall human beings have suffered from an ontological defect, manifestly a will bent on self-love. To become genuinely ethical, solidarity with one's fellow humans must be rooted in the very ontological fiber of our being. This, however, can only be effected by entering into communion with God; otherwise ethics must rely on externally imposed regulations, which, whether self-imposed or foisted on us, clash with our selfishness, causing us to rebel against them. Such moral impositions will remain, to use Luther's terms, works of the flesh. Indeed, Luther argues that one of scholasticism's greatest faults is to confuse pagan morality with Christian morality: "Vain and injurious are the speculations (of the scholastics) who teach with Aristotle that our virtues and faults adhere to the soul merely as whitewash to the wall. By this teaching they fully destroy the distinction between spirit and flesh" (*Commentary on Romans*, 116). Luther agrees with Paul that "wisdom of the flesh [mere human wisdom] is death [i.e., it brings out the worst in us, it actually provokes transgression]. Our phronesis [a Greek term Luther translates as 'wisdom']¹⁰ must be shaped by God and grounded in faith if it is to be true ethical wisdom" (*KG*, 217).

Luther also anticipates what one might call the Hobbesian ethic: "Could not laws serve to keep human depravity in check?" (*KG*, 217). The answer is a qualified no. Human laws are always based on human reason and thus prone to injustice. Even the best human laws, moreover, cannot be fulfilled to the spirit of their intent, but—as jurisprudence shows—one must always compromise at the cost of justice. At the best of times, a humanly devised legal system can prevent physical hurt and anarchy. At the worst of times, utopias implemented by those who dream that a "benign" autocrat can restore order to human society result in "revolt, unrest, and strife," as numerous examples from our history show. Still, undaunted by such failures, "human reason would like to achieve the path toward . . . a perfect political order through legal measures; yet that is impossible" (*PK*, 25). What society really needs, argues Luther, is not external legal impositions but internal conviction of neighborly love that makes restrictive laws unnecessary.

Luther's most detailed description of how love of God works itself out hermeneutically in ethical application is found in the third part of his *Commentary on Galatians* and in his *Sermons on Good Works*. First, and this might seem an obvious point, morally good behavior is judged according to God's scale. What is good, Luther claims, must be gathered from the Decalogue, not from human precept or consensus, because such always tends to be shaped in favor of those who are in power. A practical application of this principle is Luther's preaching against unethical business practices. In fact, Luther's treatises on sales practices (1520) and usury (1524) are really a hermeneutical application of the biblical commandment to love one's neighbor. Luther laments the ruling motto of businessmen to sell their merchandise for the highest possible profit. This rule is ungodly because it is based on selfishness and shows no concern for others. This rule, argues Luther, "creates room for greed and opens hell's every door and window. What does this consensus say but, 'I do not care about my neighbor . . . as long as I satisfy my own desire for profit?'" ("Von Kaufhandlung," 118). With greed in the driver's seat, the merchant actually regards his neighbor's plight as an opportunity for making a sale and enslaving him in debt. It seems as if business practice

---

10. Luther links the meaning of the Greek word to German terms that connote the heart's inclination, intent, purpose, opinion, bent of mind.

has not changed all that much since Luther's time. Luther toys with the idea of regulated pricing but finally suggests that the merchant should not charge more than the actual value of the item according to the free market plus his legitimate profit.

Luther does not naively believe that the world can actually be governed by Christian ethics. Nor is he about to divulge a theological version of Adam Smith's economic principles in order to Christianize economics; Luther states repeatedly that there are too few Christians to change the world of business. Rather he wants to warn the Christian businessman against adopting unethical practices in a largely non-Christian society and thereby giving up his newly gained freedom in Christ to become enslaved to secular economics, a system driven by the maximization of profit. Instead, those who live in the Word should consider their neighbor's plight. Although nothing speaks against their turning a profit, they should be free from the god of mammon and have a responsible but also detached relationship to work and possessions.

In Luther's view, an ethics stemming from communion with God also relativizes moral acts by preventing an ethical hierarchy. Although human wisdom elevates some moral actions while devaluing others, in God's economy "all works become equal in value. . . . All differences among the works fall away whether they are great or small, short or long, few or many" (*SGW*, 116). Thus small deeds will not remain undone simply because they do not garner recognition. Stated positively, Luther's biblical ethics lends meaning to even the smallest service, an insight closely connected with his view that one's professional service to the community is a sacred office just as much as that of a priest. Luther's relational ethics has great hermeneutic consequences: ideally a person in communion with God no longer requires rule books on interpersonal behavior, for the most natural impulse is now to love one's neighbor. To be sure, this general principle must be applied, and some may regard Luther's view as more difficult because the Christian is now saddled with the hermeneutical burden of applying the general principle of loving one's neighbor (*Nächstenliebe*) to every specific situation. Luther, however, regards such a position as hermeneutical freedom rather than bondage. Ethics that flows from a changed heart "is not bound by any work nor [does it] refrain from any. Rather [it is] like a tree, as the first Psalm has it, which bears fruit at the appropriate time, that is, according to the situation" (*SGW*, 116). Luther illustrates his point by comparing relational ethics to a marriage relationship:

> When a man or a woman is completely certain that the other accepts him in love, who has to teach him how to behave or what to do or avoid, what to say or omit, or what to consider? The mere trust in the other person teaches

him all these things. . . . There is no difference among the actions; he does the small, short, and menial [things] and their opposite equally with a joyful, satisfied, and carefree heart; however, if there is doubt of acceptance in the relationship, one begins to imagine a difference between one's efforts in order to gain affection; uncertainty about the outcome causes one's heart to be heavy and makes the work unsatisfying. (*SGW,* 116–17)

Thus ethics grounded in faith does not depend on people's approval, but one's approval by God guarantees, so to speak, that ethics will exist despite our environment's response. Neither popularity and recognition nor economic benefits should determine one's ethics. Luther argues that people often give up good works because financial circumstances seem to indicate that God has given up on them, or, if they do not believe in God, they lose faith in humanity (*SGW,* 118).

Trust in God, however, moves ethics away from abstract absolute principles and consideration of profit (economic or psychological) to a relational level. Trust in God is grounded in God's love toward humanity, which in turn is founded on God's incarnate Word, who has demonstrated God's love and has lived the first ethical principle of loving one's neighbor. To base ethics on anything else, according to Luther, is idolatry (*SGW,* 121). However, moral codes devised by humans seem to always function on the principle of winning someone's favor. In delineating true morality, Luther's conviction that Greek philosophy is fundamentally different from biblical thought surfaces once again. Western thought, he complains, has bought into the "seeking of honor and glory" advocated as the main virtue in pagan literatures. These teach that human worth should be measured according to one's quest for and achievement of honor. Such ethical systems motivated by human recognition put one at the mercy of the culturally dependent gauge of honor. Any such work, though seemingly heroic, is really blemished by selfish thirst for recognition. Not only the pagan, however, falls into the trap of recognition. Christian religiosity is an even more fertile ground for selfish ethics. Luther claims that the institutionalized church could gain its tremendous hold over Europe only because people do not trust God and seek recognition in religious works, which allows the division of society into sacred and secular: "One seeks from the devil and from human or other beings [the acceptance] that is found only in God through simply faith and trust" (ibid., 142–43).

In fact, the entire structure of the institutionalized church depends on a false hierarchy of values. Luther zeros in on the central question: why do even Christians appeal to other imaginary authorities for acceptance rather than seek communion with God and rely on his promise of acceptance? "Human pride," answers Luther. Self-concern turns us into hypocrites, makes us respecters of persons rather than of truth, and allows us to cloak injustice with the mantle of religion (*SGW*, 146–47). Luther's criticism of religion is so severe because he understands the church as the implementation of God's kingdom on earth. Relational ethics points to the reality of God's kingdom, in which God is more trustworthy than the system: "We must prove that we love God and his name and glory and his praise more than anything else, and that we trust him more and expect more good from him than from anything else. He is our greatest treasure, for whom we should risk all other goods" (ibid., 145). To behave decently and to act righteously out of fear of punishment or from the motive of gaining favor with God goes against the very nature of Luther's ethical ideal and falls under "works righteousness." Fear or appeasement as ethical motivation are the lowest form of religious belief (ibid., 119). Relational ethics, then, is independent of human recognition. It is motivated neither by fear of divine punishment nor by the desire for fame but is rooted firmly in communion with God.

Luther's Hermeneutics of the Cross

Luther's hermeneutics and its ethical impulse are anchored in his concept of the Word. To use Luther's terms, if one is not "in the Word," one can read neither the Bible nor reality correctly. Only through communion with God can the veil be lifted and the biblical text understood in the light of Christ's work. And only if one's heart is changed by divine grace can one truly fulfill the two basic ethical principles: to love God and to love one's neighbor. Most importantly, these principles cannot be grasped as abstract propositions; rather they are understood only when they are lived. Even this brief survey of Luther's hermeneutics shows the breadth of his thought and allows the following observations regarding hermeneutics and ethics.

Theological accounts of ethics are liable to a certain triumphalism, as if discoursing with God were easy and the practice of ethics nearly automatic. It is such reductionist views of ethics that Rorty justly criticizes and opposes. Luther's paradoxical view of the person in dialogue with God as torn between selfishness and godliness (classically expressed as "justified and sinner") does not allow for triumphalism. Rather ethics is an ongoing struggle of overcoming one's natural selfishness, a struggle that requires one's constant standing under the corrective influence of the Word, which is "contrary to our thinking."

Also, this account of Luther's hermeneutics challenges the claim that precritical hermeneutics is confined to method and does not consider ontological issues. I hope to have shown how deeply ontological Luther's outlook is. In fact, "ontological" may well be an unsuitable term for

Luther's insistence that our interpretation of reality must take its most basic orientation from the divine self-revelation through the person of Christ. As we shall see later, in light of recent theological and philosophical views on truth as personal in distinction to ontology, Luther's view is more closely related to the relational hermeneutics of Emmanuel Levinas and Dietrich Bonhoeffer than to ontological categories. God's self-revelation as an actual historical person requires truth categories different from those offered by our Greek ontological heritage.

Luther's view of the Bible as the word of the Word (Christ) gives his interpretative model a dynamic quality that contrasts sharply with modern debates on plenary inerrancy and inspiration. These debates in evangelical circles into which he is dragged in our day, and which are often completely detached from any deeper grounding in the nature of either God or man, resemble the arid scholasticism Luther himself detested. Luther's grasp of what one may call the linguistic or, better, the conversational and communal nature of God's word combines philosophical and theological hermeneutics and frees the scriptures to be the word of God anew in every given historical situation. Everything from the human-divine conversation (the vertical) and the human-human dialogue (the horizontal) depends on God's word.

Luther's concept of God's word also prevents his biblical ethics from freezing into a prescriptive moral code. Biblical hermeneutics is relational, as is the ethics derived from it. For example, Luther observes that Christ and the apostles reinterpret the Old Testament Decalogue for their own purposes. He can even say that Christ and the apostles establish "new Decalogues" (*WA*, 39:47). Similarly Christians cannot shun the hermeneutical responsibility of applying the command to love one's neighbor to their own particular situation. The German Lutheran scholar Paul Althaus was the first to clearly spell out Luther's "situational" ethics: "[According to Luther,] the Christian cannot arrive at the necessary decision simply by reading the directions given him in the Bible or by finding applicable statements in the New Testament or even in the sayings of Jesus. None of these are adequate in terms of a specific situation that is always different from previous situations" (*Ethics of Martin Luther*, 31). Luther certainly knew that Christians can err, and err gravely, in this process and confuse their own selfish ambitions with the guidance of God's Spirit; yet such is the price to be paid for the hermeneutical freedom granted to human beings.

Luther's writings on the church and Christian behavior constitute just such hermeneutical application. He always takes the Decalogue and the New Testament writings as his starting point, but he never simply repeats them; he translates them in light of the gospel for contemporary ears in order to apply them to culturally relevant issues in a new way. The guiding principles in this appropriation are always God's love toward humanity and the desire of the Christian to love one's neighbor. In this way, God's word is interpreted and lived out in the community. In short, biblical ethics does more than just preserve the peace, and the Christian who stands in relation to God is directed by more than a desire to maintain order and peace in society; only such an ethics, Luther argues, will persist even under the most adverse circumstances. When Christians maintain ethical behavior even under suffering and persecution, they live the theology of the cross and testify to the reality of God's kingdom. Such ethics, however, requires more than disciplined adherence to abstract propositions—only a relationship with God can sustain it (Althaus, *Ethics of Martin Luther*, 34).

Luther's Continuing Relevance

Luther remains of central importance for any debate on hermeneutics, in fact, for the relation of philosophy and theology as a whole, for it is not too much to say that Luther is a key influence in German and French philosophy. Without Luther, no Heidegger; without Heidegger, no Derrida. Indeed, the very notion of deconstruction, the patient questioning of philosophical concepts and their adequacy to express human reality fully, finds an early expression in Luther's critique of scholastic theology. Luther's antipathy to the intrusion of Greek conceptuality into theology also provides an important link between the Reformer and the twentieth-century philosopher Martin Heidegger and thus between the theological and the philosophical hermeneutical traditions.

Recent works on the origins of Heidegger's philosophy agree that, besides the writings of Paul, Luther's work exerted the greatest theological influence on the young philosopher (van Buren, "Martin Heidegger," 260). The early Heidegger shared Luther's disdain of Greek philosophy, which had imprisoned the pristine Christian experience in Aristotelian Greek concepts. In fact, it has been argued that the term "deconstruction" (*Destruktion*), which Derrida found in Heidegger, is derived from Luther's Heidelberg disputation (ibid., 163; Kisiel, *Genesis of Heidegger's Being and Time*, 101).

With Luther, Martin Heidegger rejected this impersonal abstract highest good, the God of onto-theology. Pero Brkic tells us in his monumental work *Heidegger und die Theologie* (1994) that "this God is for Heidegger an ungodly God. In onto-theological causal thinking, God loses the crucial attributes of holiness and glory, distance and nearness, hiddenness and mystery. The onto-theological God is no longer a God but a mere concept, a God over which man exerts power" (225). As late as 1957, in his *Identität und Differenz*, Heidegger claims that "the onto-theological character of metaphysics has become questionable for thinking not because of atheism" but because it is loosely based on a Christian God emasculated and distorted by metaphysics (51–52). Thus one needs to deconstruct metaphysical history in order to trace this development and free thinking from it in order to unite it with humanity's existential ground: being. Heidegger thought that Luther's *destructio* of Aristotelian scholasticism and his return to the concrete historical consciousness of primal Christianity had pointed the way to such an understanding but that the later Luther fell short of accomplishing this task (van Buren, "Martin Heidegger," 170). Heidegger finally finds the unity of thinking and being in the pre-Socratic philosophers and in German poetry.[11]

No wonder, then, that Heidegger felt drawn to Luther, for Luther's deeply relational ontology with its hermeneutic struggle for meaning, his stress on listening to a transcendent word that was historically mediated already prefigure Heidegger's existential mode of thinking, which is so different from more static modernist conceptions of knowledge. Indeed, one may argue that from Luther to Heidegger philosophy has come full circle, for both thinkers are equally removed from Cartesian and idealistic philosophy. In fact, the very foundation of Luther's thought is that knowledge and ethics are relational. The finite creature depends on God's revelation for true knowledge. *Creatus sum ergo sum*, rather than Descartes's *Cogito ergo sum*, is Luther's epistemological motto. At the same time (as our reading of Bonhoeffer will show), an extension of Luther's thought also provides grounds for a critique of Heideggerian ontology, because the Reformer's incarnational focus on the person of Christ provides a transcendence essential for knowledge that Heidegger's analysis of human existence in light of being cannot offer.

Luther's belief in the linguisticality of creation constitutes another main difference between the two thinkers. Heidegger's famous claim that language is the house of being could be stated with even more confidence by Luther. However, Heidegger's post-Nietzschean reality no longer knows the voice of God, and so, in a flattening of reality, the word of life, for Luther the beginning of all language and meaning, becomes the prison of language. Philosophical hermeneutics, as developed by Hans-Georg Gadamer, adopts Heidegger's emphasis on language; in fact, as we shall see, language takes the place of Luther's Word (i.e., God) as the hermeneutical medium. For Luther language and meaning are grounded in the Word, that is, in a God whose word upholds all creation. In Gadamer

---

11. Perhaps the clearest outline of Heidegger's program and agenda is found in his lectures summarized under the title *Einführung in die Metaphysik*, translated as *An Introduction to Metaphysics*.

the language is disconnected from this ultimate grounding. Gadamer's insight—borrowed from Heidegger—that we live in language, much like a fish surrounded by water, rightly points out the primordiality of language and the importance of concepts. However, if nothing real and binding underlies the meaning of words, if human language itself constitutes ultimate reality, then language and custom alone inform the meaning of words for each community.

If the conventional meaning of words is not undergirded by a reality that transcends convention and lends transcultural currency to the word, community values cannot be judged. For instance, Luther defined the concept of love according to the word of God. Love is defined by Christ's self-sacrifice. To love in any context means to esteem another above oneself. Without such an ultimate definition, love may mean any number of things. Luther seems to have realized that important concepts used to describe human interaction must, at least from a theological viewpoint (and that, for Luther, was the only proper one since God had created reality), be grounded in God's word. In other words, the loss of God's word is related to a loss of ethics. Luther said to Erasmus, "Take away assertions and you take away Christianity" (*BW*, 13). Without the word of God, at least according to Luther, the norm and the empowerment for doing good vanish. It is no coincidence that Heidegger never realized an ethics and that his last word is an attentive but merely passive posture of letting be (*Gelassenheit*), so different from the Pauline proclamation of God's kingdom, whose ethics of suffering and neighborly love redeems humanity and creation (Wright, *What St. Paul Really Said*, 128).

Finally, distant echoes of Luther's concept that the word proceeds from the inner word of God (ultimately equated with Jesus the Christ) to a visible incarnation of text and flesh can be heard in the writing of Hans-Georg Gadamer. The concept of the inner word, which means so much to Gadamer, and his use of the incarnation as illustration of human linguisticality are familiar sounds to the ear attuned to Luther's theology of the Word. The following chapter will trace the development of Luther's and Calvin's hermeneutics in their theological heirs. An examination of key thinkers, most of whom are central to current philosophical accounts of hermeneutic development, will help us to answer the question whether the incarnational viewpoint of Luther and the hermeneutical circle of self-knowledge set out by Calvin were faithfully observed or distorted by rigid orthodoxy in the coming generations.

3

PURITAN AND PIETIST HERMENEUTICS

The main argument of part 1 of this book is that theological herme-neutics, particularly the hermeneutics of the Protestant Reforma-tion and its intellectual heirs, cannot be reduced to a narrow, rule-gov-erned interpretive practice that applies exclusively to the reading of a sacred text. It is simply not true that modern philosophical hermeneutics is more universal because of its concern for the dynamics of human understanding in contrast with a theological hermeneutics that was obsessed with rules for scriptural practices, which quickly degenerated into the intellectual gymnastics of scholasticism.

It *is* true, of course, that theological hermeneutics revolves around the locus of the biblical text, but this is the case precisely because the text makes a claim to universality. The universal claim at the very heart of theological hermeneutics is that all reality must be interpreted in the light of God's self-disclosure, which is recorded in God's acts in history, his prophetic utterances, all of which culminate in the incarnation, death, and resurrection of the second Person of the Trinity. For better or for worse, pre-Enlightenment theology interprets human existence in light of the biblical story, a narrative it considers normative for all humanity.

Theological hermeneutics has always understood the basic theo-logical premise of the biblical narrative to be the communion between God and humanity, not a mystical or monistic unity that leads to the dissolution of the self but a participation in the community that already existed from all eternity in the Godhead itself. In retelling and applying the basic biblical story of the loss and reestablishment of human-divine communion for their respective historical horizons, precritical theologians developed an extensive intellectual apparatus of anthropology, psychology, and epistemology to explain the ebb and flow of divine-human communication. These writings were not exercises in arid scholasticism, however, but were conducted with the understanding that the vertical axis of human-divine fellowship has direct communal and political consequences. Such cherished modern notions as the separation of faith and reason or the separation of public conduct and private religious opinion were foreign to precritical theology.

The admission that such a view is preferable to the modernist separation of belief and practice is not to deny the often disastrous consequences resulting from the interconnectedness of politics and theology in the history of the Christian religion. Yet postmodern criticism has certainly taught us that modernity's faith in a neutral hermeneutical position is equally misplaced. And with this hard-won insight, we have returned to the precritical notion of "faith seeking understanding." Simply put, we all hold to an interpretive framework according to which we make sense of our experiential fragments, a plausibility structure we do not ultimately question. This is true for every kind of knowledge, whether in the natural or the human sciences. Too much has been written concerning the erroneous assumptions of scientific epistemology that have shaped epistemologies of the previous centuries to repeat it here, yet much of it may be summed up in the theological insight that knowledge of any nature proceeds by faith and follows the dynamics of belief with its convictions and personal involvement.

The recovery of pre-Enlightenment theological hermeneutics requires two avenues of research. One is to show that within their theological framework and the available knowledge base, these theologians were in fact astute and critical readers of the Bible. This avenue has already been explored by scholars such as David Steinmetz, Richard Muller, and others. Their work has forced us to rethink Hans Frei's label "precritical" for theological interpretation prior to the Enlightenment. This term is ill chosen, because it conveys the erroneous perception that Puritan and Pietist commentators did not practice grammatical-historical criticism, when in truth such critical concerns originated with biblical exegesis. Practitioners of biblical interpretation during and following the Reformation were well aware of Jewish exegesis, interacted with scientific and textual-critical theories of their day, and readily admitted corruptions of the biblical text. Thus one necessary path for assessing accurately our hermeneutical heritage must address the textual-critical abilities of these pre-Enlightenment theorists.

I want to pursue the second path of recovering theological hermeneutics by showing that not only the exegetical practice of premodern
thinkers but also its underlying hermeneutical presuppositions are worth
recovering, given the renewed interest in ethics and transcendence in
current philosophical thought. Ethics, to borrow Charles Taylor's expression, is the ability to talk about what constitutes "a good life," in
a world troubled by "a loss of meaning, the fading of moral horizons"
(*Malaise of Modernity*, 10). We will discover that Puritan and Pietist
hermeneutics derived moral confidence and norms for social activism
from an extrahuman standard and the framework of a created universe.
Philosophical hermeneutics, by contrast, fails to achieve similar moral
conviction, and its ethics is weak in the absence of such a framework.

This is not to say, however, that Puritans and Pietists present a model
we can emulate uncritically. As we have seen in the case of Calvin, Christians are often condemned by the very biblical ethics they expound. The
main point, however, is that the starting point of modern interpretation
from a nontheistic position, including philosophical hermeneutics, in
contrast to precritical theocentrism, lacks a transcendent ethical norm
such as the universal command to love one's fellow human being or the
grounding of human dignity and the preciousness of human life in the
imago Dei concept.

In this chapter, then, we will examine the heirs of Luther and Calvin, the
German Pietists and the English Puritans. Our goal is to see whether these
theologians preserve the earlier emphasis on ethics and the relational nature
of knowledge that Luther and Calvin had derived from their Christocentric
hermeneutical stance. Moreover, this section of the book aims to demonstrate that pre-Enlightenment hermeneutics was very much concerned
with the nature of human understanding and its ethical implications.

Finally, let me end this introduction with a brief comment for those who
think that English Puritans and German Pietists should not be lumped
together because their theological premises were too different. In reality
these two movements have more similarities than differences, a fact confirmed by the great influence prominent Puritan theologians had on the
development of German Pietism (Lovelace, *American Pietism*, 37, 72). For
the history of hermeneutics, it is much more helpful to view English Puritan
and German Pietist theologians as one movement of spiritual renewal that
swept through Europe as a continuation of the Reformation.

The Transition: From Luther to Flacius

My primary motivation for the retrieval of hermeneutics after Luther
is to read against the grain of the established Dilthey-Gadamer-Grondin

account of premodern hermeneutics *and* against the grain of erroneous Christian views of hermeneutic development. While the tide is slowly turning, many Christians still cling to foundationalist epistemology in their reading of the Bible and hence embrace a cognitivist-rationalist hermeneutics. In this approach, timeless concepts replace Christ as the mighty fortress Luther trusted, and battles are fought not by wrestling with the scriptures but by defending theological language and concepts that form part of our cultural identity.

In the Dilthey-Gadamer-Grondin account, this idolizing of ahistorical propositions took place as soon as theological hermeneutics was systematized after Luther. The German philosopher Wilhelm Dilthey (1833–1911) first credited Protestantism with the founding of both historical criticism and the science of hermeneutics (*Gesammelte Schriften*, 2:115). Within this context, Dilthey cited the Lutheran theologian Illyricus Matthias Flacius (1520–75) as a key figure of hermeneutical history, a status that Flacius has retained with recent hermeneutical historians (*GW*, 2:284–88; *IPH*, 23; Maier, *Biblical Hermeneutics*, 338).

Flacius's interest in systematizing and defending Lutheran doctrine derived in part from his personal friendship with Luther, under whom he was converted. Flacius quite self-consciously saw himself as living at a time when God was pleased to grant new learning so that the scriptures might be better understood than at any other time since the apostolic church. Like many other academically trained Reformers, he saw that much of the obscurity in the Bible was due not only to insufficient knowledge of the scriptures as a whole but also to unfamiliarity with biblical culture and languages. He believed that God would allow an increasingly clearer reading of his word, a process that Flacius understood to have gained tremendous momentum with the Reformation (*De Ratione Cognoscendi*, 22). Most of the practical advice for scriptural interpretation is contained in the second part of Flacius's work titled *De Ratione Cognoscendi Sacras Literas*, in which the author analyzes the stylistics, genre, and grammatical-historical and linguistic difficulties connected with reading the Bible.[1]

In sum, Flacius marks the beginning of a new era in Protestant hermeneutics, which arose when the Roman Catholic Church challenged the clarity of the scriptures on textual grounds to bolster its claim for interpretative authority. Flacius is one of the first textual apologists to

---

1. The entire work was conceived as a statement of Lutheran dogmatics based on Luther's theology as drawn from the *Commentary on Romans* and was meant to correct and supplement Melanchthon's *Loci Communes* (*De Ratione Cognoscendi*, xii). The first part of the work therefore contains Flacius's theology, while the second part deals with Bible difficulties and hermeneutics in light of the theological foundation of the first section.

admit in detail to textual difficulties and to show that they either can be overcome by sound hermeneutical rules or (in some extreme cases) must be borne until God is pleased to grant more light to the church through advanced scholarship. It is important to see Flacius's candor concerning interpretive difficulties not as the first step toward a supposedly inevitable outcome of historical criticism but rather as exemplifying the practice of critical scholarship within a framework of trust in the scriptures, which characterizes pre-Enlightenment hermeneutics.

Dilthey ascribes to Flacius a central role in hermeneutic history because Flacius represents the first systematic response to a two-pronged Catholic attack on the Protestant affirmation of the scriptures as a self-interpreting text (*Gesammelte Schriften*, 2:117).

The first line of attack attempted to present patristic views of interpretation and church authority as a unified chorus against the Reformation teachings on justification and the self-interpreting nature of scripture. Following the humanist motto "ad fontes," Protestant theologians had no trouble showing that a monolithic patristic tradition simply did not exist, let alone that it confirmed Catholic claims about the supremacy of the church's interpretive authority.

The second Catholic charge, against the clarity and sufficiency of the scriptures for matters of faith and moral practice, was less easy to defuse, and the stakes were higher: the doctrine of justification by faith alone, the main pillar of the Protestant Reformation, was at stake in the discussion about the biblical text's reliability and authority.

Protestant hermeneutics, then, arose largely in response to Catholic arguments for the church (and thus its theologians) as the final arbiter in interpretation. Such claims evoked several efforts by Protestants to provide hermeneutical ground rules for scriptural interpretation, of which Flacius's was the most sustained and influential.

Flacius wrote many polemical and historical works, but his most discussed legacy is the *Clavis Scripturae Sacrae* (1547). This work warrants Flacius's status as the founder of modern hermeneutics,[2] because in the *Clavis* he attempted to systematize Luther's practice of scripture translation and exegesis (*De Ratione Cognoscendi*, ii). Flacius's writing marks the transition from Luther's wide-ranging, often nonsystematic thought on interpretation to a hermeneutical manual. In this transition, does Flacius reduce Luther's insights regarding human understanding and ethics to mere methodological considerations?

A careful reading of Flacius shows that he remains faithful to Luther's Christocentric hermeneutics. Christ remains the heart and thus the

---

2. "Der Begründer der neueren Hermeneutik" (W. Dilthey, "Die Entstehung der Hermeneutik" [1900], in *Gesammelte Schriften*, 5:331).

hermeneutic whole of scripture by which its parts are to be read. Flacius is completely aware that the reading of the Bible demands not an objective reader but one who is deeply biased (a characteristic he shares with all the orthodox theologians featured in this study). Like Gadamer, who cautions those who oppose an objective interpretive approach to one guided by doctrinal presuppositions, Flacius is aware that successful understanding of any subject or discipline requires a consciously chosen presupposition. Flacius argues that just as understanding in general builds on a certain preknowledge, so the Bible itself demands a believing preunderstanding of God's existence and character, without one's necessarily having proved it (*De Ratione Cognoscendi*, 47). According to Flacius, a knowledge of and a relationship with Jesus Christ constitute a necessary preunderstanding that allows the reader access to the scriptures.

Flacius states that the first principle of theology is to take the biblical text's own claim to be the word of God seriously. After all, "the prophets and the entire Bible are (according to the witness of Peter in his first letter, verse 20) not a matter of individual recognition or interpretation: but as [the Bible] has been given by the Holy Spirit through the Prophets, so it must also necessarily be interpreted through his light" (*De Ratione Cognoscendi*, 31). Flacius merely touches on the role of the Holy Spirit in interpretation (a matter I will discuss in greater detail in the section on John Owen), but in the context of his teaching, the meaning is clear. The word of God is written under the supervision of the Spirit, and unless this Spirit is within the reader, guiding him as he reads, he cannot really grasp and appreciate the subject matter conveyed by the text.

Thus just as he was for Luther, the subject matter and unity of the biblical text is Jesus the Christ. He is the hermeneutical fulcrum, the beginning and the end of interpretation. Without Christ, the Bible cannot be properly understood, and if the reader has received Christ, the Bible will reveal nothing to him but Christ and that through Christ. According to Flacius, Christocentric hermeneutics distinguishes the true Christian from the traditionalist, on the one hand, and the enthusiasts (*fanatici*), on the other. It is the office of Christ to open the scriptures to the reader and illumine his heart (John 16:13), and in Christ are all the treasures of wisdom and the knowledge of God (Col. 2:3; *De Ratione Cognoscendi*, 35). In short, Christ not only provides but *is* the necessary preunderstanding for Flacius's hermeneutics: "If we turn to Christ, the veil is taken from our heart and also from the scriptures themselves, not only because we are now illuminated by the spiritual light, but also because we now hold the scope and the argument of the entire scripture in our hands, namely, the Lord Jesus himself with his sufferings and his good deeds" (ibid., 35).

Christ thus constitutes the necessary entry point into the hermeneutical circle of understanding. Flacius describes the hermeneutical circle as a process arising naturally from the way human understanding is designed: "If the human mind from the beginning understands roughly the sum of the subject matter and always keeps it before itself, it will more easily be able, while remaining engaged in the whole of the work, to grasp [or understand] the individual parts and how they relate to one another" (*De Ratione Cognoscendi*, 39). After stating this general principle of understanding, Flacius applies it to textual and biblical interpretation. Since "the rough sum of the entire Bible is Christ, for he is the fulfillment of the law, so that Christ unites and interprets the Old and the New Testament," the reader needs this "sum of the Old and New Testaments" in order to make sense of the individual parts of the text (ibid., 43). This is no different than reading any other book: "[To] have this sum of the Old and New Testaments in mind at the beginning is the most useful [thing] for the right understanding of the scriptures, just as it is useful for the exact understanding of any speaker, a comedy or some other poem, of a story or a book, to know from the outset their main concern or the scope" (ibid., 39). The overall scope of the scriptures and the starting point for any reader is Christ. Flacius, in truly Lutheran fashion, sees the dialectic of law and gospel as the foremost structure that demonstrates that Christ is the interpretive fulcrum of the Bible.

Flacius's assertion of Christ as the interpretive key and hermeneutical whole of the scriptures goes against the grain of Jean Grondin's account of hermeneutic history. Grondin believes that while Flacius retains interest in the spiritual Logos behind the scripture, linguistic and grammatical considerations as the key to access this Logos begin to dominate in Flacius's hermeneutics. On this view, Flacius sought to resolve the debate over the obscurity of scripture in grammatical knowledge: "Mastery of the letter, the gramma, was to provide the universal key to Scripture" (*IPH*, 42). Only because Grondin's interpretive framework demands that Flacius seek interpretive clarity through grammar is he then forced to conclude that Flacius failed in "constructing a purely grammatical hermeneutics" (ibid., 44). Flacius was humanist enough, of course, to see the importance of grammatical, linguistic, and historical exegesis, yet he was also theologian enough to preach two levels of clarity. Flacius's idea of a context-oriented hermeneutics comprises both the spiritual and the grammatical aspect of the text. On the surface, grammatical considerations, such as the context of a passage and the viewpoint from which it was written, play important roles. But on a deeper level, understanding depends not on technical rules but on a relation to the divine, namely, the communion with Christ. It is through him that "we hold the scope and the argument of the entire Scripture in our hands" (*De Ratione Cognoscendi*, 35).

Nor does Flacius represent the descent of theology into an obsession with timeless concepts. To be sure, theologians often turned to Aristotelian writings to borrow terminology for the formulation of clearer theological concepts so that still outstanding questions in the debate with Catholic theologians could be clarified. This did not necessarily mean that Reformation theology had already fallen prey to "Western philosophy's obsession with propositions" (*IPH*, 37). Theologians like Flacius did not forget the existential dimension of hermeneutics. But the very idea that the truth exists apart from existential appropriation, because of a transcendent divine other, required that description of this truth through language come as close as possible to the norm as taught in scripture. Flacius is therefore a good example of early Protestant orthodoxy, which was a "movement toward a lucid schema of doctrine . . . accompanied by a response to a still more sophisticated Roman polemic" (Muller, *Post-Reformation Reformed Dogmatics*, 1:32). Expression was important, for God himself had accommodated his revelation to human language.

The fact that Flacius shares Luther's view that understanding and ethics depend on one's relation to God (i.e., whether one is in or out of the word) disproves the claim that pre-Heideggerian hermeneutics neglected understanding in favor of interpretive rules. Flacius retains Luther's Christological focus as the heart of the scriptures and does not, as Grondin implies, reduce right interpretation merely to the correct application of rules. The following brief study of Puritan and Pietist hermeneutics continues to read against the grain in order to show that Luther's legacy was not destroyed by increasingly rationalist tendencies.

The English Puritans are the continuation and embodiment of John Calvin's theology, and German Pietism extends Luther's doctrines into the seventeenth and eighteenth centuries. Both movements influenced each other and belong to a wave of reformational piety that greatly impacted Europe and America. Flacius's systematizing of hermeneutical rules on the Lutheran side strongly influenced other writers of hermeneutical manuals in the English reformed tradition, such as William Perkins (1558–1602). Perkins was the first great English systematizing theologian after the Reformation, whose guidebook on hermeneutics shows many similarities with Flacius's work and therefore attests to the close connection and similarity between the hermeneutics of orthodox Lutheranism and that of English Puritanism. German Pietism, in turn, was greatly influenced by Puritan writings as the numerous translations of Bunyan and other devotional Puritan literature attests. Our focus on central hermeneutical notions will show how deeply premodern hermeneutics was concerned with the dynamics and psychology of interpretation. While the following analysis necessarily draws on either one or the other school for certain hermeneutical insights, we should keep in mind that Puritans and Pietists were surprisingly unified in holding these beliefs.

The Hermeneutic Circle

The Puritans adopted Calvin's epistemology, his hermeneutic circle of self-knowledge and knowledge of God, and made it the basis for their practical piety. Right living, according to the Puritan mind, could be achieved only through a proper perception of human existence, which in turn is possible only through a relation with the divine Creator and Maker of all things. Perkins, one of the most influential Puritan theologians, also insisted that human existence be interpreted in a dialectical movement between the human and the divine: "Blessed life ariseth from the knowledge of God and therefore it ariseth likewise from the knowledge of ourselves, because we know God by looking into ourselves" ("Golden Chain," 177). We also find Calvin's basic hermeneutical structure in the writings of the Puritan theologian John Owen (1616–83). Owen wrote that "the sum of all true wisdom and knowledge may be reduced to these three heads:—I. The knowledge of God, his nature and his properties. II. The knowledge of ourselves in reference to the will of God concerning us. III. Skill to walk in communion with God" (*WJO*, 2:80). Owen, however, further refined this thought by adding that all three components are attainable only through a relationship with Christ. "Not any of them is to any purpose to be obtained, or is manifested, but only in and by the Lord Jesus Christ" (ibid.).

This hermeneutical insight, however, was not restricted to academic theological treatises. The most popular manual of practical piety in the seventeenth century was Louis Bayly's (1565–1631) *Practice of Piety* (first edition ca. 1600). In the opening paragraphs, Bayly instructs the reader that the practice of piety consists in "knowing the essence of God" and "in knowing thy own self" (1). Bayly explains the connection of this hermeneutical circle with practical living thus:

> Unless a man doth truly know God, he neither can nor will worship him aright; for how can a man love him whom he knoweth not? . . . And how shall a man seek remedy by grace, who never understood his misery by nature? . . . And forasmuch as there can be no true piety without the knowledge of God; nor any good practice without the knowledge of man's

own self; we will therefore lay down the knowledge of God's majesty, and man's misery, as the first and chiefest grounds of the Practice of Piety. (ibid., 2)

Here we find Calvin's hermeneutical insight made the basis of practical living. Only in dialogue with the Divine can we gain true knowledge about ourselves and only then will we be able to direct our actions properly. Bayly also mentions the two important poles upon which the entire hermeneutical structure and its understanding of human existence rest: the holiness of God and the sinfulness of human beings. For the Puritans, as well as for the Pietists, true self-knowledge began with the realization that God exists, but it did not end there. The content of belief was dependent on God's character and attributes. Self-knowledge also meant the interpretation of humanity in terms of God's sovereignty and holiness with all their consequences for sinful man. This theocentric view was the hermeneutical starting point for the Puritans and the early Pietists.

Relational Epistemology

Both Puritan and Pietist theologians were pastor-theologians, trained academics who engaged intellectual trends of their time to guide their congregations through the rapid developments of new scientific concepts and philosophical ideas. This effort was, of course, made easier by the fact that science, theology, and philosophy were not perceived as separate enterprises but were understood to pursue similar questions concerning the nature of human beings and their role within nature. The whole of pre-Enlightenment theology may be summarized in the question: "What is man that you are mindful of him?" At the heart of theological thought is the question of identity, the hermeneutical desire for self-understanding, "Who am I and what is my purpose in life?" Puritan and Pietist theologians insisted, however, that this desire for meaning can be addressed only by "exteriority," that is, by knowing at least a basic answer for the why question of human existence: to glorify God and enjoy him forever. The human mind could not even begin to quench this thirst for meaning, these theologians contended, unless the focus was turned away from self toward transcendence, toward God. If human beings were made for communion with God, then why did not everyone obtain this goal? In answering this question, the Puritan theologians in particular developed a theory of knowledge in combination with a philosophical anthropology of a depth and subtlety often unat-

tained by modern approaches. The writings of the Puritan theologian
John Owen are representative of this genre.

Owen begins with the assumption that the created world depends
on the sustaining power of God and therefore assumes that all interpretive activity is a form of participation in the divine, even natural
reason. While unaided reason can give us some reliable self-knowledge, humanity's ultimate purpose is found only in God's revelation.
According to Owen, humanity was created for three reasons. The first
was "that [God] might therein make a representation of his holiness
and righteousness among his creatures" (*WJO*, 1:183). Humanity was
to be, so to speak, an ambassador for the deity to the rest of creation.
Owen argues that although God's fingerprints are all over his creation,
"none of them, not the whole fabric of heaven and earth, with all their
glorious ornaments and endowments, were either fit or able to receive
any impressions of his holiness and righteousness—of any of the moral
perfections or universal rectitude of his nature. Yet, in the demonstration and representation of these things doth the glory of God principally
consist. Without them he could not be known and glorified as God"
(ibid.). Only human beings were made in the image of God, so only we
can commune with God and reflect his character.

Second, humanity was created as a mouthpiece to pay tribute to
God's glory. Creation itself, according to Owen, "could not in any way
declare the glory of God, but passively and objectively." Creation was
like a "harmoniously well trained instrument, which gives no sound
unless there be a skilful hand to move and act it" (*WJO*, 1:183). Human
beings, however, made in God's image, were created as the loudspeaker
that would reflect the glory of creation back to the deity and intelligently
voice his praise, for "what is light, if there be no eye to see it? or what is
music, if there be no ear to hear it?" (ibid.). Third, humanity was created
to enjoy with God the beauty of creation. Human beings were made in
God's image "that it might be a means to bring man unto that eternal
enjoyment of [God], which he was fitted for and designed unto" (ibid.).
Thus in Owen's view, humankind's ultimate end, to be truly human, was
to have communion with God.

Communion, however, is by definition a personal concept and follows
the dynamics of personal relations. Consequently, if we are designed
for interpersonal communications, the way we acquire knowledge and
hence in some way our ability to reason must be patterned according
to social rather than so-called neutral, scientific categories. The reason
that we do not find the modern faith-reason split in pre-Enlightenment
theology is not because of its prescientific naiveté but because it had
not lost a relational concept of epistemology. Owen, for example, fol-

lowed the Augustinian belief that all knowledge is in some sense based on faith if we define faith as belief in a credible witness.

The Relation of Faith to Reason

It is common to describe Puritan hermeneutics in terms of a dichotomy between faith and reason. Specifically the search for meaning through communion with God is sometimes explained as a leap of faith to bridge the gap between a seemingly "nonreadable" universe and the biblical teaching of providence. The scholar John Morgan, for example, asserts that the Puritan insistence on communion with God was a "cry of the existential being for meaning in a universe which itself could provide him with none." Morgan remarks that "the puritan thus arrived at a chasm in his confrontation of faith and reason; from this dire struggle emerged his response to the external world." Morgan concludes that "the prime message of puritan Reformed Protestantism was irrational" (*Godly Learning*, 2–22).

Contrary to Morgan's claim, however, Puritans saw faith not as irrational but rather as based on credible witness. Both creation and the written word provided such testimony. Thus Morgan is also wrong in claiming that the universe yielded no meaning for the Puritan. Although natural revelation could not be said to lead toward salvation, it nevertheless served as a reminder that one lived in a created universe. The Puritans' framework of a created universe sustained by a transcendent and immanent deity allowed them to balance faith and reason. Unlike Morgan, they did not have to "read" reality through a Kantian prism that separates faith from reason. The term "irrational," for example, would not have made much sense to a Puritan theologian if used in connection with faith. A better term to use might have been "suprarational," a faith that builds on reason. Yet Morgan's misinterpretation of Puritan hermeneutics is symptomatic of our inability to understand "precritical" hermeneutics from an exclusively anthropocentric position. The tendency is to view Puritan hermeneutics either as rationalist or as mystical, whereas, unencumbered by Kant's epistemological chasm, Puritan epistemology in fact combines both characteristics. Owen's definition of faith will help to establish this thesis.

Owen defines faith as belief based on credible testimony. This thoroughly Augustinian notion of faith is strongly articulated by the later Puritans like Owen, Richard Baxter (1615–91), and William Bates (1625–99) as these divines defend what they understand to be a biblical view of human existence against the rising rationalism within the established church (Cragg, *From Puritanism to the Age of Reason*, 37). In his main treatise on the relation of faith and reason, Owen sets out to explain the nature of faith as belief in divine revelation, the self-evidencing power of written revelation, and in particular the qualities of the scriptures as the word of God (*WJO*, 4:82).[3] Owen begins his epistemological investigations by outlining three general ways "whereby we assent unto any thing that is proposed unto us as true, and receive it as such." This threefold epistemology combines knowledge by natural light, by the consideration of "things externally proposed," and by faith.

The term "natural light" refers to "inbred notions," such as the general sense that there is a transcendent dimension, and general moral categories of good and evil. These categories are objective because they are God-given. They are indeed the very basis of human apprehension: "The foundation of the whole, as of all the actings of our souls, is in the inbred principles of natural light, or first necessary dictates of our intellectual, rational nature" (*WJO*, 4:85). However, fallen human reason often fills these categories with foreign content. Although especially Greek philosophy progressed quite far in trying to reconstruct transcendent values, most conclusions arrived at through unaided reason were directly contrary to the actual truth (ibid.). Recently, Brian Ingraffia has made a similar argument. According to Ingraffia, Heidegger's positive contribution to philosophy is his exposing metaphysical constructs as onto-theology, that is, as secularized theology, rational constructs based on Greek conceptuality (*Postmodern Theory*, 9).

These kinds of metaphysics, however, should not be conflated with biblical revelation. Ingraffia contends that "the rejection of Christianity in both modernism and postmodernism has been for the most part based upon a profound misunderstanding of biblical revelation. Christian faith has all too easily been conflated with onto-theology in modernism and then criticized for being onto-theology in postmodernism" (*Postmodern Theory*, 6). Ingraffia argues that Greek rationality, upon which the nontheological elements of Western metaphysics are based, is radically different from biblical revelation, which is interested in humans only in their relationship to God (ibid., 125).

The second mode of knowing proposed by Owen is deduction: "Herein the mind exerciseth its discursive faculty, gathering one thing out of another, and concluding one thing from another" (*WJO*, 4:83). Knowledge derived from this method varies in degrees of certainty, "according unto the nature and degree of the evidence it proceeds upon." Hence such knowledge can range from mere opinion to certain knowledge (ibid.).

3. The full title of this treatise is *The Reason of Faith or an Answer unto That Inquiry, "Wherefore We Believe the Scripture to Be the Word of God"; with the Causes and Nature of That Faith Wherewith We Do So.*

The third way by which we obtain knowledge is faith. Owen defines faith as assent to something true about which we have no innate notion and about which we can make no deduction from other known principles. Faith is to believe on the valid testimony of another person: "[Faith] is our assent *upon testimony,* whereon we believe many things which no sense, inbred principles, nor reasonings of our own, could either give us an acquaintance with or an assurance of. And this assent also hath not only *various degrees,* but is also of divers kinds, according as the *testimony* is which it ariseth from and resteth on; as being *human* if that be *human,* and *divine* if that be so also" (*WJO,* 4:83; emphasis in original).

According to Owen, God's self-disclosure to humanity makes use of all three modes of knowing. For the first, God reveals himself through the mental makeup of human beings. Our capacity for self-reflection and ability to make choices or form judgments on the basis of rational argument evince the necessity of a creator who has the same qualities (*WJO,* 4:84). This conclusion echoes Baxter's statement that each person is "an index to the Godhead." Baxter is perhaps overzealous in trying to find Trinitarian elements in almost every human faculty in his exposition of the nature of God's image in a person. Nevertheless, he confirms the general Puritan teaching that rational contemplation of the human mind and body evidences a designer: "And, therefore, seeing God is known to us by this his image, and in this glass though we must not think that any thing in God is formally the same as it is in man, yet, certainly, we must judge that all this is eminently in God; and that we have no fitter notions and names concerning his incomprehensible perfections than what we have borrowed from the mind of man" (*PWRB,* 2:136).

Corresponding to the second way of knowing, that is, "by things externally proposed," God offers unto human reason ample evidence of his existence in "the works of creation and providence." We must, says Owen, use our reason aright to discern God's fingerprints in creation: "So God calls unto men for the exercise of their reason about these things, reproaching them with stupidity and brutishness where they are wanting therein, Isa. xlvi. 5–8, xliv. 18–20" (*WJO,* 4:85). The Puritan commentator Matthew Poole also refers to the reading of this book of nature: "Because it might be further objected on behalf of the Gentiles, that the notions of God imprinted in their nature are so weak, that they may be well excused; therefore the apostle adds, that the certainty of them is further confirmed by *the book of the creatures, which was written before them in capital letters*" (*Commentary,* 2:481; emphasis mine). The Puritans felt that the innate notion of God, which was evident in humanity's natural religiosity, and the cosmological evidence of a designer left humanity without excuse not to seek communion with the Divine; given this definition of reason, the Puritans considered any interpretation of reality that rejects God to go against every principle of evidence and reason. Whether one agrees or disagrees with such theistic arguments from design, this sentiment proves the Puritans' strong conviction that faith was reasonable and not irrational.

The third way of knowing is most important to Owen because it addresses the singular ability of human beings to attain knowledge beyond sensory perception by trusting the word of another. The ability to believe and act on knowledge based on testimony sets human beings apart from beasts. The other two modes of knowing function on the basis of direct evidence, either moral or empirical. Faith, however, is the most difficult kind of knowledge because it is indirect, relying on the testimony of someone else. Owen claims that the "faculty of assenting unto truth upon testimony" is "the most noble faculty of our minds." And it is to this faculty that God chose to reveal himself most fully through his written revelation (*WJO*, 4:90). Faith, then, becomes "that power of our souls whereby we are able to assent unto the truth of what is proposed unto us upon testimony. And this [God] doth by his word, or the Scriptures, propose unto us in the manner and way before expressed" (ibid., 4:85).

Owen's concept of faith as trust in credible testimony has profound consequences for hermeneutics, because it implies that all human beings exercise faith in the acquisition and handling of knowledge. Human beings, Owen argues, cannot go through life without this ability: "And if our souls did want but this one faculty of assenting unto truth upon testimony, all that remains would not be sufficient to conduct us through the affairs of this *natural* life" (*WJO*, 4:88; emphasis mine). In our daily lives, we trust those assertions the most that issue from a credible and trustworthy person. In other words, the integrity of the author of a testimony, his character and credentials, becomes crucial for the quality of knowledge thus obtained. According to Owen, God's word and character, especially as revealed in the incarnation, provide a testimony of the highest quality. For the Christian, assent to the divine revelation therefore does not consist in an irrational leap of faith but rests ultimately on trust in the verity of God's testimony: "'Thus saith the Lord' is the only ground and reason of our assent; and that assent is the assent of faith, because it is resolved into testimony alone" (ibid., 4:85).

Owen emphasizes that all three kinds of knowledge work harmoniously together in God's self-revelation: "And concerning these several ways of the communication or revelation of the knowledge of God, it must be always observed that there is a perfect consistency in the things revealed by them all" (*WJO*, 4:85). It is important to note that Owen's concept of faith is reasonable, not rational. Faith is different from reason, because it trusts rather than deduces. However, it is reasonable because there is no irrational leap into a realm of faith that contradicts all other human experiences. Instead faith opens the right perspective to judge and interpret human existence in the light of the newfound relationship to the Divine. Owen's doctrine of a reasonable faith, which corresponds to a person's psychological-existential makeup, allows him to reject what he regards as unreasonable spiritual claims, on the one hand, and merely rationalistic observations, on the other. Thus claims to spiritual revelations that directly contradict reason are to be rejected. Yet Owen also objects to reason when it oversteps its bounds and tries to conduct a reading of human existence on its own, on the basis of the book of nature alone. Though reason is useful in the acquisition of knowledge of God from the light of nature, it cannot attain to the genuine self-knowledge we find only in relational participation in the divine: "The reason hereof is, not only because there is a more full and extensive revelation made of God, his counsels and his will, in Christ and the Gospel, than in all the works of creation and providence, but because this revelation and representation of God is received by faith alone, the other by reason only: and it is faith that is the principle of spiritual light and life in us. . . . Reason alone—especially as it is corrupted and depraved—can discern no glory in the representation of God by Christ" (ibid., 1:77).

Thus without a relationship to the Divine, we cannot bring ourselves to trust the divine testimony. Instead we revert to an anthropocentric perspective by evaluating the divine witness according to our finite horizons. We "would have all things that we are to believe to be levelled absolutely unto our reason and comprehension—a principle which, at this day, shakes the very foundations of the Christian religion" (*WJO*, 1:50). Owen regards this attitude as highly arrogant and attributes it to the deficiency of our epistemological dynamic due to the influence of sin: "This apprehension . . . ariseth from the pride which naturally ensues on the ignorance of God and ourselves" (ibid.).

Ignorant of God, the human mind turns to its own limited horizon in order to explain existence and refuses any answers to the deep existential questions that revelation has to offer. Instead we are satisfied with our own limited viewpoint and acquiesce in our interpretative blindness: "Hence things philosophical, and of a deep rational indagation [searching out/investigation] find great acceptance in the world—as in their proper place, they do deserve. Men are furnished with proper measure of them, and they find them proportionate unto the principles of their own understandings" (*WJO*, 1:51). To use an illustration, we are like the angler who keeps all the small fish he catches while throwing the large ones back into the water. Asked by a passerby about the reason for his nonsensical action, he replies that his frying pan is too small. In the same way, Owen would say, we either refuse the divine message or reduce it to the limited size of our finite horizon.

Charles Taylor explains the rise of human autonomy, with its concomitant trust in human judgment on all matters, as a key ingredient of modernist culture. This new attitude toward knowledge arises from a radical shift in the concept of the self. The premodern self, Taylor argues, was "embedded in an ontic logos" (*Sources of the Self*, 301). Human beings felt surrounded by horizons of significance, all of which could be traced back to the divine Logos. The culture of modernity, by contrast, has a new identity "of disengaged reason," which is "no longer defined by a substantive rational ordering or purposes" but "prizes autonomy" (ibid., 305). Owen was almost prophetic in his fear that an unlimited exaltation of human reason would spell the demise of Christianity.

While Owen speaks thus against the reduction of knowledge to reason alone, he also rejects the subjective "inner light" position, which abounded during and after the Reformation. Owen wanted to guard against such a merely private and subjective faith by tying the content of Christian doctrine to divine revelation as found in the scriptures. The relationship with Christ grows through the contemplation of the written word: "It is not the work of fancy or imagination—it is not the feigning images in our minds of such things as are meet to satisfy our carnal affections, to excite and act them; but it is due adherence unto that object which is represented unto faith in the proposal of the Gospel. Therein, as in a glass, do we behold the glory of Christ, who is the image of the invisible God, and have our souls filled with transforming affections to him" (*WJO*, 1:157).

Owen's relational hermeneutics opposed the rationalists by emphasizing the personal and relational nature of knowledge based on a human-divine dialogue; he also opposed the inspirationalists of his day by stating that propositional knowledge, the text of the written word, is the only means by which knowledge about the divine dialogue partner can be attained. It is significant that for Owen the "beholding of the glory of Christ" in the glass of the scriptures results in "*transforming* affections" (*WJO*, 1:157). Reading is never an end in itself but always transforms the reader and results in action.

The Role of Desire

The example of William Bates shows that Owen was not alone in espousing a reasonable faith. Bates believed with Owen that the Christian religion is not contrary to reason, in the Kantian sense, but that faith in the Divine constitutes the most reasonable act a human being may perform. Faith builds on reason. At the same time, while reason is pre-paratory to faith, Bates also affirmed that only divinely given faith can reestablish humankind's dialogue with God. After all, Bates argued, the argument that faith is based on credible testimony entails that human beings were created by God with a free will, to make choices based on sound judgment. No argument will convince unless the human will, that mysterious faculty that commands all others, gives its assent: "For the arguments to induce belief, though of sufficient certainty, yet do not so constrain the mind to give its assent, but there is prudence and choice in it." Ideally "the mind enlightened by sufficient reasons that the Christian religion is from God, represents it so to the will, and the will, if sincere and unbiased by carnal affections, commands the mind not to disguise the truth, to make it less credible, nor to palliate with specious colours the pretences of infidelity. And thus the belief of it results from conviction and love" (*Complete Works*, 1:119).

A sound judgment in matters of ultimate meaning, however, involves the affections. Bates admitted that the arguments for the reasonableness of divine revelation and the Christian faith are not scientific but "of a moral nature." Nevertheless, though they "are not of equal clearness with the testimonies of sense, or a mathematical demonstration, yet are so pregnant and convincing, that the considering dispassionate spirit fully acquiesces in them" (*Complete Works*, 1:118). Thus, as in many of the later Puritans, we find in Bates an implied resistance to the application of the increasingly influential scientific method to all claims of knowl-edge and truth. Theology naturally has a vested interest in setting limits to human reason, and the theological tradition has preserved a healthy suspicion toward all attempts to elevate human reason and its exclusive trust in empirical, rational (as defined by human reason) evidence to the position of absolute autonomy. It is not surprising, therefore, that (as I pointed out in the introduction) Heidegger's and Gadamer's critique of scientific method shows theological influences.

Bates concluded that the decisive factor of our interpretive judgment is not evidence but desire. From the position that faith is not opposed to reason, Owen and Bates argued that the natural human impulse to turn away from divine revelation has nothing to do with the quality of revelation but rather with the unwillingness of the fallen human will to give assent to the subject matter of revelation. "We must," Bates ar-gued, "distinguish between what is incomprehensible to human reason and what is repugnant to it." For Bates there is no point "in the whole complexion of the Christian faith that is repugnant to reason." The problem lies rather in the inability of the fallen creature to compre-hend a revelatory message intended for a heart in tune with the divine. Even with regard to the concept of the Trinity, though "it transcends our conception . . . reason cannot prove it to be impossible" (*Complete Works*, 1:165).

According to Bates, it is not the text itself but rather the applicatory dimension of the text that makes it repugnant to us. The subject matter disclosed in the scriptures is too challenging for the reader who loathes to surrender his autonomy by acknowledging an authority higher than his own: "The pretended difficulty of belief, is but a thin transparent pretence, the difficulty of practice is the true cause of their rejecting the gospel" (*Complete Works*, 1:172). The text demands moral change from the reader and the acceptance of an authority different from his own, a step human beings deeply in love with their autonomy are unwilling to take. The Puritans contended that the rejection of the gospel as irrational is only a pretext and defense mechanism to avoid the confrontation with possible limits to human autonomy. Thus, ironically, our desire for freedom keeps us from the only truly human way of obtaining freedom, namely, in communion with God.

As the Puritan Nathaniel Vincent (1644–97) pointed out, the reader's very notion that communion with the Divine will cost him his moral and personal freedom is based on an illusion: "Sometimes the carnal heart rises against holiness, because it imagines that nothing of delight and pleasure is consistent with it, whereas indeed by being converted unto God our joy is not lost but only changed" (Kistler, *Puritans on Conversion*, 119).

It is clear that Owen and Bates made every effort to show the reasonableness of Christian faith as propounded in the written word. Faith is not seen in the Kantian sense as contradictory to reason, but rather faith develops reason to its highest capacity. Owen stated that God "doth not reveal himself by his word unto the principles of natural light, nor unto reason in its exercise; but yet these principles, and reason itself, with all the faculties of our minds, are consequentially affected with that revelation, and are drawn forth in their proper exercise by it" (*WJO*, 4:86).

In sum, in Puritan theology faith is a balance between objective and subjective factors. It is never to be equated with irrationality. Yes, the Christian faith is inseparably tied to the written word of God, but the authenticity of this word, its textual accuracy in comparison to other classical works, all these factors make it a credible testimony. Faith in this testimony is different from scientific knowledge, but as Owen argued, much of human knowledge is based on testimony rather than on our own empirical verification. Such knowledge, since it is based on trust in a credible authority, is the noblest mode of knowing that the human mind is capable of. Thus when the biblical text claims divine authority, "it giveth us the highest certainty or assurance whereof in this world we are capable" (*WJO*, 4:102).

Owen's Augustinian concept of faith provides an important insight for the dialogism advocated by philosophical hermeneutics; human dialogue is based on faith. Owen's definition of faith as belief in credible testimony makes clear that our daily attempts to understand both the indirect dialogue through text (which includes historical research) and direct interhuman dialogue depend on an implicit trust in the other's testimony. As Gadamer would put it, we anticipate completeness, that is, we anticipate that the other person or text means what it says. In order to understand, we must trust the uttered word at some level. In fact, the very notion that a testimony may be deceptive includes the basic premise of credibility; is not the ideal that always hovers in the background of Gadamerian hermeneutics and any other like-minded approaches to human relations this ideal of faith in the other's word? Finally, does not this ideal need to be anchored in a concrete referent to protect it from being questioned and destroyed as a mere social convention? For Luther, Flacius, and Owen, God provided this referent—not so much as an idea than as a reality. God's word and testimony are the measure of truthfulness and trustworthiness. After all, he had proven his faithfulness in the atoning work of the incarnation, death, and resurrection.

The Psychology of Illumination

The concept of illumination is the centerpiece of Puritan and Pietist interpretive psychology. The concept hinges on the question of nature and grace: given the Puritan doctrine of the Fall and the resulting human depravity, to what extent is our interpretive faculty affected by our fallen condition? Puritan and Pietist theologians distinguished much more carefully between sin and the condition of sinfulness. While sin is either a conscious (commission) or unconscious (omission) act of nonconformity to God's will, our sinful condition, or as the Puritans termed it, our human depravity, means the disruption of our communion with God. Hence the Westminster Confession of Faith states that on account of humanity's first sin we have fallen "out of original righteousness and communion with God, and so became dead in sin, and wholly defiled in all the faculties and parts of soul and body" (chapter 6). The spiritual Fall, then, means to be out of relation with God and results in blindness toward the things of God. The crucial question then becomes that of nature and grace: what does "defilement of all faculties" really mean? More specifically, how far-reaching are the noetic effects of the Fall? In terms of interpretation, it boils down to this: to what extent can we interpret reality and the biblical text correctly in our natural fallen state without divine assistance? Given the universal claim of the biblical narrative, these two spheres are obviously connected.

Generally, both Protestant and Catholic theology granted that the ability to read nature correctly is part of our *imago Dei*, the image of God in all human beings, a feature of God's common grace that we all enjoy by virtue of God's common grace. Yet both traditions also agree that the full meaning of creation, including the purpose of human existence, is possible only by special grace, or to use another term, by the special illumination of the Holy Spirit. By an act of God, people are drawn back into a relation with God. Puritan and Pietist theology expresses this reinstatement as the return of the prodigal son, as a family reunion made possible by Jesus the Christ's sacrificial death on the cross. It is through Christ, the Logos in and through whom all was created and by whom all creation is sustained, that philosophy and theology, nature and grace, the immanent and the transcendent come together.

Based on this belief, the Puritans and the Pietists went into great detail and depth to explain the psychology of biblical interpretation and the role of God's Spirit within it. On this topic, no one dug deeper than John Owen, without question the keenest physician of the soul, even if his writing is not particularly charismatic. His description of the Holy Spirit's role in interpretation in *Causes, Ways, and Means of Understanding the Mind of God as Revealed in His Word* (1678) provides a good example of his abilities. In this treatise, Owen explains why illumination is necessary and what it is. First, Owen proposes a model of the human psyche to explain the need for illumination. While he works from a Greek framework, Owen's model of the human soul avoids a body-soul dualism. Though there are vestiges of Aristotelian psychology (Owen privileges the mind as the leading faculty), Owen's biblicism keeps Greek philosophy at arm's length in these investigations on the human psyche; terms and their exposition follow the biblical text rather than philosophical sources. Like William Perkins before him, Owen espouses the threefold division from Paul in Ephesians 4:17–18, where the apostle speaks of the mind (*nous*), the understanding (*dianoia*), and the heart (*kardia*). According to Owen, these three elements "are one entire principle of all our moral and spiritual operations, and all are affected with the darkness and ignorance of which we treat" (*WJO*, 3:250). Owen then proceeds to delineate the effect of sin on all three faculties. He begins with the faculty of the mind, which he sees as the "leading and ruling faculty of the soul" (ibid.).

In its ideal prelapsarian state, the *nous* had God as its worthwhile object of pursuit and contemplation, so that both the will and the affections were aligned to the purpose of glorifying, serving, and fellowshipping with God (*WJO*, 3:250). In the postlapsarian state, the mind still seeks the state of rest as it formerly knew it, but because of its disoriented fallen nature, it does so by the wrong means, by engaging "in all manner of confusion; and they all end in vanity or disappointment. They offer as it were their services to the soul to bring it satisfaction. And although they are rejected one after another, as not answering as what they pretend unto, yet they constantly arise under the same notion, and keep the whole soul under everlasting disappointments" (ibid., 3:251).

The second faculty of understanding (*dianoia*) acts as *to diakritikon*, "the discerning, judging faculty of the soul, that leads it unto practice. It guides the soul in the choice of the notions which it receives by the mind" (*WJO*, 3:252). This faculty, Owen says, is even more severely affected than the mind. Since the understanding is more closely connected to the heart, the practical principle of operation and execution, it is in greater danger from sin, "for the nearer things come [to] practice, the more prevalent in them is the power to sin" (ibid.). Owen demonstrates that long before Gadamer's philosophical hermeneutics, theological interpretation clearly grasped the interconnectedness of understanding and application.

Finally, the heart (*kardia*) is the *praktikon*, the executing "practical" part of the soul that includes the will. Owen describes this faculty as "the actual compliance of the will and affections with the mind and understanding, with respect unto the objects proposed by them." He then repeats the traditional Reformed position that the light of the scriptures is "received by the mind, applied by the understanding and used by the heart" (*WJO*, 3:252). In each of these steps, the light is met with a stubborn refusal on the side of the unregenerate person to accept the saving message. The mind refuses to focus on it, the understanding will not apply it, and the heart refuses to implement the message conveyed in God's word ("an obstinate and obdurate hardness is upon the heart, whence it rejects all the impressions that come upon it from notions of truth" [ibid.]).

In other words, the faculties of the soul, originally created to receive knowledge from and commune with God, are so affected by sin that they may be said to be willfully unresponsive to light: "There is not in such persons so much as any disposition remaining to receive saving knowledge, any more than there is a disposition in darkness itself to receive light. The mind indeed, remains a capable subject to receive it, but hath no power nor disposition in itself towards it" (*WJO*, 3:252).

The solution to the dilemma is the reader's conversion to communion with God through a sovereign act of divine grace. God needs to create a new faculty that makes reception of his truth possible: conversion endows the reader with a willing disposition to accept the teachings of the text. Yet there is need for further work of the Holy Spirit. Owen teaches that our "belief in the Scriptures to be the word of God, or a divine revelation, and our understanding of the mind and will of God as revealed in them, are the two springs of all our interest in Christian Religion" (*WJO*, 4:122). Conversion takes care of the first "spring" by creating in the reader a general disposition of goodwill toward the text. But Owen also sees the necessity of illumination regarding interpretation, even after the reader's disposition has been altered.

Owen speaks of the "double act of the Holy Ghost" by which the reader is freed from repulsion by the text and also accepts it as authoritative. For the first, the Spirit "gives wisdom—understanding—a spiritual judgment," whereby the reader is enabled to "compare spiritual things with spiritual, in a spiritual manner, and to come thereby to a clear and full light of the heavenly excellency of the Word." In this way, the reader is enabled "to know of the doctrine whether it be of God" (*WJO*, 4:122). In modern parlance, the reader has received the potential to fuse with the divine horizon of meaning through the adjustment of his prejudice in favor of the divine. This change affects the interpretative approach to the text. Owen believes that without the assistance of the Spirit, the Bible will often appear less unified than it really is and its teachings will seem less urgent. However, through illumination "all the parts of the Scripture in their harmony and correspondency, all the truths of it in their power and necessity, come together to give evidence one to another, and all of the whole" (ibid.). Owen thus makes the *sola scriptura* principle largely dependent on illumination by the Spirit.

The second part of the Spirit's "double act" is to give the reader "a spiritual taste of the things themselves upon the mind, heart, and conscience" (*WJO*, 4:122). As one recognizes a pleasing taste, the reader simply knows that the doctrine taught is divine. Owen describes this assurance as the "testimony of the Spirit," which leaves such an impression on the soul that the reader "infallibly" recognizes the authority and trustworthiness of the message. Owen thus uses the term "infallibility" not so much in the sense of objective, empirically verifiable truth but in the sense of existential verification in the reader's mind and heart. It is thus from the illuminating divine aid that interpretative assurance is derived, accompanied by the willingness to apply the word to one's life (ibid., 16:327).

This interpretative independence, however, should not be misinterpreted to mean individualistic subjectivism. Owen, as in his description of faith, strives for a careful balance between illumination and outward means in the reading of the text. The Holy Spirit, says Owen, is a supreme teacher and as such makes use of the faculties God has created (*WJO*, 4:191). The scriptures are meant to teach one about one's relationship to the Divine and one's fellow human beings, but they do so without circumventing the use of one's intellectual powers. An approach that tries to suppress the use of reason is oppressive, because it wants to take control of the reader: "And hereunto the use of our own reason, the utmost improvement of the rational abilities of our minds, is required. Those who would take away the use of our own reason in spiritual things would deal with us, as we said before, as the Philistines did with Samson,—first put out our eyes, and then make us grind their mill" (ibid., 4:153). It is thus important that the reader be independent of "the authoritative interpretation of any church or person whatever" (ibid., 4:123).

Owen upholds this hermeneutical liberty against the three forces of traditionalism, inspirationalism, and rationalism, which want to substitute their authority for the interpretative liberty granted by God's illuminating work in the reader. Traditionalism makes its followers lazy through their dependency on an authority that sorts out all problems for them (*WJO*, 4:154). Such easy reliance removes readers from the difficult interpretative qualifications the Spirit requires of them. These requirements are "humility, continual prayer, meditation," and untiring study of the text. The most difficult requirement, however, is once again practical application, which demands "above all, that [readers] endeavour a conformity in their whole souls and lives unto the truths that he instructs them in." According to Owen, the divine author of the scriptures will not admit anyone into his "school" unless these conditions are met, even though the traditionalist "school" admits its students "on far easier and cheaper rates" (ibid.).

Owen rejects the hermeneutical enslavement of traditionalism as well as its opposite extreme of interpretative anarchy advocated by inspirationalists, who confuse the illuminating work of the Spirit with the inspiration granted to biblical authors and prophets. The Holy Spirit's work is not to bring new revelations but to confirm and explain what has already been written down: "We stand not in need of any new divine afflations, or immediate prophetical inspirations, to enable us to understand the Scripture, or the mind and will of God as revealed therein" (*WJO*, 4:125).

Owen denies the Quakers' argument that divine inspiration makes the written word and the hermeneutical process obsolete, as allegedly proved by the examples of the Old Testament prophets who were seized uncontrollably by the Spirit. Owen points out that the Old Testament prophets, like any other human being, needed divine illumination to interpret the meaning of their own prophecies (*WJO*, 4:125). For Owen the Quakers' insistence on an Inner Light leads to utter subjectivism and a neglect of the Bible altogether as a standard of Christian guidance (ibid., 4:167).

Rationalism, the third interpretative extreme, usurps interpretative liberty under the guidance of the Spirit by relying on reason alone. Owen diagnoses several problems with this school of thought. The most obvious is its apparent deadness to the spiritual dimension of the text. Owen anticipates the objection that many scholars with their merely rational analysis have obtained far greater knowledge than many theologians or laypersons who claim to trust in the Spirit's illuminating aid in interpretation. Does this not render such a work by the Spirit unnecessary? (*WJO*, 4:155). Owen answers this argument by once again stressing the inseparable connection of interpretation and application for theological hermeneutics and does this by carefully defining what it actually means "to know" a biblical text. Scripture, he says, uses two terms for knowledge, *gnosis* (knowledge) and *epignosis* (acknowledgment). The former, Owen argues, depicts mere propositional, or purely theoretical, knowledge, which, on its own, is useless because it does not necessitate practical application.

The term *epignosis,* on the other hand, "gives the mind an experience of the power and efficacy of the truth known or discovered, so as to transform the soul and all its affections into it, and thereby to give a full assurance of understanding unto the mind itself" (*WJO*, 4:156). "Epignotic" knowledge of God's revelation thus entails trust in the truth content of the text and therefore goes beyond mere propositional knowledge.

Owen thus clearly advocates an "affective" hermeneutics that historians of hermeneutic development, such as Jean Grondin, ascribe to Pietism in contrast to Protestant orthodoxy: "From this assertion [of an affective hermeneutic] we can see the extent to which the pietistic vision helps guard against the naive verbal objectivism discernible in Protestant orthodoxy" (*IPH*, 60). Yet Owen, one of England's greatest defenders of orthodoxy, teaches that true understanding must be gained by the help of the Spirit.

According to Owen, God, the ultimate author of scripture, must illumine the reader's inner eye to the spiritual dimension of the text. This "true meaning" is not, as is often supposed, a hidden gnostic sense, but it is the dimension of belief and application. Neither is the illumination of the Holy Spirit in the interpretative work primarily intellectual but rather affective. The Spirit not only enlightens the mind to a knowledge that is more than mere acknowledgment, but he also works an assurance of biblical teachings that shows itself in application: "That assurance, I say, which believers have in spiritual things is of another nature and kind than can be attained out of conclusions that are only rationally derived from the most evident principles; and therefore doth it produce effects of another nature, both in *doing* and in *suffering*" (*WJO*, 4:157; emphasis mine). Thus "epignotic" knowledge of the text not only enables the reader to believe in God in a relational rather than only an abstract way but also results in ethical application (ibid., 4:158).

Hence for Owen the scripture objectively reveals the will of God, but it takes "subjective revelation" or an illumination of God's Spirit to align the reader's understanding and practice with what is expressed in the text (*WJO*, 4:170). In fact, Owen claims that God designed the text in such a way that a purely rational interpretative approach goes against its very nature and purpose. He not only revealed the divine will progressively, as best suits the respective historical stage of the church's development, but also arranged its inscripturation so as to meet the reader in his or her particular life situation: "Truths have their power and efficacy upon our minds not only from *themselves,* but from their *posture* in Scripture. There are they placed in such *aspects* towards, in such conjunctions one with another, as that their *influences* on our minds do greatly depend thereon" (ibid., 4:189; emphasis in original).

It is, therefore, by divine design that the text of scripture is not put in the form of doctrines, like a systematic theology, but in the shape of "histories, prophecies, prayers, songs, letters, epistles" (*WJO*, 4:187). Owen contends that if scripture had been put in the form of catechisms and doctrinal treatises, it "would effect in us only an artificial or methodical" knowledge (ibid., 4:188). In fact, freezing doctrines in certain formulae often destroys the existential and spiritual power these teachings exert in their narrative form: "Often when men think they have brought truths into the strictest propriety of expression, they lose both their power and their glory" (ibid., 4:189).

Most importantly, cold doctrinal and creedal statements discourage the applicatory dimension that the text naturally possesses. Doctrinal creeds abstracted from the text are useful, but they can only convey a "methodical comprehension" of the text, while the applicatory dimension atrophies ("but this [rational understanding of doctrine] we may attain and not be rendered one jot more like unto God thereby" [*WJO*, 4:189]). Owen by no means disparages technical hermeneutics as long as these tools are given their proper place in interpretation.

Owen's hermeneutical approach to the text demonstrates the unfoundedness of recent claims that premodernist hermeneutics was a merely technical affair (*IPH*, 42). Owen certainly affirms the role of the arts and sciences as technical tools for interpretation: "It is true that the knowledge of common learned arts and sciences is of great use unto the understanding of the Scriptures, as unto what they have in common with other writings, and what they refer unto that is of human cognizance." He cautions, however, that to construct theology on grammatical-historical grounds alone would be "as if a man should design to make up his house of the scaffolds which he only useth in the building of it" (*WJO*,

4:157). Thus for precritical hermeneutics, mere technical rules are not enough. Instead the interpreter must also employ those nontechnical, pneumatological hermeneutical means that are congenial to the spiritual nature and content of the text.

The foremost of these spiritual means is prayer, which reminds us again of the emphasis the Puritans placed on interpretation as a dialogue between God and the reader. Prayer, says Owen, brings one into the presence of the divine so that "prejudices, preconceived opinions, engagements by secular advantages, false confidences, authority of men, influences from parties and societies, will be all laid level before it, at least be gradually exterminated out of the minds of men thereby" (*WJO*, 4:202). Prayer, moreover, inclines us "to receive impressions from divine truths as revealed unto us, conforming our minds and hearts unto the doctrine made known." In other words, the reader must remain open to the text, eager to hear what the divine other has to say. More than that, since one is listening to the divine word, once the doctrine has become clear, the reader must be ready to be "impressed" by it, that is, to be cast into the mold of the teaching. Once again, the urge for application becomes evident in this method of interpretation (ibid., 4:205).

Knowing versus Understanding

German Pietist theologians profess the same epistemological model. The fact that God created reality assures them that all epistemology and interpretation occur at some level within the Logos, within God's pervading presence. Human beings know things by the light of natural reason, which is a God-given faculty. In fact, faith is the highest form of knowledge, while scientific knowledge and method, though in themselves necessary and useful, constitute a mere shadow of the real thing. Like Owen, the Pietist theologian Philipp Jacob Spener differentiates between distanced and engaged knowledge, between mere notional and genuine understanding. The message of the word is not contrary to reason but goes beyond fallen reason.

This becomes especially clear in the encounter with the written word. The unregenerate reader may well understand the propositions of scripture as propositions but cannot grasp their true meaning. Spener admits that many people know the scriptures inside out and yet have not attained to the knowledge of God, because such knowledge is relational:

> Based on this explanation, I gladly admit that out of common grace, by which God has given man his natural understanding and left it to him even after the Fall, man may not only learn the languages [Greek and Hebrew],

but he may also understand and conceptually grasp other things belonging to words. On the basis of this natural light alone, a nonregenerate person without the Holy Spirit may, if he diligently reads and searches the scripture and contemplates its content with the help of other sources, sufficiently understand its teachings to form certain habits and to discuss and debate his findings with others as he does with other worldly knowledge that he acquires in philosophical, legal, medical, and historical books; knowledge that is obtained either by the light of reason or the words of other men. (*Die allgemeine Gottesgelehrtheit*, 10)

Spener's attributing even the rational comprehension of the word to common grace shows how close he is to Luther's and Owen's understanding that God's presence is evident in all epistemological activity. Like Owen, Spener contends that propositions such as "there is a God, and Jesus is God's son, has suffered, died, and rose from the dead, etc." are true no matter who handles them (*Die allgemeine Gottesgelehrtheit*, 15). The biblical concept of revelation and truth demands that God's truth be valid, no matter who utters it.

That there are many critics of the Bible who understand its teachings well cannot be denied, says Spener, for he has met many such people. But if every human being possesses such ability, that is, if such knowledge of the text is possible to the unregenerate, why is there need for illumination (*Die allgemeine Gottesgelehrtheit*, 16)? To answer this question, Spener formulates a difference between *Wissen* (knowledge) and *Verstehen* (understanding), the latter being possible only for one who enters into the relational aspect of biblical hermeneutics. In other words, Spener suggests the same difference between propositional and relational knowledge that also animated the Puritan epistemology and interpretation of existence. The natural man, the *anthropos psychikos*,[4] has no relation to the deity, and his knowledge about God from the scriptures thus remains propositional; it is not the kind of existential apprehension the text itself advocates as a requirement for interpretation: "However, the text says that the natural man does not understand these things, he does not grasp them; and that not merely in such a way as to say he does not participate in them while he may understand them correctly, rather the text says he *cannot recognize* [the truth]; thus even the least bit of proper recognition is lacking" (ibid., 18; emphasis in original). This darkness is due not to any fault in the text, however, but entirely to human deficiency (ibid., 92).

Again, it is important to realize that Spener, like Luther, does not advocate a distinction in propositional meaning between the Spirit and

---

4. Spener uses the same term as Owen, derived from their close reading of Paul's epistles.

the letter, as if the one would yield a divergent reading. The problem is that scripture demands a knowledge *not only* according to the letter *but also* according to the Spirit. The unregenerate reader cannot understand (*begreiffen*) the subject matter because this requires a different kind of understanding. The knowledge of God and the obtaining of a divine perspective for the interpretation of existence cannot simply be obtained by diligence (*Fleiss*): "But why does one lack understanding [knowledge of spiritual things]? [Because] it is spiritually oriented. Thus [understanding] requires a *spiritual sense, one that has been changed and illuminated by the Holy Spirit*" (*Die allgemeine Gottesgelehrtheit*, 20; emphasis in original).

The words *Sinn* and *Verstand* are critical, for they determine that Spener's hermeneutics is one with that of the Puritans. Not only is there a problem in cognitively grasping the full import of the biblical truths (*Verstand*), but the reader outside a relationship with the Divine lacks the ability to appropriate the text. The term *Sinn* carries the same sense as when Germans say, "*Danach steht mir nicht der Sinn,*" meaning "I have no inclination toward a certain activity." In other words, Spener is talking about goodwill toward the text, the unwillingness inherent in every *anthropos psychikos* to accept the authority of the divine word. Therefore, until the reader has entered into dialogue with the Divine through a change of heart, any reading ultimately remains a misreading.

Spener thus uses the same arguments to defend the clarity of the scripture as his greatest mentor, Luther, whom he quotes extensively on this position. Spener believes that to achieve a proper understanding of the text, the reader must be illuminated by the same Spirit that animated the authors of scripture (*Die allgemeine Gottesgelehrtheit*, 21). Consequently, Spener rejects the notion that knowledge sufficient for communion with the Divine may be gained from either observing the created cosmos or searching the human heart (ibid., 347).

In light of this required spiritual knowledge, Spener defines cognition as understanding: "to grasp" (*fassen*) or "to recognize" (*erkennen*) does not mean to invent something but rather to grasp a subject matter that has already been invented and presented. This *fassen* or *erkennen* is "not *mere mental assent to a proposition but trust in its truth*" (*Die allgemeine Gottesgelehrtheit*, 27–28; emphasis mine). Thus a proposition in the biblical text can be fully understood only when it is grasped in light of the meaning the divine author gave it; and this meaning is always one that demands the context of communion with the Divine: "The one who does not love God has not known God. Knowledge without love is wrong" (ibid., 40). As with Luther, Calvin, and Owen, hermeneutics is a relational rather than a technical or methodical undertaking.

Understanding does not merely entail the grasping of propositions but includes their appropriation.

To express this point in hermeneutical language: The scope of the scriptures, its heart and subject matter, requires love of God. Without this affection, biblical hermeneutics fails to provide adequate self-knowledge. The reader may cognitively grasp that he is supposed to love God and understand scripture at the propositional level. Yet only personal appropriation attains to the full meaning of the text. Thus Spener's high view of scripture and Lutheran anthropology required a doctrine of regeneration and illumination for the reading of the text. Like Perkins and Owen, he believed that divine aid is required to overcome the effects of sin. These effects are evident not just in the mind but in our very inclination. At root, a non-Christian does not understand the scriptures because he or she lacks the dynamic of personal address. As soon as one feels addressed, God is already at work in the person's psyche. Both the understanding and the general attitude toward the text must be changed before a genuine dialogue with the Divine is possible.

The Use of Tradition

Nietzsche believed that Christianity's obsession with truth had led inevitably to the death of God, that is, the death of all metaphysics famously described in aphorism 125 of *The Gay Science*. According to Nietzsche, once we have allowed the "worm" of skepticism to search for bedrock in epistemology, we soon dig through the bedrock itself merely to discover that no absolute certainty in knowledge exists (*Fröhliche Wissenschaft*, 3:428). According to this gravedigger thesis, Enlightenment philosophy is basically a continuation of Protestantism, including Descartes's search for bedrock in the *cogito ergo sum*, Hume's bedrock of sense experience, and Kant's transcendental categories. Within this scenario, precritical theology, too, is a logical precursor to the hermeneutics of suspicion embodied in the modern writings of Nietzsche, Marx, and Freud. It is certainly true that we can hear in Kant's rejection of our self-incurred tutelage (*selbstverschuldete Unmündigkeit*) echoes of the Puritan-Pietist call to interpretive independence, pitting scripture against tradition. Kant remains a good Protestant when he demands a criterion by which tradition and authorities may be judged. He deviates from pre-Enlightenment theology, however, when he makes human reason the sole judge of authority and tradition.

It is one of philosophical hermeneutics' greatest services to have reestablished the positive role of tradition that the Enlightenment had forgotten. As Gadamer teaches us correctly, human reason is, after all, not independent of tradition but can only express itself through the language of tradition. We consider something rational because our tradition validates it as such. In this Gadamer agrees with (post)modern hermeneuts of suspicion, critics of Western rationality such as Jacques Derrida and Michel Foucault. Gadamer disagrees, however, with any pretenses to disengage from tradition. It is a fundamental hermeneutical insight (and I believe a just one) that we know only via tradition. This does not mean, however, as Gadamer made clear in his response to the German philosopher Jürgen Habermas, that we cannot be critical of tradition itself. It does mean, however, that we can do so only through tradition. It is of considerable interest, then, what pre-Enlightenment theological hermeneutics made of tradition. Did it, like the Enlightenment, believe in a neutral, universally accessible space from which we could speak against tradition? Does not, in fact, the claim of *sola scriptura* entail such a belief?

We have already seen in the first chapter that the concept of *sola scriptura* should not be understood as excluding interpretive tradition and that it includes the role of the Holy Spirit in his guidance of the interpretive community. Another good locus for gauging the use of tradition in pre-Enlightenment theology is discussions of conscience. In religious controversies from Luther's slightly mythical "Here I stand" to the liturgical debates of the Reformation in Germany and England, people appealed to conscience as the final arbiter of judgment. It is not that conscience was seen as pure and unerring but rather that the main battle was between a conscience informed by atrophied tradition and one reformed by biblical study. In Puritan theology, conscience—like reason—was part of the *imago Dei*. Owen, for example, believed that "conscience is the territory or dominion of God in man, which he hath so reserved unto himself that no human power can possibly enter into it or dispose of it in any wise" (*WJO*, 4:96).

John Bunyan immortalized this notion of conscience as an a priori category in his *Holy War*: there conscience is depicted as the reminder of El Shaddai's law, a voice that Diabolus, do what he would, is unable to expel from the city of Mansoul. According to Owen, conscience's main function within the human psyche is to judge the mind in respect to God: "No power under heaven can cause conscience to think, act, or judge otherwise than it doth by its immediate respect to God" (*WJO*, 4:96). Owen does not mean that the conscience is free from either cultural influences or postlapsarian selfishness. While conscience's function as the memory of God's law cannot be entirely suppressed, the damage sustained by sin allows the conscience to be informed by tradition and education, thus by culturally differentiated values.

Whenever Owen acknowledges that tradition and education play a great part in (mis)informing the conscience, he sounds like a precursor of the Enlightenment: "I know conscience may be prepossessed with prejudices, and, by education, with the insinuation of traditions, take on itself the power of false, corrupt, superstitious principles and errors, as means of conveying unto it a sense of divine authority" (*WJO*, 4:96). Conscience may even be fooled into accepting an authority other than God as its own, such as the authority of tradition, nourished by education. The mind will then accept these false notions as the genuine transcendence of God's revelation. Thus secular notions can find access to the conscience through the mind and actually seem compatible to the malfunctioning conscience: "Wherefore, such opinions and persuasions are gradually insinuated into the mind, and are admitted insensibly without opposition or reluctancy, being never accompanied at their first admission with any secular disadvantage." They "affect, deceive, and delude the notional part of the soul, whereby conscience is insensibly influenced and diverted into improper respects and is divided as to its judging of the voice of God" (ibid., 4:97).

However, tradition and education can merely beset the "outward duties that conscience disposeth to, but none can be so upon its internal actings." Tradition and education, for example, may confuse the notions of what is right and wrong according to God's law, but they can never completely eradicate those notions themselves. The only power that can touch the innermost "springs of conscience" is the power of the Word. Because the workings of the Holy Spirit have direct access to the configuration of the system, they override all other faulty programming: "These divine convictions befall men, some when they think of nothing less and desire nothing less . . . and some when they go on purpose [to a sermon] to deride and scoff at what should be spoken unto them from [the Word]" (*WJO*, 4:97). Owen insists that the inborn hostility of man to the authority of divine revelation may be overcome effectively only by the work of the Holy Spirit. A traditional faith may do so only "notionally," but not permanently or lastingly. The word alone can break the hold of tradition and clarify misinformation accrued by education, because it speaks directly to the innermost conscience, giving the mind an entirely new direction, opening up a hitherto unknown perspective (ibid.).

In a post-Gadamerian hermeneutical context, Owen's insistence on breaking the hold of tradition sounds rather strange. Is not tradition the very canvas on which understanding takes place? Such a charge suffers, however, from its anachronistic misreading of pre-Enlightenment theology. Clearly, Owen did not know about the Enlightenment's call against tradition's authority. He himself is careful to cite many famous biblical interpreters to buttress his opinions (though he does not fear going against received opinion, including that of the church fathers, Calvin, Hieronymus Zanchius, Theodorus Beza, and others). Pre-Enlightenment theologians simply assumed that tradition played a necessary role in education. Thus Richard Baxter can write: "For young men must have teachers; they cannot begin at the foundation and yet every one learn of himself, as if none had ever learned before him: he is like to have but a slow proficient that maketh no use of the studies and experience of any that ever learned before him. And he that will learn of others, must receive their notions and words as the means of his information" (*PWRB*, 4:568). We may not, in other words, ascribe Cartesian sentiments to pre-Enlightenment theology. Descartes's very notion that we can reach epistemological bedrock by doubting everything is rejected by Baxter as foolish, given human finitude and the infinite number of things to be known. Descartes's withdrawal to doubting as the only certainty left to the human mind is unacceptable to Baxter. Instead he suggests that we admit our limitations and give up such pretences to certainty because they originate in our prideful desire for control. We should accept that we can never know anything fully, but this does not mean we do not know anything at all: "What then, because we cannot know all, shall we know nothing or deny all? Because we cannot see the whole frame of the world, in its junctures and proportion, shall we say that there is no world? . . . A beast knows not what a man is, and yet he apprehendeth that there is such a creature: and no man thoroughly knoweth what he is himself, and yet he knoweth that he is" (ibid., 2:384–85).

Baxter's conclusion is the same as Owen's: knowledge always involves trust because we cannot know with ultimate certainty. This insight should take away the pride of the Christian who mistakes the nature of God's self-revelation for abstract, mathematical certainty, for God, too, cannot be known with certain knowledge; knowledge as trust should equally squelch the arrogance of the non-Christian who cannot rest easy in rationalist proofs of God's nonexistence. The atheist is no better than the triumphalist Christian. In both cases, we find human ignorance paired with arrogance: "They think there is no such thing as communion with God because they know not what it is; nor any such thing as a spirit of prayer, because they know not what it is." Baxter's apologetic is clear: if we admit human finitude, we should also admit the existence of God, which exceeds our limited capacity. The primary mode of knowledge is trust (i.e., mediated knowledge) rather than immediate, pure certainty. We are never admitted "into the presence chamber of truth and so see her naked without delay" (*PWRB*, 2:386). We want to see rather than trust, yet "receiving truth upon trust from another" is the basis on which we form our interpretations of human existence.

As in Gadamer's hermeneutics, then, tradition is an important source of knowledge in pre-Enlightenment hermeneutics. We do not have god-like knowledge even of simple things, let alone of a proper framework for explaining reality. Certainty of that kind is inhuman. Knowledge comes via tradition, even theology. Where then is truth to be found? In the highest form of knowing, by trusting God who has made all things. The Christian must realize, however, that knowing God is also a matter of trust and that transcendence is not a matter of rational certainty but of personal relation. In other words, objective truth is not found in doctrinal equations that afford the predictability of Euclidean geography but in communion with God, a hermeneutical circle of learning and application.

Tradition and *Sola Scriptura*

Because modern readers often do not understand the premodern hermeneutical interplay between the reader, his participation in the church and interpretive tradition, and the role of the Holy Spirit, the reformational concept of *sola scriptura* remains misunderstood. The main stumbling stone is the seeming tautological nature of the Protestant claim that the biblical text itself proclaims the central message of justification by faith alone, while this very principle serves at the same time as the central interpretive presupposition that makes such a reading possible. If this charge is correct, then the Protestant Reformation advanced its own biased and historically conditioned reading under the guise of supposed timeless objectivity. Hans-George Gadamer sums up Wilhelm Dilthey's opinion: by "ultimately asserting the Protestant creedal formulae as guides to the scriptural principle of the unity of the Bible, [Protestantism] too supersedes the scriptural principle in favour of a rather brief Reformation tradition" (*TM*, 177).

Gadamer realizes, however, that some dogmatic (often unacknowledged) guideline always and necessarily guides our interpretation of texts (*TM*, 177). Gadamer, in other words, turns Dilthey's criticism of Protestant hermeneutics into the constructive insight that we must rethink our notions of objective truth, and the first victim of this rethinking how the interpretation of texts works must be the notion of truth as impersonal (abstract and detached) and timeless. The whole point of Gadamer's work is that we engage texts on the basis of our historically effected concerns and ideas. In Christian circles, this insight usually causes great unease, even fear, because we seem to abandon the safe ground of biblical revelation for the shifting sands of relativism. For surely if we admit the historical nature of *sola scriptura,* must we not also historicize *sola fide*? And if we admit that these Reformational battle cries are historically conditioned, don't we throw away not only the central tenets of Christianity but also the very method of objective reading by which we secured them in the first place?

However, I believe this opposition of historical development and truth is perhaps the biggest hermeneutical mistake modern Christianity has made. This is so, first, because it is a fundamental denial of the incarnation and its implications. God has disclosed himself to us in history, by embodying himself in Jesus. This is already a self-interpretation of God in history. Thus Christians, of all people, should be anchored in history rather than constantly trying to get out of it. Christ died to save us not from history but from our sins in order that history may be redeemed. God's condescension of coming to us in history is also the confirmation of our limitations as finite human beings: we are not God but human, and that means that we always have only a partial grasp of the whole glorious tapestry of God's self-address to us.

The Protestant Reformation certainly recovered central aspects of God's word, yet justification by grace through faith is a subtheme, albeit a crucial one, of the good news that Jesus is the Christ, the Messiah who inaugurated the new age of God's kingdom. *Sola fide* does not capture the gospel in its entirety. If that were the entire heritage of Reformation theology, it could not serve each generation, for it arose in a specific historical context to address its particular needs. At the very least, we must make this insight fruitful for our present cultural context. Simply to transpose Reformation debates and issues into our present time, as if history did not exist, not only opposes the Reformation motto of continual reformation but also gives Christianity a bad name by creating small fundamentalist factions who fight one another and the rest of the world, each residing in an isolating bubble of timelessness.

My whole argument is, of course, that both Christians and non-Christians alike have reduced the heritage of the Reformation unfairly. I have tried to show in the chapter on Luther that the interpretive principle of *sola scriptura* certainly included the use of tradition and entailed very much a sense of history. Yet at the same time, Protestantism, like any other movement, was often quick to elevate its creeds to the level of scripture, so that soon Protestant culture was shaped more by catechetical instruction than by active and lively wrestling with scripture on a daily basis. How seriously, in other words, do Christians who live by the Bible take Luther's assertion that God's word "does not allow our thinking to stand, even in those matters which are most sacred, but it destroys and eradicates and scatters everything" (*Luther Deutsch*, 1:27)?

To take Luther's injunction seriously requires the courage to examine one's presuppositions and reflect on them as possible historically conditioned constructs that we have retained for the sake of self-identity and to avoid the inconvenience of thorough reflection.

Yet if we admit Luther's method of Christian deconstruction, are we not, in fact, urging everyone to become a Derrida, a radical deconstructionist for whom nothing is sacred? How enjoyable, let alone practical, can it be to continually undermine one's position? Indeed, once we embark on this road, does it not lead inevitably to Nietzsche, nihilism, and the death of God? This understandable fear illustrates Protestantism's second major mistake of not grasping fully the *relational* nature of truth.

The great strength of Reformation theology was—and is—its emphasis on the personal relation with God as opposed to God's exclusive embodiment in a system of liturgy or even in community. At its best, the concept of a personal relation with God prevents a break between proposition and experience by insisting that the God who revealed himself historically and whose character and teaching are found in the biblical text is the same God who dwells in every believer. Deferring an exact analysis of this relationship to the last chapter of this book, I wish to point out here that Protestant hermeneutics conjoins the so-called subjective and objective sides of interpretation (the reader's experience and the text) in the second Person of the Trinity.

This interpretive principle, so foundational to Reformation hermeneutics, requires a special status for the biblical text, for unlike other texts, this text claims to be about God's self-revelation in Christ, whose Spirit also indwells the believer. In other words, the Christian reader of the biblical text is in the unique situation to have his or her interpretive projections shaped by their relationship with Christ, who is also the central focus of the text. Without this personal relationship, the reader misses the very heart of the biblical text. This has nothing to do with gnosticism, some secret insider knowledge reserved for people of particular intelligence or spiritual supermen.

Much can be gained in our reassessment of Protestant hermeneutics if we understand that the term "spiritual meaning" in pre-Enlightenment hermeneutics does not refer to a higher meaning reserved for irrational spiritualists who have given up on reality and history but instead describes the reading experience of those who have been met by God in and through history, whose reading is shaped by an ongoing participation in the Trinity. Spiritual meaning is not a meaning "hidden" behind the obvious words of the text. Rather, to use the famous Puritan analogy, it is like the difference between reading a love letter addressed to someone else and reading one addressed to you.

At the same time, however, Christian readers often forget that the correspondence between reader and text via the person of Christ is radically hermeneutical *because* it is personal. What is true of our encounter with human beings is all the more true of our encounter with the incarnate God: we will never have complete transparency. In its personal aspect, the incarnation is the very foundation of hermeneutical humility: the very essence of a personal relationship is its interpretive unfolding in time played out in a dynamic of disclosure and concealment, which marks all personal relationships. It is perhaps understandable when we reduce this personal dynamic to static propositional truths by which we then measure our faith, but it is wrong. The very nature of the personal resists incarceration in propositions. It has been the unfortunate tendency of Christianity either to embrace the personal aspect of biblical interpretation at the expense of serious textual criticism or to forgo the personal aspect in favor of rationalistic interpretation.

Tradition and Interpretive Humility

Our findings show that the Puritans and the Pietists were not precursors to Enlightenment epistemology. As in general knowledge, so in the interpretation of scripture, the kind of certainty the scientific-mathematical model promises is unattainable by humans, even undesirable because it does not suit human nature.

Neither did the reformational *sola scriptura* principle entail the rejection of tradition as such. What the Reformers upheld was the transcendence of the divine word. Owen's concern in light of the Roman Catholic insistence on final hermeneutic arbitration was to ensure some transcendent power that guarantees a critical posture toward any human authority, be it church or state. Thus for him the authority of tradition, though important, is superseded by the word, even if he recognizes the necessity of tradition for interpretation. Modern readers must be careful not to mistake the customary denunciation of tradition by Reformation theologians for a renunciation of tradition as such. The strong antitraditionalist rhetoric must be understood as a knee-jerk reaction to the church's attempt to justify poor interpretive practices by tradition.

In their own hermeneutic practice, the Puritans and the Pietists relied heavily on other interpretations but did not regard this as a problem. Their claim of *sola scriptura* is only rightly understood when seen in light of their doctrine of the Holy Spirit in interpretation. Making use of the interpretive means of tradition, language, and history, God's Spirit is nonetheless able to reshape interpretations. One is thus never caught in a vicious hermeneutic circle dictated by tradition; rather, through and from within tradition, tradition itself is reformed. The reliance on the Holy Spirit in interpretation effects interpretive humility. While the Puritans particularly are not known for humility in their judgments, Owen surprises us with a plea for tolerance that may sound strange to modern readers accustomed to the image of Puritanism as an oppressive political force. Owen insists on the interpretive humility that should come with the Christian's belief in the power of God's word.

Denying the argument that hermeneutical disputes within Protestantism demonstrate the unfeasibility of *sola scriptura,* he ascribes acrimonious interpretive conflicts to human pride. Owen certainly believes in right doctrine and the necessity to argue for it, but it is the power of truth that must convince. Comparing those who do not believe in right doctrine to sailors adrift in a storm, he asks, "But is it *humanity* [i.e., humane] to stand on the shore, and seeing men in a storm at sea, wherein they are ready every moment to be cast away and perish, to storm at them ourselves, or to shoot them to death, or to cast fire in their vessel, because they are in danger of being drowned? Yet no otherwise do we deal with them whom we persecute because they miss the knowledge of the truth; and, it may be, raise a worse storm in ourselves as to our own morals than they suffer under in their intellectuals" (*WJO,* 4:177).

It is, in other words, ethically irresponsible for those who confess to God's elective and sanctifying grace to persecute others who hold different views. It may well be that Owen comes to this insight because of his own politically disadvantageous situation, but we should not reduce his view to ideology (Yule, *Puritans in Politics*, 215 ff.). The modern notion of Puritanism as intolerant (a sentiment commonly held against Christianity and religion in general) is inherently intolerant if false. Our study of Owen shows that belief in the power of God's word and its efficacy instead provides the foundation for tolerance in interpretation.

Ethics: The Skill to Walk in Communion with God

We often think of Puritans and Pietists as rigid moralists. Moralism is concerned with moral behavior and obedience to ethical norms based on rational assent and willpower. Within a moralistic framework, ethics then becomes a body or system of rules for moral conduct. The Puritans and the Pietists, however, distinguished between ethics and morality, a distinction that has regained importance in recent hermeneutical discussion because of the influence of Levinas, whose work seeks to distinguish an original ethical experience from moral behavior as secondary to this experience (Critchley, *Ethics of Deconstruction*, 3–4).

This recent trend only returns to what Puritans and Pietists, following Luther's position, which we outlined in chapter 1, considered a fundamental. Though they did not describe it in modern terms, in Puritan and Pietist hermeneutics moral behavior flows from communion with God, a dynamic relational experience prior and conducive to moral behavior. What we moderns call morality or moral duty was known as legalism by the Puritans and as *Werkheiligkeit* (works righteousness) in German Pietism. The biblical ethics of pre-Enlightenment theologians are defined by their very opposition to legalism, the notion that one may gain, fortify, or improve one's relationship with God through the rigid observation of God's commandments. To put moral duty before one's relation with God was to put the cart before the horse. The following analysis of Puritan and Pietist notions of sanctification, or *Heiligung* ("becoming holy"), is not an ethics of duty (moralism) but rather a dynamic hermeneutical model of application that flows from communion with God. We will see that in Pietism in particular, this relational model of ethics requires an applicatory reading of the biblical text, whose strength is displayed in the social reforms of German Pietism.

The "skill to walk in communion with God," a process commonly termed "sanctification" in reformed theology, is the applicatory dimension of Puritan hermeneutics. Sanctification, the increasing restoration of a human being to the image of God, is the goal of biblical hermeneutics: "That wisdom in the mystery of the gospel, that knowledge of the mind and will of God in the Scripture, which *affects the heart*, and *transforms the mind* in the renovation of it unto the approbation of the 'good, and acceptable, and perfect will of God,' as the apostle speaks Rom.xii.2, is alone valuable and desirable, as unto all spiritual and eternal ends" (*WJO*, 4:157; emphasis in original).

Thus communion with the divine through the text should always translate into ethical action insofar as the Christian is to be Christlike in his or her moral conduct. This relation of morality to communion with the divine distinguishes the Puritan theory of ethics from moralism. Morality, for Owen, is tied to revealed truth, and truth in turn is tied to the relation with Christ. Owen disagrees with those who think that one can have morality without a relation to the divine being. The hermeneutical framework of a created universe understands all humanity to be morally obligated to the Creator, since, in federal covenant theology, Adam stood for the entire human race, which fell and sinned with him.

A decisive difference between anthropocentric and theocentric ethics, between moralism and morality, is the latter's view of humanity's universal obligation to God. For Owen, God as Creator is not only sovereign but also morally perfect, wherefore morally good behavior is ultimately only that which pleases God, not primarily that which satisfies human desires. Since God's moral law is designed to regulate social interaction for the benefit of humanity, the divine rules always meet human *needs* rather than human *desires*. This formulation sounds less rigid if we remember that Owen does not consider desire as such evil but that fallen humanity's selfishness calls for ethical principles that may contravene human egocentrism. Ideally, human desire would conform to God's image in mankind by desiring to love God and one's neighbor. However, such love, Owen argues, is possible only through communion with the Divine. The only moral behavior ultimately pleasing to God is that which grows out of a relationship with him. Of course, Owen admits, certain moral laws are evident from "the light of nature" (*WJO*, 3:633), and even atheists may adopt theistic morality when it suits their needs.

Moralism, then, views ethics from an anthropocentric perspective as that which is useful and pleasing to us rather than from a theocentric one as that which is pleasing to God. According to Owen, moralism suffers from three basic problems. First, separated from a relational dialogue with the Divine, it does not solve humanity's problems, because mere human theorizing does not dispose the heart to action. The human condition needs a radical change in disposition: "The utmost imaginations of men never reached unto that wherein the life and soul of holiness doth consist,— namely, the renovation of our lapsed nature into the image and likeness of God. Without this, whatever precepts are given about the moderation of affections and duties of moral holiness, they are lifeless, and will prove useless" (*WJO*, 3:635). It is the power of divine revelation and operation to renew persons, rather than just impose moral regulation. None of the "documents which were given by philosophers of old" ever effected such a "change on their conversation" (ibid.).

The second problem with moral philosophy relates to the implementation of "conversation," a term that translates into the modern idea of "conduct" or "lifestyle." This second major difficulty with philosophy, according to Owen, is that, while clearly spelling out some general moral principles, philosophers cannot agree on the essence of morality itself. They know by the light of nature that "others are not to be injured, that every one's right is to be rendered unto him," but "go a little farther, and you will find all the great moralists at endless uncertain disputes about the nature of virtue in general, about the offices and duties of it, about the rule and measure of their practice." What is worse, "in these disputes did most of them consume their lives, without any great endeavours to express their own notions in their conversations" (*WJO*, 3:635).

Owen charges moralism with being merely theoretical, either not daring or simply not caring to put principles into practice. The Christian reader of the word, however, has no such luxury. The universal role and rule of Christ requires that his word be obeyed: "If once it appear that Christ requires any thing of us by his word, that he hath taught us any thing as the prophet of the church, no doubt remains with us whether it be our duty or no" (*WJO*, 3:635).

The third flaw of moral philosophy lies in its "partiality." Owen argues that moral philosophy, since it springs from the minds of sinful writers, cannot serve as an ethical rule. For Owen philosophy lacks both authority and radicalness when it comes to ethics. According to him, moral philosophers are more concerned with language than with substance. "What is," he asks, "in the manner of teaching by the greatest moralists, and what are the effects of it? Enticing words, smoothness and elegancy of speech, composed into snares for the affections and delight unto the fancy, are the grace, ornament, and life of the way or manner of their teaching . . . [a]nd so easy and gentle is their operation on the minds of men, that commonly they are delighted in by the most profligate and obstinate sinners; as is the preaching of them who act in the same spirit and from the same principles" (*WJO*, 3:637). Philosophical ethics is, in other words, a "partial" philosophy, tailored to the pride of human beings, who do not want to realize that more than mere outward morality is needed to regulate human affairs. In human teaching, the root problem of alienation from the Divine is hardly addressed, and even where healthy moral principles are advocated, they lack proper foundation. Where unsound moral principles are espoused, their folly is evident from the reluctance of their propagators to implement them themselves (ibid., 3:636).

In short, moralism and moral philosophy cannot be trusted as a rule for moral conduct. Besides, Owen argues, the best moral maxims at which philosophy may arrive are already contained much more clearly in the scriptures: "I dare challenge the greatest and most learned moralist in the world to give an instance of any one duty of morality, confirmed by the rules and directions of the highest and most contemplative moralist, that I will not show and evince is more plainly and clearly required by the Lord Christ in the gospel, and pressed on us by far more effectual motives than any they are acquainted with" (*WJO*, 3:636).

Owen's principal argument here is the same as in his prior plea for the balancing of faith and reason. Morality needs to be relational, tied to the person of Christ rather than to merely abstract and rational principles. Without this foundation, morality does not make sense, because it lacks a dialogical relation to a being of moral perfection and universal authority. Hence those who want to establish ethics without divine guidance, based on reason alone, run into the danger of relativistic ethics, because in an anthropocentric turn, they have shifted the authority to human reason, and human self-understanding and moral reasoning are always inadequate because they lack genuine transcendence and are bent on self-glorification.

The Puritan argument against nonrelational ethics follows Luther's argument. Not only must there be an absolute moral demand that is not a system but a personal address by the wholly other God, but the gap between the ethical demand and the social action flowing from it requires divine grace found in communion with God. Conversion, or the "turn" of which the Puritans spoke by which human existence in every aspect is positioned to become Christlike, was something that had to begin from the "inside" out. Stoic external self-discipline without change of heart mistakes morality for grace. The Puritan Thomas Watson comments that "morality is but nature refined, old Adam put in a better dress. A moralised man is but a tame devil! There may be a fair stream of civility running and yet much vermin of pride and atheism lying at the bottom" (Kistler, *Puritans on Conversion*, 173).

Puritanism also believed with Luther that no matter what moral code we adopt, it will soon become burdensome because it goes against our human desire for autonomy and natural dislike of authority. Lack of divine grace, argues Owen, "renders obedience so grievous and burdensome to many. They endure it for a season, and at length either violently or insensibly cast off its yoke" (*WJO*, 3:622). The ethical experience of the Christian, by contrast, is marked by pleasure. While every believer is still struggling with the "old Adam," he or she is no longer under the absolute power of this influence. Owen writes: "Upon supply of [God's] grace, which gives both strength for and a constant inclination unto holy obedience, the command for it becomes equal and just, meet and easy to be complied withal . . . for I cannot persuade myself that any believer can be so captivated at any time, under the power of temptations, corruptions or prejudices, but that . . . his mind and spirit will say, 'This good I would do; I delight in it; it is best for me, most suited unto me'" (ibid.).

Understanding *Is* Application

In the history of Christianity, few other movements have demonstrated the effects of relational ethics more impressively than German Pietism, represented in our study by Philipp Jacob Spener and August Hermann Francke. The heart of Spener's hermeneutics is a text-to-action model. A genuine understanding of the text, argues Spener, much like Owen, *is* application. Spener sees a direct connection between truth and application. The proof for genuine knowledge of God and self is reformation of one's own life into the image of God and social interaction according to the model of Christ. On the one hand, he argues, God's word should be preached to strengthen the inner man. On the other hand, charitable works must result from this communion with the Divine: "Our whole Christian religion consists of the new man, whose soul is faith and whose expressions are the fruits of life, and all sermons should be aimed at this" (*Pia Desideria*, 116). Spener, and with him the theologians we have already discussed, believed in what Richard Hays has called the "embodiment" of the scriptures. Hays merely confirms Spener's reading of Paul's writings when he states that

> the Christian tradition's reading of the letter-spirit dichotomy as an an-
> tithesis between the outward and the inward, the manifest and the latent,
> the body and the soul, turns out to be a dramatic misreading, indeed a
> complete inversion. For Paul, the spirit is scandalously identified pre-
> cisely with the outward and palpable, the particular human community
> of the new covenant, putatively transformed by God's power so as to make
> Christ's message visible to all. The script, however, remains abstract and
> dead because it is not embodied. (*Echoes of Scripture*, 150)

Contrary to the popular use of the term "pietistic" as designating an otherworldliness, the father of Pietism does not teach a metaphysical dualism. For Spener understanding the text means living it, embodying the script by the power of the Holy Spirit.

Spener is convinced that only relational knowledge can produce such an applicatory manner of living. Mere theoretical approaches will fail to produce a life where social action flows from a dialogue with the Divine: "As all knowledge of God and his will according to the law and the gospel cannot stop at mere knowledge but must result in praxis and practical application, even scholarly attempts at reading the Bible to derive knowledge about God must be conducted under a holy resolution practically to apply every insight into the will of God which has been granted by his grace in one's reading" (*Pia Desideria*, 67). Spener's model for an applicatory hermeneutics is Christ himself, whose basic message, "those who love me will keep my commandments," runs through Spener's writings like a guiding thread and summarizes his hermeneutical approach.

At the beginning stands the reader's effort of personal reformation: through cultivating a relationship with the Divine, the formerly lost divine image is restored. Second, application has an intersubjective dimension: the divine directions found in the text motivate one to social interaction. There is no doubt that Spener's, and later Francke's, impressive record of social activism is founded on the summary of the Mosaic law given by Christ to "love God with all your strength and love your neighbor as yourself." Spener clearly states his position in a sermon titled *Christliche Verpflegung der Armen*. His opening lines indicate the foundation of his applicatory hermeneutics:

> Beloved in Christ Jesus. We who are called Christians and who are even remotely familiar with our Savior's commandments in the scripture know, and should know, that next to the love of God, love of our neighbor is the main virtue demanded by the law; a virtue also taught by our most beloved Savior himself, the most faithful keeper of God's law: more than that, he makes this virtue the mark of recognition by which we make known that you are his disciples, when you love one another (John 13:35). (13)

In agreement with the sermon text, Spener teaches that charitable action is not confined to the fellow Christian but also to any other person in need, because all human beings are made in God's image: "Therefore [our] neighbors are all human beings, every single one without exception and therefore those who are our brothers according to creation and in that sense have the same God as a father as we do according to Malachi 2:10" (ibid., 20).[5] Thus, as in the case of Owen, Spener's idea of tolerance and charity is firmly grounded in his biblical hermeneutics within the framework of a created universe. Spener argues that if there is a God, then reality is already determined and not created individually. Since God is eternal (*ewiglich*), his will, as expressed in the law and gospel dialectic, is universally binding for everyone at all times and thus transcends historical and cultural barriers (*Lesen der Heiligen Schrifft*, 103). Hence Spener's humanitarianism is founded on the unchangeable fact that all human beings are "made in the image of God." Heretics and pagans all are entitled to every possible aid, not because charity is a personal choice of the individual but because of the universally binding truth of common creation (ibid., 23).

Spener's insistence on social ethics is sometimes construed to show that he abandoned the teaching of justification by faith for a works-oriented religion. However, Spener himself adamantly rejects such an accusation. In most of his casuistical works, such as *Natur und Gnade* (1705), he insists that morality must flow from communion with the Divine, which in turn may only be achieved through justification by faith (14ff.). The same sentiment is stated in a series of sermons called *Die evangelischen Lebenspflichten*. Spener opens his addresses with the assertion that neither legalism nor natural goodwill will lead to charity that is pleasing to God. Instead a relation to the Divine is required be-

---

5. "Also heißen Nächste alle Menschen durch und durch ohne einige ausnahm und daher diejenigen die aus der Schöpffung unsre Brüder sind und in solchem Verstand Gott zu einem gemeinen Vater mit uns haben/nach Malachi 2/10."

cause strength for genuine social action must come from a divine change of heart. Without this conversion, Christ's commandment to exercise neighborly charity out of love for the Divine cannot be kept (xxx).

The inseparable connection between reading and application preached by Spener demands that the reader approach the text in an attitude of humility and prayer. Since the divine commandments go against the inherent egocentrism in the human psyche, prayer for divine aid to overcome these reading impediments is the first step to the reading of the text. With the aid of prayer (i.e., dialogue with the Divine), the reader is to achieve a hermeneutical attitude of humility before the text and a willingness for application. Quoting Luther at length, Spener explains that prayer must be used to invoke the help of God's Spirit, for he is the only agent who may lift fallen human reason to the heights of God's point of view. The Spirit must purify the heart and lead it to a contrite and humble position before God's text; otherwise the true meaning of the text will not be reached (*Die evangelischen Lebenspflichten*, 55).

The Spirit leads the reader into a repentant attitude to seek honestly the will of God in the text. Those who read the scriptures for merely academic interest and fame or even for entertainment should rather direct their efforts to the Greek poets and narrators, for God's word is challenging and practical and should not be toyed with (*Lesen der Heiligen Schrifft*, 60).

Perhaps Spener's most serious challenge to the Christian reader is his insistence that those who do not plan to implement scriptural teaching should not even bother to open the text. The demand of the text is always for one to enter into its world, adjust one's own view to the text, and then apply the textual insight to everyday living. The reader's progressive understanding of the text is thus inseparably tied to practical application. According to Spener, God will not grant new insights to those who do not practice what they already know to be true. Those who do not implement their knowledge are not serious about sanctification, says Spener. They want merely to tickle the old Adam (*"den alten Adam kitzeln"*); they can pray and search the scriptures all they want, but God will grant insight and growth only to serious readers. Those who obediently practice God's will are also those who will soon see the fruits of their application and will thus be encouraged to approach the text again with increased trust and eagerness (*Lesen der Heiligen Schrifft*, 71).

Thus practical piety becomes a hermeneutical precondition for successful scripture reading. Those readers who live in continuous sin will not increase their knowledge about spiritual things and practical wisdom, but those who try to live a godly life will be more likely to succeed in knowledge and spiritual growth through feeding on the text ("thus we can wisely say that a godly life is not the least means for a wholesome reading of scripture" [*Lesen der Heiligen Schrifft*, 74]). No other Pietist has heeded Spener's call to ethics more faithfully than his successor August Hermann Francke. The only real difference between these two post-Reformation reformers is Francke's initial impetuousness and recklessness in advocating reform. However, with advancement in years, Francke became more moderate. Almost more than Spener, he offers an example of social action based on a biblical hermeneutics. The two main aspects of Francke's applicatory hermeneutics are Christ as the kernel of scripture and Francke's belief that interpretation requires the use of our affections.

After his conversion experience, Francke developed what may be called his "hermeneutics of the cross." Francke, perhaps more emphatically than Spener, makes understanding of the text contingent on a relationship with Christ. More specifically, Francke declares an appropriating recognition of the crucifixion to be the key to biblical hermeneutics: "The entire scripture will remain a mystery to you unless you know the secret of the cross" (*Christus der Kern der Heiligen Schrift* [1702], in *FWA*, 246).[6] Francke is convinced that if one has genuinely grasped the meaning of the cross, then reading the biblical text will be a delight rather than a chore: "Many complain about the difficulty and the darkness of the scripture; this is the reason they do not like to read in it. The reason is the lack of love for the cross" (ibid., 247). Christ's redemptive act on the cross, which restores humanity to its original purpose of being in communion with God, is the central hermeneutical focus for Francke. Christ, he writes, is the core or kernel (*Kern*) of scripture, and since Christ is a person, a true understanding of scripture must involve a relation to that person. In another place, Francke restates the centrality of Christ for biblical interpretation by saying that "inasmuch as Jesus is the very soul of scripture and the way by which we have access to the Father, he who, in doctrinal reading, does not fix his eyes on him, must read in vain" (*Manuductio*, 99–100). According to Francke, it is necessary for understanding, edification, and application that one seek and ingest this kernel through the grammatical textual husk of scripture "for the inward sustenance and nourishment of the inner being" (ibid., 104).

Francke uses the cross not only to point out the Christocentric nature of biblical hermeneutics but also to describe its applicatory dimension. An understanding of the cross also entails the taking-up of the cross (*Auffnehmung des Creutzes*) in the biblical sense of following Christ (*Manuductio*, 104). As in Puritan hermeneutics, application is inseparable from reading; in fact, it is the main purpose of reading: "In sum; if you

---

6. "Die ganze Schrift ist dir ein Rätzel / so lange du das Geheimniß des Creutzes nicht erkennst."

take up the reading of the Bible, your sole purpose must be to become a believing and pious Christian, not only as a pretense, but with true power so that you can be sure to be accepted by God in this present world and to enjoy him eternally in the next" (*Einfältiger Unterricht wie man die Schrifft zu seiner wahren Erbauung lesen sollte* [1694], in *FWA*, 217). The true strength of biblical interpretation lies in its goal, that of becoming a pious person through an active Christianity. Not mere theory and pretense (*der Schein*) but the substance (a godly life), which lies in application, is the mark of an effective hermeneutics.

The German scholar Erhard Peschke describes Francke's hermeneutics as a "husk-kernel approach" (*Schale-Kern Schema*), a term that has become problematic at least since Schleiermacher used this term to distinguish between the unimportant historical-grammatical husk and the spiritual kernel (Peschke, *Francke und die Bibel*, 59). It is often assumed that Pietism's emphasis on the affections in combination with the husk-kernel terminology has inevitably led to loss of the text's objective meaning. A close reading of Francke's seminal treatise on hermeneutics, the *Manuductio ad Lectionem Scripturae Sacrae* (1693), will show that Francke tries to balance objective and subjective elements in his effort to withstand a rationalist interpretation that denies the affective dimension of truth.

At the opening of his *Manuductio*, Francke makes clear that the husk-kernel distinction is merely another name for the letter-spirit duality we find throughout the tradition of theological hermeneutics. Just as the Christian tradition has rarely interpreted this duality as dualism, that is, as opposing terms, Francke, too, reminds the reader that "all reading . . . respects either the letter or the spirit of the inspired writings. Separate from the latter, the former would be empty and inconsistent; but when both are united, the study of Divinity is rendered complete" (2). For Francke the textual dimension, consisting of historical, grammatical (philological), and logical reading, is meant to lead to the applicatory spiritual dimension marked by exegetical, dogmatic, inferential, and practical aspects (ibid.). The philological aspect of Francke's approach is every bit as demanding as Spener's: Greek and Hebrew should be learned properly before the student begins his study of the scriptures. The most important known languages from the eras of the Old and the New Testaments should also be learned and consulted, as should rabbinical exegesis. Particular attention is to be given to idioms in each language for a better understanding of the text (ibid., 25–27).

Moreover, in his "logical reading," the reader is to observe the genre of each text by distinguishing between epistolary form, doctrinal content, prophetic writing, and historical writing (*Manuductio*, 57). Each genre should be treated according to its peculiar structure. The epistles, for example, should be "read, reread" in the original Greek and without artificial chapter and verse divisions. "Read it," Francke suggests, "as an epistle from a friend, three or four times over without interruption, until you fully apprehend the meaning and the subject of the epistle becomes clear" (ibid., 59). Francke's advice is by no means original, as his frequent references to the writings of Dannhauer, Flacius, Franzius, and others indicate, but merely serves to reiterate the standard exhortation to painstaking philological work conducted by premodernist exegetes. Once the context (*scopus*) and main content of a text have been established, the reader can move toward the spiritual level and application of the text.

The *lectio exegetica*, or expository reading, guides the reader toward the spiritual reading of the text, the *sensus litteralis*, which Francke distinguishes from the merely grammatical *sensus litterae* (*Manuductio*, 67–68). The *sensus litteralis* is the meaning truly intended by the Holy Spirit. Francke provides the example of the second commandment, "Thou shalt not kill." The grammatical sense is clear enough, but the actual literal sense is explained by Jesus's extension of this command "to lip, life, and gesture" (ibid., 66). Again Francke makes clear that he is not advocating Protestant gnosticism: the natural man (i.e., the non-Christian) may well be able to discern the intended literal (*litteralis*) meaning, but one must nevertheless "carefully distinguish from that sense which no one can apprehend, unless divinely illuminated by the Spirit who speaks in the scriptures" (ibid., 67).

This illuminated reading, however, refers not to a different hidden meaning but to application. The one who is not in communion with God is not touched in the deepest fiber of his being. Such a person cannot be said to read a love letter, does not resonate with the necessary emotional and existential apprehension that belongs to the children of God and is necessary for genuine philanthropy. Without the help of the Holy Spirit, writes Francke, one "does not properly conceive of that genuine love to our neighbor flowing from faith" (*Manuductio*, 68). Even in his later hermeneutical writings, when Francke labels this applicatory understanding the mystical (*sensus mysticus*) or spiritual (*sensus spiritus*) sense, this dimension remains the Spirit-infused, heartfelt appropriation of the text rather than denoting a gnostically hidden signification (Peschke, *Francke und die Bibel*, 78). True understanding, for Francke, moves from self-understanding in the light of the text toward application in the social realm. The "application of the Sacred Oracles to others, whether in public or private, is attended with less trouble and more confidence after sufficient care and devotion have been used in the duty of self-application" (*Manuductio*, 131).

Francke's Affective Hermeneutics

The truly innovative aspect of Francke's hermeneutics consists in his teaching concerning the affections as interpretive aids. In "De Affectionibus," an appendix to his hermeneutical manual, *Manuductio*, Francke argues that affections such as hatred, love, anger, and sorrow lie at the very root of language. He is convinced that "unless some affection influences the heart, language would not be uttered, so that a man's words are, in fact, the index of his feelings or affections. . . . So closely, indeed, are language and affections connected together, so indissoluble is the union that subsists between them, that it would be, in effect, just as unreasonable to divide soul from body, as to separate these" (*Manuductio*, 144–45).

Since the affections are so "intimately connected with *all* language," including that of the biblical writers, one cannot adequately expound the biblical text without careful consideration of the affections that motivate the writer. Within the husk-and-kernel structure of his hermeneutics, the affections belong to the kernel, to the authorial intent, of every utterance. Those who disregard the emotions merely "watch the lips" but never "enter into the feeling" of the author (*Manuductio*, 145). These observations anticipate Schleiermacher's hermeneutics of reenactment. Francke wants to be present at the very moment when the ancient author forms his thoughts and commits them to writing. He cites with approval Spener's advice to "raise the writer from the dead and consider him alive; so as to form perfect conceptions mentally of what we cannot actually behold. When engaged in the study of the scriptures, the idea formed in the writer's mind should be carefully ascertained; the affections by which he was influenced; his state of life; and his office, at the time he penned the book" (ibid., 147).

Francke, of course, is not worried about poststructuralist criticisms of the impossibility of "investing oneself with the author's mind, in order to interpret him as another self" (*Manuductio*, 148). Instead Francke anticipates criticism from inspirationists who might argue that emotions would muddle the pure transmission of the divine word. Francke rejects such mechanical theories of inspiration and affirms the human element in scripture. For him it is "absurd" to suppose that these authors viewed themselves as mere "machines" that wrote without any feeling or perception. Instead their minds were illuminated by the Spirit and "their will inflamed with pious, holy, and ardent affections so that they wrote as they felt and as they were" (ibid., 149–50).

More reminiscent of the contemporary hermeneutical debate is Francke's answer to the charge of subjectivism. Like many other interpretation theories, as soon as one posits the reader's involvement in the emergence of meaning, one invites the charge of relativism. We are reminded of E. D. Hirsch's critical assessment of Gadamer's insistence that the reader allow language to speak: "Then whatever that language says to us is its meaning. It means whatever we take it to mean" (Hirsch, *Validity in Interpretation*, 249). Francke must defend himself against similar accusations. Does not his affective hermeneutics invite subjectivism so that "anyone might give [the text] what sense he pleased by referring it to various affections" (*Manuductio*, 150)?

Francke's answer is threefold. First, he refers to the importance of the affections for the interpretation of our daily conversations: "Daily experience testifies that even familiar conversation is capable of various interpretations according to the affections that operate" (*Manuductio*, 151).

Second, he argues that what is true in conversation is also true for dialogue with the text. Francke anticipates Gadamer's criticism regarding the application of scientific method to texts when he writes that reading with the eye of reason alone alienates the text and objectifies it on both a human and a spiritual level. These readers "do not read the word in the Spirit under whose influence it was written" (*Manuductio*, 152). It is no wonder, then, when biblical commentaries based on such objectivist readings turn out "so meager and unsatisfactory to spiritual readers." Emotions, argues Francke, are a crucial element in the restoration of God's image in the reader, and readings that neglect this dimension not only are dehumanizing but also fail to edify (ibid., 153).

Third, Francke states that this subjective element of interpretation is to be balanced with the grammatical-historical exegesis and thus is complementary rather than primary in importance. This rather reassuring argument is immediately qualified in the next segment on the affections and the "unrenewed" reader of scripture. It becomes clear that Francke incorporates his teachings on the affections into his overall husk-kernel approach. Only with the help of the Holy Spirit and with a changed heart can the reader properly appreciate the full meaning and life implications of any given text in the Bible. The "unrenewed" reader, on the other hand, understands merely on the theoretical level of natural reason.

In the course of this argument, Francke distinguishes clearly between the different natures of sacred and profane writings. For it is on the level of profane literature that the unrenewed reader can grasp the divine word. "He can apprehend the terms as they are commonly received, from the affirmation and negation, understand them when formed, and perceive the necessity of a consequence, as well in Holy Writ as in profane authors" (*Manuductio*, 155).

The scriptural texts, however, are different from other texts in that they have been written by people infused with and trained in a "habit" of soul and mind, a habit "of a soul that is endued with divine perception" (*Manuductio*, 157). In other words, at the heart of Francke's hermeneutics is an ontological difference between sacred and profane text-reader relation. Complete understanding of the biblical text requires a dimension of being in which the reader's existential disposition is aligned with that of the biblical authors, who are moved by the Spirit of God. As Francke puts it, when it comes to the spiritual meaning, "which the letter does not immediately convey, and the mind of the spirit, how is it possible for a carnal, unrenewed man to have any perception of that from which he is so entirely alienated" (ibid., 156)? This spiritual indisposition might even make it difficult to "penetrate into the sense of the letter because from the very nature of things, words and ideas are very closely related" (ibid., 157). Thus complete unfamiliarity with the spiritually motivated subject matter of scripture will also affect a merely rational understanding. Such alienation is overcome only by divine grace. Only when God's spirit resides within the reader can the horizons of the biblical text and the reader be fused.

Francke's *regulas Hermeneuticas de affectibus* is the centerpiece of his hermeneutics. In this section of the German Pietist's treatise on interpretation, we come closest to the heart of premodernist hermeneutics. Here the goodwill to understand, or in Francke's terms the change of one's frame of mind (affections), is granted as a divine gift. This hermeneutical approach recognizes that reason alone is never enough to understand, but that emotions (i.e., our like or dislike of certain subjects) play a decisive role in interpretation. The importance of affections and of one's ontological disposition also provides an explanation for the seeming ahistoricity of pre-Enlightenment hermeneutics. We have seen that these early hermeneuts do in fact take historical criticism seriously. Our reading of Francke's treatise also makes clear, however, that historical distance is far less important than the distance of the reader's being to the being of the subject matter. Thus for premodernist hermeneutics, *misunderstanding* the biblical text is the norm, while only the combination of painstaking exegetical work and reading in relation with God can lead to an understanding of the word.

Practical Hermeneutics

Francke shared Spener's conviction that a right understanding of the biblical text results in social action, and it was Spener who continued to support his younger colleague and cleared the path for Francke's career as a social reformer. Francke met Spener twice during his studies, and with Spener's help, he obtained a post at Erfurt. After this short and controversial engagement (1690–91), Francke moved to Glaucha, where he began the persistent implementation of his theories into practice. The Glauchaer Anstalten, out of which grew an internationally famous educational center, were born out of Francke's attempt to meet the challenge presented by the spiritual, educational, and economic deficit of a city still reeling from the effects of the Thirty Years' War. Poverty, sickness, a high crime rate, and almost complete indifference to religion presented Francke with a nearly impossible mission. However, faithful to his understanding that the Christian faith should translate into social action, Francke began his work.

According to an established tradition, the poor would come to the pastor's house once a week to obtain money and food. Francke used this brief opportunity to catechize his visitors. He soon recognized the illiteracy and ignorance, especially of the children, whose poverty prevented them from attending school. Francke began to raise money among his friends and also placed a can in his living room with the accompanying Bible verse: "If anyone has material possessions and sees his brother in need and closes his heart against him, how can the love of God abide in him?" (1 John 3:17; Brecht and van den Berg, *Der Pietismus*, 1:134).

The verse encapsulates Francke's entire enterprise. His biblical hermeneutics took very seriously the text's injunction to care for one's neighbor, a term Francke held to mean a person created in the image of God, whether Christian or not, and thus entitled to dignity. He soon had enough money to start a small orphanage and a school for the poor. He hired a teacher and ordered educational books. Soon wealthier burghers wanted their children to be educated in Francke's institution. Francke's financial strength increased and soon allowed him to establish an academy (1697) where students were prepared for the universities. Also, Francke added a boarding school for the children of the nobility. All these institutions served his desire to spread the Christian Pietist faith.

It would fill an entire book to trace the development and growth of Francke's institutions. Suffice it to say that by the time of his death in 1727, Francke's work had grown into an educational-industrial complex including factories, a bindery, a bookstore, and a pharmacy, where he trained his wards and integrated them into society. Moreover, Francke did much to change customs that encouraged poverty and impeded economic growth. For example, he managed to procure the right of illegitimate children to enter trades, whereas previously they were often condemned to a life of poverty.

In addition, Francke achieved practical reforms of the education system that were unprecedented. He abolished the abuse of corporal punishment, limiting it to a last resort. He encouraged the education of girls and women. Francke also originated the three-tiered school system, which is still widely accepted in Germany today. He stressed the knowledge of languages for missionary purposes; this emphasis led to his introducing Slavonic studies in his schools, the first program of its kind in Europe. Francke's bookbindery served a similar evangelistic purpose. He managed to mass produce an updated Lutheran version of the Bible, so that soon almost every household in his community possessed either an entire text or at least a copy of the New Testament.

Francke's lectures at the University of Halle were meant to propagate Christian ethics. Although from a modern perspective the selection of educational material appears narrow—Francke's explicit aim was a Christian education—he nevertheless admitted a large selection of pagan authors in Greek and Latin. In his higher-level schools, he also taught apologetics. Francke seemed to have been aware of the revolution in worldview and wanted to equip his students to deal intelligently with the increasing scientific and cosmological challenges to traditional Christian thinking.

During Francke's lifetime, this critical attitude toward philosophy prevailed even among many theologians at the University of Halle, where Francke had become a professor of theology. However, after Francke's death, a rift, barely contained during his day, between the theological and philosophical faculty at Halle erupted openly. The result was that Pietist education of the kind Schleiermacher was to receive retreated from its critical engagement with philosophical developments. Such separation of faith and reason could not possibly satisfy a curious mind, and Schleiermacher was certainly not the only one to break out of such a stifling atmosphere.

Conclusion

We have come to the end of a long but I hope rewarding section. It takes time and effort to adjust our misconceptions of our hermeneutical heritage. I have demonstrated that Puritan-Pietist hermeneutics contributes the following important aspects to interpretation theory.

First, we are, by nature, meaning-making creatures and cannot exist without purposeful metanarratives, hermeneutical frameworks within which we assemble the fragments of our human experiences into a meaningful whole. We are driven by the desire for self-knowledge, a knowledge that requires a hermeneutical circle of immanence and transcendence: knowledge of self and knowledge of God.

Second, we acquire this knowledge in part by reading the book of nature (God's creation, which bears the stamp of the Creator's splendor and intelligence) and most fully in the book of God's self-revelation (the Bible and its account of God's self-disclosure in the incarnation).

Third, knowledge in general and knowledge of God in particular are existential and relational. Knowledge, in other words, is not defined according to a modern scientific model of detached, neutral observation, but knowing requires that the knower be involved with the thing known. Knowledge also requires trust. It would be hard to find anyone in the history of Christian thought who has emphasized human finitude and its consequent interpretive limitations more than the authors of the theological and devotional literature resulting from the Protestant Reformation. Richard Baxter in his treatise *The Reasons of the Christian Religion* (1666) laments the finitude of human understanding: "But alas! how poor and uncertain a thing is man's understanding! How many are deceived in things that seem as undeniable to them! How know I what one particular may be unseen by me which would change my judgment and better inform me in all the rest?" (*PWRB*, 2:76). The human mind, argues Baxter, is much too bound up in this historical world to make deductions and to form a perspective that transcends its finite horizon. To make universally valid truth statements concerning human existence, the mind would have to take into account all existent facts. One would need a godlike omnipotence that transcends time and historical boundaries, a position that is humanly impossible. He concludes: "This is not well; but it is a disease which sheweth the need of a physician, and of some other satisfying light" (ibid.).

Fourth, self-knowledge also requires doubt; however, unlike the Cartesian model of seeking epistemological bedrock through systematic doubt, which leads to solipsism and has been criticized justly by postmodern philosophers, Puritan-Pietist epistemology follows the motto "faith seeking understanding." These theologians understood that knowledge comes from an interpretive process that rests on an exterior knowledge base that is not transparent to us and that we cannot control. The Puritans and the Pietists believed this transcendent source of knowledge to be the divine Logos, which had entered history in the incarnation and person of Jesus. For them knowing the purpose of human existence required a personal relation with this Logos, something that cannot be achieved but must be granted by grace. This interpretive model does not recognize a split between faith and reason but defines reason in terms of relational (or sociological) categories of purpose, love, trust, and involvement.

Fifth, contrary to modern notions of knowledge as accumulation of information, pre-Enlightenment theology embraced the rather humanistic notion that knowledge and reading should issue in wisdom.

Conventional notions of knowledge such as "civil wisdom and prudence, for the management of affairs" or "[a]bility of learning and literature," though important, are "of no use at all to the end and intent of true wisdom" (*WJO*, 2:80). Instead the source of this wisdom is the Divine. This is the important link to scripture as revelation that makes Puritanism such a genuinely hermeneutical movement. Every area of human life is influenced by the reading, interpretation, and application of the biblical text, of God's word revealed to humankind.

Sixth, Puritan and Pietist epistemology did not neglect but rather required a detailed account of human understanding. Its basic premise was that human understanding had been deeply affected by its alienation from God: humanity was created for communion with God, and the loss of this relationship renders humans aimless and blindly groping for a purpose in life. In this state, the interpretation of human existence becomes subjective, because without the divine object of conversation, the universe is "flattened" or "silent," to use Taylor's expression. Since understanding is defined as occurring in relational-existential terms rather than as mere contemplation, correct self-understanding is possible only in relation with God. This relation, however, requires divine illumination. In this model, self-understanding is never static but evolves dynamically from communion with God through the applicatory hermeneutics described in this chapter.

Puritan-Pietist hermeneutics constitutes a continuation of the theological hermeneutics established by Luther and Calvin, whose relational quality derives from its Christological emphasis on interpretation. The following chapters chart the hermeneutical consequences of theology's departure from this particular focus.

Part 2

The Silencing of the Word

4

THE SECULARIZATION
OF THEOLOGICAL HERMENEUTICS

From Ethics to Moralism

The interpretive framework of pre-Enlightenment theological hermeneutics was challenged by the intellectual movement known as the Enlightenment. Like all labels, this term should not be used as an accurate
description of a historical event but rather as a convenient shorthand for
an intellectual and cultural tendency that has profoundly shaped Western
culture to this day. The common denominator of English, French, and German Enlightenment streams is the basic assumption of self-illumination.
The liberation of the self from ecclesial authority implied that autonomous
human reason replaced the premodern dependence on divine illumination for all knowledge. Christian thinkers were seduced by the lure of
epistemological bedrock, the kind of absolute certainty in knowledge that
has become known as foundationalism. In part this development resulted
from the increasing importance and independence of science.

Natural science, formerly inseparable from God's sustaining activity in
creation, increasingly followed a mechanistic model in which unalterable
laws of cause and effect encouraged a view of God as an engineer who
was happy to observe the workings of his invention from a distance. The
Enlightenment was by no means a generally atheistic movement. Britain
and Germany did not share the anticlericalism of the French intellectuals.
A crucial difference, however, between Enlightenment and pre-Enlightenment theology was the former's inversion of faith and reason by turning

faith into a rational affair. Natural theology became highly popular because it exalted the order of nature, in place of revelation, as proof of God's existence, making reason the foundation of religion since reason recognized order in nature (Gardner, *Kant and the Critique of Pure Reason*, 5).

British empiricism relied on sense experience as the foundation of our perception of reality, while Cartesian philosophy embraced radical, methodological doubt as the safest foundation for certain knowledge. Neither rationalism nor empiricism, however, escapes a mind-body dualism, and both methods are a departure from the earlier theological motto of "faith seeking understanding." Unlike modernist epistemology, "faith seeking understanding" had assumed that the acquisition of knowledge always depends on a transcendent condition for such knowledge.

The Enlightenment soon ran into trouble on a number of issues. For example, while both scientists and philosophers (and rationalist theologians) claimed reason as their foundation, they nevertheless often came to different conclusions about the structure of reality. The double effect of this disagreement was that the reliability of reason as epistemological authority became questionable and the rift between science and metaphysics widened.

Another significant blow to the Enlightenment viewpoint was the empirical skepticism of Hume, which reduced all knowledge to sense impression filtered through developed mental habits that then evoke the appearance of interpretive consensus. Hume's work challenged Kant to present an alternative to rationalism and empiricism in order to defend the Enlightenment. Kant's first major work, *The Critique of Pure Reason*, sought to establish the task and limitations of human reason in order to make room for faith, so that each might inhabit its proper sphere. This he accomplished in his second work, *The Critique of Practical Reason*, in which he postulates the ideas of God, freedom, and immortality as a priori categories of practical reason, that is, of the moral use of reason (*Critique of Practical Reason*, 141). A positive development in Kant's second critique is his effort to establish substantive criteria for moral behavior. He speaks strongly against morality based on feeling, a veiled attack against the morality of sensibility advanced by Shaftesbury and Hutchinson, but also a distancing from a certain form of Pietism and its obsession with self-examination.[1] Kant argues that feeling alone cannot provide a solid basis for moral decisions. The will should never be "in the service of the inclinations" but instead is subject to the causality of an absolute moral

---

1. In his biography of Kant, Ernst Cassirer notes that Kant was influenced by two kinds of Pietism: the Pietism of his parents, which he found praiseworthy in its calm serenity and neighborly love, and a Pietism advocating a regulated and mechanized self-scrutiny and excessive display of religious feelings (*Kant's Life and Thought*, 17–18).

law, conforming to which may then result in feelings of pleasure (ibid., 171). This law, however, is not found in the realm of the senses but is "the fundamental law of supersensible nature and of a pure world of the understanding. . . . The moral law is the sole determining ground of the pure will" (ibid., 227).

Kant rightly seeks a normative base for the human values that lend purpose to our existence, but he does so at the cost of the primary ethical experience of pre-Enlightenment hermeneutics. Whereas Puritan and Pietist ethics had a relational character and could be expressed in social categories such as trust and dialogue, Kant moves ethics into the realm of the impersonal. Kant's ethics is indeed ethics of duty that, in order to correspond to the pure category of freedom, must be free from any historical and sensible influence. This lack of historical and relational categories is the real problem of Kantian ethics, not its supposed denial of human sinfulness.

Kant believes, quite to the contrary, that humanity is greatly plagued by self-centeredness. In fact, he argues that our conception of moral freedom as choice and, ideally, as the pursuit of happiness shows how egocentric our ethical goals are. These desires, however, should in no way ground the ethical demand: "Now the moral law, which alone is truly objective . . . excludes altogether the influence of self-love on the supreme practical principle and infringes without end upon self conceit which prescribes as laws the subjective conditions of self love" (*Critique of Practical Reason*, 200). Thus respect for the moral law can never be the incentive for morality. Instead this incentive is the conviction of reason, "a pure sense-free interest of practical reason alone" (ibid., 204).

These citations are meant to convey the cerebral, rationalist flavor of Kant's morality. For Kant, our very humanity is defined by our being moral agents who respect the moral law for its intrinsic authority conveyed to us by the discipline of reason. Kant ends up sounding very much like the apostle Paul prior to his conversion: "Duty and what is owed are the only names that we must give to our relation to the moral law" (*Critique of Practical Reason*, 206).

Thus with Kant we have arrived at an inversion of pre-Enlightenment theological ethics. Kant's view of ethics is precisely what Puritan and Pietist theologians prophesied against. An ethics of duty, they argued, would occur when the primary ethical relation to God is lost. Again, John Owen most clearly foresaw this danger. In a chapter titled "Corruption or Depravation of the Mind by Sin," Owen states that the foundation for moral duties is the reconciliation of the fallen creature with the Divine. Scripture "grafts all duties of moral obedience in this stock of faith in Christ Jesus" (*WJO*, 3:279). However, the prejudice of our fallen minds "inverts the order to these things" (ibid.). Those who read the Bible without knowing God will inevitably "cry up" moral principles they are already familiar with from their upbringing. But such readers do not have the slightest idea what the foundation of these duties is. When those readers turn to the Bible, they believe the only useful information to be found there is the very moral codes they have imbibed through their upbringing in a Christian tradition, because they cannot perceive Christ as the true scope of the Bible. Owen's observations deserve extensive quotation, for he virtually forecasts the result of much biblical criticism in the Enlightenment:

> These [moral duties] they make the foundation, according to the place which they held in the law of nature and covenant of works, whereas the gospel allows them to be only necessary superstructures on the foundation. But resolving to give unto moral duties the pre-eminence in their minds, they consider afterward the peculiar doctrines of the gospel, with one or other of these effects; for, first some in a manner wholly despise them, reproaching those by whom they are singularly professed. What is contained in them is of no importance, in their judgment, compared with the more necessary duties of morality, which they pretend to embrace; and, to acquit themselves of the trouble of a search into them, they reject them as unintelligible or unnecessary. Or, secondly, They will, by forced interpretations, enervating the spirit and perverting the mystery of them, *square* and fit them to their own low and carnal apprehensions. They would reduce the gospel and all the mystery of it to their own light, as some; to reason, as others; to philosophy, as the rest. . . . Hereby advancing morality above the mystery and grace of the gospel, they at once reject the gospel and destroy morality also; for, taking it off from its proper foundation, it falls into the dirt,—whereof the conversation of the men of this persuasion is no small evidence. (*WJO*, 3:279–80)

Owen prophesies that without a relation to Christ, biblical morality will degenerate into moralism and mistake the result of faith (morality) for its source (faith in God). About one hundred years after Owen penned those words, Kant wrote in the preface to the first edition of his *Religion within the Limits of Reason Alone*: "Morality thus leads ineluctably to religion, through which it extends itself to the idea of a powerful moral lawgiver, outside of mankind, for whose will that is the final end (of creation) which at the same time can and ought to be man's final end. If morality finds in the holiness of its law an object of the greatest respect, then at the level of religion it presents the ultimate cause, which consummates those laws, as an object of adoration and thus appears in its majesty" (5–7). Just as Owen had predicted, Kant inverts the relationship between religion and morality.

Kant's misunderstanding and consequent reinterpretation of the Reformation teaching on conversion as the basis for the application of revelational knowledge become evident in the course of his argument, during which he preaches a full-fledged gospel of moralism and reinterprets the biblical doctrine of regeneration in terms of a voluntary decision to moral improvement. To some degree, Kant argues, a person may become morally responsible by altering his behavior for the better. But, Kant goes on,

> if a man is to become not merely legally, but morally a good man (pleasing to God), that is, a man endowed with virtue in its intelligible character (*virtus noumenon*) and one who, knowing something to be his duty, requires no incentive other than this representation of duty itself, this cannot be brought about through gradual reformation so long as the basis of the maxims remains impure, but must be effected by a revolution in the man's disposition (a going over to the maxim of holiness of the disposition). He can become a new man only by a kind of rebirth, as it were a new creation (John III, 5; compare also Genesis I, 2), and a change of heart. But if a man is corrupt in the very ground of his maxims, how can he possibly bring about this revolution by his own powers and of himself become a good man? (*Religion within the Limits of Reason Alone*, 5–7)

Here the Reformation theologian would answer, he cannot; it is a work of divine grace and intervention. Kant, however, opts for a moralistic salvation by works. He sees no need for regeneration: "Yet duty bids us do this, and duty demands nothing of us which we cannot do" (ibid., 43). One cannot help but recall the discussion on the freedom of the will between Luther and Erasmus, in which Erasmus aligned himself with Kant when he said: "What purpose, however, should all these commandments serve, if no one is able to keep them in any way?" (*Vom freien Willen*, 37). Luther replied that this tension between the law's demand and our inability to keep it is the very purpose of the law. It is meant to point out our helplessness and need for communion with God (*BW*, 135). Kant, in this sense, revives the Erasmian standpoint and grants the human will the ability to choose the good. Thus Kant argues that one achieves a "change of heart" by making the conscious decision to live a morally good life, while outwardly the progression of moral improvement will always lag behind that decision in practical execution: "That is, he can hope to find in the light of that purity of the principle which he adopted as the supreme maxim of his will, and of its stability, to find himself upon the good path of continual progress from bad to better. . . . From this follows that man's moral growth of necessity begins not in the improvement of his practices but rather in the transforming of his cast of mind and in the grounding of a character" (*Religion within the Limits of Reason Alone*, 43–45).

Kant preaches the stern moralism of the Enlightenment. Moreover, Kant's categorical imperative, however rational it may appear, lacks a real foundation. Kant does not ground human rationality in God, something pre-Enlightenment theologians expressed in terms of God's natural light; thus Kant's assumption that human reason is universal and transcends historical-cultural differences becomes very problematic. After all, whose reason are we talking about? Has not reason justified highly inhuman practices in the past?

What is even more problematic, however, is Kant's lack of a *relational* concept for ethics. In light of Owen's concept of morality as dependent on communion with the Divine, Kant's moralism is a good example of the self-imposition of moral laws that Owen had mentioned earlier in his treatise. As history has shown, Kant's stern moralism did not last and was scornfully denounced not only by Schleiermacher but also by Nietzsche and his postmodern followers.[2] Hence Owen is already a critic of the Enlightenment before Romanticism, and he condemns the modernist reliance on human knowledge and its confidence in reason before postmodern criticism appears on the world stage.

We may conclude that, contrary to a common misconception of Puritanism, widely propagated by historians and novelists (such as Hawthorne in his *Scarlet Letter*), Puritan theology as expounded by Owen did not propagate moralism but was severely critical of such an attitude. This is not to deny that Puritanism could easily degenerate into mere moralism; in fact, that is exactly what often happened in the subsequent chapters of European and American history. However, the early Puritans were highly critical of such developments, and to equate the term Puritan or Pietist with callous, rigid insistence on mindless "moral" behavior is a perversion of pre-Enlightenment ethics.

The premoderns, in fact, found nothing more deceptive and detestable than morality based on reason alone. For them morality could be based only on a dialogue with the Divine made possible through regeneration. The "turn" of which they spoke, where the "whole man" was to be changed in attitude and behavior into at least some likeness to the Divine (Christ), was internal first, external second. Much of Puritan discourse was devoted to exposing a merely "external" morality. The Puritan Thomas Watson, for example, wrote in 1656 that deception in this matter "will often make a man take morality for grace. Alas, moral-

2. The development of morality from premodernism to postmodernity in light of changing hermeneutics has been nicely summarized in Roger Lundin, *The Culture of Interpretation: Christian Faith in the Modern World* (Grand Rapids: Eerdmans, 1993), 84–88.

ity is but nature refined, old Adam put in a better dress. A moralized man is but a tame devil! There may be a fair stream of civility running and yet much vermin of pride and atheism lying at the bottom" (Kistler, *Puritans on Conversion*, 173).

Owen agrees, arguing that self-imposed morality, or in fact any ethical code that is merely intellectually accepted, soon becomes burdensome, because it goes against the human desire for autonomy. We naturally dislike authority, says Owen, and only through divine grace will we willingly obey the divine authority. "Want [of grace] is that which renders obedience so grievous and burdensome to many. They endure it for a season, and at length either violently or insensibly cast off its yoke." Obedience to moral law must be made willingly, and this can occur only when the heart has been changed through divine grace (*WJO*, 3:622).

Owen's concept of morality as grounded in personal relation with the Divine tries carefully to balance the objective and subjective elements in interpretation. His approach provides a contrast to rationalist morality, the Enlightenment version of ethics, on the one hand, and to subjectivist ethics, an approach taken by some strands of Romanticism, on the other. The moral theory of Jean-Jacques Rousseau (1712–78), though not paradigmatic for all Romantic thinkers, provides a good example of subjectivist morality. In his famous chapter on the vicar from Savoy in *Émile* (1762), Rousseau argues for a natural law written in every person's conscience.[3] The vicar rejects philosophy as well as divine revelation in favor of "a different guide," namely, an inner light (388).

This inner light is in effect nothing more than the Puritan conscience that has been cleansed of its moral defect. "The conscience never fails," the vicar exclaims, "it is the true guide of human beings. . . . I don't have to consult anyone but myself concerning my actions: whatever I sense to be good is good, whatever I sense to be bad is bad: the conscience is the best of all casuists" (*Émile*, 418). The good vicar does not need communion with God through regeneration. All one requires for sound moral behavior is to look within. Such teaching is not only reminiscent of the Quakers' Inner Light, but it also leads to what Owen condemns as man-centered ethics. Rousseau, and with him much of Enlightenment philosophy, is no longer in need of a genuine dialogue with the Divine. The book of nature still shows irrefutable evidence of a divine creator, and no unbiased reader could fail to conclude from contemplating God's works that the universe was purposefully designed (ibid., 396). But there

3. The attempt to read the vicar's confession as essentially Rousseau's own view seems justified in light of Ernst Cassirer's observation that all of Rousseau's work is concerned with the moral progress of human society according to an inner light of nature (*Question of Jean-Jacques Rousseau*, 76–78).

is no need for dialogue with him. Moral certainty is man's endowment, and virtue is his "birthright" (ibid., 240).

In effect Rousseau turns the doctrine of original sin on its head by stating that man is naturally good but becomes corrupted through society and civilization. Only when he frees himself from those influences can the clear voice of conscience speak. Both natural reason and sentiment will then prompt the will to act on these inbred principles (*Émile*, 419).[4]

We see here the beginnings of the concept of human progress, affirmed by inner reason and sentiment, which will reappear in Schleiermacher's theology. Rousseau argues rightly that if man's basic inclination is toward the moral good (an assumption that also assumes that we all know innately what the good is), dialogue with the Divine through the scriptures becomes obsolete. In fact, man has become like God because of his infallible conscience: "Conscience! conscience! Divine instinct . . . infallible judge of good and evil who gives human beings god-likeness" (*Émile*, 425). Dialogue with the Divine through prayer has become superfluous. Where the Puritans argued for the need of divine aid for moral development, Rousseau's vicar states, "Neither do I ask of him the power to do right; why should I ask what he has given me already?" (ibid., 459). Likewise, scripture is superfluous, for it can only affirm the sentiments that are already resident in the human conscience. Also God has given each and every human being the will to obey these moral impulses.

By contrast Owen argues that only the regenerate are given the basic willingness to obey God's law out of love: "Upon supply of [God's] grace, which gives both strength for and a constant inclination unto holy obedience, the command for it becomes equal and just, meet and easy to be complied withal" (*WJO*, 3:623). In communion with the Divine, one realizes the justice of the command, because one willingly acknowledges its authority and usefulness. Even then, however, there remains part of the "old Adam," which makes obedience sometimes difficult (ibid.). Nevertheless, the change wrought by regeneration and the indwelling of the Holy Spirit enables the regenerate to follow the voice of their regenerate spirit: "Let us but, upon our proposal of it unto us, consider what our minds and hearts say to it, what answer they return, and we shall quickly discern how equal and just the command is; for I cannot persuade myself that any believer can be so captivated at any time, under

---

4. Rousseau designates this inbred principle as the conscience: "Il est donc au fond des âmes un principe inné de justice et de vertu, sur lequel, malgré nos propres maximes, nous jugeons nos actions et celles d'autrui comme bonnes ou mauvaises; et c'est à ce principe que je donne le nom de conscience" [There is therefore at the bottom of our hearts an innate principle of justice and virtue by which, in spite of our maxims, we judge our own actions or those of others to be good or evil; and it is this principle that I call conscience] (*Émile*, 422).

the power of temptations, corruptions or prejudices, but that . . . his mind and spirit will say, 'This good I would do; I delight in it; it is best for me, most suited unto me'" (ibid.).

Rousseau's teaching is merely a secularized revision of earlier Protestant thought. Rousseau takes the regenerate heart of Calvinism and makes it the natural condition of every human being. In doing so, he sets a precedent later followed by many German Enlightenment thinkers. The premise of the morally good heart formed the basis for the belief, also advocated by Rousseau in *Émile,* that the right education will afford moral improvement. The poets and dramatists of the German Enlightenment believed, for example, that aesthetic education would morally reform lives. Gotthold Ephraim Lessing (1729–81), for instance, went so far as to claim in his *Die Erziehung des Menschengeschlechts* that written revelation itself had been superseded by man's now awakened reason as a once necessary step in human moral development.

It becomes increasingly clear that the question of epistemology, at least in the realm of ethics, is closely connected to that of anthropology. The secularization of relational morality is expressed in terms of the inner moral light, the heart. Owen, the Puritan, recommended listening to impulses of the *regenerate* heart, the heart that desired to adhere to divine revelation. Moreover, the conscience needs to be informed by the word of God. From Owen's perspective, Rousseau's advice to listen to an inner voice would be deadly, because he appealed to the "voice" of the fallen, *unregenerate* heart, which has at best some vague notions regarding the transcendent law of God: "There are sundry moral duties, which I instanced before, which the light of nature, as it remains in the lapsed, depraved condition of it, never extended itself to the discovery of. And this obscurity is evident from the differences that are about its precepts and directions" (*WJO,* 3:635). In other words, Owen rejects the notion of Rousseau's sentimental deism that there is an innate natural law that we would follow if we only got in touch with our inner selves.

As we have seen, Owen would agree with Rousseau that we can glean general notions regarding human conduct from the "light of nature," but those ideas are mere general moral aspects that never point to the existential root problem, humanity's alienation from the Divine. Prior to the healing of this breach, all morality is merely a nonrelational imposition that will soon become burdensome. Moreover, without the principle of God's inward grace, we would never feel inclined to obey willingly authority other than our own. The Puritans believed that this inward grace is conveyed through the work of the Holy Spirit.

Kant's transcendental idealism with its division of reality into things themselves and appearances and his stern duty ethics evoked much criticism from the Romantics. The most incisive criticism came from theologically motivated thinkers such as Johann Georg Hamann and Johann Gottfried von Herder. Herder, for example, detested the rationalistic obsession with tidying up reality and knowledge into rational categories to match the clarity of Euclidean geometry. For him the contrast Kant erected between faith and reason was a profound fallacy, and he maintained that there is no knowledge without belief at its base (Berlin, *Magus of the North*, 35). Among the most important theological critics of the Enlightenment emerging from Romanticism is the theologian Friedrich Schleiermacher (1768–1834), a key figure in both theological and philosophical hermeneutics.

From Transcendence to Immanence

My assessment of Schleiermacher's contribution to hermeneutics is shaped by the basic premise of this book: pre-Enlightenment hermeneutics, its shortcomings notwithstanding, grasped the only defensible foundation for hermeneutics and ethics by grounding the interpretation of reality in the incarnation. While pre-Enlightenment theologians did not work out the implication of the incarnation in terms of our present debate concerning interpretation and ethics, their focus on the incarnate Word of God provided the important category of *personal transcendence*, which allows us to reconfigure the concepts of reason, knowledge, and truth in relational terms.

The personal transcendence of the universal Logos, who became the paradigmatic human being while retaining his nature of the eternal Logos, allows for both otherness and sameness, for both individuality and universality, the elements crucial for hermeneutics and ethics. In fact, the incarnation allows us to say that hermeneutics *is* ethics, if all interpretation is indeed grounded in the divine Logos that is the incarnate Word of God. The pre-Enlightenment interpretation of human existence rested, however, on the Christian doctrines of creation, Fall, redemption, and their implications for human understanding and conduct. The question that guides our reading of Schleiermacher is how his changes to reformational theology affect the view of the incarnation and thus all hermeneutics.

My argument briefly stated is this: while Schleiermacher effectively replaces Kant's dualism of faith and reason, of the phenomenal and the noumenal world, the very monism by which he accomplishes this feat forces him to give up the transcendence pre-Enlightenment hermeneutics had derived from the incarnation. If one is willing to resist the separation of Schleiermacher's theological and philosophical views (and works) and rather hold them together, one will find that despite all his

warmth and fervor, Schleiermacher loses the objective pole of hermeneutics that his theological predecessors had found in the incarnation.
While his monism is effective in combating the division of faith and reason
that Kant had set up, it pays a high price for this success: the transcendence of God's incarnate and spoken Word is reduced to an immanent
world. Schleiermacher effectively flattens the hermeneutical circle of
knowledge of God and knowledge of self on which pre-Enlightenment
theology had insisted.

In responding to the Kantian dualism of faith and reason, Schleiermacher offers an interconnected view of reality that harmonizes religion
with the emergent science. Religion becomes part of an organic whole
and yet is the primary discipline for discovering ultimate meaning.
In this harmonization of faith and reason, Schleiermacher evades the
conflict of transcendent divine realities and concepts such as humanity's
separation from God by making nature the realm of grace. As his biographer Dilthey explains, Schleiermacher seeks ultimate connections
that lend unity to the multiple fragments of human experience: "The
world is not only to be explained in its finite causal relations, but it
is also supposed to be understood as an all-comprehending piece of
art in its own eternal harmony, as it mirrors itself to that spirit which
focuses on the vision and feeling for the holistic, for the one" (*Gesammelte Schriften* 13/1:323).

Schleiermacher's intention was clearly to achieve a world picture
that resisted either materialism or idealism. He writes, "The union of
idealism and realism is the entire goal of my striving, and I have tried
to make that clear in the *Speeches* as well as in the *Soliloquies*" (*Dialektik*, 11). This desire to overcome the Kantian phenomenal-noumenal
division is also reflected in his philosophical system described in his
lectures on dialectics for the philosophical faculty in Berlin (1811). All
knowledge, Schleiermacher insists, is based on the knowledge of God.
God is not a postulate of knowledge but lies at the very heart of the idea
of knowledge. The knowledge of God is the very foundation of all other
knowledge (ibid., 23). The absolute is here described as God, and our
knowledge of God is found in our knowledge of the world: "As soon as
we find a trace of the one, we also have the basic character of the other"
(ibid.). All knowing is hermeneutical in that we interpret God when we
interpret the world. "Our knowledge about God is thus only complete
with the world vision. As soon as we have a trace of the one, we also have
the basic pattern of the other. To the extent to which the world vision is
incorrect, the idea of the godhead will also remain mythological" (ibid.,
25). This view allows Schleiermacher to unite the human and the natural
sciences into one coherent epistemological enterprise. Neither theology
nor art can be split off from the sciences. On the contrary, "although

there is a difference between art and science, it seems to grow smaller the higher one advances" (ibid.).

It is wrong to view Schleiermacher as an intentionally secularizing thinker. He remained a Christian philosopher and a philosophical theologian. For him all knowledge rests in the philosophical insight that the world is interconnected and that human reason arises from this monistic construct (*Dialektik*, 4). Thus, contrary to Kant, the most universal and the most particular forms of knowledge (philosophy and natural science) have the same foundation (ibid., 5). Beyond the general principle of the unity of all being, Schleiermacher insists, nonetheless, on a separation of science and theology. Particular theological pronouncements should not meddle in the affairs of scientific research. Nevertheless, the scientist in his activity is tracing God.

In a way, Schleiermacher pursued Dilthey's dream of establishing a universal basis for both human and natural science. Schleiermacher's motivation for such an undertaking was to gain knowledge of the Divine: "We are therefore engaged in the formation of the living beholding of the godhead insofar as we work on the completion of the natural sciences" (*Dialektik*, 31). Natural sciences help to inform us about the workings of the universe in their intricate connections; thus science serves as the way to God. But what kind of a God does it seek? It is true that Schleiermacher overcame the faith-reason dualism of the Enlightenment, and he managed to establish a beautifully organic and interconnected picture of knowledge and human existence—but at what cost?

The price Schleiermacher paid is the objective, historical side of the Christian faith and thus the genuinely relational categories required for true ethics. The unique word of God is reduced to the impersonal monistic common ground on which Schleiermacher's system rests. And yet it is precisely this monistic view that enabled Schleiermacher to construct his dialectical general hermeneutics.

Schleiermacher defines dialectics as "the principles of the art of philosophizing" (*Dialektik*, 4). To philosophize is, in turn, defined as the "achieving of an insight [or knowledge] in conjunction with a clear awareness of how it came about" (ibid.). Schleiermacher calls philosophizing an art, because a piece of art is "a particular in which the whole is immanently present, and which contains an infinite" (ibid.). Schleiermacher's use of philosophy comprehends all metaphysical speculations that attempt to generate knowledge of the whole. These are the most pure form of art.

The other sciences, he argues, are less pure, because in them formal concerns of method often come between the subject matter and its presentation. However, this difference is only perceived, because there is ultimately no opposition between method and knowledge, as these merge in the most lofty ideas: "Although there exists an opposition between science and art, it seems to diminish the higher one ascends" (*Dialektik*, 4). For example, no one can have an idea of God without knowing "how this highest idea is expressed in the individual, or how the relation of the absolute is to the particular" (ibid., 5).

How, then, is knowledge of the highest things possible? The answer to this question contains the seed of Schleiermacher's hermeneutical circle. "All knowledge," he argues, "depends on original knowledge [*ursprüngliches Wissen*]." Every individual already possesses this knowledge, albeit unconsciously (*auf unbewußte Art*): "Original knowledge exists in everyone as a power that can be raised to the level of consciousness" (*Dialektik*, 9). Thus all interpretation, in fact, all knowledge, moves from the whole to the part. The vague notion of the highest knowledge (the whole) is constantly refined and further awakened by added knowledge from particular disciplines (ibid., 10). The source of this precognitive whole is "God" or rather Schleiermacher's universal God-consciousness. So the circle closes itself: each individual has in himself the seed of the highest knowledge, a dormant *God-consciousness*.

Education in the natural sciences and the humanities contributes to the refinement of this whole until the individual sees in all clarity, at least for a moment, the interconnectedness of all things. That, for Schleiermacher, is the knowledge of God and the very basis of hermeneutics. Mere philosophical assessments of Schleiermacher's hermeneutics fail to see that he never relinquishes the idea that hermeneutics remains a religious affair. He concludes his lectures on hermeneutics by reminding the listener that

> even if the hermeneutic task in relation to the N.T. text seems very subordinate, compared with the totality of the object of the whole task of the Christian church . . . it is yet on the other hand the most universal interest that is attached to the hermeneutic task, and we will be able to say with certainty that if the universal religious interest were to die, the hermeneutic interest would also be lost. Our view of the relationship of Christianity to the whole of humankind and the spiritual clarity with which this has developed in the Protestant church is the guarantee of that. (*Hermeneutics and Criticism*, 157)

Schleiermacher's theory is very attractive because in overcoming the dualism of faith and reason, it allows for the harmony between faith and science and hence provides good grounds for the unity of all education as participating in progressive self-knowledge. Those who actually achieve a glimpse of the interconnectedness of all things, that is, those who realize their God-consciousness or sense of ultimate dependence, are inspired to artistic creation, worship, and charitable activity.

This notion of inspiration enables Schleiermacher to suggest a general hermeneutics. Based on his monistic worldview, he considerably widens the meaning of inspiration to encompass all manifestations of genius, that is, of that spiritual link that resides in each human being as a reflection of, and connection with, God, the world Spirit (*Weltgeist*). All important aspects in Schleiermacher's hermeneutics, the linguistic, divinatory, dialectical, or grammatical-historical dimensions of his thought, ultimately hinge on the notions of *Weltgeist* and *immediate God-consciousness*. It is in relation to one's approximation to the All that human progress and understanding are to be measured.

Schleiermacher makes this abundantly clear in the "Concluding Observations" to his lectures on hermeneutics in the winter of 1826–27. For him hermeneutics is an all-encompassing undertaking for the betterment of humanity. According to Schleiermacher, history supports this assumption because "an attentive observation of history also teaches that since the reviving of the sciences, the occupation with interpretation contributed the more to the mental developments to all sides the more it dealt with the very principles of [interpretation]" (*SW*, 4:204). Interpretation needs to concern itself with the manifestations of the Spirit in language and in writing. Schleiermacher distinguishes three gradations (*Stufen*) of interpretation, each step representing an increasing understanding of the impressions and reflections of the world soul in writing.

The first and lowest stage is mere historical interest (*Geschichtsinteresse*), where one is interested only in the event itself without trying to understand the grammatical or psychological dimensions of the text. The second stage of interpretation is motivated by aesthetic interests (*künstlerisches oder Geschmacksinteresse*). Here the reader may be pleased by the rhetorical fireworks of the text or with its form. This is a very narrow focus, says Schleiermacher, and is mostly the occupation of the educated. The third and highest interest one can have in interpretation is the speculative-scientific in combination with the religious. By scientific (*wissenschaftlich*) is meant an exact and deep-reaching analysis of all aspects of the text: "The scientific examines the subject matter at its deepest root" (*SW*, 4:205).

Both the scientific and the religious interest issue from the highest faculties of the human spirit, and both make us realize the importance of language. Speech, we remember, is for Schleiermacher the manifestation of thought, yet it also shapes thought because we cannot think without language (*SW*, 4:205). Therefore, a good interpreter seeks to determine exactly how the writer and even humanity in general operate in the formation and use of language (ibid.).

But Schleiermacher's thinking goes beyond a mere technical reconstruction. After all, language is the medium through which the *Weltgeist* seeks its expression: "Language should picture the innermost thoughts of the Spirit" (*SW*, 4:444).

Language, therefore, is what guides the individual in his or her moral spiritual development, because we get in touch with the *Weltgeist* through language. Thus the technical aspect of hermeneutics serves as a conductor to the spiritual-psychological "pulse" of the author. Both are "most closely interconnected, because language guides and accompanies the human being in his development" (*SW*, 4:444). Therefore, careful grammatical exegesis is required to get to the point at which we resonate with the author's expression of immediate self-consciousness. In short, hermeneutics in its dialectical oscillation between grammatical and divinatory elements is an important tool because language serves as the conduit of immediate self-consciousness and thus to true self-knowledge.

Finally, Schleiermacher's monism also allows him to construct this self-knowledge as ethical. Much in Schleiermacher's hermeneutics enhances human dignity. Understanding is indeed ethical because it respects the desires and expectations of the author and thus fosters community. Every human utterance is treated as an expression of our shared universal reason, and this transcendental, transempirical premise of one common reason that connects humanity is actualized and confirmed by every successful communication. Schleiermacher's monistic vision of sociality as an interconnected web, in which we are tied to one another and connected to the world-all, does indeed merge realism and idealism. This organic view of human reality allows him to reject the Enlightenment preoccupation with propositional knowledge and advocate a relational model of knowing. His participatory model of reality, however, comes at the sacrifice of transcendence and difference. This leveling effect of Schleiermacher's monistic construct is also evident in his description of understanding.

Schleiermacher provides a much more positive view of understanding than does the postmodern hermeneutics of suspicion, which has learned from Nietzsche to distrust any attempt to understand something because the will to understand is merely a thin disguise for the will to power, the desire to force another's thought into the interpretive mold of our own hermeneutical framework. Yet it is in Schleiermacher's very effort to construe self-knowledge as ethical that the severe consequences of his monism emerge most clearly. It becomes increasingly clear that his concept of understanding operates on the reduction of transcendence to immanence, of difference to sameness. In the end, Schleiermacher sacrifices individuality to understanding. While reason only manifests itself in individuals, the goal is ultimately to overcome individuality for commonality, a move toward sameness. For Schleiermacher the road to human solidarity and salvation lies in sameness: "The closer each one comes to the universe, the more each one communicates himself to others, the more completely they become one; no one retains a mere individual consciousness, but everyone shares that of the other at the same time. They are no longer merely human beings but also humanity, and disclosing themselves, triumphing over themselves, they are on the way to genuine immortality and eternity" (*SW*, 4:352).

The troubling aspect of this hermeneutics is not so much that it assumes common ground in understanding but that understanding requires the elimination of difference. Moreover, this sameness resembles more a Platonic than a Christian idea of the cosmos in its ultimately impersonal matrix, the great cosmic world All. Schleiermacher's laudable effort to make hermeneutics ethical and knowledge relational fails because his participatory model of reality lacks the personal transcendence former theologians had found in the incarnation. No matter how much Schleiermacher seeks to establish an ethical model of interpretation, without the incarnate Logos at the center of reality, all Pietistic fervor is mere emotionalism. None of Schleiermacher's warmth in talking about Jesus in his more devotional works can regain the real personal categories so necessary for the relational nature of truth and understanding found in pre-Enlightenment hermeneutics. His "idealistic monism," even if attenuated by its emphasis on experience, has already excised the historical reality of God's self-revelation assumed by Puritan and Pietist theologians, for whom understanding was anchored in the incarnation (Brown, *Jesus in European Thought*, 132).

Only in the incarnation does the idealist-realist problem, which has plagued the history of philosophy from its inception, find a true resolution. The incarnation provides common ground for our experience of truth and understanding by positing as its source the universal Logos and truth-giving light of God. At the same time, God's self-revelation as a real human being in history also cures this synthesis of the immanent and the transcendent of its Hegelian presumptions to absolute self-consciousness. Truth in light of the incarnation remains completely interpretive and genuinely dialogical because of its personal quality. No one has discussed this problem more wisely than Dietrich Bonhoeffer, with whose help I will try to sketch out an incarnational hermeneutics in the last part of this book.

Schleiermacher's monism also effects an important change from earlier formulations of morality as the mediation between an ethical demand and its translation into moral action. For the Puritan and Pietist tradition, reading was inseparably linked to social action. Interpretation of the biblical text and self-knowledge were possible only as enactment, not as contemplative theory. Not only did interpretation have to be motivated by the right relation with the Divine, but reading the scriptures and devotional literature also had to result in social action. As Matthew Henry puts it: "In a word, [we] must walk closely, consistently, courageously, and constantly, in the faith *and practice* of the gospel" (*Commentary*, 6:726; emphasis mine).

For the premoderns, even meditation is never an end in itself. The Puritan Nathanael Ranew (1602–78) wrote in his manual on meditation: "For all duties and holy performances there is great necessity of meditation, in some due measure, for a due, wise, warm, lively, and spiritual acting them, acting from the right principle of grace within, by the right rule, eyeing the word, and to the right mark and end, salvation: real and vigorous performing in this sort must have some good allowance of pondering what we are to perform" (*Solitude Improved by Divine Meditation*, 192). Meditation and the reading of the text constitute a fountain for action. Ranew exhorts, "Keep this fountain open and still running; this is the water to drive the mill, the wind that moves the sails, the spring in the watch that carries all the wheels, and keeps them going" (ibid., 195).

The Puritans' felt need to translate reading into practice is further evidenced by Henry Scudder's manual for Christian life, *The Christian's Daily Walk*: "You are commanded to walk as Christ walked, 1 John ii.6; and it concerns you so to do, if you would approve yourself to be a member of his body: for it is monstrous, nay impossible, that the head should go one way, and the body another" (24). Philipp Jacob Spener echoes the Puritan teaching when he says that not only "his own support and gain, but also the glory of his God and the welfare of his neighbor should be the object of all that [the Christian] does in his station in life" (*Pia Desideria*, 60). In the same vein, Francke admonishes his listeners that faith needs to translate into action: "Just as the experience increasingly strengthens faith, so love to one's neighbor is increasingly strengthened and multiplied through faith" (*Vom rechtschaffendem Wachstum des Glaubens*, in *FWA*, 283). Francke's *Stiftung* in Halle remains a monument to the earnestness of his conviction that Christian faith and social action are inseparable.

For premodern theology, this ethical demand of fulfilling the law of charity remains an impossible demand because of sin, the disruption of communion with God. As Luther has taught us, the gap between the moral demand and its implementation is bridged by faith. Faith, however, should not be defined in Enlightenment terms as an attitude of mind or an irrational belief contrary to reason. Rather to have faith is to be in right relation with the Divine, expressed variously as "new life," "walking with God," "communing with God," or "trusting in God."

These terms indicate a radical change in the disposition of the center of our being such that one is tempted to speak of an ontological change. Concrete moral action was thus an inseparable part of a person's new relation to God in Christ. As Steven Charnock puts it: "It is as impossible for the new creature to sin by the influence of habit, as for fire to moisten by the quality of heat, or water to burn by the quality of cold. It is as impossible for that habit to bring forth the fruits of sin, as for the sun to be the cause of darkness or a sweet fig-tree to bring forth sour fruit" (*The Nature of Regeneration,* in *WSC,* 3:119).[5]

Schleiermacher, however, in his effort to distinguish true religion from mere morality, practically eliminates the radical gap between the ethical demand and its implementation, or—to restate this in theological terms—between sinful human nature and the fulfillment of the law to love God and one's neighbor. The chasm between ethical demand and sinful human agent is reduced to mere ignorance. As a result, what earlier theology had described as regeneration or the new birth becomes a mere recognition of one's God-consciousness, something the human agent had possessed all along.

Schleiermacher's monistic hermeneutics is an important turning point in hermeneutic history. While his monistic ontology is by no means original, his reinterpretation of traditional Christianity in terms of that framework is the link in the history of hermeneutics between the Reformed hermeneutics of the Puritans and the early Pietists, on the one hand, and both liberal theological hermeneutics and the philosophical hermeneutics of Gadamer, on the other.

Schleiermacher retains the Pietist aversion to abstract knowledge but loses the earlier interplay between subjective reader response and the corrective role of the biblical text. His concept of a monistic interconnected universe serves as the foundation for his hermeneutics. As a result, he changes the traditional theory of inspiration from a God-directed specific influence to a general principle; the idea of progressive revelation of one essential message to a concept of progressive human spiritual development of successive manifestations of God-consciousness, with Christ being the supreme model of such human achievement; and finally, the biblical anthropology that depended heavily on the concept of original sin and human depravity to an idea of sin as mere forgetfulness of one's potential *God-consciousness.*

---

5. This does not mean that Puritans taught perfectionism. As Charnock immediately observes, "Yet as there is darkness in the air, though the sun be up, by the interposition of thick clouds, so is there darkness in the new creature from the habit of sin in the soul, which is not only a lodger, but an unwelcome inhabitant: Rom. vii.20, 'Sin that dwells in me' still, and acts according to its nature, though much over-powered and weakened by degrees by that habit of grace" (*WSC,* 3:119).

The results of these foundational changes are far-reaching. For the reader, hermeneutics no longer requires an attitude of humility toward the biblical text. The fact that each human being is a microcosm of the whole, and in that sense part of the Divine, puts the reader and the author on the same level. In the absence of the genuine exteriority that premodern hermeneutics found in a transcendent God, the author, the reader, and the Divine are part of the same system. In effect Luther's cosmic Word is already silenced and has been replaced by the more inclusive idea of *Welt-All*. As a result, the reader focuses no longer on one author, God, or the Holy Spirit, who inspired the scriptures equally, but rather on particular authors who express the experience of oneness with the universe most purely. Thus the canon of scripture is, in principle, infinitely expandable: "The holy scriptures have become the Bible out of their own power, *but they do not prohibit any other book to be or become also a Bible,* and whatever was written with the same power could easily be added [to the sacred writings]" (*SW*, 4:395; emphasis mine).

Schleiermacher's hermeneutics remains Christocentric, because it is through laying hold of Christ that one is empowered to higher levels of God-consciousness. However, Christ is no longer seen as the necessary bridge between man's sinfulness and God's holiness. The otherness of God is greatly diminished and man's sinfulness redefined as a low state of consciousness. While Schleiermacher remains an important theological critic of the Enlightenment and Kant's duty ethics, his work distorts both theology and ethics. As Thielicke points out, in Schleiermacher "religion and ethics seem finally to be linked only at the level of motives, not of programs of action. They meet only in the basic sphere of anthropology, where our self-understanding is at issue" (*Modern Faith and Thought*, 211). Even though ethics is the theoretical foundation of Schleiermacher's hermeneutics, his lectures on this subject unfold not a program for action but merely a sophisticated cultural philosophy.

This construct centers, similar to the ethical conceptions of Shaftesbury and Francis Hutchenson, on the natural imbalance of society and the individual and their striving toward harmony. Schleiermacher does not offer specific moral commandments (he, in fact, dismisses them) but holds that human reason will gradually overcome the tension between the desires for egocentrism and communal participation within human beings (Scholz, *Ethik und Hermeneutik*, 131). In the progress toward a balance between individualism and communal interest, hermeneutics, the art of understanding, plays a crucial role. Since no culture or community can exist without symbols, which must be communicated and understood, language and interpretation are crucial for moral progress. Each communication or utterance consists of the given linguistic medium and of the particular imprint of its author, elements that correspond to Schleiermacher's grammatical and psychological aspects of interpretation.

We can see, then, that Schleiermacher's hermeneutics is not only inseparably linked to his idea of moral progress, but it also retains an important aspect of premodern hermeneutics, namely, that understanding is itself ethical. Understanding is ethical because it "effects community" by paying careful attention to the voice of the other (Scholz, *Ethik und Hermeneutik*, 141). In contrast to premodern hermeneutics, however, Schleiermacher no longer bases this goodwill toward understanding on the spiritual foundation of God's regenerating grace and the Holy Spirit's power but on human reason and universal moral progress.

Nevertheless, while Schleiermacher has eradicated the incarnational ground for understanding found in earlier hermeneutics, his insistence that understanding is ethical preserves an insight modern philosophical hermeneutics has lost. In his famous Parisian "nonencounter" with Derrida, Gadamer does not understand Derrida's correct insight that willingness to understand the other is bound up with a "metaphysics of the will" (Gadamer, "Reply to Jacques Derrida," 53). Gadamer does not believe that understanding must be ethically grounded. For him the effort of goodwill, the Platonic ευμενεις ελεγχοι, means merely that "one does not go about identifying the weaknesses of what another person says in order to prove that one is always right, but one seeks instead as far as possible to strengthen the other's viewpoint. . . . Such an attitude seems essential . . . for any understanding at all to come about. This is nothing more than an observation. It has nothing to do with an 'appeal,' and nothing at all to do with ethics" (ibid., 55). Yet the Gadamer-Derrida encounter itself demonstrates that one cannot, in fact, simply presuppose Gadamer's humanistic curiosity and courtesy for all life situations. There will always be those who are indifferent, who do not want to listen, or who want to deliberately twist one's words. Such refusal is based on an ethical choice not to heed the other's voice. In this context, Schleiermacher's realization that understanding is in fact a moral (*sittlich*) activity is a useful correction to Gadamer's apparent insistence on understanding as nonethical.

In stark contrast to premodern hermeneutics, however, Schleiermacher's social and cultural philosophy depends not on the revealed word of God and the need for regeneration but on his belief in organic moral progress. Schleiermacher departs from the premodern theological concepts of human depravity and the need for regeneration to provide unselfish moral impulses. His basic premise of teleological development toward the good built into the cosmos allows him to locate the original sources of both Christianity and ethics within every human being. Schleiermacher has thus virtually eradicated the premodern doctrine of sin.

When the Puritan turned to examine himself, he saw deviation from an external moral standard, a natural selfishness that could be overcome only by divine help and a close personal relationship with the deity through Christ. Schleiermacher, however, obliterates the distinction between the object of knowledge and the inquirer. The Puritan turned the eyes inward to arrive at self-knowledge in light of the external word. Schleiermacher finds both light and knowledge within. For him, God-consciousness *is* self-knowledge. Thus he flattens the former epistemological circle of "self-knowledge through the knowledge of God" by removing a truly "other," external source of knowledge, which may serve as a corrective to human interpretation of the self and the universe.

In Schleiermacher's own theology, the loss of transcendence in his interpretation theory leads to a crisis of the word. Thielicke, for example, observes that since Schleiermacher does not see the reader as the recipient of the word, as in premodern theology, but rather as the producer of divinity, all of us are, in this sense, divine (*Modern Faith and Thought*, 274). Schleiermacher's immanentism does not really allow the word to address the reader in the same corrective and deconstructive way Luther had suggested. The predictable consequence is that the text does not really assert itself over against the reader, but rather, as we have seen in the case of Schleiermacher's own biblical exegesis, it is dominated by the reader, who reads his own experience into the text. Thus hermeneutically Schleiermacher's greatest weakness is that by rejecting an objective transcendent Divine, he entrenches a subjectivism in hermeneutics whereby the text loses its power to speak.

Schleiermacher's Impact on Hermeneutics

It is impossible to do justice to the complexity and the rich implications of Schleiermacher's interpretation theory. We must restrict ourselves briefly to an overview of his importance for current hermeneutic theory. His work is generally recognized as constituting a turning point in both theological and philosophical hermeneutics. The qualitative assessment of this turning point, however, differs greatly in the respective disciplines of theology and philosophical hermeneutics. In fact, it has been claimed that while Schleiermacher marks a fundamental shift in hermeneutical history, the nature of this shift still seems far from settled (Birus, "Hermeneutische Wende?" 213). We will turn first to his effect on modern theology.

Most theologians acknowledge Schleiermacher's impact on modern theology. Even if Schleiermacher has not made an original contribution but has synthesized already existing theological sentiments into a systematic theological construct, he remains the "father of modern Protestant theology" (Tillich, *History of Christian Thought*, 387).[6] Karl Barth, arguably the most eminent voice of twentieth-century theology, has criticized Schleiermacher's contribution as detrimental to the proclamatory nature of the word. Our own analysis of Schleiermacher's theological position confirms Karl Barth's judgment (shared by Emil Brunner) that Schleiermacher's subjectivism constitutes a distinct departure from reformational theology.

Karl Barth, who wrestled all his life with Schleiermacher's thought, felt keenly Schleiermacher's departure from reformational anthropology. Barth concludes that

> fundamentally there is nothing supernatural here—Christ too is an act of nature, a final development of its spiritual power. . . . In the last resort, even the divine Spirit is only a supreme enhancement of human reason. Thus revelation is neither absolutely supernatural nor absolutely suprarational. . . . Concepts like that of a fallen nature that needs redemption and is not finally capable of spiritual acts like revelation, or darkened reason that cannot finally experience its supreme enhancement in the divine Spirit, seem not to exist at all for [Schleiermacher]. (*Theology of Schleiermacher*, 242)

Schleiermacher's husk-and-kernel approach also encourages the isolation of positive revelation into a private realm of personal belief. It is true, of course, that he sought to overcome a faith-reason dualism by unifying all knowledge as striving toward religion. Unfortunately, however, his hermeneutics requires that religion be stripped of all particularity and reduced to a nondescript God-consciousness.

In the end, Schleiermacher's own conception of religion becomes the exegetical straightjacket that determines what counts as the true spiritual kernel and what may be discarded as mere human husk. Schleiermacher believes strongly enough in his ability to differentiate between true and false God-consciousness to criticize the writers of the Gospels for not always adequately relating Christ's experience, as in the case of

6. Paul Tillich recognizes a decisive turning point in the history of theology in Schleiermacher, for "theology was faced with having to make the basic decision, whether the attempt to construct a synthesis out of all the elements in theology we have described is the right way, or whether a return to the orthodox tradition with some modernizations is the right way. If the latter method is followed, then of course Schleiermacher has to be abolished; but if the former, then Schleiermacher remains the founder of modern Protestant theology" (*History of Christian Thought*, 387).

the apostle John, "who shared Christ's basic views very *inadequately*" (*SW*, 4:394; emphasis mine). One may justly ask how Schleiermacher can criticize John's basic views of Christ when cognitive criteria and propositional statements have been largely removed by his own system of thought. Numerous other similar examples show that for all its richness, Schleiermacher's hermeneutics indeed encourages an authoritative stance toward the text. In the end, the educated and supposedly historically more advanced consciousness of the interpreter rather than the text determines meaning.

The interpreter's superiority over the text under the guise of neutrality, or even worse, in the sincere belief of freeing God's truth from historical and cultural inadequacies, was to become the ethos of the historical-critical school, Rudolf Bultmann's demythologizing, and the division between the historical Jesus and the Christ of faith. It is therefore imperative for our recovery of theological hermeneutics to avoid Schleiermacher's monism and subjectivism as much as rationalist neutrality in interpretation.

While theology laments the high price of religious particularity that Schleiermacher paid for a general hermeneutics, philosophy has eagerly welcomed his interpretation theory as a positive watershed in hermeneutic development. In philosophical hermeneutics, Schleiermacher has been credited with establishing hermeneutics as a general method, disconnected from biblical exegeses (Palmer, *Hermeneutics*, 40).[7]

Indeed, Schleiermacher viewed his own lectures on hermeneutics as a novel attempt to construct a general hermeneutics that undergirds all other "specialized hermeneutics" (*H*, 95). As Schleiermacher puts it, "neither theological nor classical hermeneutics represents the essence of the matter. Rather hermeneutics itself is something greater out of which these two types flow" (ibid., 179). As Hendrik Birus points out, Schleiermacher's explicit claim to originality for this new path is rendered doubtful by Herder's criticism of rationalism, in which he lays the groundwork for Schleiermacher's view of language and divinatory interpretation ("Zwischen den Zeiten," 26). Our reading of Pietist hermeneutics has shown that both Herder's and Schleiermacher's views have strong precedents in Francke's affective hermeneutics.

Nonetheless, Schleiermacher's systematic exposition of important hermeneutic themes has ensured his dominance as a transitional figure for philosophical hermeneutics. For example, we find in Schleiermacher's

7. Richard Palmer states that Schleiermacher's "conception of a general hermeneutics marks the beginning of the nondisciplinary 'hermeneutics.' . . . It might almost be said that hermeneutics proper here emerges historically from its parentage in biblical exegesis and classical philology" (*Hermeneutics*, 40).

notes already the centrality of language for hermeneutics. "Language," he writes, "is the only presupposition in hermeneutics, and everything that is to be found, including the other objective and subjective presuppositions, must be discovered in language" (*H*, 51). Even notions of tradition and historically effected consciousness, which are central to Gadamer's hermeneutics, are prefigured by Schleiermacher's attention to language-shaping influences. For Schleiermacher thinking occurs in language, yet at the same time language shapes thought. Hermeneutics and rhetoric are thus "intimately related" because "every act of understanding is the reverse side of an act of speaking, and one must grasp the thinking that underlies a given statement" (ibid., 97). At the same time, however, our linguistic heritage (*Angeborenheit der Sprache*) modifies the spirit and thus the thought of the speaker (ibid., 99). These references to the linguisticality of understanding show that Schleiermacher anticipates important issues of current hermeneutical discussion, and it is not surprising that since Gadamer's *Truth and Method,* Schleiermacher has received more attention from philosophers than from theologians. This attention, however, suffers from a curious neglect of Schleiermacher's theological convictions.

Gadamer, for example, clearly acknowledges Schleiermacher's important contributions to grammatical and psychological exegesis (*TM*, 184). He seems well aware of the spiritually charged foundation of Schleiermacher's hermeneutics, as several statements suggest. Gadamer mentions, for instance, that Schleiermacher's hermeneutics depends on "a pre-existing bond of all individuals" (ibid., 189).[8] He also mentions that Schleiermacher extends the hermeneutical circle of part and whole, which had been used by the philological school of Friedrich August Wolf and Georg Ast, to "psychological understanding, which necessarily understands every structure of thought as an element in the total context of a man's life" (ibid., 190).

However, Gadamer does not give the reader the necessary background to understand why Schleiermacher can make such claims. Gadamer presents Schleiermacher's monistic background in implicit and very moderate terms without explaining the thoroughly spiritual-theological foundation of Schleiermacher's principles. Gadamer makes it sound as if Schleiermacher merely recognized common human qualities on the basis of which he can claim a universal hermeneutics (*TM*, 191). Gadamer neglects to tell us that Schleiermacher's achievement of a general

---

8. Gadamer also links Schleiermacher's concept of divination to the conception of the spiritual interconnectedness of humanity: "In hermeneutics, what corresponds to the production of genius is divination, the immediate solution, which ultimately presupposes a kind of con-geniality" (*TM*, 189).

hermeneutics requires his monistic metaphysics. A full disclosure of Schleiermacher's metaphysics invites, of course, a comparative critique of ontology that cannot be done without theology. It is understandable that Gadamer's Platonism leads him to avoid this discussion. However, Schleiermacher's own work makes clear how important metaphysical presuppositions are for the construction of a general hermeneutics. Hence for our recovery of theological hermeneutics, an exchange of philosophy and theology on ontology is exactly where conversations about interpretation theory will be most fruitful.

Schleiermacher clearly presents a departure from Reformation theology. Even though he understood himself in all sincerity to be "a servant of the Word," how different is his hermeneutics from that of the Reformation (*SW*, 2:883)! His conception of hermeneutics and ethics required significant redefinitions of cardinal theological concepts. Most importantly, he lost the radical divine transcendence of premodern hermeneutics and thus the ultimate ground for both hermeneutics and ethics. This process of secularization continues in the twenty-first century. Understanding the importance of theological presuppositions for interpretation theory will help the reader to see the many unacknowledged theological assumptions that underlie Gadamer's hermeneutics and expose the lack of ethical transcendence in his philosophical hermeneutics.

Gadamer's philosophical hermeneutics depends on Heidegger's philosophy, and Heidegger conducts interpretation in an explicitly atheistic framework. Working consciously from a Greek rather than a Judeo-Christian worldview, Heidegger and Gadamer have successfully exposed and criticized modernity's reduction of truth to scientific methodology. Particularly Gadamer's analysis of Enlightenment misconceptions of interpretation in his main work *Truth and Method* has been path-breaking in this regard. Yet despite these achievements, philosophers and theologians alike have remained unsatisfied by Heidegger's view of the human subject and by Gadamer's interpretive theory. The former is deemed not human enough, the latter too naive in its assertion of the possibility of self-knowledge. I will argue that both deficiencies are the result of unacknowledged theological assumptions that disrupt and subvert the supposedly atheistic overcoming of theological hermeneutics. It is to this chapter in hermeneutic history that we now turn.

5

GADAMER'S PHILOSOPHICAL
HERMENEUTICS

The most difficult aspect of recovering a theologically and biblically motivated hermeneutics for our time is to recognize fully the achievements of nontheological sources, yet the theological notion of common grace, that all truth is God's truth, requires nothing less. As so often in the history of the church, non-Christian thinkers provide the most clear-sighted framing of the issues and the best conceptual and analytical tools. In the history of interpretation, such credit must be given to the work of Martin Heidegger and his student Hans-Georg Gadamer. Without question their work, more than Nietzschean and deconstructionist strands of thought, contains resources for a workable theory of interpretation. Ironically, however, their work in turn depends heavily on theologically motivated sources such as Augustine, Aquinas, Luther, Kierkegaard, and Dostoyevsky.

Heidegger and Gadamer have consistently employed these sources to criticize the modernist epistemological paradigm; particularly Gadamer has worked all his life to make Heidegger's notion of the hermeneutic circle fruitful for epistemology in the humanities by articulating in numerous essays the basic insight that human knowledge is by nature interpretive rather than apodictic in a scientific sense.

In this chapter I will show that much of Gadamer's thought is indebted to theological sources and that his work is inherently unsustainable without them. Even my critical evaluation, however, is driven by the conviction that truth as interpretation is the only correct foundation for a theological hermeneutics simply because it is the only theologically defensible position—we are finite human beings and not gods. As Garrett Green rightly points out in his *Theology, Hermeneutics, and Imagination*, it is high time Christians realized the opportunity that the crumbling edifice of modernity's reason-faith dualism offers for getting beyond the objectivist-relativist dichotomy, which still frames most of the popular debates on interpretation (205).

Self-examination is, of course, the hardest task of all, and it may be some time yet before the broader Christian community is at ease with a nonfoundationalist account of knowledge. Yet an incarnational hermeneutics must reject a rationalist account of knowledge if it wants to recover a theological model of interpretation that is faithful to biblical Christianity. I believe that Gadamer is a helpful ally in recovering theological hermeneutics because he, too, is in search of a hermeneutics that affirms self-knowledge. Recognizing current interpretive paradigms and the advantage offered to theology by philosophical hermeneutics' criticism of scientific objectivism is imperative if we are to avoid expending our energy in useless and avoidable battles. We must understand the main concepts of philosophical hermeneutics to assess their value from a theological perspective.

The Gift of Hermeneutics: To Be Human Is to Interpret

The foundational insight of Gadamer's philosophy is the universality of hermeneutics. Gadamer has learned this insight from his teacher Heidegger ("Reflections," 10). The universality of hermeneutics means simply that human knowledge, or more basically, human contact with reality, is not immediate but mediated. Often theological critics of Gadamer and Heidegger lose patience at this important starting point and launch into near hysterical warnings against relativism. Such cries not only demonstrate ignorance of Heidegger's explicit aim to overcome modernist subjectivism, but theological tirades against the interpretive nature of all human knowledge also overlook Heidegger's clarion call to worldview thinking. Heidegger and Gadamer believe that the very point of hermeneutics is foundational thinking.

Heidegger reminds us that every discipline, including theology, must practice first-order thinking. According to Heidegger, every academic discipline must continually rethink its foundational concepts and become aware of their historical origin and development. Concepts, he argues, do not just appear but are time-bound descriptions of our world (*SZ*, 10). In this case, such thinking requires that we define what we mean by mediated and immediate knowledge. When we do this, we find that Gadamer's claim to the universality of hermeneutics is linked to a critique of scientific epistemology at the beginning of the twentieth century.

Science, Gadamer argues, has bequeathed to us a very problematic model of human knowledge. While scientific epistemology has been hugely successful in harnessing the secrets of nature for human use, it falsely reduces knowledge to an absurd standard of objectivity. Because philosophical developments adapted for the sciences have been undeniably successful in improving our knowledge and technological progress, we only count as true that which is neutral and verifiable in a scientific sense. This is foundational*ist* rather than foundation*al* thinking, and it originated in the philosophical position of René Descartes, who had attempted to find the bedrock of all knowledge in the irreducible position of indubitable doubt. Descartes himself was not quite as sure concerning this bedrock as the accepted story of this development suggests; he realized that he could not sufficiently ground and explain his capacity for reasoning or the idea of infinity in a finite human mind. Nevertheless, the upshot of his rationalism, the notion that only value-free facts are true knowledge while all other forms are merely subjective impressions, still dominates much of Western consciousness.

When the scientific method is transposed from the laboratory into philosophy and made the shibboleth of knowledge, we not only deny the historicity of concepts and worldviews but also create an unsuitable measure for truth in general. Friedrich Nietzsche criticized Western rationalism, whose worship of concepts he viewed as nothing but a forgetfulness-of-prior-invention mentality. Modern academics, Nietzsche argued, first invent concepts, ideas, and categories of classification only then to forget their human origin by treating them as discoveries of timeless principles and absolute certainties. As everything with Nietzsche, his exaggeration makes the valid point that human knowledge is finite and perspectival and that forgetting this amounts to claiming the status of a god.

Martin Heidegger takes up Nietzsche's criticism of the sciences, but his phenomenological stance allows him to affirm self-knowledge rather than deny it. Rather than fall in with Nietzsche's hermeneutics of suspicion, Heidegger claims that we can overcome the absurd reduction of human knowledge to scientific objectivism by realizing that so-called subjective knowledge is actually the first order of knowledge. Rather than thinking that we begin with neutral empirical knowledge (the objective side) to which we then add value and meaning (the subjective side), Heidegger argues that human beings know primarily existentially or interpretatively. Humans, in other words, are not mathematically oriented machines who process reality through a grid of Euclidean geometry or by numerical codes and exact scientific categories; instead human beings see reality based on moods, environment, culture, and training.

Heidegger gives numerous examples of this. We do not register, for example, the chirping of birds and the rumbling of cars as technical noise measured in decibels but precisely as the "chirping bird" and the "rumbling car." Hearing coincides with interpretation (*SZ*, §14, 163–64). Neither do we see objects primarily as measurable entities in their geometrical dimensions but rather as meaningful for human comfort or discomfort (a chair for seating, a pen for writing, a glass of water for drinking, etc.). In short, we always perceive things *as* something. Objects, ideas, and situations always have some kind of meaning for us from which our perception starts. While these meanings can always be changed and expanded on, to say that we first see with a "naked" eye and then add subjective judgments of meaning is demonstrably false. The sciences, argues Heidegger, and Gadamer follows him in this, cannot themselves provide interpretive frameworks; true science excels at experimentation and verification, but it cannot or should not tell us what scientific discoveries mean in terms of human existence. This is the task of thinking, which, for Heidegger, is the exclusive province of philosophy.

Heidegger's criticism of science is part of a larger undertaking, his so-called *Fundamentalontologie*, which one may roughly translate as the attempt to rewrite the history of the interpretation of being in order to discern the meaning of existence in general. Whatever one may think of this endeavor itself, whether it is a secular theology or simply a misguided interpretation of Western intellectual history as an ontological failure, theology should take up two elements of Heidegger's work. We have already mentioned the first one as Heidegger's admonition to worldview thinking. Theology must historicize the intellectual horizon within which it operates. To interpret God's word correctly, we must understand the influences that shape our understanding and our way of approaching God's word.

The second element of Heidegger's thought, adapted for hermeneutical theory by Gadamer, is Heidegger's criticism of the philosophical error that underlies scientific methodology and whose application to the human sciences (and especially to theology) is disastrous. At issue is what Richard Bernstein has aptly identified as "the Cartesian Anxiety," the view that identifies objective knowledge, defined in terms of scientific epistemology, with truth and rejects any alternative as a surrender to relativism (*Beyond Objectivism and Relativism*, 228).

Perhaps the single most important issue in recovering theological hermeneutics is the overcoming of this objectivist-relativist divide, which continues to dominate discussions on interpretation. Cartesian foundationalism is alien to a biblical notion of knowledge because it is allergic to the historical embodiment of knowledge. Knowledge derived from the world of history with all its flux and contingency makes us uneasy, and it is no wonder that a scientific rather than a biblical paradigm of knowledge continues to inform the cries of modern evangelicals for absolute truth and certainty. An incarnational hermeneutics, however, must take its orientation from the fact that God entered history without compromising transcendence. We will see a fuller explanation of this incarnational hermeneutics in our discussion of Bonhoeffer, who insists that self-knowledge is available to us only in history, culture, and language because God manifests himself within those media.

It is time that we expose our obsession with disembodied knowledge for what it really is: an idolatrous desire for an independent and neutral knowledge that is not given to human beings. It is the kind of knowledge the serpent promised to Adam and Eve. In his commentary on the temptation scene, the Puritan poet John Milton rightly judged the desire to know as God knows to be simultaneously intoxicating and dehumanizing. In Milton's description, we find our primeval parents, having fallen for the serpent's lie, "as with new wine intoxicated both / They swim in mirth and fancy that they feel Divinity within them breeding wings / Wherewith to scorn the Earth" (*Complete Poems and Major Prose*, 1007–10). Milton has it right: the rationalist concept of knowledge is an inhuman fancy. To scorn the earth, to deny the finitude and historicity of our ideas, to think ourselves above what Gadamer calls the historically effected consciousness is nothing but the desire for divinity. And yet this intoxication continues to distort theological discussions on hermeneutics.

To assert the hermeneutical nature of human existence to evangelical audiences inevitably elicits the Cartesian anxiety—how can I know with certainty? As Bernstein points out, Descartes writes not only as a philosopher but also as a Christian. It is often overlooked that Descartes's quest for a fixed Archimedean point outside of history is more than a philosophical or epistemological device but is first of all the meditation of the Christian soul to secure human existence from the vicissitudes of life by anchoring existence in God (*Beyond Objectivism and Relativism*, 18).

Yet when Descartes's quest is taken out of the Christian context and viewed solely as epistemological method, a host of problems result. First of all, the starting point of knowledge becomes transcendental. "I doubt, therefore I am" without reference to a creator effectively institutes an interior-exterior gap between the human mind and its environment. I know that I am, but how do I know things around me really exist? The answer concerning the material world must be "by trial and error"—the scientific method. Things become real when our subjective perception has been confirmed or corrected by empirical data.

In the world of concepts and ideas, however, such scientific method is virtually useless. How does one define love, honor, and decency according to this method? It is here that the Heideggerian criticism of scientific objectivism becomes useful. Based on the phenomenological tradition begun by Edmund Husserl, Heidegger denies the Cartesian split between the mind and reality. Heidegger believes it is wrong to conceive of phenomena as inherently deceptive. We do not in the first instance perceive reality as an optical illusion whose true nature is revealed to us only through scientific discovery. What we perceive is essentially what we get. This does not mean, however, that we perceive things fully or completely: "'Behind' the phenomenon of phenomenology is essentially nothing different [from what we perceive], but that which is to become phenomenon may well be hidden" (*SZ*, §7, 36).

The distortion, however, is not in the object but a consequence of our finitude. Phenomena may be concealed for various reasons. They may be completely unknown to us and so cannot be recognized. Conversely, they may be all too well known and buried under layers of traditional interpretation. In this case we *seem* to know the object but in reality do not (*SZ*, §7, 36). For this reason commonsensical or seemingly "immediate" perception is not always the most reliable. It is the task of phenomenology (indeed, of philosophy) to clear away mistaken interpretations by carefully peeling away former layers. This *Destruktion* has the positive goal of letting terms and concepts speak again in their original context (ibid., §6, 20).

For Heidegger this phenomenological method must be in the service of ontology, the deepest question of all, the question of the meaning of being as such. While we do not have to follow Heidegger in his equation of philosophy with ontology and ontology with phenomenology (*SZ*, §7, 35), I believe theology should accept the promise of phenomenology to overcome the subjectivist-objectivist divide and to embrace the hermeneutical nature of our existence. As Heidegger puts it: "The Logos of phenomenology of human existence has the character of *hermeneuein* [interpretation]" (ibid., 37).

To be human is to interpret. This is not a flaw but a gift; it is part of who we are. Ultimately, of course, this concept must be worked out for theology in terms of the universal Logos, the wisdom that was with God in the beginning and incarnated itself in the historical God-man Jesus the Christ. This undertaking remains a task for the last chapter. Before construction, however, comes deconstruction. Gadamer has developed Heidegger's basic insight into his own philosophical hermeneutics. We must now turn to a critical analysis of his work in our continuing effort to trace theological concepts in interpretive history for our recovery of theological hermeneutics.

Gadamer's Augustinian Hermeneutic

> Christology prepares the way for a new philosophy of man, which mediates in a new way between the mind of man in its finitude and the divine infinity. Here what we have called the hermeneutical experience finds its own, special ground. (*TM*, 428)

> Certainly the humanistic experience of God cannot do justice to the claim of the Christian concept of God. However, when modern philosophizing begins to walk the old paths of thinking, perhaps the thinker can learn again to recognize familiar content in the concept of God. (*GW*, 10:358)

In his early writings, Gadamer is in dialogue with theological thought because theology provides an important source for philosophical thinking. Only here, Gadamer insists, do we find answers to those questions that go beyond our finite horizon, questions of guilt, death, and the fatedness of human existence (*GW*, 10:350, 359). He also regards theology's insistence on transcendence and on an existence that supersedes individual being as a bulwark against modernist individualism (ibid., 10:358). One must recognize, Gadamer argues in another essay, that Western thought is rooted in two primordial words, in the Greek Logos and the word of God, proclaimed and interpreted by the philosopher and the prophet (*Kleine Schriften*, 202).

Gadamer's earliest thinking in the 1920s was, in fact, triggered and influenced by the relationship between philosophy and theology (*GW*, 10:249). Indeed, the relation between philosophy and theology remains an important element not only for understanding Gadamer's thought but also for delineating its inherent problems. I want to show that Gadamer relies at crucial moments in the development of his philosophical hermeneutics on the prophet rather than on the philosopher, on the Christian Logos rather than on the Greek one. In his later writings, however, Gadamer seems to forget (or repress) his earlier interaction with theology and conveys the impression that his thought relies exclusively on Plato and Aristotle ("Reflections," 25). Yet Gadamer's hermeneutics, and especially its later practical development, cannot really function without the Augustinian Logos Christology, from which Gadamer derives his view of reason and language.

Gadamer relies mainly on two theological elements for his view of language and interpretation. The first is Augustine's Logos Christology.

Augustine's doctrine of illumination, the idea that human rationality is grounded in the divine Logos, as well as its concomitant incarnational notion of the "inner word," decisively shapes Gadamer's view of language and reason. The second main theological influence is a Pietistic notion of self-understanding. Gadamer models hermeneutic experience on the theological insight that explanation and understanding are one. He learns predominantly from German Pietism that exegesis is always motivated by application—a text means because it means to me now, that is, the notion of truth as a contemporizing word event. At the same time, however, self-understanding retains an element of objectivity as a revelation of being that arrives from the "outside" and thus counters the existentialist notion of truth as mere self-understanding ("Heidegger and Marburg Theology," in *PH*, 208).

Reason and Language

Despite the obvious theological influences in his work, Gadamer ostensibly philosophizes in a nontheistic framework. He tells us that his work has always been driven by two interests: hermeneutics (the art of understanding) and practical philosophy, an interest that became more pronounced after his retirement in 1968 ("Reflections," 26). Gadamer's discussions of these two main interests are in turn dominated by the concepts of rationality and language. In fact, Gadamer's whole philosophy may be boiled down to his view of human reason and its linguistic embodiment. Gadamer insists that a proper conception of reason and language safeguards the reader from the misunderstanding of his philosophical hermeneutics displayed by "method fanatics" (scientists, structuralists, and neopositivists) and "ideology critics" such as Habermas (ibid.). Against both groups, Gadamer insists that his philosophy is neither relativistic nor naively metaphysical but rather embodies a radical openness to an understanding of our world on the basis of language and reason. Linguisticality, Gadamer is convinced, "constitutes a human capacity inseparably linked with rationality as such" (ibid., 25).

The main pillars of Gadamer's philosophical hermeneutics are thus language and reason. In developing his view of language, Gadamer makes it very clear that his philosophical hermeneutics is not a metaphysics but a reflection on the immanent mediation of the universal and the particular through language. Gadamer's belief in a universe in which God no longer provides the ground for the correspondence between the perceiving subject and the perceived object is documented in two places. In his 1960 essay "The Nature of Things and the Language of Things," Gadamer recognizes the superiority of classical metaphysics and, indeed, theology in their overcoming of the modernist subject-object divide in the divine mind. "To be sure," Gadamer says, "classical metaphysics' concept of truth—the conformity of knowledge with the object—rests on a theological correspondence. . . . Just as the soul is created to encounter beings, so the thing is created true, that is, capable of being known. An enigma that is insoluble for the finite mind is thus resolved in the infinite mind of the creator" (*PH*, 75). At the same time, however, Gadamer asserts that "philosophy certainly can no longer avail itself of such a theological grounding and will also not want to repeat the secularized versions of it, as represented by speculative idealism with its dialectical mediation of finite and infinite" (ibid.). Yet Gadamer recognizes the necessity of this subject-object mediation and asks: "Are there finite possibilities of doing justice to this correspondence? Is there a grounding of this correspondence that does not venture to affirm the infinity of the divine mind and yet is able to do justice to the infinite correspondence of soul and being? I affirm that there is. There is a way that attests to this correspondence, one toward which philosophy is ever more clearly directed—the way of language" (ibid.).

Thus the centrality of language for Gadamer's hermeneutics is based on its role as a substitute for the divine. Language is no longer a secondary manifestation of the human spirit alongside art, law, and religion "but represents the sustaining medium of all of these manifestations of the spirit" (*PH*, 76; see also *GW*, 2:72). Gadamer, in other words, is satisfied that language itself indicates the "commensurateness of the created soul to created things" but no longer worries about *why* this is so. Language is the medium that encompasses all beings insofar as they can be expressed in words. Gadamer follows the later Wittgenstein in viewing language not as an instrument but "as the element in which we live, as fishes live in water" ("Reflections," 22). We are not masters of language but are surrounded by it and by the things that are revealed through language.

Gadamer's substitution of language for a divine presence or meditation as the explanation for knowledge (the correspondence of mind and world, soul and being) begs the question why language has the ability to accomplish this task. How do we know that language is a trustworthy medium of mediation? This question is not moot, for it concerns speech-act theory as much as recent efforts at reconstructing rational and ethical communicative principles, predominantly Habermas's concept of communicative action.

As deconstructionists point out, the irreducible metaphoricity of language does not allow for stable meaning. How is it, then, that language can still convey knowledge? Given the metaphoricity of language, which Gadamer, too, sees not as a hindrance but as an essential ingredient in meaning-making, how can we abstract from the multiple shades of meaning the best possible one unless we intuitively grasp and extract from the midst of these possible meanings the one that pertains to the matter at hand? In other words, what guarantees the connection between word and referent? It is well known that deconstruction, for example, stipulates a certain loss or even violence in the very origin (*arche*) of language. For Derrida, at least, writing—that is, any language—"cannot be thought outside of the horizon of intersubjective violence" (*Of Grammatology*, 127). Derrida's "confession of faith," which grounds his hermeneutics of suspicion, is contrary to Gadamer's creed of confidence, a faith in human reason and language.[1]

The Inner Word

Gadamer secures his view of language by adopting the Augustinian revision of Platonism. In *Truth and Method*, he establishes the covenant between word and referent by turning to Logos Christology. For a description of the nature of language, Gadamer first turns to the Greeks, only to find that Greek philosophy does not want to admit this relationship "between word and thing, speech and thought" but rather tries to rescue thought from the dominance of speech. Gadamer finds a more suitable way to describe the relationship of word and thought in Christian word theology, the concept of the eternal *verbum*. The Christian idea of the incarnate Word, he believes, "does more justice to the being of language, and so prevents the forgetfulness of language in Western thought from becoming complete" (*WM*, 422; see also *TM*, 418).[2]

Language is a key element in Gadamer's epistemology. Gadamer is interested in how we can know historically and how this knowledge, a nonsubjective knowledge that differs from the measurable scientific knowledge, is transferred in the human sciences.[3] More specifically his concern is the transfer of this knowledge, of truth, through language. In conversation with texts from past and present, such insights or truths

1. "Is not language more the language of things than the language of man?" (Gadamer, *PH*, 77; *GW*, 73). I am indebted for this insight to J. K. Smith and his outstanding theological engagement with Derrida in *The Fall of Interpretation*, 123.

2. My translation on this point differs from the Weinheimer/Marshall edition, which translates Gadamer's present future "so daß die Sprachvergessenheit des Abendlandes keine vollständige werden kann" as past tense. Gadamer seems to see the Christian concept of the word as an ongoing bulwark against the forgetfulness of language.

3. In his discussion of artwork, Gadamer describes the task of hermeneutics as the bridging of human and historical distances between spirit and spirit (or mind and mind [*Aesthetik und Hermeneutik*]; *GW*, 8:1).

emerge concerning a subject matter. In fact, as Gadamer makes clear in part 3 of *Truth and Method,* the central concept "fusion of horizons" has the character of a conversation (*WM,* 392). In this conversation, truth reveals itself to the listener through concept and language. Concepts and language are neither mere tools nor exact representations of their referent.

In his discussions of Greek and Christian thought, Gadamer tries to formulate a view of language that lies somewhere between the models of language as an arbitrary sign system (*Konventionalismus*) and language as an exact representation of objects (*Abbildungstheorie*). In this effort, he enlists the help of theological speculations on the incarnation. Perhaps the most important insight Gadamer gleans from theology is that thought is not necessarily self-reflexive. Theology clarifies the relation of mind or spirit (*Geist*) to thought and word. In Logos Christology, the inner word of the Trinity, the Son, did not emanate from and was not created by God the Father; in the same way, the inner word of the spirit/mind is not created (*gebildet*) in an act of reflexivity. If someone thinks and thus says something, he refers to some thing (*die Sache*). "In truth, there is no reflexivity involved in the formation of the word, for the word does not express the mind but the intended subject matter [*die Sache*]. The formation of the word originates in the content of the subject matter itself [*im Sachgehalt selbst*]. . . . The word is not expression of the [human] mind, but approaches the *similitudo rei* [likeness of the thing]" (*WM,* 430). Thus for Gadamer the truth about things is somehow fully present in the mental word.[4]

Logos theology also helps Gadamer explain the quality of this "revelation" through language. The model of the incarnation describes certain qualities of language (*WM,* 425). The mystery of the Trinity reflects the miracle of language insofar as the word, which is true because it accurately describes a state of affairs, is not directed toward itself. Like the incarnation, language's very nature is revelatory and proclamatory. The paradox of Christ's essential equality with God and his simultaneous individual, personal (historical) existence serves as a model for the plurality of linguistic signifiers that somehow converge in the depiction of a thing. Gadamer argues that here we encounter more than a mere analogy, because the relation of speaking to thinking "corresponds in all its imperfection to the divine interrelation of the Trinity. The inner word of the mind is as equal in essence with thought as is the Son with the Father" (ibid.; see also *TM,* 421).

Thus theology, in contrast to Greek thought, allows Gadamer to establish the event character and process quality of the word. Christ, the

4. Nowhere is Gadamer closer to Heidegger's view of apophansis, of Being (i.e., truth) revealing itself through language.

incarnate Word, is a single speech act, yet insofar as he is also a truly historical event (*Geschehen*)—unless one falls into Nestorianism—it is also perceived from various human perspectives in its manifestations. In preaching, too, the word event occurs in many different forms yet is one word nonetheless. Gadamer here clearly alludes to Luther's concept of the Word behind the written word. Different from propositionally known truths, the preached word is thus always *relationally* connected to the incarnate Word and its effects on the listener. Just like the divine word, the human word also has such event-character. Gadamer uses this analogy for the process of concept formation (*Begriffsbildung*).

Gadamer explains that Aristotle believed that the formation of concepts, although arising from our finite horizon, nonetheless proceeds toward the elucidation of the subject matter. Common concepts are formed by convention, but these conventions are based on the natural common agreement of what is good and right (*WM*, 436). Thus Greek philosophy discovered language's natural ability to form concepts based on what is extracted from experience as common and thus perceived as universally true. The radically new dimension that theological reflection makes accessible is one in which the word is a *process* whereby the unity of the subject matter is brought to *full* expression. The theological model, according to Gadamer, best understands our finitude. That thought is discursive is quite obvious. The theological concept of the inner word, however, understands that our finite reason cannot grasp a concept or idea in its entirety; instead our finitude requires that our knowledge be formed dialectically in an inner conversation (ibid., 426).

Is the inner word, then, nothing but the discursive nature of our thought? And if so, does not this discursive nature run counter to intuitive knowledge and hence destroy the Trinitarian analogy? Gadamer draws on Thomas Aquinas's Logos formulations at this point to show that discursivity does not necessarily entail linear succession (which would be opposed to the Trinitarian analogy). Rather when we think, we do so in an intellectual "emanation," which contains many concepts at once and does not really require temporal sequencing in the strictest sense (*WM*, 427). Thus, in contrast to Platonic Logos conceptions, the word is not formed after knowledge has been attained in the mind; rather the word is the gradual enactment of revealed knowledge (*Vollzug der Erkenntnis*) and thus a process.

Thus far the prophetic Logos has secured language's objectivity, its event character, and even its plurality and creativity. Contrary to those who confuse Platonism with Christian theology and lump both together as logocentric fallacies, Gadamer turns to the Christian Logos to assure stability of meaning amid a plurality of signifiers. Gadamer tells us that Platonism, not its Augustinian revision, associates material diversity with spiritual loss of purity and presence (*WM*, 438). Plato's logocentrism values thought over speech and sees writing as a devaluation of the spirit, of pure thought and full presence.[5] Logos Christology, in contrast, celebrates the plurality of meaning as the common creative power of the divine and the human, a concept that allows Gadamer to maintain the word's fullness in the midst of an unfolding linguistic diversity. Just as the incarnate (external) Word is not a lesser manifestation of the Godhead than the Father or the Spirit (internal word), the plurality in which the human mind (the inner word) unfolds itself does not present a dilution or lessening in value. Gadamer finds in Logos theology that "the Word is not a different order of being than the Spirit, nor a diminished, weakened version of the same. This insight constitutes the superiority of the Christian philosopher over the Platonists. [For him] the plurality in which the human spirit unfolds is neither a deviation from the One nor a loss of at-homeness" (ibid., 439).

Drawing on the fifteenth-century theologian Nicolaus Cusanus, Gadamer argues that in our thinking process, we form words, and this word formation is formally analogous to the relation of God the Father and God the incarnate Son. The plurality of concepts and signifiers is, in fact, a sign of the creative power of the human spirit, which unfolds and contains the order of being (*Wesensordnung der Dinge*). Gadamer adopts Cusanus's view that the plurality of expressions are all derivations from an ideal concept. Gadamer leaves open the exact nature of this *vocabulum naturale* and what kind of relation words have to it, but he affirms the basic view that "the individual words of one language share a final commensurability with that of every other language insofar as all languages unfold from the unity of the mind" (*WM*, 441). Theological speculation thus yields the following model: the external manifestations (the concepts) of the inner word, the thing in itself, are all valid because they refer equally to the subject matter. Just as the incarnation is a full representation of God even in its historicity, and just as the preached external word still accurately reflects the kerygma, so the human spirit recognizes the truth of the thing in itself, the subject matter among its many varying designations (ibid., 442).

Gadamer makes it very clear that all his metaphysical and theological detours have the sole purpose of methodological devices. He repeats in *Truth and Method* his earlier statement: there is no divine intellect that beholds both the known and the knower; historical research may not be guided by theological principles. Gadamer, in short, endorses the Heideggerian exclusion of theology from hermeneutics. Finitude means

5. While Derrida criticizes this view of language, one wonders if he does not in some sense remain indebted to the Greek way of thinking by attributing violence to language and interpretation (Smith, *Fall of Interpretation*, 129).

philosophizing unsupported by revelation, a view Gadamer repeats in his autobiographical essay in 1996 ("Reflections," 31).[6] If we keep in mind Gadamer's dependency on theological models for his thought, however, such assertions seem rather doubtful. Given his own explanation for the connection between the mental word and the subject matter, Gadamer's resorting to theological language at key moments in the development of his thought is perhaps less descriptive than indicative of the genuine home of hermeneutics—the Christian Logos.

The Word Strikes Again: The Event Character of Interpretation

Gadamer's reliance on theology also becomes apparent in the applicatory dimension of his hermeneutics, in the notion of understanding. Gadamer affirms that all understanding should be self-understanding, "to which German Pietism referred as *subtilitas applicandi*" (Dutt, *Hans-Georg Gadamer im Gespräch*, 10). At the same time, however, Gadamer wants to avoid the Enlightenment's autonomous subject with its inevitable subjectivism. He does so by resorting, once again, to the vocabulary of theology: "The hermeneutic event," he says, "is possible only because the word, which has come to us in tradition and to which we must listen, really strikes us as if it spoke to us and addressed us ourselves" (*WM*, 462). Appropriation and interpretation are the same in this language event. The kind of knowledge gained through language is not objectivizing knowledge but, as in the case of the divine word, *participatory knowledge*. What is true is true according to its being; it exists in the presence of an eternal spirit, and only then is it possible for the finite human mind to recognize, to know it. Knowledge is thus participation in being known (*Zugehörigkeit*; ibid.). This participation characterizes the hermeneutic experience and allows Gadamer to articulate and solve what he calls "the hermeneutical problem" of intersubjective communication across historical and cultural boundaries.

The event character of an argument, a plan, a text is its self-evidence that there is something true about it that we discern even before we reflect on it critically (*WM*, 485). Thus understanding is the event or arrival of truth. For in understanding, Gadamer asserts, "we are drawn into an event of truth and arrive, as it were, too late, if we want to know what we were supposed to believe" (*TM*, 490). To show how close this

---

6. While the context of Gadamer's remark is his denial of a zero point of knowledge or absolute knowledge, his conclusion that human existence must remain "unsupported" by revelation surely includes God's self-revelation in the incarnation.

formulation comes to Augustine's view of understanding, listen to these words of Augustine (from *On the Teacher*) to his son-pupil Adeodatus: "But when we have to do with things which we behold with the mind, that is, with the intelligence and with reason, we speak of things which we look upon directly in the inner light of truth which illumines the inner man, and is inwardly enjoyed. . . . Even when I speak what is true and [the listener] sees what is true, it is not I who teach him. He is taught not by my words but by the things themselves which inwardly God has made manifest to him" (*Earlier Writings*, 96).

Augustine also teaches the importance of question and answer, which Gadamer also considers indispensable for the elucidation of a subject matter. Truth, for Augustine, is like an event that is conceived in its entirety but that we can see only with the mind by exploring it from various angles. Thus in Augustine, the Socratic method of question and answer works because God allows human reason to intuitively grasp truths without being fully able to articulate them: "The reason [for the listener's inability immediately to grasp the whole] lies in his own weakness. He is unable to let the light illumine the whole problem. Though he cannot behold the whole at once, yet when he is questioned about the parts which compose the whole, he is induced to bring them one by one into the light" (*Earlier Writings*, 97).

Logos Christology, in other words, can ground a hermeneutics of confidence in God's sustaining and active presence in creation. Logos Christology proposes that our minds and the world were designed by the same maker to be compatible. Language was designed to articulate this knowledge and to permit humans to communicate both with God and with one another. Gadamer articulates hermeneutical experience most clearly and strikingly when he borrows from this theological vocabulary. Perhaps this is the case because what Gadamer describes as the hermeneutical experience finds its proper grounding and home in a theological view of being and language. Gadamer thankfully accepts the theological reinterpretation of the Greek metaphysics of light and harvests its insight for the hermeneutical experience, in which "the light that causes everything to emerge in such a way that it is evident and comprehensible is the light of the word" (*TM*, 483; see also *WM*, 489).

Gadamer admits that this Logos doctrine has guided his entire hermeneutical inquiry.[7] Gadamer, in fact, discerns in Augustine's interpretation of Genesis a basic element of hermeneutical experience, "according to

7. "I myself depend on Augustine's appropriation of the Stoic's teaching of the inner logos . . . for in this Christian message any doubling of the world (mimesis) is avoided. The inner speech is not the pattern for the external speech but the whole is a process of unique, mysterious structure. One should not call it Platonism" (*GW*, 8:418).

which the multiplicity of what is thought proceeds only from the unity of the word." Moreover, theology also yields the event character of the word. These insights are then formulated as the two basic pillars of hermeneutic experience: first, "that both the appearance of the beautiful and the mode of being of understanding have the character of an event," and, second, that "the hermeneutical experience, as the experience of traditionary meaning, has a share in the immediacy which has always distinguished the experience of the beautiful, as that of all evidence of *truth*" (*TM*, 485; emphasis in original).

Logos and Tradition

Without its theological context, Gadamer's appropriation of Logos theology becomes problematic as the unresolved debate between Habermas and Gadamer on the issue of tradition makes clear. According to Gadamer, it is Habermas's inability to recognize Gadamer's definition of tradition as socially and historically embodied reason that leads to their misunderstanding: "Habermas, in my opinion, . . . unjustly restricts my conception of tradition to the 'cultural tradition'" (*TM*, 485). Yet the debate is not solved by Gadamer's clarification that tradition does not mean culture or historical period. In his most recent remarks on this issue, he writes: "For we live in what has been handed down to us, and this is not just a specific region of our experience of the world, specifically what we call the 'cultural tradition' which only consists of texts and monuments and which are able to pass on to us a linguistically constituted and historically documented sense. No, it is *the world itself* which is communicatively experienced and continuously entrusted (*traditur*) to us as an infinitely open task" ("Reflections," 29; emphasis in original). The issue becomes much clearer once we realize that Gadamer uses "tradition" almost synonymously with "human reason," which reveals and recognizes through language—albeit conditioned by a cultural horizon—truths concerning our world. That tradition translates basically as human reason also explains Gadamer's optimism regarding Habermas's concern that the closed hermeneutical circle does not allow one to import criticism from outside this circle and thus break free from ideological or technological entrapment.

Gadamer's replies to this complaint converge with his increasing interest in practical philosophy. He draws chiefly on Aristotle and Plato to construct his idea of ethics. Richard Bernstein nicely summarizes Gadamer's implicit trust in human reason: "When Gadamer appeals to the concept of truth to justify what he has to say about the relevance of Aristotle, phronesis, and the tradition of practical philosophy to our hermeneutical situation, he is implicitly appealing to a concept of truth which (pragmatically speaking) comes down to what can be argumentatively validated by a community of interpreters who open themselves to tradition" (*Philosophical Profiles*, 68). In other words, truth is recognized in dialogue, as the beautiful is recognized by the beholder when it appears. This, however, is only possible because for Gadamer, "even relativism which seems to reside in the multiplicity of human languages is no barrier for reason, whose 'word' [or logos] all have in common" ("Reflections," 29). In light of Gadamer's appeal to human reason as the guide to truth, Habermas's concern is not addressed by merely shifting from the level of tradition to that of universal human reason. Gadamer still cannot tell us how we are able to deduce from conflicting traditions the guiding principles for practical decisions. Whose reason are we appealing to?

As we have seen, Gadamer derives essential elements of his argument from theological rather than philosophical notions. He is very clear in his insistence that hermeneutical experience can be explained by borrowing from the Logos concept while rejecting its theological foundation (*TM*, 484). This insistence brings us back to his earlier warning against returning to theological metaphysics or its secularized cousins: Gadamer detaches the theological foundation to argue that Logos Christology best explains our linguisticality, yet he has arrived at the fact that things are so on the basis of theological formulation of the Logos.

In short, has not Gadamer's own historically effective consciousness led him to define hermeneutical experience in an Augustinian way? Is that perhaps why he simply cannot understand how deconstruction has a different way of looking at texts, a different hermeneutical experience, a different faith ("Reply to Jacques Derrida", 55–57)? When Gadamer and Derrida met for the now infamous 1981 conference at the Goethe Institute in Paris, Gadamer failed to see the validity of Derrida's comment that insistence on the goodwill to interpretation requires an ethics. For Gadamer, our ability to communicate and basic human solidarity require a listening ear; this has nothing to do with ethics, but "a good deal to do with the difference between dialectic and sophistics" (ibid., 55).

In defending himself against the "sophist" Derrida, Gadamer does, in fact, use his theological conceptualization of the hermeneutic experience to reject the accusation that philosophical hermeneutics falls prey to the Platonic philosophy of presence, which characterizes all Western thought. Gadamer insists that Derrida ignores Gadamer's own critique of Greek philosophy and the crucial role of the theological Logos concept in this critique (*Phenomenology of Ritual and Language*, in *GW*, 8:419).[8]

---

8. "My own attempts represent a continuation of Heidegger's thought, insofar as they seek a way from our linguisticality to leave Greek metaphysics behind" (*GW* 8:419).

Gadamer, of course, may mine Christian Logos theology for the construction of his hermeneutics without any obligation to its larger theological context, which revises Plato's abstract correspondence theory of truth by positing the mystery of the Trinity at the heart of knowledge, community, truth, and ethics. As I have pointed out, however, when Gadamer moves from description to prescription, that is, when he makes his hermeneutics a universally applicable principle and a practical philosophy, problems stemming from a decontextualized adoption of Logos Christology appear, and context can no longer be ignored. It matters a great deal how things are when it comes to knowledge and to trusting language and, finally and most importantly, to ethics. To use Gadamer's own terms, it matters greatly what kind of natural environment (*Umwelt*) forms the basis of our language world (*Welt*; *Sprachwelt*).

If, contrary to Augustine's assumption, the world is not created and sustained by God, then naturalism is the unpleasant alternative. Such, for example, is the presupposition of Richard Rorty's neopragmatism,[9] according to which truth is nothing but convention and language merely a tool in the game of survival. For Gadamer, by contrast, the word normally can be trusted to reveal true aspects of human existence. A naturalistic conception of the world, however, does not warrant such an optimistic view. It is subject to what has become known as "Darwin's doubt," that is, Charles Darwin's unease concerning the evolution-based mind's ability to generate reliable data. Thus much of what Gadamer presupposes depends on crucial anthropological assumptions that need to be clarified.

Gadamer, in short, interprets by faith. Jean Grondin, one of the best interpreters of Gadamer, reluctantly comes to the same conclusion. In his *Introduction to Philosophical Hermeneutics*, Grondin mentions Gadamer's debt to the Augustinian Logos concept.[10] Grondin explains that philosophical hermeneutics' claim to universality is derived from Augustine's concept of the inner word. Grondin wants to make "emphatically clear," however, that the inner word is no "private or psychological inner world existing prior to its verbal expression. Rather, it is that which strives to be externalised in spoken language. . . . There is no preverbal

9. "Pragmatism starts out from Darwinian naturalism—from a picture of human beings as chance products of evolution. This starting-point leads pragmatists to be as suspicious of the great binary oppositions of Western metaphysics as are Heidegger and Derrida" (Rorty, "Remarks on Deconstruction," 16).

10. Jean Grondin in his essay "Gadamer and Augustine" acknowledges the debt that both Heidegger and Gadamer owe to Christian thought for the insight that behind every spoken word lies an inner word: "This essential insight was found by Heidegger and Gadamer in Augustine's *De trinitate*, a text highly valued by both" (*Sources*, 140).

world, only world oriented to language, the world which is always to be put in words, though never entirely successfully" (*IPH*, xv).

While this warning restricts universality to the immanent or even technical level of understanding (in contrast to Heidegger's more mystical totality of being, which makes itself known through language), a few pages later Grondin, employing the thought of Paul Ricoeur, likens philosophical hermeneutics to "critically informed faith" that "concerns itself with truth claims that disclose the possibility of meaning—and thus with the *verbum interius* behind every explicit meaning." Grondin concludes that "this faith in meaning, without which language would remain empty of significance, can lay claim to universality" (*IPH*, 15).

Philosophical hermeneutics, then, confesses faith in language and meaning. Unless one is satisfied with fideism, with faith in faith, Gadamer's faith, as I have tried to show, is plausible only in a theological context that can account for this trust in our meaning-making abilities. For Augustine faith in meaning is not blind but grounded in the incarnate Word of God. Augustine does not believe in a preverbal word either; for him, in a much more concrete and yet at the same time more profoundly mystical sense, reality is defined by the divine incarnate Logos.

Gadamer's faith in human reason becomes progressively more apparent and problematic when he appeals to language and hermeneutic understanding as facilitators of moral progress. In his afterword to the third edition of *Truth and Method*, Gadamer describes tradition as being "not the vindication of what has come down from the past but the further creation of moral and social life; it depends on being made conscious and freely carried on." Gadamer rejects an ideal of eventual total enlightenment toward which we progress, yet he seems to affirm a process of emancipation through hermeneutical understanding (*TM*, 570). In the absence of a universal ethical norm, Gadamer's practical philosophy assumes a general human solidarity, although he realizes that we are far from a common human consciousness (*GW*, 4:225). He suggests that global economic or environmental disasters could foster the solidarity necessary for binding truths and moral action (ibid., 4:227).

Again one may ask: according to what anthropological theory should a crisis bring out the best in people? The records dug up for the filming of *Titanic* have certainly shown, as have recent events in Kosovo, Rwanda, and many other countries, that crisis situations testify to human depravity rather than to human goodness. Thus, as John Milbank has argued, if only in a footnote, the overall benign nature of Gadamer's dialectic of understanding is without basis. From a theological perspective, however, the Gadamerian correspondence between word and meaning makes sense, language may be viewed as reliable because it is so designed, and moral progress remains at least possible despite a fallen human nature because "the Christian hermeneutic circle is benign via the incarnation and the cross" (Milbank, *Word Made Strange*, 120).

Premodern hermeneutics, by contrast, was able to ground the trustworthiness of language in the idea of *imago Dei*. Human beings are created in the communicative image of God. At the same time, the fallen, sinful nature of humanity explains the elements of provisionality, deception, and egocentricity that pose an obstacle to perfect knowledge and moral progress. Especially in the realm of ethics, theological anthropology and its discourse of conversion to a new humanity provide a dimension missing from Gadamer's practical philosophy.

The Way Forward: Learning from Gadamer

We can learn much from Gadamer. His philosophical hermeneutics presents the best possible starting point for a recovery of theological hermeneutics. As I have tried to show, theologians in the Reformation tradition spend much of their effort in delineating theories of interpretation in light of their intellectual culture, and thinking Christians must do the same today. Theologically informed theories of interpretation must get beyond the objectivist-subjectivist divide, which still informs theological debates on interpretation, and move toward a sense of truth as embodied. Gadamer's philosophical hermeneutics takes us a good part of the way in the right direction. The following paragraphs outline what I believe to be the incontestable benefits of Gadamer's insight that to know is to interpret.

First, Gadamer reminds us of our human finitude. It is certainly ironic that theological hermeneutics should require this reminder since Gadamer's position is nothing less than a return to the classic Christian epistemological creed "faith seeking understanding." Contrary to idealist and Christian fundamentalist dreams of a pure, ahistorical consciousness, which is often equated with "the self," philosophical hermeneutics reminds us of our humanity, our embeddedness in history and culture.

Theological hermeneutics should embrace this insight even if it is principally derived from Heidegger's concept of "thrownness," which is rather cold and inhuman and yet is essentially correct: we are born into language, customs, and a heritage of ideas that we did not choose. This concept certainly gains a much more benign aspect when stated within a Christian interpretive framework, in which thrownness is rather a careful placement by a good creator God. Whether one states this theologically or atheistically, however, the result for interpretation theory is the same: we are historical beings with a finite interpretive horizon shaped by fears, interests, and desires that are human in the sense of being both common to humanity across all ages *and* specific to our current cultural climate. To return to the traditional theological view of knowledge as divided into the book of nature and the book of revelation, whichever book we read, we read motivated by a certain interest. Neutral, uninterested knowledge does not exist.

Second, we should follow Gadamer in rejecting the modernist division of subjective opinion versus hard scientific fact. Even the indubitable individual facts of science make sense only within a larger story or framework that is narrated from a certain perspective. It is here that Gadamer joins hands with Michael Polanyi's efforts to convince scientists of the large degree to which tacit knowledge plays a role in supposed value-neutral findings. Polanyi shows that

> the processes of knowing (and also of science) in no way resemble an impersonal achievement of detached objectivity. They are rooted through-out (from our selection of a problem to the verification of a discovery) in personal acts of tacit integration. They are not grounded on explicit operations of logic. Scientific inquiry is accordingly a dynamic exercise of the imagination and is rooted in commitments and beliefs in the nature of things. It is a fiduciary act. . . . Its method is not that of *detachment* but rather that of *involvement*. (*Meaning*, 63; emphasis in original)

Polanyi's crucial insight is that knowledge exists only within frameworks of meaning and that integration of experience into these horizons of signifi-cance requires imagination. Polanyi realizes that this integrative work is linked to poesis, to the creative act of integrating all subsidiary impressions into a coherent whole. Thus "works of science, engineering, and the arts are *all* achieved by the imagination" (ibid., 85). To phrase it in the language of interpretation theory, knowledge is indeed interpretation. This means that framing the debate concerning valid knowledge as a scientific fact versus imaginative insight merely obscures the real issue, namely, the focus on the integrative frameworks we employ for meaning-making.[11]

For Gadamer and Polanyi, knowledge cannot be divided into the fac-tual truth of science and the subjective truth of the humanities. Nor can we define rationality along those lines. The view that meanings achieved in the humanities are simply works of the imagination (even if brilliant

11. This focus allows Polanyi to avoid the demonizing of technology and blame a scientistic worldview instead: "It was not technology that produced the totalitarian ide-ologies which brought the disasters of the twentieth century into being, along with the feeling of absurdity and the contempt for human society that are current today. We may thank the scientific image of the world, as reflected in the modern mind, for these" (*Meaning*, 105).

ones) and that only the meanings achievable in science express reality is tenable only if one allows the possibility of neutral, uninvolved knowledge of pure detachment and objectivity. Such knowledge, however, is not available to human beings. As Polanyi tells us, we achieve meaning by integrating individual perceptions into a meaningful whole, that is, by interpreting them. And interpretation is the work of the imagination in science every bit as much as it is in poetry.[12] For this reason, Polanyi concludes, "we must judge the quality of a 'scientific' world view by the richness of its imaginative integrations, just as artists judge the quality of their own productions in art" (*Meaning*, 107).

Third, we can learn from Gadamer to redefine human rationality as participating in transcendence. Like Polanyi, Gadamer insists that meaning-making is part of our humanity. Drawing on Greek thought as mediated by the German philosopher G. W. F. Hegel, Gadamer holds that any division of rationality into scientific fact and mere subjective contemplation is wrong. Instead both science and philosophy serve reason. Gadamer insists that we must get over German idealism's equation of reason with the internal possession of an isolated self and recover the Greek notion of rationality as the very structure of being in which we share. Reason, in other words, is not human self-consciousness opposed to an irrational universe but our participation in the very structure of the universe, its Logos.

His participatory view of reason allows Gadamer to retrieve and claim for hermeneutics the Greek notion of *theoria*. Theory in this sense is not distanced, detached contemplation but participatory reflection. The Greek term *theoria*, Gadamer tells us, originally meant participation in the delegation sent to a festival for the sake of honoring the gods. Thus theory cannot mean unbiased and distanced contemplation. Instead the distance proper to *theoria* "is that of proximity and affinity." *Theoria* meant not to watch from afar but "is a genuine sharing in an event, a real being present" (*Reason in the Age of Science*, 18). Thus reflection as participation in the rationality of being offers "another way in which a human heightening of awareness penetrates and discovers itself—not the way inward to which Augustine appealed but the way of complete self donation to what is outside in which the seeker nevertheless finds himself. To have seen and retained this notion of Greek rationality is Hegel's great contribution to philosophy" (ibid.). With Hegel, Gadamer

12. Polanyi distinguishes between the insights of the humanities and those of the sciences, however, in this way: Using products of scientific imagination takes very little imagination. It doesn't require much imagination to fly a plane or use a telephone. To understand a piece of art or a poem, however, requires much more imagination and active re-creation (*Meaning*, 85).

posits what he calls "the exigence of reason, which presses us to keep on bringing about the unity of our knowledge" (ibid.). The task of self-understanding is ever before us. Under this umbrella, all disciplines labor, the sciences, the arts, and philosophy.

His belief in the universality of reason allows Gadamer to retain the humanist desire for self-knowledge and yet affirm the radical historicity of human knowing. Contrary to Hegel and idealism, however, Gadamer holds to the embodiment of reason in language, and this is the second major aspect of his thought that theological hermeneutics ought to take on board. For Gadamer, the rationality of being manifests itself in the character of language; hence his famous statement, "being that can be expressed is language." For if human reflection participates in the rationality of being, it does so through language. That is why Gadamer insists, as we have seen, that the infinite mediation of soul and being is accomplished by language.

While adherents of the Nietzschean strand of postmodern philosophy may be dismayed by an assertion of being's rationality, theological hermeneutics should recognize here the same dynamics as presented by John's Gospel, in which the Greek notion of the Logos is appropriated for Jewish-Christian theology and the rationality of being is identified with the incarnation. The only difference is that Gadamer rejects the medieval grounding of word-thing relation in the mind of God, but he does so not because of a militant atheism but because he desires to avoid an instrumental view of language. Gadamer's view is not incompatible with a theological view of language, if such a theological view is incarnational and if it is not still ridden by Cartesian anxiety, the obsessive need to bridge the Kantian gap between the reality and the thing itself.

Fourth, theology must fully adopt Gadamer's insistence on the linguisticality of interpretation. If theology must believe in some form of universal reason, which I believe it does if it wants to be faithful to biblical Christology, the second important element theological hermeneutics must incorporate is a noninstrumental view of language along the lines of Gadamer's language philosophy.[13] Gadamer's view of language follows logically from his view of reason. We remember that while Gadamer holds to the universality of reason, he also believes in its historical embodiment in language.

Gadamer "translates" Heidegger's thrownness into the hermeneutical experience of understanding. We encounter reality and learn about ourselves only in and through language. We are thrown into a culture and its

13. Gadamer explains his view of language most fully in the essays "Mensch und Sprache" (1966), "Sprache und Verstehen" (1970), and "Wieweit schreibt Sprache das Denken vor" (1970).

linguistic tradition, and only in language does understanding take place. The linguisticality of human understanding is, in fact, the basis for the universality of hermeneutics as the only human way to experience the world: "Understanding is inseparably tied to language [*sprachgebunden*]; that is how one should understand the universal claim of the hermeneutical dimension" (*GW*, 2:231). Because human understanding moves within a culturally and historically shaped linguistic medium, issues, concepts, and ideas present themselves to us on the ground of a certain familiarity. Thus hermeneutic experience (and this includes our reading of written texts as much as the text of nature) begins with the familiar rather than the unfamiliar: "It is always an already interpreted and in its relations ordered world into which experience breaks as something new that topples whatever had guided our former expectations, which, even in doing so, becomes part of our experience" (ibid., 2:230).

Theological Concerns about Gadamer's Philosophical Hermeneutics

Even this brief description of the hermeneutical experience makes clear that Gadamer's "hermeneutical consciousness" differs markedly from the Cartesian and idealist notion of consciousness as isolated and ahistorical. The dialectic move from the familiar in its encounter of the strange with its consequent incorporation of the new into a broadened horizon of understanding combines Gadamer's well-known notions of the hermeneutical circle and the fusion of horizons. Despite many criticisms of the universal claim of Gadamer's hermeneutics, I believe that the articulation of a viable theological hermeneutics requires essential agreement with Gadamer's position.

Two main criticisms have been raised against Gadamer's position, and both have important implications for theological hermeneutics. The first issue is, again, that the linguisticality of our understanding leads to relativism. The second, and more justified, criticism is that the fusion of horizons denies radical transcendence and entails the assimilation of another view or position into one's own and so annihilates difference. How serious are these challenges? If they are justified, does not hermeneutics pose a threat to the recovery of theological hermeneutics?

To say that our consciousness is linguistically structured and to claim that our linguistically shaped preunderstanding of the world is the necessary starting point of understanding merely acknowledges the incarnation of the human mind in historical reality. To say that we live in language, however, is not the same as to say that we are imprisoned by language. This would be true only for an instrumental view of language in which language is reduced to a system of signals we employ mechanically at will. Gadamer, on the contrary, emphasizes the creative power of language by which we build on and transcend our inherited language and concepts. Human experience teaches us that "although one lives entirely within a language this is no relativism because an imprisonment in one's language is not possible—not even within one's own mother tongue." Instead both our own language and human linguisticality in general allow an infinite expansion of the human conversation and concept formation. Thus, contrary to historicism and cultural relativism, Gadamer insists that the differences in languages in all their historical particularity are witness to the universality of reason (*GW*, 2:230).

If the fear of relativism is unfounded, does Gadamer's philosophical hermeneutics pose a threat to transcendence? Gadamer's protestations notwithstanding, there are those who agree with his linguistical and interpretive view of human knowledge and yet fear the latent assimilative element in his hermeneutic philosophy. This is not only the main line of attack of Levinasian philosophy in all its manifestations but also a matter of concern to Christian theologians who want to preserve God's otherness and who fear that hermeneutics can recognize only the familiar.

Lesslie Newbigin, for example, acknowledges the dynamics of the hermeneutic circle for all human knowledge but doubts that its emphasis on familiarity provides an adequate model to describe what is involved in the encounter between scripture and our culture (*Foolishness to the Greeks*, 51).

Newbigin believes that the biblical emphasis on the radical discontinuity between all human wisdom and the revelation of scripture together with the New Testament emphasis on the veiled or even repulsive nature of its teaching to the heart untouched by God implies "a relationship between pre-understanding and understanding that is (to put it no more strongly) not adequately represented by the model of the hermeneutical circle. It implies a profound discontinuity—not just a circle but a chasm" (*Foolishness to the Greeks*, 52). In other words, while Gadamer's hermeneutic circle is operative in Christian and non-Christian communities, it cannot account for the radical change in outlook demanded by the Bible itself, a change described most vividly in the resurrection metaphor of Paul.

Unfortunately, this criticism cannot be refuted conclusively from Gadamer's work because Gadamer's relation to theology remains ambiguous. Gadamer follows Heidegger in rejecting dogmatic theology as a positive science. Especially in his later years, when he thinks more seriously about the role of the great world religions in solving current global crises, Gadamer tends to dismiss dogmatism altogether, but he also favors the view that all religions are in search of transcendence; this transcendence, whatever we may want to call it, resists dogmatic formulations and thus presents the limits of human knowledge. According to the later Gadamer, it is the task of humanity to rally around this insight in order to acknowledge religion as a fundamental factor in self-understanding and yet resist the notion that there is one correct religion.

In addition, while we find in Gadamer's work the affirmation of Christianity's uniqueness, he never resolves the question whether philosophical hermeneutics encompasses theology or whether theology is based on a revelatory phenomenon that lies in some sense outside the province of hermeneutic philosophy. Gadamer clearly asserts the truth claim of Christian theology against Greek mythology, for example. While Greek stories such as the one in which Zeus suspends disobedient gods from Olympus by chains until they obey his will are entertaining, they "do not possess the value of facts nor, unlike Christian theology, do they have the value of truth" (*GW*, 10:213). And one of the truth claims of the Christian revelation is, after all, that of universality. As we have seen in the previous chapters, the tradition of the Reformation unanimously followed Paul in believing that this claim is incompatible with the idea that mere human understanding can even begin to understand the meaning of the incarnation, because such understanding is a divine gift.

We cannot, however, lightly dismiss Newbigin's concern about God's otherness but must carefully consider how Gadamer's hermeneutics can help in recovering a theological hermeneutics. Philosophical hermeneutics is by far the best account of human knowledge, and the discipline of theology is, after all, the human examination of divine revelation. Some argue that philosophical hermeneutics is in fact a return to the only possible Christian paradigm of knowledge as faith seeking understanding and to the essential insight that all understanding is also self-understanding. Philosophical hermeneutics, with its critique of uninvolved, detached knowledge, is the best starting point to construe what Fred Lawrence (following Rowan Williams) has aptly termed an "integral Christian hermeneutics." Integral Christian hermeneutics learns from Gadamer's hermeneutic philosophy that "even independently of divine revelation and grace, the human quest for meaning is shaped as 'faith seeking understanding.' In making manifest the ever mysterious nature of human self-understanding in time, Gadamer opens up philosophy to theology, and challenges theology to be philosophical" (Lawrence, "Gadamer, the Hermeneutic Revolution, and Theology," 193). To put it another way, hermeneutic philosophy reminds Christian theology that understanding is incarnational: it cannot be separated from its human dimensions of being in time, of historical conditionedness and human error.

On the other hand, while Lawrence is correct in believing that hermeneutics promises to open philosophy to theology, philosophical hermeneutics by its very nature cannot provide the radical transcendence theology requires if it is to preserve God's otherness in his address to humanity. Philosophical hermeneutics operates in the sphere of the Greek rather than the divine Logos and fails to acknowledge the second half of the hermeneutical circle that Augustine bequeathed to the Christian tradition, namely, that there is no knowledge of self without *knowledge of God*. The tension between knowledge of self and knowledge of God forms the focus of the next chapter. I have chosen this focus because it best describes the current debate in interpretation theory between so-called radical hermeneutics and philosophical hermeneutics. It is no coincidence that this central issue hearkens back to the hermeneutical circle of the Reformation tradition, for both are linked by the heritage of humanism.

The Reformers, too, were humanists in the sense that they recognized two things. First, because Christian revelation is passed down in writing, theology requires philology, love of the text. In their understanding of the incarnational nature of revelation, God discloses himself never "purely" but incarnationally, so that the scripture follows the very principles of the incarnation in its human and divine elements. The text is both human and divine. Neither is the text a mere shell with hidden meanings behind the text itself, nor should it be treated as divine. Careful grammatical-historical exegesis is inseparable from the God-given truths it contains. Both theology and philosophical hermeneutics seek self-knowledge through texts and recognize the value of tradition, particularly textual tradition. I have tried to show that Gadamer, much like Heidegger, is indebted to theology for key principles of his work, and yet theology is greatly indebted to philosophical hermeneutics for its careful philosophical discussion of how "faith seeking understanding" is the universal structure of human knowing. Gadamer's hermeneutics is a hopeful humanism that espouses a careful but optimistic account of self-knowledge.

Second, unlike Gadamer's humanism, the theological humanism of the Reformation was consciously ethical, based on the divine transcendence human understanding encounters in the incarnation. For two decades, this lack of transcendence and its implication for ethics has become the central focus of criticism against Gadamer's philosophical hermeneutics. The work of Emmanuel Levinas is at the center of this debate, and in the following chapters, we will examine his thought and the deconstructive criticism to which his ethical impulse has provided the central idea of radical transcendence. Levinas is important for the recovery of theological hermeneutics because his work challenges philosophical hermeneutics' claim to universality and makes it possible to imagine a hermeneutics that depends not on the impersonal Logos of being but on the Word made flesh.

6

THE ETHICAL HERMENEUTICS
OF EMMANUEL LEVINAS

We are used to a philosophy where the confirmation of self is the principle of subjectivity and where spirit is equivalent to knowing, that is to say, to the gaze which takes in things, to the hand which takes and possesses them, to the domination of beings. I think, on the contrary, that in man this ontology is interrupted or can be interrupted. Within the vision I am developing, human emotion and its spirituality begin in the for-the-other, in being affected by the other. The great event and the very source of its affectivity is in the other!

—Emmanuel Levinas, *Is It Righteous to Be?*

This chapter is intended as an introduction to the thought of the Jewish philosopher Emmanuel Levinas (1916–95), whose insistence that ethics is the foundation and goal of human thought is an important element in our recovery of theological hermeneutics. Levinas is of crucial importance to our project because of his uncompromising demand for radical ethical transcendence. A theologically sensitive reader may well ask, why choose Levinas and not Karl Barth? Does not Barth in his uncompromising return to Reformation theology also preach radical transcendence? Moreover, does not his Christian conviction make him a better choice for recovering theological hermeneutics?

Levinas, however, offers two important aspects that make him indispensable for our particular project. First, I have insisted throughout this book that the recovery of theological hermeneutics necessitates the dialogue between philosophy and theology. Levinas understands this need better than Barth, and he also interacts consistently with the philosophical thinkers who have shaped hermeneutical development, Husserl and Heidegger in particular. At the same time, Levinas is a profoundly Jewish and religious thinker who bridges the concerns of theology and philosophy.

Another, perhaps even more important reason, however, is that Levinas is an ethical thinker par excellence. The very heart of his philosophy is ethics. Like Karl Barth, Levinas proclaims transcendence and radical difference, but unlike Barth, he seeks this transcendence not in God but in the human other. This is decisive because locating transcendence within humanity actually places Levinas in greater proximity to the incarnational theology of Dietrich Bonhoeffer (with whom we will conclude our recovery of theological hermeneutics) than to the lofty starting point of Barth's theology. As is well known, Barth shifted his position to a more incarnational theology only late in his career.[1]

Yet while Levinas shares with Bonhoeffer a focus on human existence and hence on ontology, unlike Bonhoeffer, his work offers a sustained critique of exactly those ontological beliefs that drive the philosophical hermeneutics of Heidegger and Gadamer. In fact, Heidegger serves Levinas as the main target of what he sees as the general malaise of modern philosophy, namely, the pursuit of truth and the development of ontology based on a free and autonomous self. Contrary to its purpose, philosophy has become "tantamount to the conquest of being by man over the course of history." By reducing to understanding cognition all that is other, philosophy marches toward the total heteronomy of understanding; the pursuit of knowledge is thus identical with complete immanence.

For Levinas, challenging the Western ontology of sameness is not an empty academic notion but a task demanded by history itself. Whenever our irreducible humanity is placed in the service of some greater, anonymous totality, we invite human tragedy. Levinas believes the best example of this is Martin Heidegger's involvement with National Socialism. Levinas believes that "Heideggerian ontology subordinates the relation with the other to the relation with Neuter, Being, and it thus continues to exalt the will to power." For all his criticism of modernity

---

1. In his last writings, Karl Barth took a position similar to Bonhoeffer's. Somewhat repentant of his earlier ahistorical emphasis on transcendence, Barth writes that "we do not need to engage in a free-ranging investigation to seek out and construct who and what God truly is, and who and what man truly is, but only to read the truth about both where it resides, namely, in the fullness of their togetherness, their covenant which proclaims itself in Jesus Christ" (*The Humanity of God*, 47).

and technological thinking, Heidegger's ontology "maintains a regime of power more inhuman than mechanism." Levinas identifies this power as the pagan notion of being, an anonymous neuter that is "ethically indifferent, as a heroic freedom, foreign to all guilt with regard to the Other" ("Philosophy and the Idea of the Infinite," 103–4).

For the Jewish philosopher Levinas, Heidegger's philosophy is intrinsically pagan and inhuman; the value of Levinas's critique of hermeneutics lies in its constant reminder that philosophy, including hermeneutic philosophy, is never ethically neutral. For Levinas, Heidegger's philosophy and his involvement with fascism are the culmination of Western philosophy's customary blindness to this fact: "Heidegger not only sums up the whole evolution of Western philosophy. He exalts it by showing in the most dramatic way its anti-religious essence become a religion in reverse. . . . In Heidegger atheism is paganism, the pre-Socratic text anti-Scriptures. Heidegger shows in what intoxication the lucid sobriety of philosophers is steeped" ("Philosophy and the Idea of the Infinite," 104).

This short introduction should make Levinas's significance for hermeneutics and ethics clear. For one, Levinas's elevation of ethical transcendence to the shibboleth of human thought is arguably the single most important impetus behind philosophy's current obsession with otherness. Moreover, the theological inspiration of Levinas establishes common ground for a dialogue between theology and philosophy. Ethics becomes the common concern of both.

By ethics, however, Levinas does not mean moral rules and guidelines but a metaethics of absolute transcendence. This transcendence is not an abstract ideal or a concept but arises from the real and immediate encounter with our fellow human beings, the "skin-to-skin" proximity in which all one's immediate self-affirming ambitions, whether intellectual or physical, are checked by the moral demand to put the other first. Ethics is thus first philosophy, the ground and goal of all philosophical investigation. If one agrees with Levinas that ethical transcendence comes before all else, then hermeneutics must also serve ethics. In other words, Levinas preaches to hermeneutics the need for ethics. It is, however, a dangerous sermon, for its message threatens the very existence of philosophical hermeneutics. After all, if ethics is first philosophy, then ethics is also prior to hermeneutical philosophy; and since hermeneutics lays a claim to universality, ethics and hermeneutics are from the outset in competition for universal validity. The title of this chapter may indeed appear self-contradictory to the reader familiar with Levinas's thought: can we even talk about a Levinasian hermeneutics when he criticizes hermeneutics as another totalizing system?

Yet just as Gadamer's hermeneutics finds its ultimate fulfillment in theological hermeneutics, Levinas's relentless insistence on ethical transcendence as the ground of human thought has its proper home in the provenance of theology. Incarnational theology alone offers what Levinas desires: an ethical (i.e., personal) transcendence that does not compromise otherness in providing common ground for human knowledge and self-understanding.

The Heart of Levinas: Totalities Are Inhuman

Levinas's philosophy is deeply influenced by the Holocaust because this event embodies the singular failure of human conscience to uphold the absolute dignity of every human being. As long as ethics depends on human consciousness, the very structure of human thought will always find a way to rationalize and hence destroy the supremacy of human dignity—Auschwitz may again become possible. For Levinas this possibility exists as long as we seek the meaning of existence and the meaning of humanness against a greater totality. Thus the central thematic of Levinas is to shelter the unique identity of every human being against any possible totalities, to affirm the uniqueness of our humanity. Levinas's philosophy is thus fundamentally a humanism, or as he would put it, a "humanism of the other human being."

When Levinas diagnoses the fundamental problem of Western thought as loss of humanness, he targets our inability to conceive of thought and knowledge other than within closed, totalizing ways. In line with other critics of Western culture (Nietzsche, Heidegger, Derrida), Levinas believes that in the "Hellenic-Judeo-Christian tradition," thought and experience, our engaging and processing of reality, have always been based on the idea of totality. In hermeneutical jargon, we might say that we can only think in terms of parts and wholes. The integration of our sense experience into a meaningful whole requires such operation, but Levinas wants to resist the reduction of meaning to this dynamic because it signals the loss of transcendence (*AT*, 40). We have seen this problem in Schleiermacher, whose striving for a monistic common ground results in the reduction of difference to sameness. Meaning, in Schleiermacher's thought, is achieved by flattening transcendence to immanence. Levinas identifies this tendency to purchase meaning at the cost of transcendence as the root of evil in Western thought: to think and know means to think and know in terms of a totalizing whole outside of which reality makes no sense to us. His whole work aims to find a different, more human, more ethical way of thinking about meaning.

Levinas distinguishes between two main strands of totalization. One is the Cartesian, or rationalist, paradigm, which amounts to a totality without reality (*AT*, 44). The price exacted for the Cartesian retreat into the intuitions of reason as the absolutely certain starting point is that of an empty rational formalism without ontological traction. The inherent problem of rationalism is that it posits an absolute rational totality for the possibility of thought and then has trouble reconciling this rational construct with the empirical world. Levinas credits Kant with identifying the problems of such a rationalist starting point. Kant has shown that reason demands to know the final causes of conditioned facts. Yet reason finds these ultimate grounds in the ideas of the world and of God, ideas that go beyond the sensible and empirically verifiable. Thus these ideas express no real being, and when reason tries to give these ideas ontological significance, the result is irrational nonsense, contradictions (antinomies) of thought.

Levinas concludes that for Kant "in the ideas of totality, reason thus loses its cognitive value. Its pretension to know is illusory" (*AT*, 45). As long as we define reason as the ability to integrate all facts and ideas without contradiction, a gap separates knowledge and truth, because truth requires the ideal of totality that experience doesn't provide. Knowledge of empirical facts is thus neatly separated from comprehending reason. We have seen in the previous chapter how Schleiermacher solved this problem by means of an ontological monism, the interconnectedness of being, but this, too, resulted in a totality and the loss of transcendence.

In this Levinasian genealogy of totality, Hegel initiates the second strand of totalizing interpretation by reintroducing historicity into thinking. According to Levinas, Hegel succeeded in recovering a connection between being and reason by returning to the Greek Logos tradition. Hegel pulled idealism back into the realm of history and so recovered the Greek notion that rather than an abstract reservoir of universal reason apart from the real world, the totality of being is "the essence of being itself," so that any given image, concept, or idea offers only an abstract and partial aspect of the real (*AT*, 41). Yet Hegel does not go far enough. Even in this welcomed historical scheme, truth is only truth when it relates to the whole of being—another totality. For Hegel, as is well known, this totality was progressively revealed as reality's relentless progress toward the total self-consciousness of the world spirit. The relation of the whole and the part was ultimately resolved into a complete cosmos of progressive history. As Levinas puts it, Hegel's system "would leave nothing outside of itself. It would be freedom" (ibid.). At the end of Hegel's march toward enlightenment stood "total presence of being to itself or self-consciousness." For Levinas the end of history in Hegel is marked by "a lucid and free humanity, of which the nineteenth century believed itself to be the glorious dawn" (ibid.). Yet this supposed liberation of humanity toward civilization and freedom is for Levinas the death of originality and difference and therewith the death of the human.

For Levinas the call to ethics and the deconstruction of the deeply ingrained totalities in Western thought are not mere academic exercises but a full-blown humanism. Only with an ethical concept of the subject and of knowledge can we avoid the dehumanizing tendencies in our society. Levinas cites the intellectual development in the university, the fountainhead and guardian of knowledge, as a tragic example and a warning against the neglect of ethics as the foundation of knowledge. For example, with the disappearance of the self in structuralism and poststructuralism, knowledge itself has become meaningless. The current crisis of the human sciences in general and of philosophy in particular demonstrates the urgent need to uphold the absolute unique value of the ethical human relation as the measure of all things.

Levinas reminds us that the human sciences were founded on the concept of human dignity, essential for all human intellectual and social activity. His concern is that the death of the human subject that dominates philosophical discourse in the human sciences inevitably entails the death of human dignity and thus opens the gates for inhumane atrocities. Levinas doesn't miss the deep irony that research in the humanities has focused on the death of the human and found renewal and strength in a number of obituaries: the end of humanism and the end of metaphysics, the death of the human and the death of God (*HM*, 85).

Levinas distances himself from all dehumanizing modernist or postmodernist theories of selfhood that share the ill-conceived assumption that true selfhood coincides with consciousness and that true knowledge is perception rather than intuition. Western intellectual history makes it hard to resist Levinas's argument that our intellectual quest for an autonomous self as consciousness actually backfired because it has led to the dissolution of the self. While traditional modernist conceptions of subjectivity and knowledge aim to establish the human subject as an autonomous will that masters its environment, they culminate in the exact opposite with the postmodern critique of modernity: the dissolution of the self. According to Levinas, the root problem, addressed by neither modernity nor its radicalization, postmodernity, is the reduction of the human self to consciousness and the concomitant reduction of knowledge to cognition.

Levinas is convinced that only a different subjectivity, an ethical self, will allow us to devise a more human way of knowing. The mistaken identification of the self with consciousness is unethical because it is self-centered: it knows no mode of existence other than self-preservation. In this context, Levinas always refers to Spinoza's term of *conatus essendi,* because it exemplifies for him the inhuman quality of knowledge through totality.

Spinoza's pan-monism, reality as one god-substance, requires that each object share God's necessary attributes. Since self-preservation in his being is one of God's attributes, Spinoza believes that "each thing, in so far as it is in itself, endeavours to persist in its own being" and then relates this shared ontological characteristic to our ability to intuit the essence of things (*Ethics*, 3:6, as quoted in Garret, *Cambridge Companion to Spinoza*, 123). Spinoza's monism demonstrates most clearly what other totalitarian conceptions of the self and knowledge often merely assume: the acquisition of knowledge serves self-mastery and seeks to master all else in its wake. Modern research in the humanities, for Levinas, still reflects this idea of adding increasingly to a body of knowledge in the hope of reaching a sum total of complete clarity in the quest to eliminate any ambiguity.

We will deal with Levinas's view of hermeneutics more explicitly later, but his account of intellectual history allows us to anticipate that hermeneutics, for him, continues the Hegelian tradition of totality even though it is a more open-ended totality. He argues that even the Heideggerian and Gadamerian notion of the hermeneutical circle is modeled too much on the text as something that can be progressively understood, even if it resists final interpretation (*AT*, 49). While philosophical hermeneutics breaks with "Cartesian habits of understanding," it is still implicated in totalizing the human because here the part is still validated in light of a totality, however tenuous, rather than possessing independent validity. Levinas's critique of hermeneutics is thus motivated by his insistence on the intrinsic and independent dignity and value of each human being that is required for the humane. That is why Levinas wants to conceive the human subject and knowledge beyond totality, in a new relation of human being to human being that founds all other knowledge and politics: "Humanity, would not be, on this view, one domain among those of the real, but the modality in which rationality and its peace are articulated wholly otherwise than in the totality" (ibid., 51).

We can see how important the thought of Levinas is for recovering theological hermeneutics. His philosophy addresses the two central elements we have identified as necessary for interpretation: the knowledge of self and the knowledge of God. Philosophically this means that without transcendence self-knowledge is impossible. Levinas calls philosophy back to a radically *ethical* transcendence and puts our social relation at the center of meaning. Levinas calls hermeneutics back to what matters: a detailed description of the self and its dependence on ethical transcendence for self-knowledge. Yet as a post-Heideggerian thinker, he is also keenly aware that meaning occurs within language and history through communication. The following analysis of Levinas crystallizes his concern with crucial hermeneutical issues: subjectivity, knowledge, language, and aesthetics.

Levinas's Incarnational Subjectivity

Creation Is Good: The Ego in Enjoyment, or Levinas's Good Atheism

Levinas develops his alternative subjectivity through a phenomeno-logical analysis of its two constituent elements: the natural self and the ethical self. He argues that the interaction of human beings with nature and with one another yields two inseparable facets of human selfhood, the ego (natural self) and the I (ethical self). We need to pay close attention to Levinas's painstaking analysis to avoid the common misreading that the ethical imperative of the other threatens to eliminate the self. Levinas, on the contrary, establishes the necessity of an independent "atheistic" self at the biological level of existence. This "ego" is then limited by the ethical call of the other to establish the nobler, ethical "I."

In trying to distance selfhood from monistic constructs at the most basic biological level, Levinas introduces the central notion of separa-tion. In opposition to sheer naturalism, on the one hand, and to Heideg-gerian ontology of thrownness and self-preservation in a cold, hostile environment, on the other hand, Levinas's subject emerges as "egoism of enjoyment" (*TI*, 175). Human existence differs from animal existence through this most basic, noninstinctual level of reflection that is both biological and spiritual. We make a home for ourselves in this world first of all by enjoying its provisions. This "dwelling" is our primary mode of maintaining ourselves in enjoyment (ibid., 37). In this activity of finding our place in the world, we encounter objects not in rational reflection but as things that either aid or resist our endeavors to satisfy bodily needs of subsistence and spiritual needs of self-identity. We are, in effect, trying to identify our environment as useful to our consump-tion in enjoyment.

In this concrete egoism, we define ourselves in separation from the world. Levinas also calls this low-level mode of nonreflective conscious-ness "sensibility," an intuitive knowing that defines human existence (*Dasein*) prior to Heidegger's reflection on the meaning of being. Theo-logically, Levinas's account of enjoyment reflects the biblical notion of a good creation in contrast to Heidegger's hostile climate of thrownness. With the idea of primal enjoyment, Levinas also consciously distances himself from what he sees as Heidegger's mere utilitarian relation to objects as instruments (ready to hand or ready at hand) for our projects.

It is important to understand Levinas correctly at this point. Even at the level of our primary bodily needs, the ego is defined not in opposition to nature but as an independent entity that reduces the meaningless mass of our environment to meaningful objects for our subsistence. We thus turn meaningless flux and difference into sameness not for the sake of serving any totalizing scheme, such as conquering nature for a greater cause of empire, national glory, and honor, but rather for the sake of enjoying its material bounty. This starting point is crucial because it establishes the self neither in opposition to nature nor with reference to any greater totality that would encompass both nature and the self (*TI*, 38). Levinas argues that either starting point would jeopardize the basic metaphysical impulse he finds at the heart of human existence, our desire for a "relationship with the absolutely other" (ibid.).

To enable this relationship in separation, outside of any totality, either physical or metaphysical, Levinas establishes the ego as our "individuation through happiness," by which he hopes to rescue identity from its dependence on totalities such as Heidegger's being or National Socialist dreams of common racial identities, because here the independence of the ego always disappears in larger participatory structures by which it gains its identity. Levinas's main concern is to establish an autonomous self at the most basic ontological level. The ego of enjoyment is not a consciousness supported by enjoyment but consciousness *as* enjoyment, "a movement toward oneself" (*TI*, 118).

Levinas calls this autonomy of the self in enjoyment "atheism," a term that he uses in a positive sense. Atheism means the breach of totality, the establishment of a self in the solitude of enjoyment. In enjoyment the self is not subordinated to being, as in Heidegger, but exists on its own unique terms. Levinas states his opposition to Heidegger's ontology clearly: "The existent would then not be justiciable to the 'comprehension of being,' or ontology. One becomes a subject of being not by assuming being but in enjoying happiness, by the interiorization of enjoyment which is also an exaltation, an 'above being.' The existent is 'autonomous' with respect to being; it designates not a participation in being, but happiness. The existent par excellence is man" (*TI*, 119).

The atheistic ego of separation, however, is immediately qualified at the physical level by the transcendent phenomenon of ethics. Even while it is a thoroughly biological activity, enjoyment is already a form of reflection. This does not mean that enjoyment is reducible to reflective thought, as if we would give meaning to objects only on reflection. Rather enjoyment itself constitutes and directs reflection. Eating, for example, is not reducible to the concepts of taste, muscle movement of jaw and tongue, and other sensations that would constitute the "consciousness of eating" (*TI*, 129). We cannot, in other words, reduce our biological relation to the world in terms of either naturalism (reality is nothing but biochemical events) or reflection (things only have meaning in thoughtful reflection). Rather we encounter transcendence within immanence. Already at the physical level, our egoism is limited by the transcendence of the other, an imposition of another ego whose needs limit one's immediate enjoyment. Ethics, for Levinas, thus begins at the most primordial, skin-to-skin relation, in which tearing the very food I enjoy from my mouth and giving it to the other is the appropriate definition of ethics and the most human response to the other.

Levinas thus envisions a self that consists of two parts: the "ego" in enjoyment and the "I" effected by the ethical call. These two constitutive parts of the self, the autonomous ego and the ethical "I," are not related dialectically. Any dialectic would compromise radical transcendence by making the self intelligible only within a greater framework. Separation thus becomes a key element in Levinasian subjectivity. Only an independent self in enjoyment whose existence does not depend on the other ensures separation. Yet this ego cannot be hermetically sealed to the ethical call from the other, even in its total separation. How is this possible? The solution is that the idea of infinity is found at the very heart of the ego itself. In this sense, "egoism, enjoyment, sensibility, and the whole dimension of interiority are necessary for the idea of Infinity, the relation with the Other which opens forth from the separated and finite being" (*TI*, 148). As Levinas puts it, "In the separated being, the door to the outside must hence be at the same time open and closed. . . . Interiority must be at the same time closed and open. The possibility of arising from the animal condition is assuredly thus described" (ibid., 149).

Levinas's solution, however, requires a theological premise. His atheism is not at all atheological. On the contrary, Levinas maintains that his view of the self is possible only with the theological notion of creation ex nihilo. To see this connection, we must remind ourselves once again of Levinas's aversion to totalities and his yearning for radical transcendence. He argues that we can only come up with a full-bodied self of enjoyment that is yet irrevocably called to ethical responsibility when both parts coexist not as dialectical opposition but as unity. This unity of the atheistic self (ego) and the ethical self (I) is possible only in a creationist account (*TI*, 148).

According to Levinas, only theology provides this model. God creates man as dependent on him, but this very creaturehood actually gives human existence its freedom from totalizing systems: "But the idea of creation ex nihilo expresses a multiplicity not united in a totality; the creature is an existence which indeed does depend on an other, but not as a part that is separated from it. Creation leaves the creature a trace of dependence, but it is an unparalleled dependence: the dependent being draws from this exceptional dependence, from this relationship, its very independence, its exteriority to the system" (*TI*, 104). Levinas does not define our creaturely status negatively as finitude but positively as ethical limitation. To be human is to be open to infinity, to the ethical call that defines us, but this call in no way diminishes the reality and importance of our physical existence. Yet only when this ethical call, by which the truly human "I" emerges as the limitation of the ego, comes from the outside can infinity (transcendence/the ethical) withstand the invasion of totality, "in a contradiction that leaves a place for the separated being" (ibid.). Contrary to the charge of critics who accuse Levinas of disemboweling the self, his view of creation opens the door for a complex subjectivity in which the natural self forms part of the full human identity imparted to us by the ethical transcendence of the other.

We have seen that Levinas can establish this necessary paradox only on theological grounds. He insists, in fact, that only "religion" can articulate an ethical ontology in which human existence is defined by its independent dependence on the other. Levinas finds this relation, the idea of infinity, already foreshadowed in ancient Greek philosophy but fully expressed only in the religious notion of creation ex nihilo.[2] From this biblical perspective, Levinas can claim that "the ultimate structure of reality" is not ontology but "religion, where relationship subsists between the same and the other despite the impossibility of the Whole—the idea of infinity" (*TI*, 80).

In light of deconstructionist dilutions of Levinas's theological foundations, it is important to realize the importance of theology for his ethical philosophy. The full validation of the immanent and the transcendent at the same time depends on creation ex nihilo. This paradoxical relation "exists divinely" as "religion" in stark contrast with totalizing conceptions of reality in which either the finite or the infinite suffers loss (*TI*, 104). When Levinas talks about an atheistic subject, he means that the subject is free in its distinctness from God and others. At the same time, however, Levinas seeks an incarnational subject that is not self-sufficient but whose true human identity exists only through the address by another. This ethical call, which founds our true human identity, is not an abstract ideal but occurs truly "in the flesh," in the midst of rubbing shoulders with our fellow human beings.

2. Levinas finds the idea of infinity in Plato, "in the transcendence of the Good with respect to being" (*TI*, 80).

The Incarnate Subject: Substitution, or Oneself as Another

Levinas's atheistic ego, the self in the separation of enjoyment, requires the limitation of radical transcendence for the foundation of our truly human subjectivity. The incarnation of this transcendence in the midst of the ego's enjoyment is the ethical call away from solipsistic self-satisfaction toward substitution. The self becomes a true, human self only when it extends outward as a self-for-the-other.

Levinas elaborates this incarnate subjectivity as substitution most fully in chapter 4 of *Otherwise Than Being, or Beyond Essence*. Levinas links the kenotic self, the subjectivity of "oneself-for-another," with the idea of an incarnate subject. This incarnate subject needs to be fully physical and yet different from the merely biological or sociological. The self has to be incarnated as physical because "only a subject that eats can be for-the-other, or can signify. Signification, the-one-for-the-other, has meaning only among beings of flesh and blood" (*OB*, 74).

Yet this truly physical self, the self we previously described as independent ego in enjoyment, is neither the Cartesian "animated body" nor the naturalist body with emergent mental higher functions. Rejecting both materialism and mind-body dualism, Levinas proposes an "incarnate subject." He argues that we are animated not by mind or instinct but by another soul, by the *ethical relation* to the other, by proximity, by sensitivity as exposure. This ethical exposure at the level of sensibility is not merely a prequel to the intuition of consciousness but its very foundation. Levinas's point is that neither consciousness nor thought but ethical relation is the first order of human existence:

> The non-thematized proximity does not simply belong to the "horizon" of the contact, as a potentiality of this experience. Sensibility—the proximity, immediacy and restlessness which signify in it—is not constituted out of some apperception putting consciousness into relationship with a body. Incarnation is not a transcendental operation of a subject that is situated in the midst of the world it represents to itself; the sensible experience of the body is already and from the start incarnate. The sensible, maternity, vulnerability, apprehension—binds the node of incarnation into a plot larger than the apperception of self. In this plot I am bound to others before being tied to my body. (*OB*, 76)

The incarnate subject, this unity of enjoyment-ego and ethically determined "I," begins not in an abstract idea of God but in concrete human relations. This grounding allows Levinas's subject full participation in space, time, history, and language without surrendering its transcendent ethical identity to these elements.

Besides incarnation, the most theologically significant term for this Levinasian subject-in-relation is *substitution*. Substitution is a controlling idea in *Otherwise Than Being*[3] and remains a defining term in his later work. Levinas sees indeed a certain confluence of incarnational Christian theology and his own thought because for both, "the idea of substitution—in a certain modality is indispensable to the comprehension of subjectivity" ("A Man-God," in *Entre Nous*, 59).

For Levinas, an ethical—and thus a properly human—vision of reality depends on the substitutionary subject, a self defined by radical transcendence (exteriority), irreducible to ontology, reflection, or consciousness:

> To see in subjectivity an exception, putting out of order the conjunction of essence, entities and the "difference"; to catch sight, in the substantiality of the subject, in the hard core of the "unique" in me, in my unparalleled identity, of a substitution for the other; to conceive of this abnegation prior to the will as a merciless exposure to the trauma of transcendence by way of a susception more, and differently, passive than receptivity, passion and finitude; to derive praxis and knowledge in the world from this nonassumable susceptibility—these are the propositions of this book [*Otherwise Than Being*] which names beyond essence. (*OB*, xlviii)

Levinas does not preach the dissolution of self found in some Eastern religions but the irreducible identity of each human being. Paradoxically, the very core of who we are and human praxis and knowledge depend not on self-assertion but on the "trauma of transcendence," the ethical call. This paradox of a passively received identity as the only avenue to authenticity links his work with Heidegger's search for authenticity in *Being and Time* and with Dietrich Bonhoeffer's response to Heidegger. Bonhoeffer, as we shall see later, also addresses our need for authenticity and anticipates Levinas's complaint that Heidegger's plea for authenticity remains cruelly caught in the self-referential structures of being and human consciousness. For Levinas, authenticity that secures our true humanness must originate outside of ontology, so that human selfhood escapes "the fate of essence" (*OB*, 8). Nonetheless, this ethical origin of selfhood cannot be nothingness but lies beyond the opposition of essence and nothingness and is something that calls the subject into being as an "ego of incomparable unicity [i.e., authenticity]" (ibid.). Levinas knows that his search for the irreducible uniqueness of the ego pushes the envelope of our imagination, and yet he insists that the only truly

---

3. Levinas developed this concept first in the 1967 essay titled "Substitution," and its companion essay "Language and Proximity" (in *Basic Philosophical Writings* [Bloomington: Indiana University Press, 1996], chaps. 5 and 10).

human concept of the self is "a unicity that has no site, [one] without the ideal identity a being derives from the kerygma that identifies the innumerable aspects of its manifestation, without the identity of the ego that coincides with itself, a unicity withdrawing from essence—such is man" (ibid.). The self gains its unity, its identity as self, not from within itself but from the outside, from the call to exist for the other.

Instead of a subject that is defined by self-control through knowledge acquisition, Levinas offers a subject that is defined by the abnegation of control and mastery. Levinas describes a kenotic subject, a subject that derives its irreducible identity through the limitations of self-consciousness, control, and agency. Levinas is not arguing that the subject does not possess these qualities, but denies that they establish the subject. Put positively, he is concerned with the foundational identity and character of the self. The self does not come into being as solitary consciousness that then looks about itself and establishes its identity through knowledge of things. Rather the self is called into being in passivity. Levinas's basic point is that "the identity of the I is not the result of any knowledge whatsoever; I find myself without looking for myself" (*RB*, 49). Levinas's various terms for describing this kenotic self, "the face, proximity, election, substitution, hostage" are meant to emphasize the passivity and exteriority that found the subject. Levinas's subject is *called* to be subject and instituted as ethical subject by its address from the other. The truly human subject comes to be only in this ethical, social relation.

Levinas illustrates this concept of a kenotic self and its passively derived identity with theological examples. In the Old Testament, the nation of Israel's very identity consists in being called by God, in its election as the nation through which God will address all humanity. This election, this call, is unilateral; it can be denied but not unmade. This seems to be the basic pattern of divine covenants in the Old Testament. The stories of Noah, Abraham, and Israel exhibit a pattern of calling that persists into the New Testament. The unique identity of an individual or a nation is conveyed by an authoritative address from God. Levinas adopts this biblical pattern for his philosophical discussion of true ethical selfhood. Just as in Israel's history God elects and calls the nation and individuals to their true identity, so the human self and its identity come into being through the electing call of the other.

In theological terms, one might say that in Levinas the self is gained by first losing itself. The ineluctable, unrefusable ethical demand, the voice of God in the face of the other, is prior to conscience, prior to the will, prior to intentionality, prior to intuition, and prior to representation in consciousness. It is, in short, on the "hither side of being, of ontology," where all these categories have traction. Similar to the notion of subjectivity that we have seen in premodern hermeneutics,

Levinas's subject is not autonomous or self-affirming but is born in passivity, is called whether it likes it or not. The subject is defined not in contrast to nonbeing or being but by its ethical relation with the other. This other "diverges from nothingness as well as from being. It provokes this responsibility against my will, that is, by substituting me for the other as a hostage. All my inwardness is invested in the form of a despite-me, for-another. Despite-me, for-another, is signification par excellence. And it is the sense of the 'oneself,' that accusative that derives from no nominative; it is the very fact of finding oneself while losing oneself" (*OB*, 11). Ethical transcendence thus is the beginning of true self-knowledge and of meaning itself. Unless the self is drawn away from itself by the intervention of an exterior address, meaning and knowledge simply remain in the circle of solipsism.

The Meaning of Substitution: Responsibility

On the basis of this incarnate subjectivity, Levinas contends that meaning begins not in reflective consciousness but in the interhuman, ethical relation. The incarnate subject, the subject as substitution, is the very ground of meaning and self-understanding. If we ask Levinas for a definition of the human, he answers that "humanity, to which proximity properly so called refers, must then not be first understood as consciousness, that is as the identity of an ego endowed with knowledge or (what amounts to the same thing) with powers." Instead Levinas appeals to a subjectivity older than knowledge and power, a proximity that is "no longer in knowing in which these relations with the neighbour show themselves, but do so already in narration, in the said, as an epos and a teleology" (*OB*, 83).

As Simon Critchley has pointed out, Levinas offers a subject in the truest sense of the term's Latin root, *subjectum,* that which is thrown under the authority of the other (*EPS*, 51). Levinas's increasingly violent terms for describing this relation should be taken with a grain of salt. These overstatements signal his insistence on an extroverted, outward-directed subject that originates in exteriority and remains protected from being turned into an instanciation of universal reason or any totality whatever. Levinas insists that no dialogical, reciprocal, or dialectical mediation occurs in this relation. Radical ethical transcendence is maintained only when the ethical demand is a one-way street from the other to oneself. "Who then came to wound the subject, so that he should expose his thoughts, or expose himself in his saying? He is subject to being affected by the other, and this being affected, by reason of its very irreversibility, does not change into a universal thought. The subject affected by the other cannot think that the affection is reciprocal, for he is still obsessed with the very obsession he could exercise over him that obsesses him. Not to turn into relations that reverse, irreversibility, is the universal subjectness of the subject" (*OB*, 84). So if there is anything universal about the subject, it is that it is not universal. Our inability to comprehend either ourselves or the other fully is not an ignorance that must be overcome. This ignorance "bears witness not to the naivety of a humanity still incapable of thinking," nor does it refer to Heidegger's "everydayness of man, fleeing concepts and death in an original identity prior to all mediation." Rather this ignorance points to the "preoriginary hither side of abnegation," which announces "a one-way relationship. . . . The immediacy of the other, more immediate still than immediate identity in its quietude as a nature—the immediacy of proximity" (ibid.).

This one-way relationship means that I am responsible for the neighbor irrespective of his approach: "The knot of subjectivity consists in going to the other without concerning oneself with his movement toward me." This means that beyond all necessary reciprocal relations "I have always taken one step more toward him—which is possible only if this step is responsibility. In the responsibility which we have for one another, I have always one response more to give, I have to answer for his very responsibility" (*OB*, 84).

This responsibility is not reducible to a common humanity, to race, to ethnicity, but transcends all these ontological categories. The kinship with my neighbor is "outside of all biology, 'against all logic.'" For Levinas, even common humanity as a basis for humanism is not enough. The kinship is not "because he would be recognized as belonging to the same genus as me that he concerns me. He is precisely *other*. The community with him begins in my obligation to him. The neighbor is a brother." So here proximity also becomes fraternity. And this fraternity is an obligation we turn away from at the cost of psychological damage: "A fraternity that cannot be abrogated. . . . Proximity is an impossibility to move away without the torsion of a complex, without 'alienation' or fault. This insomnia is the psyche" (*OB*, 87). Levinas's ethics thus rests on a biblical concept of fraternity (equality as addressed by radical otherness) rather than the liberal humanist concept of a common rational humanity. The kinship with my neighbor is "outside of all biology, against all logic" (ibid.).

This kinship as ethical obligation is what Levinas calls the "face." This term does not refer to an actual visage but to ethical transcendence: the other calls me, breaks up my self-enclosed mental space and serenity, interrupts my sense of time, always presents a disturbance, is irreducible to my objectifying gaze, always appears as the total disruption of common presence. The "face," this synonym for proximity and obsession, is the way in which the other approaches me and claims me before any a priori structures can model or shape my interpretation of reality. In our human relations, we necessarily reduce this face to an image, to objectified and received concepts. Yet the face originates from beyond this ontological realm. It comes in its proximity as a command "as though from an immemorial past, which was never present, began in no freedom. This *way* of the neighbor is a face" (*OB*, 87). The face in its ethical transcendence is "the very birth of *signification* beyond *being*" (ibid., 90; emphasis in original).

The face has the power to disrupt my self-complacency; it limits my self-enjoyment by imposing the need to serve another human being. It is at this ethical juncture that meaning begins. Real meaning thus lies not in straight reference but in its interruption.[4] Originary meaning, for Levinas, lies in ethical transcendence rather than in conceptual knowledge: "Substitution is signification. Not a reference from one term to another, as it appears thematized in the said, but substitution as the very subjectivity of a subject, interruption of the irreversible identity of the essence. It occurs in the taking charge of, which is incumbent on me without any escape possible. Here the unicity of the ego first acquires a meaning—where it is no longer a question of the ego, but of me. The subject which is not an ego, but which I am, cannot be generalized, is not a subject in general" (*OB*, 13–14). The subject emerges as "hostage" to the irrevocable call by the other to ethical responsibility.

Hostage to the Other? Concerns about Levinas's Subjectivity

Levinas's violent language of usurpation by the other sounds worrisome. It usually raises two objections. The first addresses the quality of human existence. If this ethical imperative defines humanity, am I in effect always walking about like a scolded dog, afraid of pleasure and enjoyment, waiting in complete self-denial for the demands of the other? The answer is no. For Levinas the subject is both enjoyment and its disruption. Levinas moves knowing to the level of sensing (not necessarily feeling), where the subject is founded by the never ceasing tension between enjoyment and its interruption. We enjoy reality, the world, love, and life in a deep sense of identity and being oneself for oneself. However, at the same time there is what Levinas calls the

4. We find here, in Levinas's subjectivity as substitution, the origin of Derrida's rejection of meaning as full presence and his insistence over against Gadamer on the breach as the origin of our interpretive experience.

"denucleation," or coring out of the self. The happiness of the self for itself is subverted by the same sensibility: "There is a non-coinciding of the ego with itself, restlessness, insomnia, beyond what is found again in the present" (*OB*, 64).

Moreover, the limitation of self-enjoyment is necessary for our human identity. Levinas tries to show in detailed phenomenological analyses of consciousness, memory, and time that at the heart of human experience, we find inexplicable boundary experiences rather than control and mastery. Rather than correlation and sameness, we find disruption and breach, yet these mean something because they point us to ethical transcendence as the origin of all human communication and meaning. Even if such meaning is nonsense within mathematical and logical models of reason, the primordial sense is the ethical demand for substitution, which calls the "I" of enjoyment to its ethical identity, "that sense which is the-same-for-the-other." This signification cannot be achieved by contemplation. It does not lie in "elevated feelings," nor can we obtain it by contemplating the beautiful. Instead meaning in sensibility *is* sense, not as elevated feelings but as in "a tearing away of bread from the mouth that tastes it, to give it to the other" (*OB*, 64).

Perhaps Levinas's unselved self draws so much criticism because we are indeed so accustomed to an autonomous self that we sooner put up with the dissolution of the human subject than accept Levinas's unpleasant alternative; subjectivity as choice and performance, at least, leaves us free to choose our subjectivity rather than saddle us with a subject that finds a definite ethical identity only through another. Perhaps it is Levinas's insistence on the religious model of an inescapable calling to an ethical commitment, this lack of choice that is most offensive to a Western consciousness accustomed to define freedom as choice. Do we not define even love, the foundational ethical emotion, as an emotion we respond to and convey by choice? For Levinas, by contrast, love is not eros but agape, not erotic but ethical. "Love," he argues, "does not begin in the erotic. In love without concupiscence, in the disinterested love of responsibility, the beloved one is 'unique in the world' for the one who loves" (*RB*, 229).

Levinas almost invariably sums up his notion of love as ethical responsibility with Father Zosima's phrase in Dostoyevsky's *Brothers Karamazov*: "Each of us is guilty before everyone and for everyone, and I more than all others" (*RB*, 56). This is love as ethical obligation, what Levinas calls the "'originary constitution' of the I or the unique, in a responsibility for the neighbor or the other, and the impossibility of escaping responsibility or of being replaced" (ibid., 229). Just as God, a personal being, calls individuals and nations in the Old Testament to responsibility, each human being embodies this call to another.

For Levinas, the impossibility of escaping this call and responsibility is the exact opposite of enslavement. It is "not a servitude but a being chosen" as the foundational act for human identity and dignity. This thought, however, is found not in egoistical philosophies preoccupied with establishing an autonomous self but in religion, for "religions that have recourse to this term, *chosenness*, see in it the supreme dignity of the human" (ibid.). For Levinas "charity or mercy makes it possible for man, created in God's image, to be 'otherwise than being'" (ibid., 231). Consequently, to be human is to be ethical, and to be ethical means to be irrevocably called to neighborly love. "The only absolute value is the human possibility of giving the other priority over oneself." This principle is not restricted to any particular religion but is the universal ground for true humanity (ibid., 170).

Drawing on biblical language, Levinas argues that this primordial ethical relation is one of holiness and peace. Holiness means that "the meaningful appears and signifies and has its importance above all in my relation with another person." While this limitation of my selfishness is traumatic, it nonetheless signifies peace rather than violence. Levinas maintains that "the first intellectual act is peace. Peace, understanding by that my solicitation for the other person. Peace precedes my manner of thinking; it precedes the desire to know, . . . it precedes objective thematization." In fact, Levinas redefines rationality not as conquering knowledge but as the pacific ethical rapport of one person to another (*RB*, 56).

The second common objection against Levinas's description of the subject as hostage to the other follows from the first. If I am called to give unconditional priority to my neighbor, how can this be peaceful when the other has evil intentions? Should we show this radical hospitality to anyone, even to the devil? Answering this objection also makes clear the major difference between Levinas and Derrida. For Levinas the ethical demand by the other is ultimately grounded in a Judaic version of the *imago Dei*. Our obedience to this ethical demand is predicated not on the other's moral conduct but on the fact that he or she incarnates a divine command. This is what the concept of *imago Dei*, the image of God, means for Levinas:

> To be made in the image of God means not that one is God's icon but that one finds oneself in its trace. The revealed God of our Judeo-Christian spirituality shows himself only in this trace. To approach [God] does not entail following this trace, which is not a sign. It means, instead, to approach the others [fellow human beings] who exist in the trace of this illeity. Through this illeity, which has its place on the hither side of calculations and reciprocal relations of economy and world, being signifies.

A meaning without finality that cannot be satiated by happiness. ("Die Bedeutung und der Sinn," in *HM*, 59)

Levinas always reminds us that he is a Jew, not a Christian. In the Jewish worldview, relation to the transcendent deity is maintained "without God entering into the world" (*RB*, 278). Yet Levinas also lives by the Old Testament and its demand for social justice. Hence the relation to God is indescribable without reference to one's concern for the other. In the absence of the divine incarnation in Christ, the only incarnation is the trace of God in the face of the other, the *imago Dei*. Levinas explains that his thesis "consists in affirming that sociality is a rapport entirely other than that which is established and that sociality itself is commanded by the word of God, which is the face of the other" (ibid.).

Levinas's notion of the face shows how inseparable his philosophizing is from his theology. When he says that the relation of the other is the beginning of meaning, of the intelligible, he links this relation to God: "In the other, there is a real presence of God. In my relation to the other, I hear the word of God. It is not a metaphor. It is not only extremely important, it is literally true. I am not saying that the other is God, but that in his or her face I hear the word of God" (*RB*, 171).

To say, then, that Levinas's ethical philosophy exposes us to the arbitrary will of another human being, or to imply with Derrida and Caputo that hospitality is unconditional, misconstrues Levinas's emphasis on the ethical imperative as grounded in God himself. While we certainly cannot know whether an angel or a devil knocks on our door, we open the door because both are subject to God's law of neighborly love (Caputo, *On Religion*, 11). For Levinas, at least, the essence of our humanity is found in passivity, but this passivity is protected by God himself. While Levinas realizes that the unconditional ethical demand of the other may seem arbitrary, he believes that the ethical quality of the word justifies this inequality: "It may appear arbitrary; unless it be—in the word addressed to the other man, in the ethics of welcome—the first religious service, the first prayer, the first liturgy, the religion out of which God could first have come to mind and the word 'God' have made its entry into language and into good philosophy" (*GM*, 151).

Yet some questions remain. For one, God still remains a rather vague concept, and the Christian concept of the incarnation as historical grounding for God's goodness provides a more historical framework for transcendent ethics. Moreover, Levinas does not really address the question of how this radical transcendence gets translated into moral action. To use Lutheran language, Levinas sets up the law (heeding the ethical demand) and bothers little with grace (how can I obey an impossible command?). The demand for ethical responsibility serves Levinas well philosophically, because it gets him around the age-old question whether human beings are individuated by matter or by form. Levinas can say that individuation occurs in ethical responsibility.

And yet the theological context of ethical transcendence as the word of God in the face of the other haunts Levinas's work. He is stuck with a theological problem: while the ethical call is prior to the will, what makes the will willing to implement it? How can we heal the wound of the ethical law? Disingenuously, Levinas leaves this "consoling side of ethics" to religion; and yet even in doing so, his parting comments sound legalistic. Levinas recognizes that "what responsibility as a principle of human individuation lacks is that God perhaps helps you to be responsible. . . . But to deserve the help of God, it is necessary to want to do what must be done without his help" (*RB*, 170). But how, one may ask, do I get to the point of wanting to do what is good? And has not Paul, trained in Jewish theology, told us that even his good intentions were thwarted by his own sinfulness and life's circumstances? How do I handle these ethical failures? While Levinas's emphasis on personal agency is laudable, he lacks the premodern pneumatological element. Luther, for example, followed Paul in emphasizing the Holy Spirit as the divine agent who indeed helps us to be responsible and whose assurance of our acceptance by God enables an ethics outside the vicious circle of duty ethics, or works righteousness, as Luther called it.

And yet Levinas's emphasis on ethical transcendence is crucial for the recovery of theological hermeneutics. Ethical transcendence founds the interpreting subject and, as we shall see in the next segment, also determines the kind of knowledge adequate for this subjectivity.

Knowledge Conceived Otherwise

Levinas's rejection of subjectivity as primarily consciousness is inseparable from what he regards as the malaise of epistemology, namely, that perception is the origin of knowledge. In other words, Levinas's redefinition of the subject as ethical elicits the question: "What kind of knowledge is appropriate to an ethical subject?" Levinas tries to answer this question by modifying Edmund Husserl's phenomenological notion of intentionality.

In his early works, Levinas appropriates Husserl's phenomenology to show that intention is prior to and already at work in perception. It is in intentionality rather than in perception that the origin of knowledge is found. Intentionality is not only prior to perception but also pervasive throughout the process of knowing. Perception already grasps, possesses. Perception wants to identify an object within a totality in order to classify and master it. Intentionality, by contrast, signifies distance as much as accessibility and allows the distant to be given rather than seized. Husserlian phenomenology is crucial because it allows objects, and also other human beings, to reveal themselves to us.

Yet Levinas also sees the limitations of phenomenology from an ethical point of view. In intentionality the object reveals itself only within a conceptual grid, a "thematized" notion, and so becomes reduced to one's own interpretive framework. This is particularly problematic in encountering other persons and their self-expressions, whose unique differences are threatened by the anticipatory structure of intentionality.

Levinas criticizes Husserl's phenomenology because it still desires full self-presence as the ideal of knowledge rather than founding knowledge on the boundary experience of ethical transcendence. Levinas takes his departure from the limits of self-knowledge rather than from aspirations of self-reflexivity. He believes that Husserl's phenomenology still misreads Kant's barrier to transcendental reflection, the fact that the self could not get behind itself and look at itself, as a dark spot that would be illuminated eventually. This, Levinas believes, was the arrogance of Romantic philosophy and also of later idealism: confidence in the self's power to illumine everything. Levinas, by contrast, believes in the positive value of the transcendental barrier. The fact that conscience, in reflection, can actually have a sense of its own operation without the ability to articulate this blind spot is a breach that points to the ethical dimension. This breach in consciousness refuses identification or pointing to an origin. It is in the truest sense of the word anarchic: it cannot be categorized or ordered (*AT*, 18–19).

This anarchy or irreducibility is not, however, "disorder as opposed to order," some kind of chaotic precognitive element prior to the ordering of consciousness. The anarchy of the ethical "brings to halt the ontological play, which, precisely qua play, is consciousness, where being is lost and found again, and thus illuminated." This anarchy touches and influences the ego, and consciousness cannot lay hold of it. The breach in consciousness, in other words, confirms Levinas's notion of the subject as proximity. Proximity as subjectivity is a form of an ego that is "unable to conceive what is 'touching it.'" That is why "the ascendancy of the other is exercised upon the same to the point of interrupting it, leaving it speechless." Levinas calls this anarchic dynamic "persecution" (*OB*, 101). Thus the self is established in the interiority of consciousness but not by consciousness's affirming its autonomy and rule. Instead the self is established by putting in question its very independence and control (*AT*, 21). And so for Levinas, crucially, self-knowledge begins in difference with a breach, not in sameness.

This anarchy goes against Husserlian intentionality. Levinas realizes that Husserl's "intentionality of consciousness does not designate voluntary intention only," yet nonetheless, Husserl's undertaking as a whole still runs on the attitude and tracks of rationalism and voluntary intention: "The given enters into a thought which recognizes in it or invests it with its own project, and thus exercises mastery over it." Levinas argues to the contrary that consciousness never reaches full self-reflexivity. This denial of total self-awareness, however, is not merely a weakness, a sign of our finitude, but rather points positively toward the ethical realm beyond or prior to consciousness. Husserl's anticipatory intuition failed in its hastiness to "see" an object to take note of this irreducible surplus that allows phenomena to appear (*AT*, 21).

On Levinas's account of philosophy, Husserl's student Heidegger too failed to recognize the ethical importance of boundary experiences in human perception. After modifying Husserl's intentionality, Levinas also radicalizes Heidegger's notion of temporality as a breach that points to the ethical relation as the foundation of knowledge. Levinas insists that, applied to consciousness, Heidegger's definition of temporality provides evidence yet again for the fissure or breach within our knowing and perception that points to the preontological ethical realm.

Heidegger distinguishes between an existential and a vulgar sense of time because he believes that our common sense of clock time, which controls our lives, is actually secondary to our apprehension of time in its existential dimension. Temporality is more originally determined by our state of being than by the clock. This is why, for example, good times seem short while ordeals (like close readings of Heidegger) never seem to end, even if both endure for the same measurable length of time. For Levinas, however, even existential time, the ontological notion of time, is founded in turn on the preontological. He points out that Heidegger's supposed deepest ontological sense of time still thematizes events and objects by abstracting them from the absolute flow of time. By making temporality part of my experience of something *as* something, the irreducible difference of temporality is turned into sameness by becoming part of my existential experience. Events and objects in time only have meaning for me because they have already been turned from their preontological saying into the realm of being (*OB*, 37).

Levinas agrees with Heidegger that human beings are beings in truth because they have consciousness and language to express reflective acts. Yet contrary to Heidegger, Levinas does not think man's power to say (to reflect and name entities) is in the service of being because true meaning begins in the concrete personal relation. It is on this deeper foundation that all ontology rests (*OB*, 38). Levinas is deeply concerned about Heideggerian ontology, because it subsumes humanity under being. Human existence tends to have value for Heidegger only insofar as it serves being rather than enjoys the intrinsic dignity Levinas deems essential. Only when human beings are intrinsically valued, only when each individual has a unique dignity independent from totalities of being or even of religion, is the primacy of the ethical ensured. For this reason, Levinas anchors the truly human in the ethical, which is prior to consciousness and its conceptualizing tendencies. Heidegger's foundational ontology explains human existence as interpretive of being, but for Levinas this is merely the surface of the deeper ethical level whose presence we recognize in the cracks of consciousness and temporality. The ethical (which Levinas will later call "saying" in contrast to the ontological realm, the "said") "is the first fissure visible in the psyche of satisfaction" (*GM*, 106).

Even in our ability to know, we find such fissures. Levinas's analysis of human consciousness in time aims to demonstrate that the origin of knowledge is not ontology but ethics. The temporality of consciousness, which makes representation possible, also points to that which resists representation, that which is not captured in essence (and being). By its very nature of succession, time makes memory and representation possible, but it also presents us with an insurmountable diachrony of time. Because memory (apprehension and recognition) work in time, there is also a lapse of time, "something irrecuperable, refractory to the simultaneity of the present, something unrepresentable, immemorial, pre-historical." Simply put, our memory is not a finite copy of eternity but exists in time (*OB*, 38). This is not a weakness of human beings but the nature of time, "the impossibility of the dispersion of time to assemble itself in the present, the insurmountable diachrony of time" (ibid.). This means that Levinas deducts (or finds evidence of) the ethical saying in the nature of the temporal. This evidence lets Levinas conclude that the ethical relation, or saying, is not merely a correlative of the ontological realm (language, culture, texts, history, etc.) and exhausted in it but rather that the diachrony points to a signified, a referent or meaning that lies beyond being and ontology (ibid.).

Standing in the tradition of phenomenology, Levinas consciously modifies this tradition in light of his biblical heritage. Phenomenology, unless it is conceived *ethically* rather than *ontologically*, cannot escape the dehumanizing consequences shared by all immanent approaches that deny ethical transcendence as the foundation of philosophy. According to Levinas, phenomenological analysis itself points us to the boundary experiences in human consciousness that reveal the deeper ethical relation that is the beginning of knowledge. In his later works, Levinas argues increasingly for this ethical knowledge, whose origin is prior to ontology and which can neither be measured by nor contained within its register. Levinas suggests a model of knowledge that takes its direction from the other's ethical demand, that is, an epistemology of revelation rather than discovery. By grounding knowing in ethical transcendence, Levinas finds that epistemology is bound up with the desire for the other. Contrary to its own convictions, even Cartesian or scientific epistemology is driven by desire, albeit by its perversion. Our hankering for ahistorical, absolute knowledge stems from the misconstrual of desire as finite and satiable. Our unchecked desire for autonomy in its search for satisfaction through total comprehension distorts our paradigm of knowledge. In ontological models of knowing, desire is perverted as satisfaction in knowing, so that to know is to master a subject to the point of no further surprises.

Levinas, by contrast, seeks to reinstitute knowledge based on desire for transcendence. For him, desire is by definition never satisfied. Since desire is desire for the other, satisfaction as "coming-to-rest" would mean my comprehension of the other and hence the cessation of his or her transcendence. Knowledge as satisfaction of desire leads inevitably to the loss of transcendence. Instead Levinas wants to establish transcendence at the very origin of knowledge. This transcendence is the irreducible difference of the object, its resistance to be fully known by the self. In beginning knowledge with ethical transcendence, Levinas wants to preserve the unpredictability in knowing, a way of sensing in which knowledge is not dulled by "lived adequation of thought to its object in thought, the identification of the Same, satisfaction" (*AT*, 4). Knowledge conceived otherwise pursues an ideal of wonderment of the dissatisfying, when my expectations are not fulfilled, when my horizon is shaken, my perceptions overturned. Only when knowledge begins in asymmetry, in "the disproportion between cogito and cogitatum," does knowledge become objective. Knowledge can avoid subjectivism at its very origin only on a model of knowledge as revelation. Levinas finds this transcendence

in a thinking that finds itself thinking more than it can embrace, the blinding bedazzledness of the gaze by an excess of light and a bursting of knowledge in adoration. . . . Beyond the objective, which is always already correlative to a prior "aim" and intention to discover—behold an other that *reveals itself*, but that does so precisely in surprising the intentions of subjective thought and eluding the form of the look, totalitarian as presence—eluding the transcendental synthesis. An exceptional idea of the Infinite that has escaped being, and of a presence stronger and more venerable than the totality. An idea that cannot, by virtue of the "ontological argument," be peremptorily relegated to presence, to being that is locked within the totalizing look, nor to some other world, nor some empty heaven. (*AT*, 4)

The empty heaven is the Greek Logos, this impersonal rationality we find in Plato's realm of ideas, in Enlightenment rationalism, and which still persists in Heidegger's account of knowledge. Even in Heidegger's fundamental ontology, authentic knowledge is the individual's standing in the truth of being. The shepherd of being, this messenger poet, is the servant of impersonal being rather than the servant of concrete and ethical human being.

In contrast with these conceptions of knowledge as impersonal, Levinas redefines reason and knowledge in personal terms. Knowledge and meaning begin in the ethical relation, with the concrete intersubjectivity of social life. Especially in *Totality and Infinity*, Levinas laments the depersonalization of philosophy, the loss of the ethical in knowledge: "Philosophy itself is identified with the substitution of ideas for persons, the theme for the interlocutor, the interiority of the logical relation for the exteriority of interpellation. Existents are reduced to the neuter state of idea, Being, the concept" (88). Philosophy must reverse this trend and pursue a model of knowledge as *ethical*, that is, not of minds in touch with the universals through knowledge or individual consciousnesses in touch with objects but as persons in relation. Since Levinas is fixated on Heideggerian ontology, he regards ontology as impersonal, and this impersonal realm has no place for the human face of knowledge. This grand neuter of being can only be avoided in an alternative view of existence as persons in relation. Yet Levinas does not want this desire to be mistaken for a new theological Pietism: "To wish to escape dissolution into the Neuter, to posit knowing as a welcoming of the Other is not a pious attempt to maintain the spiritualism of a personal God, but is the condition for language without which philosophical discourse itself is but an abortive act, a pretext for an unintermitting psychoanalysis or philology or sociology, in which the appearance of a discourse vanishes in the Whole. Speaking implies a possibility of breaking off and beginning" (ibid.). Levinas's point is clear: without ethical transcendence knowledge becomes either a subjectivist monologue or the tyranny of the impersonal. Levinas does not reject truth, knowledge, and meaning but recasts them in relational terms.

Not the Greek Logos, not impersonal rationality, but persons in relation form the matrix of our knowledge. Levinas's position thus opens up a way to conceive of tradition and its teachings as fundamentally ethical. The world, says Levinas, comes to me through the other in a master-teacher relation. We have already seen that Levinas rejects a Platonic model of knowledge, according to which the soul remembers concepts based on its preexistence in the realm of ideas. Thus knowledge can be arrived at not maieutically but in conversation with the other: "Teaching is not reducible to maieutics; it comes from the exterior and brings me more than I contain" (*TI*, 51). Contrary to Rousseau's model of education, which depends on our common access to a pool of universal reason and ideas that are then teased out of the student through questions, Levinas believes that knowledge is attained by others teaching us. This is a far more historically and hermeneutically oriented view of knowledge than rationalism or idealism offers.

Much like Gadamer's hermeneutics, Levinas's account of knowledge begins in the concrete shared social life. Persons in relation rather than abstract ideals of reason determine the quality of our knowing. Recent work on Gadamer's hermeneutics shows how close and yet how far apart Gadamer's and Levinas's positions are on this issue.[5] Both thinkers desire transcendence and difference for overcoming subjectivism and yet value tradition and language as the only possible conduits for our knowing. Nonetheless, the different sources from which these positions are developed prevent a complete reconciliation of their thought. The main source of Gadamer's philosophical hermeneutics is the Greek Logos in contrast to Levinas's biblical conception of radical ethical transcendence as the word of God in the face of the other. As Levinas puts it, "My point of departure is the meaningful, in which the human is held before all system." Meaning is articulated neither originally nor exclusively in knowledge. Knowledge is not the place of the meaningful; rather "in the obligation toward the other there is a meaning." Against the Greek Logos tradition, Levinas wants to "think reason otherwise" on the basis of the biblical tradition, for which "man is not a rational animal . . . [but] resembles God" (*RB*, 271–72).

These two different sources explain their different emphases even if both situate knowledge in concrete human relations. Gadamer begins with correlation, with common ground, but works hard to ensure difference and plurality in understanding. Levinas, by contrast, begins with radical difference and then has considerable trouble explaining common ground and conceptual knowledge without compromising transcendence. The main argument of this book continues to be that both require an incarnational Christology in order to get what they want. The next chapter on the relation of philosophical hermeneutics and deconstruction will explain this problem more fully.

Before we examine the challenge of radical hermeneutics, however, we still must deal with Levinas's view of language because it demonstrates most clearly the tension between ontology and ethics that is at the

5. See James Risser's excellent article on the commonalities and differences concerning solidarity in Gadamer and Levinas in "Shared Life," *Symposium* 6, no. 2 (Fall 2002): 167–80.

heart of Levinas's philosophy and the quarrel between hermeneutics and deconstruction.

Incarnation or Docetism? Levinas on Language

In its demand for an ethical reconceptualization of the self and knowledge, Levinas's ethical philosophy is characterized by its opposition to ontology. However, as Derrida has correctly pointed out to Levinas, his ethical philosophy cannot do without the very ontological terminology it denounces. Derrida's criticism forced Levinas to face the central problem of his entire undertaking: how can we talk about the other? This tension between ontology and ethics is particularly significant for Levinas's conception of the subject as incarnating the ethical relation to another: how can we talk about the other and give ethics concrete contours without violating the very transcendence that grounds ethics in the first place? Derrida's challenge puts Levinas's philosophy to the critical test. Can the absolutely other incarnate in being without loss of transcendence?

Theology has faced this same problem with God talk. How can we talk about God, the wholly other, without reducing him to an idol? Does not the same conceptual language we use to describe God freeze-frame him into human conceptions and thus "put God in a box" of our imagination, which is limited not only by finitude but also by the noetic effects of sin? Indeed, the very character of each theological school depends on how it approaches this dilemma. Otherness and sameness, divinity and humanity converge in the incarnation, God's perfect expression of himself within the realm of being. In this sense, he has talked to us in "person." Whether and how we can talk about God depends on our interpretation of this event.

The interpretation of this human-divine event has often been victim to extremes. So-called liberal theology tends to "immanentize" God and reduce the incarnation to a divinely inspired moral example. We have seen this in Schleiermacher's theology. Karl Barth has leveled a scathing criticism at this approach and countered with the radical transcendence of God. Yet Barth's approach also shares Levinas's problem. After establishing the radical transcendence of God, he has difficulty in bringing God to earth and thus in fully validating history. Another extreme is apophatic, or negative, theology, which claims to know nothing positive about God.

This difficulty also haunts Levinas's undertaking. Because he cannot conceive of an ontology that would allow both radical transcendence *and* its valid ontological expression in history and human culture, transcendence cannot fully incarnate in ontology. And yet as I have shown, Levinas pursues an incarnational model of subjectivity and knowledge. This model, however, begins with the breach of transcendence and fails fully to incorporate transcendence within the human sphere of language and reason, because such accommodation is by definition a loss of transcendence.

We have seen that for Levinas "good phenomenology" seeks out boundary experiences in phenomena to show that all human activity depends on the primordial ethical relation. If, however, meaning, reflection, knowledge—and now language as the embodiment of thought—depend on ethical transcendence, how can we articulate the ethical-ontological relation without compromising transcendence? Like Heidegger before him and Derrida after him, Levinas opts for new terminology to avoid as much as possible the interpretive baggage of traditional metaphysical terms. In his discussion of language, our ability to communicate the ethical, Levinas has chosen the terms "saying" and "said" (*le dire, le dit*) to articulate the relation between the ethical and the ontological sphere.

Levinas devotes an entire book, *Otherwise Than Being, or Beyond Essence*, to this problematic. Essentially, the term "saying" stands for the ethical, the face-to-face relation. This ethical saying is incarnated in the ontological "said," that is, in human structures of communication of language, texts, and art. Levinas formulates this relation very carefully: "The one-for-the-other, saying, is on the point of changing into an intentional consciousness, a formulation of truths, a message emitted and received." Yet sensibility, the ethical exposure cannot be reduced to conceptual meaning. "In this caress proximity signifies as proximity, and not as an *experience* of proximity" (*OB*, 80; emphasis mine). Saying, the ethical relation of proximity that defines the human subject, is at the very beginning of human systems of signification. Thus the "incarnation of the subject," its birth and identity as the "I" that is called to serve the other, is the basis for human communication. Levinas's concession to Derrida is the admission that the ethical saying is incarnated in the ontological signifying structures, in the said, that is, in language (ibid., 79).

If Levinas is correct in his assumption that ethics is the origin of communication and meaning, two important questions arise. First, if Levinas rejects the Greek Logos as universal rationality in favor of an ethical Word ultimately grounded in the divine call, where does this leave hermeneutics? Philosophical hermeneutics, after all, is rooted in the Greek Logos of being.

And, second, even if we can work out a relationship between ethics and hermeneutics, in which hermeneutics governs the domain of the said but remains under the constant challenge of the ethical saying, what is the actual, positive content we gain from this? What concrete knowledge is conveyed in language?

Levinas offers an answer to these questions by building, again, on the phenomenological tradition. He concedes to phenomenology that language is apophantic (i.e., revelatory). Rejecting an instrumental view of language, Levinas believes that the meaning of language "is not the simple expression of thought held to exist prior to it, to which it would conform." Instead language is indeed "an order of phenomena destined to do the same work as that of thought: to know and to reveal being." So far Levinas stands in the phenomenological tradition for which language incarnates reason. Levinas believes with the phenomenological tradition of Husserl, Heidegger, and Gadamer that language is apophansis, the concealing-revealing "locus of truth"; yet for him, beyond idea, concept, and the content of proposition "*apophansis* signifies as a modality of the approach to the other person" (*OS*, 142).

Levinas does not contest that concept and proposition, knowledge of terms, are important for our legitimate success in human enterprises. There is, in other words, room for a "positivist" interpretation of language: "One can take an interest, consequently, in the *said*, in its diverse genres and their diverse structures, and explore the birth of communicable meaning in words and the surest and most efficacious way of communicating it. Thus one can attach language to the world and to being, to which the human enterprise refers; and thus attach language again to intentionality" ("Hermeneutics and Beyond," in *GM*, 105).

Yet Levinas thinks that in philosophies of language from Plato to Heidegger, language's role in revealing knowledge has been unduly stressed to the neglect of the ethical role of language (*OS*, 141). While it is true that the ethical saying depends on the said for its appearance, Levinas wants to begin with the ethical to "bring out an intrigue of meaning that is not reducible to the thematization and exposition of a *said*." After all, propositions are primarily an address to another, not merely the revelation of content. Communication, at least for Levinas, is not principally an exchange of propositional truth but an approach to our fellow man. Communication "is capable of ethical significance to which the statement itself of the Said is subordinate." Therefore, the primary role of language is to reveal proximity rather than the "uniting of minds in truth." Language points to "a sociality that is irreducible to *knowledge* of the other." That is why Levinas is opposed to empty rhetoric or eloquence if it does not spring from the ethical relation and its demand for responsibility (ibid., 142).

What then transpires in language? Language, when it merely conveys content, can easily become empty sound, no different than unintelligible noise. To this reduction of language, Levinas opposes the living ethical word. What really matters in language is the social relation, the real presence of the other (*OS*, 149). Yet this presence is not the romantic fusion of minds but the transcendence of the living word proffered by another person. This ethical word does not primarily convey content or fuse us with another mind but puts us in relation with irreducible otherness: "It is to the extent that the verb [i.e., the ethical saying, the word] *refuses to become flesh* that it ensures a presence among us" (ibid.; emphasis mine).

This sentence points to the fundamental problem of Levinas's philosophy from an incarnational point of view: Levinas simply cannot conceive of a transcendent word that would be fully present and yet remain irreducibly transcendent. While he embraces a kenotic subjectivity, he cannot conceive of such a possibility for God. Certainly, Levinas talks about the descent of God in the face of the other. For him the living ethical word of God comes to me in my neighbor first. "The divinity of God is played out in the human. God descends in the face of the other," and its single but all-important revelation is "thou shalt not kill" (*RB*, 236).

And yet this descent is not the indwelling and consequent participation of divine transcendence in the flesh. For Levinas, God cannot become human flesh as in the Christian idea of incarnation. Applied to language and ethical philosophy, this means that the transcendence of the ethical word is compromised when it appears in the ontological realm. For this reason, Levinas rejects the language of participation and talks about the ethical-ontological relation as "a relation without relation" (*TI*, 80). He argues that "the comprehension of God taken as a participation in his sacred life, an allegedly direct comprehension, is impossible, because participation is the denial of the divine" (ibid., 78). Levinas's reason for this tenuous ethical-ontological relation is fear of idolatry. By guarding the transcendence of God and his invisibility, Levinas also seeks to guard social justice because we can only know God through others.

While Levinas's affirmation of God's transcendence and communal knowing are extremely important and positive values, his insistence on God's invisibility ends up opposing the living ethical word to the written sign, even to language itself. It is good, of course, that on this basis he rejects a merely instrumental view of language—self-expression is not merely the manifestation of a thought (*OS*, 149). And yet, Levinas can never quite free himself from the dualism of living word and frozen textual sign, "in which language is already transformed into documents and vestiges" (ibid.).

Levinas's revival of the spirit-letter dualism in ethical terms has important consequences for his view of art and literature. His dilemma is that communication in texts and languages always threatens the extinction of the living word, and yet this is the only way for the other, the ethical to emerge. To appear at all, the saying must be incarnated in the said; the living ethical presence of the other must ascend through ontology in order to be present. The ethical saying, he concludes, "must spread itself out and assemble itself into essence, posit itself, be hypostatized, become an eon in consciousness and knowledge, let itself be seen, undergo the ascendancy of being. Ethics itself . . . requires this hold" (*OB*, 44).

This ascendancy of the saying in ontology occurs on three levels. First, the deep saying (the primordial ethical call and signification), then its inspired said, in which the saying articulates itself and is constantly on the verge of collapsing into the said, and finally a third, superficial level of the said, in which the said becomes "a pure theme" that is "exclusively designed" as static concept.

Levinas argues that language is a system of nouns or concepts by which we identify things and that the remainder of language is a sign system that designates objects' identities and their interrelations. For Levinas this is the ontological level of language most removed from the ethical saying, a level represented by art: "Art is the pre-eminent exhibition in which the said is reduced to a pure theme, to absolute exposition, even to shamelessness capable of holding all looks for which it is exclusively designed. The said is reduced to the Beautiful, which supports Western ontology." In this sense, art is "the birthplace of ontology" (*OB*, 40–42).

Yet this most superficial level of representation coexists with a deeper level of the said. Standing in the tradition of phenomenology, Levinas principally agrees with Gadamer that language is the house of being, or that "being that can be expressed is language." Language is not merely a secondary tool for expressing more immediately present thoughts. When we make predicative statements, we are not merely using a sign system that points out things we could also recognize without language. Rather "being is a verb," which doesn't name but *enacts* being in time: "In the predicative proposition [the verb] is the very resonance of being understood as being" (*OB*, 40).

While language, texts, and art as ontological *said* indeed tend to obfuscate the ethical *saying*, they are also its only way of appearing, and the proper place of this appearing is human communication. Language at its most dynamic level is this tension between ontology and saying. Language is both noun and verb, same and other. Language can be conceived as "a system of nouns identifying entities" that designates and thus arrests. However, it can equally be conceived "as the verb in a predicative proposition in which the substances break down into modes of being, modes of temporalization. Here language does not double up the being of entities, but exposes the silent resonance of the essence" (*OB*, 40).

This more dynamic level is Levinas's description of Heidegger's idea of art as revelation or Gadamer's word event, where meaning resides in the *how* of appearing rather than in some meaning *behind* the artwork. For Levinas textual exegesis and art criticism are necessary to uncover this ethical how. Written texts and art tend to "freeze" the living word and thus require the voice of the critic to free it again. Only when we "wrench experience away from its aesthetic self-sufficiency" through a living voice do we hear the ethical word again. Literature and human art in general bear within themselves traces of the spirit of the infinite, the human spirit or ethical relation that animates language and artistic expression. Writing, for Levinas, is inspired by the fundamental ethical relation that constitutes human existence before all else.

It is this inexhaustibility of the living word within the text that constitutes "the marvel of writing," in which an infinite richness of meaning preserves the voice of the other that teaches. In this sense, literature is like the Holy Scriptures: just as the voice of God inspires the Bible, so the voice of the other inspires human writing. That is why Levinas can claim that the Holy Scriptures and "the national literatures of our civilization rest just as much within the infinite possibilities of hermeneutics." For Levinas "Goethe's Faust, Shakespeare's tragedies, The Divine Comedy, Racine, Corneille, and Molière" all are inspired by the spirit that "solicits, from beyond the light of knowing, a reflection originating in the interhuman, in the relation to the face, where God first comes to mind" (*RB*, 232). Levinas sees art criticism and interpretation as the guardians of this ethical relation. This guardianship is, in fact, the function of philosophy: it is the phenomenological reduction that seeks out the saying in the said.

Levinas believes that the constant self-renewal of art and art criticism keeps the ethical-ontological tension alive and points to the intersection between saying and being: "In the inexhaustible diversity of works, that is, in the *essential renewal* of art, colors, forms, sounds, words, buildings—already on the verge of being identified as entities, already disclosing their nature and their qualities in the substantives that bear adjectives—recommence being" (*OB*, 40).

Interpretation, or exegesis, has the same function. It prevents the artworks and text from petrifying into a completely soundless said—to recall again the levels of the ethical word's ascendancy through ontology. The preontological saying resonates in the said as its essence, always in danger of ossifying into a completely dumb idol of empty communication. It is the task of hermeneutics to awaken and make resound the essence of the said. "It is this call for the exegesis" which brings "the modality of the essence said in the work back to the depth of the essence *properly so-called* . . . [which is] the verb, the logos, that resounds in the prose of predicate propositions" (*OB*, 41). This logos, basically the place where Heidegger and Gadamer encounter being, is merely the site beyond which the ethical is found. We must begin with these ontological structures, which are hard enough to ascertain. However, we require a further phenomenological reduction "of the said to the saying beyond the logos, beyond being and non-being, beyond essence, beyond true and non-true" (ibid., 45). This "utopia of the human" means that the human is a place nowhere in ontology but in the ethical responsibility evoked by proximity to my fellow human being (ibid.).

It is time to assess what we may gain from Levinas's view of language, texts, and art for the recovery of theological hermeneutics. Just as he did with his conception of the subject, Levinas tries to rescue language from becoming inhuman. Language is not a vehicle for thought, nor is human self-expression in texts, art, and culture something that should ensnare us in pleasurable contemplation. Instead Levinas revives, at least in a qualified sense, the premodern notion of the word as relational transcendence. In the word, the other comes to me and teaches me, beyond any objectification or measurable knowledge. Language defined as ethical word is focused not on myself but on the other; it is not contemplation or reflection but prayer: "By the proffered word, the subject that posits himself exposes himself and, in a way, prays" (*OS*, 149). Language, for Levinas, is the very embodiment of human solidarity. He believes with Gadamerian hermeneutics that "the generality of the word institutes a common world," but it does so only because "the ethical event at the basis of generalization is the underlying intention of language" (*TI*, 173). Levinas certainly agrees with philosophical hermeneutics that language is the locus of truth and that its role is to "know and reveal being" (*OS*, 140). But for Levinas language is not first a sharing of concepts or subject matter but a sharing of humanity in which we "offer the world to the Other" (ibid., 174). Language is not merely one meaningful human action among others, but it is a primordial ethical donation, our "offering of contents which answers to the face of the Other or which questions him, and first opens the perspective of the meaningful" (ibid.).

Levinas teaches us that like subjectivity and knowledge, language is grounded in ethical transcendence. It is important to note that Levinas's view of linguisticality relies heavily on theology. While theology begins for Levinas in the face of the other (*RB*, 271), human communication testifies to our being made in the image of God, something premodern hermeneutics termed *imago Dei* and which Levinas revives with his notion of à-Dieu. The fact that God's transcendence reverberates (rather than being mediated!) in one's social relation with other human beings opens a new vista for thinking, language, and meaning: "The way in which God takes on meaning in the I-You relation, to become a word of language, invites us to a new reflection." It is not, he warns quickly, "as if the other man must be taken for God or that God, the Eternal Thou, be found simply in some extension of the You" (*GM*, 151). Rather we should understand that in dialogue the unequal emerges. In other words, for Levinas communication begins not with dialogue but with ethics. Only then can we ensure transcendence as "a modality according to which, in dialogue, or more precisely in ethics of dialogue, in my deaconship with respect to the other, I think more than I can grasp" (ibid.).

In Levinas's phenomenology of transcendence, language, too, presents us with another boundary experience that points to the infinite in us. The true ethical word thus breaks, for the sake of humanity, with any easy commonality or dialogue. It breaks with any ontology of sameness. The meaning of the human is found precisely in what lies beyond our ability to grasp, "beyond that which man can be, beyond that which he can show himself" (*GM*, 167). This transcendence that I find in the other's address to me is "the regime otherwise than being" (ibid., 168). In the voice of another human being, God comes to mind. In the other's face, we find the trace of "God who loves the stranger, of an invisible, unthematizable God, who expresses himself in this face" (ibid., 166). Yet the other is not a God surrogate. Rather the trace of God in the face of the other comes as the ethical call to responsibility. Revelation, for Levinas, is that "love of the other man." Our relation to the absolute is an ethical relation (ibid., 168).

While Levinas's ethical philosophy has many affinities with word theology, what role does it allow for interpretation? If texts actually incarcerate the living voice, the face of the other in whom we may see the trace of divine otherness and perceive transcendent ethics, what are we interpreting for? On the one hand, Levinas affirms the need for interpretation for preserving the ethical essence, the living word proffered through the text; but does this reduction of the text to the ethical allow for content? We can sympathize with Levinas's fear that in reducing art and texts to pleasure, the verb of the living word has become the noun of abstract form and contemplation. When we adore art for its beauty alone, aesthetics becomes anaesthetics.

Levinas concedes the need for interpretation because criticism and interpretation make visible to us "the spoken word of a living being speaking to a living being [which] leads the image with which art was content back to fully real being" (*OS*, 149). Yet if we reduce art and texts to that single element, do we not end up with a reduction similar to the one Levinas warned against? Is there, after all, any disclosure of knowledge in language? To use Levinas's words, "what does it matter? Reduced to its essence, language is perhaps the fact that one sole word is always proffered, which does not designate a being that is thought" (ibid.). Does intellectual content matter? Is not what matters the ethical saying that is beyond thought? Why should we interpret if "this Saying [*le dire*] is delirium [*est délire*]"? The epiphany of the saying in the said of conceptual language is "ambiguity or enigma," so why do we read and interpret?

Yet Levinas insists that his ethical philosophy is not sheer apophasis (negative knowledge) because its positive content is responsibility for the other. In a late interview, Levinas confessed his embarrassment concerning the question to what extent even the Bible constitutes positive revelation. Levinas is clearly uneasy with positive religious content, but he still offers his own positive kernel: "The law of God is revelation because it enunciates: 'Thou shalt not kill,'" a command that Levinas enlarges in traditional fashion to mean "thou shalt do everything in order that the other may live. . . . All the rest is perhaps an attempt to think this" (*RB*, 272). Theologically, this is indeed the crucial question that haunts Levinas's work: how clearly has God revealed his will to humanity?

Yet Levinas's insistence on radical transcendence threatens not only theological hermeneutics but also the general validity of concrete textual exegesis. Pious phrases such as "language is the fact that always one sole word is proffered: God" leave hermeneutics with very little, almost nothing to do. Should we reduce all texts to à-Dieu, to help your neighbor? If so are we not, in fact, saying adieu, good-bye, to interpretation?

In the discussion of language and particularly of art and texts, Levinas's fundamental weakness emerges: without an incarnational theology in which otherness is incarnated without loss of transcendence, an adequate conception of aesthetics is impossible. We have seen that philosophical hermeneutics models interpretation on the experience of art, because our experience of the beautiful is indeed the foundation of interpretation. Yet we sympathize with Levinas: aesthetics requires chastening by ethics. However, in the absence of an incarnational foundation, ethics will ever remain opposed to aesthetics or, at best, feel threatened by it.

While Levinas endorses interpretation to the limited extent of guarding the saying in the said, he has fundamental reservations concerning philosophical hermeneutics and its ontological claims. We must understand these general reservations to explain the relation of Derridean deconstruction and Gadamer's philosophical hermeneutics.

Levinas's Critique of Hermeneutics

No current discussion of hermeneutics, either theological or purely philosophical, can ignore Levinas's recovery of ethical transcendence if only because it provides the main impulse for deconstructionist criticism of philosophical hermeneutics. Beyond this immediate significance, however, Levinas is particularly important for the recovery of theological hermeneutics because he is a fundamentally humanistic and religious thinker.

He is humanistic because he is sincere and uncompromising in his attempt "to think the ultimate structures of the human" (*RB*, 54). Against the prevalent cultural antipathy toward metanarratives, Levinas is enchanted by truth and meaning, which he recognizes as universal constituent elements of our humanity.

Levinas's humanism is religious because he defines the human being as fundamentally religious. He understands Western culture as a tree with two roots of different sensibilities: Greek and Hebrew culture. Both have a different measure of what constitutes humanity:

> Next to Greek philosophy, which promotes the act of knowing as a spiritual act par excellence, man is he who seeks truth. The Bible teaches us that man is he who loves his neighbor, and that the fact of loving his neighbor is a modality of meaningful life, of thinking as fundamental—I would say more fundamental—than the knowledge of an object, than truth as knowledge of objects. In this sense, if one estimates that this second manner of being religious engenders thinking, I am a religious thinker. I think that Europe is the Bible and the Greeks, but it is also the Bible which renders the Greeks necessary. . . . I say sometimes: man is Europe and the Bible, and all the rest can be translated from there. (*RB*, 53)

Levinas believes in the necessity of retrieving the Hebrew concept of humanity. While he agrees that Greek is the conceptual language of Western philosophy, and in this sense the Bible and Hebrew spirituality require philosophical translation into the Greek, Levinas's project is driven by the biblical concept of ethical transcendence. This theological inspiration makes Levinas so important for our project because it disrupts both modern and postmodern conceptions of truth and meaning. Levinas's central hermeneutical thesis is that meaning is inseparable from human spirituality. While he agrees with philosophical hermeneutics that meaning, the question of self-knowledge and purpose of our existence, is central to our humanity, Levinas gives full weight to the spiritual-ethical foundation of meaning.

Levinas's whole undertaking is a hermeneutical humanism that asks for the meaning of the human and defines the human as being called by the other into an ethical relation through which God comes to mind. True human freedom is achieved when we realize that true humanity is to be human in relation to others to whom we are ethically obligated: "By way of this freedom the humanity in me, that is to say humanity as the I in its [toward-God] à-Dieu, signifies despite its ontological contingency of finitude and the enigma of its mortality . . . in the inalienable responsibility, the uniqueness of the elected." This call constitutes true human identity, which raises each person to a dignity and excellence "irreducible" to our roles on "the social stage of history" (*GM*, 170).

Levinas's ethical philosophy provides us, from within philosophy, with a theologically inspired critique of hermeneutics whose remoteness from Christian fundamentalist tendencies gives new hope for a theological hermeneutics that can appeal to both philosophy and theology alike.

Levinas's ethical philosophy and Gadamer's hermeneutics both acknowledge the fundamental human desire for meaning. Levinas criticizes hermeneutics, however, for overlooking the ethical origin of meaning. Gadamer locates meaning in the Greek Logos and Levinas in the ethical Logos of interhuman relations, which is, ultimately, an incarnation of the divine Logos. For Gadamer, as we will see in the next chapter, meaning is the exigency of a universal rationality, a Logos inherent in being in which we participate and because of which we want to understand things in a meaningful way.

For Levinas, in contrast, meaning begins in the spiritual, "in the initial fact that man is concerned with the other man." The ethical moment of personal, ethical transcendence is "the first notion of signifying, to which reason may be traced, and that cannot be reduced to anything else. It is phenomenologically irreducible: meaning means" (*AT*, 173). Meaning begins in sociality and cannot be derived from—or abstractly expressed by—fundamental ontology. Thus "meaning is not defined formally but by an ethical relation to the other person in the guise of responsibility for him or her" (*OS*, 93).

Levinas defines meaning as transcendence and transcendence as meaning, "a meaning . . . beyond what man can be and show himself," and a meaning that is revealed in the transcendence of the face. The face is "meaning beyond doubt. Not sign or symbol of the beyond; the latter allows itself to be neither indicated nor symbolized without falling into the immanence of knowledge." The ultimate meaningful word is the face of the other, which alone "translates transcendence to us." In short, meaning is ethical transcendence, and this transcendence is itself an expression of God, the site of where the word "God" becomes meaning, the place of "the first prayer, of the first liturgy" (*OS*, 94).

Levinas distances himself from both hermeneutics and deconstruction by insisting that meaning is primordially incarnate in humanity rather than in any theoretically graspable sense. In his view, hermeneutics falls short of ethics by trying to assimilate this personal transcendence into an interpretive framework, and deconstruction fails by denigrating temporality. Levinas believes that Derrida's notion of *différance* "attests to the prestige that eternity retains in his eyes, the 'great present,' *being*, which corresponds to the priority of the *theoretical* and the truth of the theoretical, in relation to which temporality would be a failure" (*AT*, 173; emphasis in original). For Levinas, Derrida's critique of Western rationality remains wedded to Platonism. He considers his own thought more appreciative of history. In line with an incarnational theological hermeneutics, Levinas locates the beginning of meaning firmly in the concrete temporal and historical social sphere.

This appreciation of history shows strong affinity with Gadamer's philosophical hermeneutics. Gadamer emphasizes history just as strongly in the concept of historically effected consciousness, the idea that our prejudgments are shaped by our mental and cultural environment. This starting point, however, does not preclude our transcendence of it. The hermeneutical circle is not a vicious circle but an interpretive spiral of ever-widening circles in which the reshaping of questions in accordance with the object provides ever greater insights. Levinas recognizes this openness but still believes that hermeneutics is not radically transcendent enough. Its "open notion of totality" still depends on a projection of a whole to understand the part, and however provisional this projection may be, the fact remains that each particular makes sense only in light of a whole, of a totality (*AT*, 49).

Besides hermeneutics' inability to imagine a meaning unencumbered by the dialectical relation of part and whole, Levinas is also suspicious of its interpretive premise that only same can understand same. He sees this sameness in the hermeneutic dynamic of fore-understanding and its revision. These concepts try to recognize that we already antici-pate the structure and meaning of a text in order to then revise these projected meanings based on careful study of a work. Levinas finds this model misleading. He claims that, in fact, hermeneutics models mean-ing and interpretation too much on the experience of understanding texts, which is then expanded to a universal structure of understanding. Hermeneutics fails to construct interpretation on a truly human model of interaction.

Moreover, Levinas is convinced that the central hermeneutical notion of fusing horizons meets its defeat in the irreducible otherness of the personal. In direct human conversation, ethical transcendence works directly against the hermeneutical concept of fusing horizons. The ethi-cal relation does not allow "return to oneself." The ethical meaning, "as signification of the-one-for-the-other . . . is not a configuration produced in the soul. It is an immediacy older than the abstractness of nature. Nor is it a fusion; it is contact with the other" (*OB*, 86).

This slender contact as a trace of the saying in the said nonetheless packs enormous ethical punch. It is the trace whose irrevocable ethical call "obsesses the subject without staying in correlation with him, without equalling me in a consciousness, ordering me before appearing, in the glorious increase of obligation." No correlation! On these grounds, Levinas is suspicious of hermeneutics, which states that interpretation must begin with correlation. For Levinas this hermeneutic tendency overlooks "modalities of signification irreducible to the presents and presences, different from the present, modalities which articulate the very *inordinateness of infinity*" (*OB*, 94; emphasis in original).

Hermeneutics, because it focuses on the Greek Logos of rationality and listens to the voice of being, cannot decipher these signs of infinity: these are "not the signs that would await ontological interpretation, nor some knowing that would be added to its 'essence.'" Levinas thus produces a fundamental challenge to the universality of hermeneutics: interpretation finds its Waterloo at the ethical level, the very ethical foundation that gives rise to interpretation in the first place.

The hermeneutic circle is disrupted and interpretation fails because its ontological categories of understanding simply have no traction on ethical reality. The proper approach to the ethical reality is not interpretation but substitution (*OB*, 94). This is because in the ethical relation, we are not dealing with meaning conceived as knowledge in the conventional positivist sense, not even in the hermeneutical sense in which, too, knowledge begins with personal involvement. Rather the ethical moves in the register of spirituality, "no longer understood on the basis of knowing" (ibid.).

In the face of the other, hermeneutics' claim to universality is, so to speak, defaced, because its ontology is unable to account for the phenomenon of the face. Levinas concludes that "the-one-for-the-other in proximity does not form an ontological conjugation of satisfaction. The capacity of a being, and of consciousness, its correlate, is insufficient to contain the plot which forms in the face of another" (*OB*, 97). On Levinas's account, hermeneutics is unable to recognize the ethical ground of interpretation because its Greek roots assume an anthropology and epistemology that are incompatible with ethics.

While Levinas acknowledges Heideggerian subjectivity as an improvement over a modernist subject of total self-assurance, this subjectivity still proposes a schema in which "the self loses itself and finds itself out of an ideal principle, an arche; in its thematic exposition being thus carries on its affair of meaning." The problem, in other words, is Heidegger's subject, which is never really altered in Gadamer. Both understand subjectivity as consciousness that participates in being. As long as man is in any way the mouthpiece of greater, impersonal reality (i.e., universal rationality or being), true ethical transcendence perishes in the pursuit of an "ideality towards sameness" and becomes an exercise in certainty "which remains the guide and guarantee of the whole spiritual adventure of being" (*OB*, 99).

Independently from Derrida, Levinas thus launches his own charge of logocentrism against philosophical hermeneutics. He accuses hermeneutics of participating in the Greek Logos of rationality, and in this broad sense of logocentrism or *Logos-centrism*, Gadamer is guilty as charged. Contrary to the Greek model of interpretation, Levinas insists that in the ethical relation meaning begins not with the self posing questions but with the self being put in question. In total loss of self-control, "consciousness is affected before forming an image of what is coming to it, affected in spite of itself." This, of course, is contrary to Gadamer's claim that hermeneutics begins with some common ground or correlation, something that speaks to me because I recognize it.

As it turns out, Levinas's criticism of hermeneutics is part and parcel of his attack on Greek ontology. Levinas sees the universal claim of hermeneutics with its heavy dependence on the Greek Logos as threatening the ethical relation prior to all understanding. The difference between Levinas and Gadamer is not a disagreement concerning ultimate comprehension. Gadamer explicitly denies final and complete understanding. The real difference is that Levinas grounds understanding in the radical difference of ethical transcendence rather than in the friendly congeniality of universal rationality, however hermeneutically it may be conceived. Levinas concedes that it is only in this realm of understanding that conversation of and about the other can take place. Language is, after all, the house of being (Heidegger), and being that can be expressed is language (Gadamer). Yet for Levinas the house of being is erected on the foundation of the human other, on ethics; ontology only exists because of ethics.

Levinas's ethical philosophy questions the primacy of central hermeneutical positions: the hermeneutical circle with its anticipation of completeness, language as revelation of being or truth (i.e., adherence to a Greek paradigm of truth broadly defined), the priority of dialogue, the idea that understanding begins with correlation rather than difference, the notion of prejudgments and fore-structures as guiding our interpretations, and, finally, the central hermeneutical concept of fusion of horizons.

In short, for Gadamer's claim that being human is to interpret, Levinas substitutes the claim that our true humanity lies in ethical responsibility. It is my argument that Levinas's challenge to hermeneutics is both badly needed and yet highly problematic. Levinas is an ally in our recovery of theological hermeneutics because he contests hermeneutics' claim to define human understanding. He sees clearly that philosophical hermeneutics arises from a mainly Greek and neopagan framework that lacks a convincing ethical foundation. Levinas's critique cuts to the heart of the matter when he points out that in the constant tension between Greek and Judeo-Christian thought in Western thought, hermeneutics is Greek rather than Jewish. The Greek Logos does not know the radical ethical transcendence that Levinas knows from his own Old Testament background.

This does not mean, however, that hermeneutics has lost its validity. I maintain that Gadamer's account of understanding is the best account of human understanding to date but that it lacks the ethical foundation Levinas provides. Even in its clear recognition of otherness and the social relation, philosophical hermeneutics does not begin with radical transcendence. Gadamer's concern for openness and for the other, which are already themes in *Truth and Method*, are not primordial. Like Heidegger's thought, Gadamer's hermeneutical philosophy overcomes subjectivism and offers the wholesome concept of truth as revelation. Both help us to see truth not as a human construct but as something larger into which we are taken up. That is why all arguments against Gadamer's supposed relativism are unfounded.

Yet Levinas correctly senses that Heidegger's and Gadamer's notion of truth is animated fundamentally not by the human and personal but by the Greek Logos. Even this impersonal Logos, however, allows for a solid critique of idealism. Levinas's reading of hermeneutics as merely another form of idealism is thus simply wrong. Gadamer, in fact, denounces idealism's tendency to "construct truth in its entirety from self-consciousness" as leading to scientific objectivism (*Reason in the Age of Science*, 14). Moreover, the Greek Logos is interpreted differently by Gadamer and Heidegger. Gadamer is less "mystical" than Heidegger. His being is not Heidegger's being, for which humanity is the place of being's self-revelation (Safranski, *Ein Meister aus Deutschland*, 410).

Again, for all its problems, Levinas's theologically inspired ethical critique of philosophical hermeneutics exposes crucial weaknesses in philosophical hermeneutics: it lacks anthropology, and it lacks the radical transcendence of ethics, of an infinity that is not rational but relational. This is what Levinas's critique contributes to our recovery of theological hermeneutics. On its own understanding, Levinas's ethical philosophy provides a natural theology of transcendence that wants to show "the transcendence in natural thought in the approach to the other" (*AT*, 177). Levinas helps us to see that all our interpretive activity, whether we read the Bible, study history, or read novels, is to gain knowledge of self and knowledge of God. Natural theology is vital for interpretation, but as the premodern interpreters already knew, transcendence does not begin in human reason but in the ethical, in the personal communion with God that founds all human rationality and understanding. Theology ought to agree with Levinas that revelation, not contemplation (which remains necessary, of course), is the first order of hermeneutic experience.

Based on our reading of Gadamer, the combination of hermeneutics and ethical philosophy then seems plausible enough: language and texts are inspired by the ethical human relation and should be interpreted in this context. Interpretation is the legitimate and necessary activity of being in the world as long as hermeneutics has an ear for its ethical origin. Hermeneutics and ethics, I suggest, should strive for a joint venture that can support Gadamer's openness toward the other in understanding, on the one hand, and Levinas's love of texts and his inspirational model, on the other. For some, however, such a balancing act is impossible because hermeneutics always compromises radical ethical transcendence. This suspicion about hermeneutics has been most clearly expressed by John Caputo, who rejects Gadamer's philosophical hermeneutics in the name of "more radical" deconstructionist hermeneutics.

More specifically, Caputo denies the possibility of self-knowledge, which is, after all, a central concern of philosophical and theological hermeneutics. While Caputo draws much on Levinas, he also alters Levinas's basic trajectory. I have argued that what makes Levinas attractive to hermeneutics is his insistence on the ethical. Yet while Levinas interprets ruptures in seemingly coherent structures such as time and consciousness as boundary experiences that point toward an ethics of neighborly love, Caputo, following Derrida, falls in love with the breach itself. Deconstruction violates Levinas's philosophy by first stripping the ethical of the little content it had and reducing it to difference for difference's sake. This weapon of irreducible difference is then wielded against philosophical hermeneutics and, in Caputo, against the very notion of self-knowledge. After assessing the challenge of radical hermeneutics, I will show that a theological hermeneutics (and Caputo writes, after all, in the name of theology) does not have to align itself with Caputo's deconstructionist denial of self-knowledge in order to uphold otherness and ethics in interpretation.

7

HERMENEUTICS AND SELF-KNOWLEDGE
The Challenge of Radical Hermeneutics

From Levinas to the Ethics of Deconstruction

I began this book with an assessment of premodern hermeneutics to show that the central terms of the debate have never really changed. The central issues in the history of hermeneutics have always been self-knowledge and meaning. I have argued against the view that premodern theological hermeneutics is merely a local application of a more universal philosophical hermeneutics. The Reformers and their successors discussed questions of understanding as worldview questions. The crucial difference is that for them, self-knowledge, meaning, and ethics were possible only within an ontology of a personal infinity, the transcendent God. Philosophical and theological developments have done much in the last centuries to obscure this view.

With Levinas, however, philosophy and hermeneutics have been called back to radical transcendence as a necessary source for self-knowledge. Yet Levinas also writes after a period of immense human suffering. The difference is that whereas formerly transcendence was unquestionably found in the biblical God, yet now centuries of human suffering and self-extermination on a scale unknown to earlier ages have led to a distrust of a positive theology that sometimes occasioned and often sanctioned inhuman actions. It is equally true, however, and yet often overlooked,

230

that theology, and not atheism, is the very ground from which resistance to inhumanity has sprung up time and time again to seek a restoration of human dignity not by denying its centrality but by affirming the uniqueness of the human as the ground of ethics.

In light of a full century of disenchantment with theology, I believe the right approach to theological hermeneutics is one of cautious optimism, one that takes thinkers like Levinas and Gadamer seriously as advocates for meaning and ethics. They are advocates of transcendence, and transcendence is needed for self-knowledge. We find in these thinkers a return to the recognition of a full hermeneutical circle in which meaning is pursued in light of transcendence. Their insistence on the possibility of meaning and self-knowledge, however, has not gone unchallenged. In a curious twist of events, Levinas is turned against Gadamer, but not before he has been divested of his theological sensibilities. It seems that Heideggerian atheism, the idea that theology is unable to think critically, is still alive and well in academic writing, even under the name of apophatic theology.

While Levinas's criticism of Western ontology and rationality has been eagerly welcomed, particularly by adherents of deconstructionist philosophy, his theological foundations have come under attack with equal vigor. In a strange instance of conditional deconstructionist hospitality, Levinas is turned against Levinas to retain ethical transcendence without its necessary theological foundation. The admirably clear and honest work of Simon Critchley brings this emasculation of Levinas to light.

In his most recent essay, Critchley argues that one should resist the temptation to regard Levinas's theological convictions as the key to his writing because he is both a philosopher and a Talmudic scholar (*CCL*, 23). Yet he also realizes that Levinas "wants to leave the climate of both Heidegger's philosophy and an entire Greek tradition, in order to return to another source for thinking, namely the more Biblical wisdom on unconditioned respect for the other human being" (ibid., 26).

Critchley's warning is justified insofar as Levinas's rich insights cannot be reduced to theology. However, his warning also reminds us to guard against atheistic misreadings of Levinas that deny the centrality of theology for his philosophy. While Levinas is not a theologian, one simply cannot read Levinas or accept his ethics without also accepting its theological inspiration. Levinas's philosophy is theologically inspired and is, in this sense, theological through and through. This does not mean that Levinas "does" theology but that his philosophy is impossible without it and depends on a fundamental theological insight, namely, that human beings are made in the image of God. It seems to me that Critchley's attempted separation of theology and philosophy is what Levinas's ethics warns against.

With characteristic clarity, Critchley identifies Levinas's central idea "that the relation to the other cannot be reduced to comprehension and that this relation is ethical, structuring the experience of what we think of as self or subject" and, one should add, our knowing (*CCL*, 25). Yet this "big idea" stands or falls with its theological inspiration. Even the division between philosophical and confessional writings, which Levinas himself seems to favor, is typically modern in that it splits intellectual integrity into faith and reason. Levinas's "big idea" becomes most clear and concrete when he draws nearest to its theological source. Note, for example, his description of a subject beyond the ontological register as the incarnation of God's Word in the face of the other:

> There is no separation between the father and the Word; it is in the form of speech, in the form of an ethical order or an order to love that the descent of God happens. It is in the face of the other that the command-ment comes which interrupts the progress of the world. Why would I feel responsible in the presence of the face? That is Cain's answer when he is asked: "Where is your brother?" He answers: "Am I my brother's keeper?" That is the face of the other taken as an image among images, when the word of God it bears is not recognized. We must not take Cain's answer as if he were mocking God or as if he were answering as a child "It isn't me, somebody else did it." Cain's answer is sincere. Ethics is the only thing lacking in his answer; it consists solely of ontology: I am I, and he is he. We are separate ontological beings. (*RB*, 171–72)

In this way, Levinas anchors his subjectivity even outside the other in God as the utter goodness that gives meaning to the face of the other. For this reason, Levinas does not hesitate to use rather radical terms such as "hostage" to describe our relation to the other. The other stands in for the ultimate other, the good, God. The theological implications of Levinas's language are important for hermeneutics because they move us toward an incarnational hermeneutics, a conception of rationality and knowledge that I will explain more fully in the last chapter of this book.

Levinas warns us that his incarnational ethics is not another onto-logical proof for God's existence, nor does he want to turn the other into God or God into merely the highest ethical principle (*AT*, 108). Levinas's God remains profoundly the *Deus absconditus*, the invisible God whose trace we see in the face of the other. Nonetheless, he is the ultimate ground of ethical transcendence. Levinas is not interested in the nature of God but in the ethical demand resulting from him. In fact, it is crucial that God remain disincarnate for transcendence to remain radical and unpredictable. Only when the ground of transcendence is radically free, by eluding our intellectual grasp, does it remain truly transcendent.

God's radical freedom is also why Levinas rejects the modern notion of faith and its demand for immediate certainty. For him even the existential theology of Kierkegaard defines faith in this way and hence remains trapped in a "dialectical wavering" of faith and uncertainty, oscillating between highs of satisfaction and lows of unhappiness. Levinas thus rejects the very same qualities of faith cherished by deconstructive appropriations of his thought. We shall see later that Kierkegaard is one of Caputo's models for radical hermeneutics, whose embracing of radical uncertainty remains implicated in this preoccupation. Levinas suggests that we turn away from the preoccupation with self and certainty, turning instead from self to other, "to a psyche still incapable of thoughts in which the word *God* takes on meaning" (*GM*, 109–10).

All this is to say that any effort to detheologize Levinas does more harm than good by emphasizing once again the self and its anxieties rather than turning the gaze away from ourselves toward transcendence. And yet from such secularized versions of Levinas's ethics, deconstructionist challenges are issued to hermeneutics. This chapter will show that the two main challenges against hermeneutics by Jacques Derrida and John Caputo, for all their philosophical sophistication, become most clear when seen as a weaker, detheologized version of Levinas's criticism of hermeneutics. The basic challenge issued by this secularized ethics is the accusation that hermeneutics relies on assimilating tendencies in its pursuit of self-knowledge. Derrida's misreading of Gadamer's hermeneutics as logocentric is best understood in this way, as is Caputo's line of attack that hermeneutics' basic starting point of correlation violates radical ethical transcendence, the otherness of the other.

Caputo writes in the name of theology and ethics (under the banner of Derrida) and employs Levinas to argue for a deconstructionist hermeneutics. This "more radical hermeneutics" glories in its rejection of self-knowledge and derives its verve from the conviction that the only thing we can know about ourselves is that self-knowledge does not exist. Following this interpretation, hermeneutics cannot accept difference because it always wants to integrate and assimilate the unknown into the known in its quest for self-understanding. It is not without irony that Gadamer evokes a theological conception of self-understanding in defense against deconstructionist arguments.

These two challenges are best outlined and understood as arguments for an immanent transcendence that doesn't get off the ground, or, as Levinas might say, a transcendence that does not probe deeply enough to see the trace of God in the face of the other.

Derrida's Challenge

Gadamer's main concepts were developed during a time when philosophy was reshaped by a new focus on language. We have seen how central language is to Gadamer's work and how he adopts and perfects the insight of his teacher Heidegger that language is the house of being. We know that Gadamer developed his views on the linguisticality of human existence and understanding independently from French linguistic philosophy. Gadamer's main work, *Truth and Method*, the fruit of a long and successful teaching career, was written before Derrida launched deconstruction, with its central argument that Western rationality is logocentric, that is, that it privileges the spoken word over writing in its desire for absolute, certain truth.

While Derrida uses Nietzschean and Heideggerian insights to critique Western rationality from within the particular linguistic teachings of French structuralism, he makes essentially the same point as Gadamer, namely, that language is central rather than instrumental in human understanding and that human reason is not some pure interface with being. Truth in language is not the immediate contact of a Platonic ideal with the mind; truth is not the unmediated and full ahistorical presence of a voice to the inner ear. Like Gadamer, Derrida attacks the absolute self-presence of consciousness, the purity of the inner voice of reason: "Since absolute self-presence in consciousness is the infinite vocation of full presence, the achievement of absolute knowledge is the end of the infinite, which could only be the unity of the concept, logos, and consciousness in a voice without *différance*. *The history of metaphysics therefore can be expressed as the unfolding of the structure or schema of an absolute will-to-hear oneself speak*" (*SP*, 102; emphasis in original).

For Derrida the entire history of Western metaphysics is characterized by the desire for the full presence of the voice. Western philosophy's obsession with universal reason, the Greek Logos, is merely a particular manifestation of the fundamentally human desire for unmediated presence of meaning found in the voice. Derrida explains that "logocentric philosophy is a specifically Western response to a much larger necessity which also occurs in the Far East and other cultures, that is, the phonocentric necessity: the privilege of the voice over writing. . . . When words are spoken, the speaker and the listener are supposed to be simultaneously present to one another; they are supposed to be the same, pure, unmediated presence" (Kearney, *States of Mind*, 167). In Derrida's view, the Western philosophy of language has always seen writing as subversive to this full presence. Derrida, by contrast, wants to show that the supposedly immediate exchange of meaning in language is every bit as subversive and mediated as writing.

It is important to keep in mind the larger point of this seemingly obscure philosophical discussion. Like Nietzsche's and Heidegger's criticisms of Western philosophy, Derrida addresses the epistemological crisis peculiar to post-Cartesian philosophy: how can I know reality? If this question sounds like unnecessary philosophical gymnastics to the Christian reader, it might help to translate this problem into the question, How can I know God and his revelation? The departure from the premodern theory of knowledge ("faith seeking understanding") initiated by Cartesian philosophy ("doubt seeking understanding") had been inadequately addressed by Kant's three critiques until Edmund Husserl's phenomenology was hailed as overcoming the mind-reality divide. Phenomenology's call "back to the things themselves" reestablished the conviction that reality and God revealed themselves more or less faithfully to the observer. Heidegger's existential phenomenology was seen by many as the improved version of Husserl because it added the existential-interpretive dimension Husserl had lacked. Derrida denounces these attempts to reestablish trust in human reason as logocentric ruses to eradicate ambiguity and difference.

The Origin of Logocentrism: Derrida's Critique of Husserl

It is unfortunate, however, that Derrida believes Gadamer's philosophical hermeneutics to be implicated in logocentrism. This prejudice stems from his alignment of Gadamer with Husserl's phenomenology, which Derrida attacks as another logocentric self-delusion in the human quest for stable meaning. He argues that Husserl's entire project stands or falls with the claim that expression and meaning are inseparable. For Derrida, Husserl's trust in reason as ordered toward truth (that perception is essentially trustworthy if not uncomplicated) merely repeats the cardinal error of Western reason, the desire for full presence.

Derrida's argument is complicated, but it is essentially an argument about language, even if it is about the inner dialogue of our minds when we perceive ideas and objects in consciousness. We recall that for Derrida the fundamental flaw of Western metaphysics is the impossible desire for unmediated knowledge and clarity, a desire represented in our predilection for the directness of voice over the ambiguity of linguistic signs and writing. In other words, not logocentrism (the obsession with reason as immediate inner word) but the necessity of *phonocentrism* is the fundamental flaw of human perception. Derrida believes that "logocentric philosophy is a specifically Western response to a much larger necessity which also occurs in the Far East and other cultures, that is, the phonocentric necessity: the privilege of the voice over writing" (Kearney, *States of Mind*, 166).

Derrida's sweeping general claim is that we tend to equate truth and meaning with immediacy, with unmediated contact, and that we believe we find this "pure, unmediated presence" in the spoken rather than the written word. In this view, "when words are spoken, the speaker and the listener are supposed to be simultaneously present to one another; they are supposed to be the same, pure unmediated presence. This ideal of perfect self-presence, of the immediate possession of meaning, is what is expressed by the phonocentric necessity" (Kearney, *States of Mind*, 166).

As a consequence of this desire for unmediated truth, writing is perceived as uncertain and unstable because of its spatial and temporal distance from the author's voice. Writing is suspect because it depends on interpretation; "it can have different meanings as opposed to a single unifying one." In European philosophy, this immediacy was uniquely equated with reason and epistemology, and Derrida finds this weakness at the heart of phenomenology. For Derrida, Husserl's phenomenology favors the immediacy of the inner voice and relegates history, time, and the real world to a lower, less immediate status of truth. Derrida finds this distinction in two places in Husserl: in his division of signs into indicative and expressive, and in his view of time.

First, Derrida attacks Husserl's division of signs into indicative and expressive categories. For Husserl an indicative sign is anything that merely points toward the ideal object intended by the mind without actual animation by intention. As Derrida puts it, "Having its 'origin' in the phenomena of association, and always connecting empirical existents in the world, indicative signification in language will cover everything that falls subject to the 'reductions': factuality, worldly existence, essential non-necessity, non-evidence etc." (*SP*, 31). Derrida suspects that the customary Western distrust of the physical body and temporality motivates this distinction. Husserl's opposition of body and soul depends ultimately on his interpretation of language: "Here we find the core of indication: indication takes place whenever the sense-giving act, the animating intention, the living spirituality of the meaning-intention is not full present" (ibid., 38).

By contrast, expression, Husserl's second kind of sign, "is a sign charged with meaning" (*SP*, 32). Expression is anything that is expressedly animated by an intention. Thus involuntary facial expressions and bodily gestures, for example, are excluded, as is unintentional speech. Derrida observes that for Husserl "all speech, or rather everything in speech which does not restore the immediate presence of the signified content, is in-expressive" (ibid., 40).

Derrida argues that Husserl's indication-expression distinction implies that all speech functions as indication rather than expression. Pure expression is only the lived experience of the solitary mind. The inner monologue has no need or purpose for indication, for the sign, because it is immediately self-present. For Derrida, Husserl thus falls prey to the "obstinate desire to save presence and to reduce or derive the sign, and with it all powers of repetition" (*SP*, 51). With this argument, Derrida's crusade against Western metaphysics begins. Western metaphysics is driven by the desire for pure presence and hence sees the written sign as derived from the more original and immediate mental experience. In Derrida's own words, "the sign is from its origin and to the core of its sense marked by this will to derivation or effacement. Thus to restore the original and non-derivative character of signs, in opposition to classical metaphysics, is, by an apparent paradox, at the same time to eliminate a concept of signs, whose whole history and meaning belong to the adventure of the metaphysics of presence" (ibid.).

This desire for presence goes back to Plato, who sheltered the ideas as immediately present truths from the contingencies of history. Derrida pursues the opposite goal. He announces the end of metaphysics and the precedence of writing over speech, of difference over sameness. Applied to phenomenology, Derrida's crusade against logocentrism issues in the accusation that Husserl privileges the voice over writing (the sign) in the interior monologue that guarantees the immediate self-presence of phenomenology. The voice transcends the vagaries and difference of any other "signifying substance" (*SP*, 77). Derrida believes that for Husserl the inner voice, my meaning intention, is not subject to any division. "It does not risk death in the body of a signifier that is given over to the world and the visibility of space" (ibid., 78). The inner voice never ventures outside the ideal object or ideal meaning and accesses true meaning immediately without mediation by the physical world or language.

The second main line of Derrida's criticism attacks Husserl's notion of temporality. What finally slays the Western dragon of unmediated knowledge is temporality. In typical deconstructionist fashion, Derrida turns Husserl against himself. Derrida questions Husserl's inside/outside separation in phenomenology because of Husserl's own account of time. Husserl himself knew that even in interior conversation, in the monologue of consciousness, we rely on memory and images. These in turn rely on metaphors from sense experience, without which we cannot imagine or intuit anything at all. While Husserl wants to avoid the use of metaphors because they draw on the exterior world, Derrida denies this possibility.

The weakness in Husserl's schema is memory. For things to have meaning, we compare the perceived object to our memory and its traces of possible meanings: "Sense, being temporal in nature, as Husserl recognized, is never simply present; it is always already engaged in the 'movement' of the trace, that is, in the order of 'signification'" (*SP*, 85). The purest inner ideal meaning only exists because of prior sense experience, and thus the inner voice is not exempt from the influence of time, space, and history. As soon as we imagine or intuit, temporality and space are right there with it: "Hearing oneself speak is not the inwardness of an inside that is closed in upon itself; it is the irreducible openness in the inside; it is the eye and the world within speech" (ibid., 87). In terms of our linguisticality, there is no pure nonlinguistic meaning. Expression and indication are always intertwined (ibid.).

The Real Source of Derrida's Challenge

Derrida's criticism of Husserl is by no means original. In one way, it is merely a restatement in linguistic terms of Heidegger's charge that phenomenology cannot shut out ontology. In another way, however, Derrida's critique depends on Levinas's ethics. Certainly, Derrida's criticism also depends on his interpretation of Plato as believing in full presence rather than the mediation of truth through language. Derrida opposes Plato to Aristotle on this issue, a view disputed by Plato scholars, Gadamer among them. The essential point, however, is that Derrida arraigns Western thought for its cover-up of difference, a motivation that could be Nietzschean, but which, on account of its ethical desire for justice, stems from Levinas. Derrida tells us that deconstruction, for all its frequent *use* of Nietzschean vocabulary, "is, in itself, a positive response to an alterity which necessarily calls, summons or motivates it" (Kearney, *States of Mind*, 168).

Sounding ever more Levinasian, Derrida continues, "Deconstruction is therefore a vocation—a response to a call. The other, as the other than self, the other that opposes self-identity, is not something that can be detected and disclosed within a philosophical space and with the aid of a philosophical lamp. The other precedes philosophy and necessarily invokes and provokes the subject before any genuine questioning can begin" (Kearney, *States of Mind*, 168). Deconstruction turns out to be an application of Levinas's radical ethical transcendence and ethical subjectivity.

Derrida, in other words, reads Husserl through Levinas's eyes. Where Husserl sees sameness, Derrida wants to affirm difference; where Husserl sees mental acts unaffected by time, Derrida wants to insert time-lag or deferral. This is the origin of the Derridean term *différance*, which combines the words to differ and to defer. With this term, Derrida addresses what he sees as Husserl's transcendental idealism, the notion that true meaning is the true and present relation of thought and object, a relation characterized ultimately by sameness. Derrida's program resists any meaning outside language or any sign system.

For Derrida, by contrast, meaning does not exist outside language, and even within language, signs and concepts defer any final definition of meaning ad infinitum. Our thinking moves by necessity in language and linguistic tradition, to which we cannot take an outside position but from within which we seek meaning and understanding. Yet like Levinas, Derrida does not consider the impossibility of unmediated truth to imply meaninglessness. Instead he wants to complicate our received notions of meaning as certain knowledge and straightforward object-referent construct. Derrida has consistently denied that his position implies a denial of meaning. Asked in an interview to explain whether his concept of *différance* implies the complete self-referentiality of language, he replied:

> It is totally false to suggest that deconstruction is a suspension of reference. Deconstruction is always deeply concerned with the "other" of language. I never cease to be surprised by critics who see my work as a declaration that there is nothing beyond language, that we are imprisoned in language; it is, in fact, saying the exact opposite. The critique of logocentrism is above all else the search for the "other" and the "other of language." . . . Certainly deconstruction tries to show that the question of reference is much more complex and problematic than traditional theories supposed. It even asks whether our term reference is entirely adequate for designating the "other." The other, which is beyond language and which summons to language, is perhaps not a "referent" in the normal sense which linguists have attached to this term. But to distance oneself thus from the habitual structure of reference, to challenge or complicate our common assumptions about it, does not amount to saying that there is nothing beyond language. . . . Deconstruction is not a disclosure in nothingness [i.e., is not a nihilism] but an openness towards the other. (Kearney, *States of Mind*, 173)

Derrida's reply shows at least that he believes in something beyond language, but he is also certain that its articulation for finite beings is only possible from inside language. It is the task of philosophy, then, to deconstruct our systems of reference so that we are not completely controlled by them. In this sense, it is certainly true that the primary motive of deconstruction is to critique ideology.[1]

1. See Jean Grondin's *Hans-Georg Gadamer: Eine Biographie* (Tübingen: Mohr/Siebeck, 2000), 369.

Gadamer's Reply to Derrida

Gadamer understands Derrida's concern in charging Husserl and Heidegger with logocentrism well enough, but he insists that Derrida's accusation of logocentrism demonstrates the French philosopher's misreading of the German phenomenological tradition. In his writings on deconstruction, Gadamer has been at pains to establish his philosophical hermeneutics as a philosophy of finitude that is neither logocentric nor a closet essentialism. In fact, Gadamer insists that he and Derrida are much closer in objective, if not in spirit, than Derrida cares to admit. If reason is linguistic and the unfolding of meaning in language occurs hermeneutically, Gadamer makes the same claim as Derrida: we never hear a pure, unmediated voice. For this reason, Gadamer dismisses Derrida's charge of logocentrism against the German phenomenological movement embodied in Husserl, Heidegger, and himself as wrongheaded.

Derrida's point is that expression, which in Husserl is not a sign or an indication but has an immediate ideal meaning, is also susceptible to signs (and hence to difference and deferral of meaning) and that the past "now" of retention contradicts the presence or identity of the present "now" (the early Husserl believed that we can have full access in consciousness to the intentionality of others by recalling their words or ideas and making them present to us). In short, Derrida argues against Husserl's sense of pure contact with the phenomenon in consciousness because of the mediated nature of all knowledge and the temporal dimension of consciousness.

Gadamer insists that in both cases Derrida reads neither Husserl nor Heidegger closely enough. For starters, by 1910 Husserl himself had already abandoned the idea that expression and meaning are one and the same. Heidegger and his students had also long abandoned this notion: "The teaching of the unity of expression and meaning, which triggered Derrida's criticism, was long behind us" (*GW*, 10:128). By directing his criticism against the early Husserl, Derrida flogs a dead horse.

Moreover, since Derrida reads Heidegger through Husserl, his understanding of Heidegger (and thus of Gadamer) is distorted (*GW*, 2:371). Derrida's charge of logocentrism against Heidegger, and consequently against Gadamer's hermeneutics, is hamstrung by Derrida's fixation on the "platonic static sense of one ideal meaning," (ibid., 10:129) which applies, however, neither to Heidegger nor to Gadamer's own work. In fact, Gadamer completely agrees with Derrida that even the inner voice of conscience requires interpretation. He disagrees, however, with Derrida's view of language as split into its constituent parts of word and meaning.

After all, while understanding is intrinsically dependent on our choice of words, we don't listen to our own or others' *words* to the exclusion of what they want to express. Neither do we listen to voice as such. For Gadamer understanding and meaning depend not exclusively on the sign but on that which the sign, the words, the conversation try to get at, the subject matter. This is the essence of communication and understanding (*Verständigung und Verstehen*). In other words, we fish for meaning, project a meaning, and cut through the thicket of words almost intuitively to understand *what* someone is trying to say. Gadamer fully agrees with Derrida's notion of difference, but he does not need to evoke "writing" as a primordial element that causes difference. Gadamer sees no need for Derrida's concept of *écriture* because *lecture*, reading itself, is ambiguous enough—reading "in which the written is on its way to language" (*GW*, 10:128).

Gadamer's definition of the word "understanding" (*Verstehen*) further clarifies his rejection of Derrida's logocentric label for hermeneutics. Understanding means to stand in for someone, to be someone's advocate.[2] The one who stands in our place does not repeat what we said or dictated but speaks our cause, our concern, or subject matter as another to others. Certainly difference is implied here, Gadamer says. In this sense, Gadamer's statement in *Truth and Method* should be understood thus: "To understand means to understand differently" (*Wer versteht, muss anders verstehen*). To understand differently, then, merely means that one appropriates what has been said to be able to pass it on. Gadamer is thus not guilty of the Derridean critique that his work depends on an ahistorical, timeless Platonic notion of presence.

Gadamer goes further, however, and questions Derrida's concept of *écriture*, the notion that any supposed immediate presence of voice is already implicated in a sign system. For Gadamer writing itself (even in the broad sense of the signification system in which Derrida uses the term) requires the voice for its actualization. Gadamer insists that "one cannot read writing without understanding, that is, without articulating it and thus without adopting an occasional intonation and modulation that anticipates the meaning of the whole. Only in this way can writing return to speech [*sprechen*] (which does not have to be reading aloud). The actualization of writing always demands interpretation in the sense of interpreting understanding [*deutendes Verstehen*], just as the word that is directly spoken to me demands an interpreting understanding" (*GW*, 10:129). In that sense, hermeneutics does not grant an immediacy of even the spoken word. All utterances demand interpretation from the very beginning. The dialogical nature of hermeneutics means that any

2. "*Für jemanden stehen*" (*GW*, 10:129).

utterance is subject to appropriation and interpretation in the process of understanding.

Gadamer also believes that Derrida misunderstands the temporal dimension of hermeneutics. Derrida seems to think of time in terms of a split between time past and time present. But is the multiplicity of meaning really to be found in the facticity of the sign (Derrida), or is it not rather found, with Gadamer, in constituting meaning through the facticity of speech and answer (*GW*, 10:126)? For Gadamer, Derrida's criticism of Heidegger is not nuanced enough. Aristotle, Plato, and Heidegger can, of course, be accused of a logocentrism in the broadest sense, but this is a Logos-centrism, that is, a belief in a basic rationality of the universe, not, however, in a simple word-referent structure of certainty. And while Derrida may certainly label their implicit ontology the temporal character of "presence" in the broadest sense, Gadamer concludes that the accusation of unmediated presence, of logocentrism against hermeneutics, makes no sense whatsoever in light of the temporal criticism that Heidegger applied to Greek ontology (ibid., 10:127).

Gadamer reminds us that Heidegger's basic concept of time, which determined all his later work, and his criticism of onto-theology stem from an early seminar on Paul's letter to the Thessalonians, whose notion of *parousia* Heidegger wanted to make fruitful for philosophy. In the same way that Paul exhorts the congregation not to demand the immediate return and presence of the Savior, the entire analysis of *Being and Time* rests on the futurity of *Dasein*. *Dasein*'s mode of being is future oriented and not presence oriented. Thus Heidegger finds in Paul's notion of time an important existential dimension for his deconstruction of the presence-oriented view of time, which dominates the West with the rise of science, the measurable clock time Heidegger comes to call "vulgar time." Moreover, Heidegger appropriates Kierkegaard's insight that one cannot understand "out of time" in a "distanced" manner (*mit Abstand zu verstehen*). Kierkegaard criticized the church of his time for treating the Christ event merely historically without making it present. Heidegger has used this sentiment in his criticism of the atemporality of reason and logic. Given these considerations, Derrida's reduction of Heidegger's complex thinking on temporality to logocentrism appears highly questionable to Gadamer.

Hermeneutics Is Logos-centric

In essence Gadamer accuses Derrida of misunderstanding both the Greek tradition and Heidegger's appropriation of it. In his blind zeal to flush out logocentrism at all cost, Derrida overlooks that neither

Heidegger nor Gadamer hold to a full and complete presence of meaning or elevate some inner, pure, unmediated voice over an unreliable linguistic utterance. Just because Gadamer speaks about Logos does not mean he is logocentric. Gadamer's modified version of the Greek Logos concept (in which rationality is linguistic and dialectical) contains both proximity and distance, the moment of reflection, of distancing oneself from the immediate reaction to the present. Since reason is embodied in language, all human language has the character of conversation and the inherent dynamic of proximity and reflective distance.

In addition, Gadamer explicitly distances himself from Heidegger's view that conversation is tainted by the threat of inauthenticity and defines the essence of language as conversation, a conversation whose very nature resists complete domination by either the speaker or the addressed but in which the subject matter emerges. Gadamer believes that "this is a superior experience, insofar as it goes beyond Heidegger's *Jemeinigkeit* of Dasein and its seduction by the world [*und seine Verfallenheit an die Welt*]. There is no subjective consciousness, either in the speaker or in the addressed, that is able to completely comprehend [*umfassen*] that which emerges in conversation" (*GW*, 10:128).

Gadamer fails to see how such a concept of language is either phono- or logocentric. After all "it is not the art of hermeneutics to nail down someone to what someone has said but to gauge and receive that which he actually wanted to say" (*GW*, 10:129). The problem lies rather with Derrida's fixation with a Platonic-static sense of an ideal-unified meaning, which he sees in everything that is not deconstruction. A fine ear can clearly detect Gadamer's subtle accusation: is it not Derrida who wants to "nail down" hermeneutics to the schema of presence and is unable to grant it a full hearing?

Gadamer's careful analysis of Derrida tries to show that hermeneutic philosophy pursues the same goal as deconstruction. The difference may just be a question of terminology. In his reflections on Derrida's work, Gadamer has pointed out the superiority of the "inner word" to Derrida's notion of *écriture*. Like the inner word, Derrida's *écriture* also tries to guard against illusions of univocal word-thing reference. Yet Derrida's inability to articulate a positive structure of reference and his consequent suspicion of hermeneutics' ability to do so are evidence that deconstruction is itself logocentric. According to Gadamer, Derrida's Levinasian anxiety that the fusion of horizons in understanding and conceptual formulations occludes and represses otherness shows that deconstruction associates language and conversation with loss of transcendence (*GW*, 10:130).

Gadamer concludes that to associate hermeneutic understanding with assimilation or identification betrays deconstruction's own idealistic, logocentric motivation (*GW*, 10:130). A proper understanding of the Greek Logos and hermeneutic philosophy should recognize that fusion of horizons does not mean assimilation: "When I speak in my own work of the necessity that in all understanding one's horizon fuses with that of the other, I am certainly not talking about a lasting and identifiable oneness; rather, [the fusion of horizons] occurs as ongoing conversation" (ibid.). The hermeneutical notion of conversation, based on the model of the inner word, is not assimilation but allows for an infinite unfolding of the subject matter without loss. The point is not return to the one but, as in the incarnational model, an originary unity whose rich implications continue to unfold. Gadamer's philosophical hermeneutics is indeed not logocentric but Logos-centric and in this sense guards the manifold manifestations of the word as much as deconstruction.

In the end, Gadamer's ever more finely honed concept of truth as the fusion of horizons has even convinced Derrida that hermeneutics and deconstruction agree on the infinite deferral of final meaning. Gadamer tells us that "in the end, Derrida has completely agreed with me after I told him in Naples that the horizon of the horizon fusion in interpretation is not something we can ever reach and so cannot occupy a metaphysical position. The horizon of interpretation changes constantly, just as our visual horizon changes with every step we take" (*Lektion des Jahrhunderts*, 67).

But if hermeneutics and its central concept of horizon fusion avoid logocentrism, do they avoid interpretive violence? Even if hermeneutics does not want to "nail down" the other, is it not still essentially committed to the ancient Greek belief that understanding requires familiarity, that only same understands same? After all, hermeneutics' claim that knowledge comes to us only as interpretation is hardly controversial; most contemporary philosophers and theologians share this turn from rationalist conceptions of absolute truth to a more dynamic, hermeneutical model.

What remains in question, however, is the universal claim of philosophical hermeneutics and its dependence on the Greek rather than the Judeo-Christian Logos. Based on its Greek-inspired ontology, hermeneutics remains an interpretive model of recognition. Even in its full recognition of the alien and of difference, Gadamer's hermeneutics is a dialectical mediation between the alien and the familiar. It is true that interpretation fuses horizons by integrating the alien into the universality of the logos. Contrary to Derrida's allegations, however, Gadamer has always insisted that this fusion does not assimilate the alien into the familiar. Differently from Hegel, Gadamer's adoption of Heidegger's radically temporal-historical framework does not aim at an eventual resolution of things. As Gadamer indicated, horizon fusion is merely a moment of encounter that allows us to understand something alien without eradicating its difference.[3]

For Levinas, however, hermeneutics still rests on Greek ontology, which is essentially an impersonal, unethical construct. Levinas, as we have seen, diagnoses philosophy's neglect of ethical transcendence at the heart of subjectivity and knowledge as the central malaise of Western thought. Consequently, he insists on an ethical enframing of interpretation. Gadamer does not understand this desire. For him respect for the other is merely a basic requirement for anyone who wants to listen.

My argument is, in short, that after Gadamer's response to Derrida's criticism and their rapprochement late in their careers, the central unresolved issue between hermeneutics and deconstruction remains ethical transcendence. Does interpretation begin in ethical transcendence (Levinas) and so in radical difference (Derrida), or can interpretation do without ethics and abide serenely in the ontological realm of Heidegger's and Gadamer's Greek logos? I have argued that the ethical impulse for justice at the heart of deconstruction is itself derived from the philosophy of Emmanuel Levinas, whose ethical philosophy and its central concern to preserve the uniqueness and dignity of the other has greatly influenced Derrida. We detect Levinasian terms and the Levinasian distaste of sameness and totality throughout Derrida's writing, from Derrida's early work on Husserl to his later work on friendship, hospitality, and faith.[4]

Derrida's mature work has increasingly turned to these religious and ethical topics that some see, and I believe correctly, as an outgrowth of an original ethical impulse that motivates all of Derrida's work. Simon Critchley, for example, has argued convincingly that Derrida is best read as an ethical thinker, if, as Critchley rightly points out, "ethics is understood in the particular sense given to it in the work of Emmanuel Levinas" (*ED*, xiii). As Critchley shows, not only has Levinas exerted a powerful and continuous influence on the development of Derrida's thinking, but in fact, Levinas's ethical imperative is also that of Derrida.

When we understand deconstruction as a variant of Levinas's ethical philosophy, we can also understand its value independently of its misreading of Gadamer's philosophical hermeneutics. Even if Derrida's

3. James Risser has correctly pointed out that Gadamer's idea of understanding rests on a non-assimilative notion of logos in which, much as in the rhetorical figure of metaphor, identity and difference can coexist. See "Die Metaphorik des Sprechens." In *Hermeneutisch Wege* (Tübingen: Mohr/Siebeck, 2000), 187–89.

4. Bruce Ellis Benson also notes this in his recent book *Graven Ideologies: Nietzsche, Derrida, and Marion on Modern Idolatry* (Downers Grove, IL.: InterVarsity Press, 2002). In a footnote, he remarks that "though most readers have not noted the connection, Jacques Derrida['s *Speech and Phenomena*] is clearly indebted to Levinasian concerns" (111).

criticism of hermeneutics as logocentric (privileging voice over writing) is false, the underlying Levinasian point that hermeneutics is *Logos-centric*, that it begins on the Greek premise, however modified, that reason is common to all human beings, remains valid. The basic contention between deconstruction and hermeneutics remains: should interpretation begin in correlation, with the premise of common ground, or in radical difference, in the breach? This question, we remember, was Derrida's challenge to Gadamer in 1981. Is hermeneutics able to conceive a meaning that begins with breach and difference rather than an interpretive context of sameness and the incorporation of new insights into an existing, albeit ever-changing, framework ("Three Questions to Hans-Georg Gadamer," 53)?

It is my ongoing contention that only a *theological* hermeneutics based on the doctrines of the incarnation and the Trinity can offer such an integrative approach. Levinas, as I have tried to show, allows us a glimpse at this theological option but only if we fully appreciate the biblical inspiration of his ethical transcendence. Yet current philosophers of ethics are reluctant to see the full implications of Levinas's theological roots. Instead they make every effort to reduce his biblically inspired ethical transcendence to a less offensive form of atheist transcendence.

Very Little, Almost Nothing: The Secularization of Levinas

We have seen that Levinas's ethical transcendence has already made an impact on hermeneutics through Gadamer's first encounter with Derrida in 1981 at the Goethe Institute in Paris. The only crossing of swords at this "nonencounter" was Derrida's claim that hermeneutics presupposes an ethical stance it cannot justify and Gadamer's defense that willingness to listen has nothing to do with ethics but everything to do with the basic mechanics of communication.

Both Gadamer and Derrida have since voiced their disappointment concerning this encounter. Most recently, in his Heidelberg address commemorating Gadamer's death, Derrida confesses that he did not really engage Gadamer in Paris but that this failed dialogue turned out to be more successful than a harmonious meeting could ever have been (*UD*, 5). Derrida believes to have learned from Gadamer that deconstruction and hermeneutics are not enemies but two sides of a beginning dialogue. They are, in fact, two inseparably connected phases of interpretation. While hermeneutics focuses on understanding, deconstruction focuses on that which limits understanding.

Derrida's exposition of Paul Celan's poetry in this speech pays homage to hermeneutics but also points out that he himself is not a hermeneut but a deconstructionist. Hermeneutics, Derrida explains, is the careful interpretation of the text under consideration of its rhetorical-linguistic structure and cultural-historical context. Sounding much like Levinas, Derrida argues that hermeneutics itself, however, is occasioned by the irreducible excess of texts, "which withdraws itself from any assembling through a hermeneutics. Rather through this, first hermeneutics becomes necessary" (*UD*, 17). Deconstruction, in contrast to hermeneutics, focuses on this irreducible excess and sees its task in questioning the comfort of hermeneutics.

It is hard not to read Derrida's concluding words as the Levinasian call for ethics. Should we not, asks Derrida, think the world from the perspective of an absence of initiative grounded in an I-Thou relation? This is one of the questions Derrida "would have liked to ask Gadamer in calling for help." He states, "In order to orient our thinking, to aid us in this dangerous task, I would have recalled how much we need the other and how much we will continue to need him; how much we must carry him and be carried by him, there where he speaks in us even before we speak" (*UD*, 32).

Derrida here recalls hermeneutics to the transcendence of the personal human relation, the otherness, alterity, or ethical saying urged on philosophy by Levinas. We have seen that for all his refusal to mount an apologetic for the Abrahamic God in his philosophical writings, Levinas nonetheless traces in the irreducible excess that which resists final interpretation and comprehension, the other whose ethical claim on us is ultimately grounded in God. Simon Critchley has well described Levinas's God: "The transcendence of the divine in Levinas is the alterity of the trace, an order irreducible to presence and the possibility of incarnation. Levinas's God is not the God of onto-theo-logy, but rather, . . . God 'is' an empty place, the anarchy of an absence at the heart of the community. . . . Levinas writes that it is 'thanks to God' that I am an Other for others" (*ED*, 228).

Thinkers like Derrida and Critchley are attracted by Levinas's ethics because it is a metaethics that leaves open the question of concrete moral application. Simon Critchley points out that "Levinasian ethics does not seek to tell us how we ought to act, nor does it even claim to offer a normative system or procedure for formulating and testing the acceptability of certain maxims, judgments or values" but rather "an ethics of ethics" (*ED*, 255–56).

In the speech presented here, Derrida confirms Critchley's belief that the role of deconstruction is to be the guardian of this openness. The whole idea of deconstruction is that while all meaning occurs within a historical-linguistic context without recourse to an ahistorical, ultimate referent, there occurs within this context and within each text a rupture that resists final interpretation. After all, Levinas himself understands Derrida's work in this way when he writes that through Derrida's "deconstruction of presence, the testimony of consciousness to itself loses its Cartesian privilege. . . . What appears truly in deconstructive analysis as a lacking to self is not *the surplus* (which would be yet another promise and a residuum of ontology) but the *better* of proximity, an excellence, an elevation, the ethics before being or the Good beyond being" (*Proper Names*, 60–61; emphasis in original).

Derrida and Critchley share Levinas's anxieties about ontology and Western metaphysics, but their atheism does not allow them to anchor ethics in God. This lack, coupled with a strong awareness that we cannot leave the language of metaphysics and ontology, brings about negative formulations of ethics and subjectivity. Critchley, for example, argues that philosophers should try to reshape metaphysics from within and remain "metaphysicians in the dark" by following the ethical impulse and facing the agony of applying this indeconstructible justice to the political and social dimension of life.

Critchley, who, like Derrida, openly admits his atheism, is a careful expositor of Levinas but rejects his theological sensibilities; in fact, he seems to think Levinas would be rather better off without them (*VL*, 82). Certainly, deconstruction and "metaphysics in the dark" can teach us much concerning human finitude with its ambiguity, and we should heed their warnings against triumphalist and self-congratulatory stances on ethics, politics, and decision making. Yet Critchley, offended by Levinas's theological source for transcendence, reduces Levinas's divinely inspired transcendence to atheist transcendence, "the primal scene of emptiness, absence and disaster, what [he is] tempted to call atheist transcendence" (ibid., 83).

Atheist transcendence means that Critchley wants to flatten Levinas's transcendence by cutting off the slender thread that ties Levinas's subjectivity to God. While Critchley accepts Levinas's argument that transcendence must be understood in terms of a social relation, he rejects the very assumptions in Levinas's work that give it depth and promise: "First that the relation to alterity can be understood ethically in some novel metaphysical sense and, second, that this ethical relation has theological implications (i.e., the trace of illeity)" (*VL*, 82). Instead Critchley follows Derrida in settling on difference for difference's sake. He brackets the "ethico-metaphysical consequences" of Levinas's radical transcendence and reduces it to a "formal notion" (*EPS*, 278), to an aporia akin to Derrida's messianic, "an unconditional, apriori, universal dimension of experience—the messianic—which is undeconstructible" (ibid., 111).

Critchley is fully aware that the cardinal weakness of Levinas's thought, its "open wound," is the great gap between his ethical ideal and reality, between its radical transcendence and implementation (ibid., 113). And yet instead of wrestling with the theological implications of this weakness, Critchley follows Derrida's reduction of Levinasian ethics to a "reflective, emancipatory critique" (ibid., 114). Ethically inspired philosophy thus becomes again the Socratic gadfly whose subversive activities keep the political powers on their toes in the name of justice.

One may well ask whose justice we are talking about. While it is precisely the point of deconstructive ethics to offer a pure justice without any definition, a justice compared to the messianic whose power consists in its refusal to appear, such apophatic oracles are not faithful to the spirit of Levinas's ethical philosophy. Apophatic visions of justice fly in the face of Levinas's own convictions. I have tried to show how much Levinas's teaching depends on theological doctrines. His incarnate subjectivity requires the doctrine of creation ex nihilo (*TI*, 63). Likewise, the qualification of the "good violence," of the ethical demand as peaceful, depends on its grounding in the biblical God.

Above all, however, Levinas himself insists that his ethical philosophy is not negative theology but revelatory theology with its single message from on high, the call to serve one's neighbor. Given Levinas's own account of ethics and justice, the attempt of deconstruction and its followers to cleanse his philosophy of that foundational element is akin to removing a vital organ from a person's body and still expecting it to function. This problem becomes quite clear in Critchley's work. His atheistic, deconstructionist ethics cannot acknowledge that Levinas's otherness is linked to the biblical God of justice. While Critchley accepts Levinas's social starting point of ethics, an immanent transcendence, he cannot understand Levinas's belief that this transcendence is characterized by the good: "I do not see why such alterity then received the predicate 'goodness'" (*VL*, 81).

One reason, at least, why this alterity can be called good is Levinas's conviction that God has created the world and that human beings are in some sense made in God's image, as free creatures whose simultaneous freedom and dependence is the divine gift of their humanity. Human identity is defined by radical ethical transcendence because "an infinity that does not close in upon itself in a circle but withdraws from the ontological extension so as to leave a place for a separated being *exists divinely*" (*TI*, 104; emphasis mine). When Critchley wrongly surmises that Levinas's rejection of ontologically driven theology (or onto-theology) is a rejection of creation ex nihilo altogether, he replaces Levinas's Jewish sensibilities with his own atheistic ones (*EPS*, 68). Critchley writes that Levinas "de-theologizes" the theological concept of creation ex nihilo, when, in fact, Levinas uses this very concept to distinguish his thought from both onto-theology and the Greek logos that underlies Heideggerian ontology: "To affirm origin from nothing by creation is to contest the prior community of all things within eternity, from which philosophical thought, guided by ontology, makes things arise as from a common matrix. The absolute gap of separation which transcendence implies could not be better expressed than by the term creation, in which the kinship of beings among themselves is affirmed, but at the same time their radical heterogeneity also, their reciprocal exteriority coming from nothingness" (TI, 293). Critchley is correct to affirm that Levinas's notion of creation resists totality, but this is not because it is de-theologized but because it is full out Jewish theology. His very idea of infinite desire of the other, "the relationship between strangers," is affirmed across the idea of creation ex nihilo. This doctrine guarantees that need is replaced by desire which opens "the possibility of a sabbatical existence, where existence suspends the necessities of existence" (ibid., 104).

Levinas's whole point is that God comes to mind through the ethical call that limits one's selfishness in irrefusable service to one's neighbor. Levinas is wary of dogmatic theology because he fears the arrogance of theology and doctrine on account of which we lose ourselves in theological definitions and systems while the widow continues to starve. His caution against positive theology has very little to do with deconstruction's penchant for radically apophatic knowledge. As I have shown earlier, "Thou shalt not kill" is the positive universal norm for Levinas's ethics. Rather than losing ourselves in the idolatry of discussing and portraying God, we should serve God by turning to our neighbor with a helping hand.

Unlike Critchley, Levinas does not separate theology and philosophy but sees the latter as coexisting with—and preparing the way for—the former. What sets Levinas apart from other theologians is his attempt to find this structure of holiness, our ethical constitution as one-for-the-other, in the very fabric of philosophy, questioning philosophy's equivocation of knowledge and spirituality from the ground up. Levinas's effort to show spirituality as ethics at the very heart of reality and as the foundation of human existence supports his claim that his "language is not simply a sermon; it is also an attempt to philosophize" (RB, 54).

Given Levinas's own convictions, to cut off his ethics from its theologically inspired roots and transplant it into a deconstructionist ethics, however concretely oriented toward human sociality and justice, excises the uniqueness from Levinas's work, its otherness, and thus reduces it to the sameness of all other philosophical systems or nonsystems that exclude theology. Critchley writes that he has tried very hard to listen "for many years" to the voice of theology and the Divine that arises in Levinas's ethical relation but has now become quite deaf to it (VL, 82).

Given many Christians' talent for annoying seriously thinking people, Critchley's deafness to this voice is understandable, but Levinas's ethics without this dimension lapses into merely formal and hence empty piety. The philosopher Alain Badiou has clearly identified the tendency of thinkers like Derrida and Critchley to derive from Levinas an ethics of the right to difference (the asymmetry) but insists that they cannot have this without also accepting Levinas's religion. For difference can be upheld only when it is anchored in an ultimate Other. Badiou sees clearly Levinas's guarantee against the collapse of ethical transcendence into sameness is the "altogether-Other," which is "quite obviously the ethical name for God" (*Ethics*, 22). If there is one central notion in Levinas's philosophy, it is this: "There can be no finite devotion to the non-identical if it is not sustained by the infinite devotion of the principle to that which subsists outside it. There can be no ethics without God the ineffable. In Levinas's enterprise, the ethical dominance of the Other over the theoretical ontology of the same is entirely bound up with a religious axiom; to believe that we can separate what Levinas's thought unites is to betray the intimate movement of his thought, its subjective rigour" (ibid.).

Badiou believes, and I agree with him, that we cannot de-theologize Levinas but have to accept that his is a non-Greek ethics based on a Jewish faith and that ethics is by definition "a category of pious discourse" (*Ethics*, 23). He argues against Critchley's attempt to secularize Levinas, especially in view of politics. According to Badiou, such attempts yield "a dog's dinner. We are left with a pious discourse without piety, a spiritual supplement for incompetent governments, and a cultural sociology preached, in line with new-style sermons, in lieu of the late class struggle" (ibid.).

It is true that Levinas's resistance to dogma seems to justify the label "apophatic" for his thought. We should be careful, however, not to mistake negative theology for agnosticism. Levinas's resistance to dogmatic theology should not be taken as a denial for the profoundly theological basis of his thought. For Levinas, in the face of the other, God comes to mind. Based on his nontheistic hermeneutical stance, Critchley pursues Levinas's ethics in the opposite direction, not "the transcendence of the Good beyond Being or the trace of God, but . . . the primal scene of emptiness and disaster, what [he is] tempted to call, rather awkwardly, atheist transcendence" (*VL*, 83). Critchley thus aligns himself with a venerable line of philosophers, Nietzsche, Heidegger, and Derrida among them, who for all their professions of justice and otherness cannot bear the otherness of theology. Interpreted in Levinasian terms, this move to forestall the disrupting voice of theology indicates an attitude of self-preservation, a refusal to engage theology for fear that it might actually have something to say that disrupts the pleasant comfort of God denial.

Now, given the history of Christian theology and, more to the point, the caricatures of theology—which, too, hold a grain of truth—as self-satisfied, socially irrelevant academic discipline or, perhaps worse, as society-destroying, meddling fundamentalism, the exclusion of theology from the current discussion of ethics and hermeneutics is understandable. I suspect, however, that this rejection is at least partially, if not mainly, motivated by an unwillingness to engage theological traditions thoughtfully and on their own terms.

The Judeo-Christian tradition is unique in the sense that such an engagement requires a personal relation with God, an ethical relation that consists in God's call through which subjectivity is founded not on one's own terms but on God's. I will outline this further in the last section but suffice it to say for now that a thick conception of theology as personal relation may well allay Critchley's fears of theological arrogance and provide a model of knowing that is both hermeneutically acceptable and ethically satisfying. While I sympathize with Critchley's suspicion of otherworldly, abstract metaphysical constructs beyond being, an incarnational hermeneutics based on the God who actually became human being and yet remains at the same time the completely transcendent other offers a hermeneutical ontology that affirms the human need for meaning without allowing a totalizing grasp of any interpretation.[5]

Critchley's ethics of deconstruction has found a theological advocate in the theologian-philosopher John Caputo. He moves beyond Critchley's cautious "metaphysics in the dark" to an open rejection of metaphysics in celebration of unknowing. Caputo calls this "radical hermeneutics" and challenges us finally to give up the notion of self-knowledge. It is to his challenge we turn next.

Dancing with the Devil: Radical Hermeneutics and Self-Knowledge

At least since the Delphic oracle's summons, *"gnosi seauton,"* the desire for self-knowledge has animated philosophers and theologians

5. An incarnational hermeneutics thus addresses directly Critchley's concern about the task of interpretation. In *Very Little, Almost Nothing*, Critchley reiterates his earlier argument in *Ethics of Deconstruction* that hermeneutics is the task of articulating the "meaning of meaninglessness," an impossible but necessary task. This is, in effect, atheist transcendence, a position that, with all the respect I have for Critchley's impeccable scholarship, is deeply dehumanizing because it pits an inherent human drive of meaning-making against the essential meaninglessness of the universe and then demands justice and ethics "for no reason," in the face of this meaninglessness (*VL*, 138). In this sense, Critchley is, in effect, the secular version of Caputo's negative theology (ibid., 151–52).

alike. The inscription on the Greek temple, "know thyself," warns us that without self-knowledge, without the interpretation of our being (*Daseins-interpretation*), we are blind concerning our existence in this world. "Know thyself"—this has been the central question for humanism, that is, for the human sciences and their ancestor, medieval and Renaissance humanism.

With the Protestant Reformation, an important development occurred in the ancient quest for self-knowledge. Luther's exegetical work in particular recovered the biblical and incarnational focus on God for interpretation and so reintroduced personal-relational aspects into the quest for self-knowledge. The Reformation debate between Erasmus of Rotterdam and Martin Luther demonstrates that the debate concerning self-understanding became sharply focused on the quality of self-knowledge.

The dispute between Erasmus and Luther concerning the freedom of the will was all about whether we could gain adequate self-knowledge through the light of reason or through divine illumination. Erasmus, we remember, claimed that reason is the God-given armor by which we know ourselves and wage war against the flesh in order to attain virtue, while Luther likened reason to an armor of straw that cannot resist the fiery breath of the devil. Only in encountering Christ and understanding ourselves as completely dependent on him do we know how weak we actually are and that our only hope lies in clinging to him (Werner Welzig, introduction to Erasmus's *Enchiridion*, xx).

This Reformation debate shows that the question of self-knowledge is also one about human autonomy. Erasmus's insistence on reason as a reliable source of self-knowledge was denied by Luther because for him, true self-knowledge meant to see oneself in need of Christ; if reason were able to reveal this, then who is to say that Pelagius wasn't right after all: we could not only know but also save ourselves by means of reason. Luther's comment addresses the question of self-knowledge and autonomy: for Erasmus, self-knowledge seemed to imply self-control, whereas for Luther, the first step of self-knowledge was to recognize one's total dependence on a transcendent God as the source of illumination.

Even more importantly, however, Luther insisted that the source of transcendence for the only kind of illumination that yields adequate self-knowledge must be personal. Luther's insistence that only by the help of God, and then finally in communion with God, can human beings come to genuine self-knowledge introduced the category of personal transcendence into the discussion about illumination and self-knowledge.

Thus the debate between Luther and Erasmus contained in seed what I see as the crucial question concerning self-knowledge today: is self-knowledge even possible without the notion of a personal God who transcends the totality of being, or to put it more philosophically, is self-knowledge possible without real transcendence, without, to use Levinas's term, radical exteriority?

Luther and Erasmus's exchange may seem insignificant compared to our modern predicament. At least they still acknowledged the fundamental human desire to interpret our existence in the larger context of the world, the call to self-understanding. The central question in recent hermeneutic discussion has become whether such desire is even legitimate. The most outspoken advocate against self-knowledge is Caputo in his latest work on hermeneutics, titled *More Radical Hermeneutics: On Not Knowing Who We Are*. According to Caputo, the very frustration of the human desire for self-knowledge is the driving force of hermeneutics, at least of his brand of radical hermeneutics, a mixture of philosophical hermeneutics and deconstruction:

> Thus the hypothesis, both impudent and timid, that wends its way through these studies is that we do not "Know" ourselves or one another, that we do not "Know" the world or God, in some Deep and Capitalized way that yields the capitalized Secret. *That* if anything is *who we are*, the ones who do not know who they are, and whose lives are impassioned by the passion of that non-knowing. . . . That Socratic, Kierkegaardian, and Derridean knowledge, that passion of non-knowledge and structural blindness, I argue throughout is the most salutary form knowledge can take. (*MRH*, 5)

Caputo's radical hermeneutics is the inevitable result of accepting the loss of transcendence and meaning, the very stance I want to argue against.

Nonetheless, Caputo's well-articulated opposition to self-knowledge is of great service because it allows us to clearly identify transcendence as the central problem of self-knowledge in modern philosophy. Kant knew the challenge he faced in trying to assess the limits of pure reason when he wrote that the most difficult aspect of this task was self-knowledge (*Kritik der reinen Vernunft*, [A] 7).

Kant did not solve but merely systematized the basic problem of knowing the self: the need for but the inability to articulate transcendence, that is, how can reflecting consciousness know anything outside itself? Self-knowledge (or self-understanding) is the attempt of the self to understand itself. The peculiar problem of this situation is that in order for this self-knowledge to be real, it must refer to something that is greater than the reflecting ego. The self is object but also condition of thought. As soon, however, as thought begins to articulate these transcendent boundaries that guarantee transcendent knowledge about oneself, they cease to exist as boundaries. Transcendence has become absorbed into consciousness. As long as this transcendence resists assimilation into consciousness and remains absolute limit, we have transcendence, but we cannot really say anything about it. Kant clearly points out the epistemological paradox of modernity: we require transcendence to ensure an objective pole for genuine self-knowledge, but we cannot, by definition, allow positive content for this transcendence. This means, however, that self-knowledge remains ultimately unverifiable.

There are two possible reactions to this problem of self-reflection. One can either accept the limitations of self-reflection and admit that we cannot really say anything substantive about the self (Kant), or one can forgo real transcendence and make the self the arbiter of reality, which means condemning it to immanence (Bonhoeffer, *Akt und Sein*, 32–33). Philosophical idealism took this latter route, and it is this construct that deconstruction has rightly attacked, sometimes to the point of Caputo's denial of any illumination of the self. Caputo's resignation to darkness may be an understandable reaction to idealism, but it also requires a resolute entrenchment in the final aporia of transcendental reflection.

For Caputo the transcendental barrier is the unnameable source of everything about which we cannot speak. It is the secret at the heart of Caputo's hermeneutics: "For me, hermeneutics simply means the necessity of interpretation. . . . A more radical hermeneutics means that the necessity of interpretation is driven by the absolute secret" (*MRH*, 3). The absolute secret is radical antifoundationalism, "the secret that there is no Secret." It is "this absolute secret that no one knows, and that is not a matter of knowing, that impassions hermeneutics and drives hermeneutics on" (ibid., 2). Not knowing who we are, being "cut off from the secret," we are faced with the inescapability of hermeneutics (*On Religion*, 20).

In terms of religion, Caputo's "more radical hermeneutics" signals a return to Schleiermacher's "religious kernel" approach. All religions are animated by the secret, namely, by divine love, which finds many different expressions, all of which are legitimate interpretations of the inexpressible secret. Caputo calls this contourless belief "religion without religion." Religion without religion does not deny truth, but it denies positive knowledge. Its creed is radical openness; its beginnings are in difference rather than sameness.

Of course, like most people who are passionately for religion but afraid of positive religious content, Caputo means well. He writes against fundamentalism and religious rationalism in order to advocate a religion of action rather than words. To love God is not to reflect on him in conceptual theology but to act justly and to stay clear of all the "complications of human religion" (*On Religion*, 138–39).

Caputo's reformulation of Augustine's question, "What do I love when I love my God?" into "*How* do I love when I love my God?" despite its good intentions, signals also the rejection of Augustine's hermeneutical circle of self-knowledge and knowledge of God. There is no "how" without a "what" and thus a radically open notion of God also leaves one without any definition of humanity or ethics. The bottom line of this religion, its nonnegotiable cornerstone of faith (if we may still call it so), is the confession that "we do not know what we love when we love our God" (*On Religion*, 108). It is clear that Caputo does not desire this bottom line, as his rejection of "New age poppycock" clearly indicates. Nor does his doctrine of ignorance concerning self-knowledge dismiss the importance of learning. It remains unclear, however, how Caputo's agnostic hermeneutics is able to prevent exactly the profusion of "religious nonsense" he wants to avoid (ibid., 136).

To use Derrida's earlier distinction, Caputo is a deconstructionist before he is a hermeneut. Like Derrida, Caputo enshrines difference or otherness at the heart of reality. Again like Derrida, he avoids the distinct ethical quality of this otherness; he avoids Levinas's direct revelation of God's command "thou shalt not kill" and erects instead an idol of difference to which he sacrifices self-knowledge.

We should, however, not condemn him too quickly. Caputo's ethical intent is humane and honorable: radical hermeneutics will save us from violence. Our inability to formulate or hold absolutely to any convictions will somehow produce peace. Radical openness to new possibilities will have the opposite effect of fundamentalism. That is why ethics must remain radically open rather than descriptive. Open mind, open future. Levinas's transcendental ethics, in other words, cannot be prescriptive. The function of ethics is solely to "optimise the possibilities of human flourishing and minimize violence, by allowing for the invention of new forms and the coming of things we have not foreseen" (*MRH*, 10).

For Caputo the notion of divine revelation is by definition linked to fundamentalism and hence to violence. When religion can abandon dogma and embrace nonknowing, the world can sleep more easily. This "more devilish hermeneutics" suggests nonknowing as the only way "to keep us safe when it comes to God and religious faith, whereas holier hermeneutics, which thinks that God has whispered in our ear," makes Caputo nervous. Caputo wants to keep faith safe from knowledge because for him the only true religion is the Kierkegaardian "leap-of-faith religion," an Abrahamic hope against hope. One wonders, though, whether Abraham would have hoped against hope if he had not known from previous experience that God kept his promises.

Given that Caputo's ambition is to make Derridean doctrine fruitful for theology in creating a more radical hermeneutics, his concerns about Gadamer's philosophical hermeneutics are predictably similar to Derrida's critique of hermeneutics as assimilating rather than upholding difference. Consistent with his renunciation of self-knowledge, Caputo is suspicious of Gadamer's hermeneutic philosophy because he still talks a great deal about self-knowledge and hence appears too confident about reason and its results.

Caputo, nonetheless, acknowledges certain common traits of Gadamer and Derrida. He sees clearly that both "share a common commitment to the interchange between what Levinas calls the 'same' and the 'other,'" between one's own and the other's interpretive horizon. Caputo has also come to see that Gadamer defines hermeneutic consciousness as the risk of letting the other come on his own terms, in a gesture of hospitality. For Gadamer, "hermeneutics means to hear and welcome the coming of the other, both in person and living dialogue, and in the great texts and works of art of our tradition" (*MRH*, 42).

Yet Caputo still fears that Gadamer's idea of finitude is not radical enough. Gadamer's notion of finitude cannot conceal a "latent theory of essence." His finitude of understanding is not as radical as Derrida's *différance*. While Gadamer *talks* about welcoming the other, his herme-neutical notion of fore-understanding could never handle unexpected guests. According to Caputo, hermeneutics still suffers from Hegelian infinity, in which difference is ultimately resolved into sameness, into a deeper substantial unity.

Caputo sees this suspicion confirmed in Gadamer's interpretation of modern art forms that resist traditional aesthetics of representation. And yet Gadamer, driven by his desire to close the gap of difference, fails to recognize that modern art wants to point out disruption. For him modern art is merely an invitation to toil harder in order to fuse horizons and reconcile differences. This is Gadamer's good infinity, his Hegelianism: all differences are eventually assimilated within the horizon of all art's inexhaustible potentiality of meaning (*MRH*, 49). That is why, in Caputo's final analysis, Gadamer's interpretive risk is minimal. Gadamer's risk always stays "within the bounds of sense" (ibid., 53).

Like Derrida's, Caputo's objection to hermeneutics is fueled by "a passion for non-knowledge and structural blindness," and like Derrida, Caputo inherits this passion from Levinas. Caputo follows deconstruc-tion, opposing to Gadamer's dialectic of assimilation a Levinasian model of asymmetry in which "the other comes toward me with the power of a claim, with the force of a disruption whose otherness I cannot ap-propriate or assimilate" (*Demythologizing Heidegger*, 212).

Caputo claims that Derrida's insistence on difference is more radical than Gadamer's "edifying finitude," a facticity without bite. Gadamer's hermeneutics is too measured and benign and cannot extend hospitality to real otherness. Deconstruction, by contrast, "is bad and makes no bones about it. It dines with sinners and thieves." Continuing the theological metaphor, Caputo likens Gadamer's hermeneutics to a Sunday sermon in which we hear only the expected. Deconstruction, by contrast, is the sermon of self-dissolution that puts us and our expectations radically in question and constantly preaches that "we do not know who we are—that is who we are. There is no Secret—that's the only secret" (*MRH*, 55). On Caputo's account, deconstructionist hermeneutics opens its arms more widely in a radical hospitality that would even invite the devil.

Moreover, Caputo also overstates the difference between Gadamer and Derrida. If it is true that Derrida has come close to Gadamer in his view that interpretation presupposes faith in human communication, Gadamer has also come closer to Derrida in acknowledging radical transcendence (*MRH*, 5). In fact, I believe that in the end, there is no essential difference between Caputo's more radical hermeneutics and Gadamer's philosophical hermeneutics. Both embrace the hermeneutical nature of knowledge, and both suggest a final transcendental barrier when it comes to ultimate truths or religion.

The following sections will show that Caputo need not worry about Gadamer's infinity because philosophical hermeneutics also tries to avoid religious fundamentalism through nonknowledge. Even so, Gadamer's notion of Socratic nonknowing, or *ignoramus*, upholds the possibility of self-knowledge while denying certain knowledge about ultimate religious claims. Moreover, I want to suggest a path that makes self-knowledge possible in two ways. First, in order to solve Kant's problem, we need to recover the premodern hermeneutical category of the personal for self-knowledge. I believe this is possible by using Levinas's critique of Western philosophy—his category of otherness—as ethical transcendence.

Second, in order to refute the denial of self-knowledge by radical hermeneutics, we must show that the category of the personal as ethical transcendence is actually more radically hermeneutical than what either Caputo or Gadamer thinks possible. My argument is roughly this: Insights about who we are as human beings unfold hermeneutically. To gain true insights we require transcendence, true exteriority. Finally, this exteriority is relational, because the limits of our understanding, which make understanding possible by saving it from subjectivism, are imposed on us by the alterity of the other person, which is, in turn, grounded in the alterity of God in his self-revelation to us. We will turn to this final point in the last section of this book.

Self-Knowledge as Hermeneutical

Caputo's hesitations notwithstanding, we can learn from Gadamer a great deal about the hermeneutical nature of self-knowledge. Gadamer establishes, first of all, that self-knowledge, the question of who I am, is fundamentally a hermeneutical question. He reminds us that every human being is faced with the task of orienting himself or herself in the world, and hence "understanding is understanding oneself in the world" (*GW*, 8:345).

Thus "in the last analysis, *all* understanding is self understanding" (*PH*, 55).[6] The term "world" in this context does not connote the individual objects or sense experiences that make up the planet we inhabit but the horizon of meaning that combines these fragments into a meaningful whole. Indeed, since sense impressions must be interpreted for us even to conceive of terms like "planet," "universe," and "environment," we do not have a world apart from interpretation. At the same time, the world is never given to us as a whole but rather as a partial horizon. It is the mark of our finitude that we never have a godlike view of the world but that reality discloses itself only partially (*GW*, 8:345). Gadamer's insistence on the linguisticality of this interpretive self-orientation in the world is too well known to repeat it here. This interpretive access to the world unfolds in language.

As a careful student of Heidegger, Gadamer knows the problems of self-reflexivity, and his work follows Heidegger in overcoming Cartesian subjectivism and German idealism (*GW*, 2:40). For this reason philosophical hermeneutics insists on the transcendent nature of interpretation. Self-knowledge acquires objective value only if it is inspired by something greater than ourselves. This is why the experience of art is representative for the hermeneutic experience. The very nature of art, Gadamer claims, exemplifies human self-knowledge, for art carries us beyond ourselves (*PH*, 54). It does so not in detached contemplation but in our participation in the picture or text (*GW*, 8:387–88).

Gadamer's work has been described as Platonic, Hegelian, and Heideggerian. It is, however, also distinctly Kantian because it is marked by the tension between the limits of reflection and the simultaneous assurance that we are not caught in a circle of self-reflexivity. As we have seen, Gadamer addresses this problem clearly in the third part of *Truth and Method*. Through the tradition of theology, more precisely through the tradition of Augustine's theory of illumination, Gadamer can break out of the subjectivism that hampered the transcendental reflection in German idealism.

Like the divine Logos, the inner word in philosophical hermeneutics is a true presentation of the subject matter in the mind and *also* manifests itself (is incarnate) in the historical particularity and interpretive multiplicity that mark our finitude. Just as Christ, the eternal Logos, is

6. See also *GW* 2:40–41.

for Augustine the divine light by which all human reason operates, so Gadamer's inner word is the light in, by, and through which the subject matter (*der Sachverhalt*) comes to light (*WM*, 430).

If we take this most promising section of *Truth and Method* and combine it with Gadamer's insistence that all understanding is in the final analysis self-understanding, his optimism concerning self-knowledge is well founded in a critical hermeneutical realism. As I have argued, however, this realism is possible only theologically and is found neither in Greek thought nor in any other religion that does not possess the novel idea of divine incarnation.

In fact, when Gadamer defends his concept of self-knowledge, he takes recourse to the classical Protestant description of self-knowledge. In his essay on this topic, "On the Problem of Self-Understanding," Gadamer makes clear that he refers to an originally theological concept that was distorted by idealism into the notion of self-consciousness. Gadamer tries to recover the original theological sense of self-understanding as experience of transcendence. Just because understanding means by definition that "unconscious elements involved in the original act of knowledge be brought to consciousness" does not mean that understanding requires or results in assimilation.

The paradigm for this experience of transcendence is, once again, the Christian model for self-understanding: "It is not, therefore, as a sovereign self-meditation of self-consciousness but rather as the experience of oneself that what happens to one and (from the theological standpoint) what takes place in the challenge of the Christian proclamation, can remove the false claim of Gnostic self-certainty from the self-understanding of faith" (*PH*, 49).

Contrary to theology's alleged tendency to assimilation and sameness, Gadamer believes with theology that understanding "involves a moment of 'loss of self,'" which he outlined in his famous example of the game as a description of hermeneutic experience. This is essentially an experience of transcendence, of being confronted by—and taken up into—something greater without losing one's individuality or identity. Gadamer is drawn to the theological definition of self-understanding as dependent on grace. He recognizes clearly that the self-understanding of faith is most assuredly determined by the biblical notion that faith is not a human possibility but an act of divine grace that happens to the believer. Gadamer wants to recover this important theological insight for his critique of the scientific method, which has distorted self-understanding into self-possessive certainty. To combat such a subjectivist notion of self-knowledge, Gadamer appropriates the original theological notion for hermeneutics: "We can formulate this idea as a theoretical generalization by saying that the individual self, including his activity and his understanding of himself, is taken up into a higher determination that is the really decisive factor" (*PH*, 54).

This absorption into something greater than oneself is not a "loss of self-possession" but the "free buoyancy of an elevation above oneself." This experience of self-understanding is the opposite of self-possession or self-realization, however, because here the understanding or augmentation of the self is passive: "The self that we are does not possess itself; one could say that it 'happens.' And this is what the theologian is actually saying when he asserts that faith is an event in which a new man is established. The theologian says also that we must believe and understand the Word, and that it is through the Word that we overcome the abysmal ignorance about ourselves in which we live" (*PH*, 55). For Gadamer philosophical hermeneutics shares with theology the belief that self-understanding is a dialogue with others through texts, and he fully realizes that theological self-understanding depends on the dialogue with the Divine through text. Gadamer believes the same structure is found in human communication, which is always real dialogue because one is confronted with something greater than oneself: "It cannot be denied that such an actual conversation (Gespräch) contains elements of chance, the favour of surprise and in the end also of buoyancy, even elevation, which belong to the essential character of game" (ibid., 57).

Conversation and even language itself thus have for Gadamer a dynamic, ever-changing, and developing quality. "The life of language," he writes, "consists in the constant playing further of the game that we began when we first learned to speak. A new word usage comes into play and, equally unnoticed and unintended, the old words die. This is the ongoing game in which the being-with-others of men occurs" (*PH*, 56). We should not mistake this comparison of understanding and language to mean that life is merely a game in which self-understanding does not matter. To do that would be to read Gadamer as a French rather than a German philosopher. For Gadamer a game is nothing frivolous. Gadamer, in common with Levinas and even the later Derrida, shows a deep seriousness about life, and he sees self-knowledge through tradition as a means to orient ourselves within the human community.

Given Gadamer's account of self-knowledge, there is no need for "more radical" hermeneutics and its denial of self-knowledge. Gadamer explicitly follows a theological model of self-understanding that converges with Caputo's "I don't know who I am." Nor does Gadamer have a bad infinity. As the next section shows, Gadamer denies our knowledge of ultimate meaning, or religion, as much as does Caputo's deconstructionist hermeneutics.

Self-Knowledge Requires (Religious) Transcendence

Gadamer helps us to see, then, that as a hermeneutical question, the question of self-understanding leads to the question of transcendence. To the end of his life, Gadamer remained silent about the real possibility of transcendence, although his entire work may be understood as an exploration of such transcendence (Zimmermann, "Ignoramus," 211). In his later writings from the 1990s on, and partially influenced by his encounter with Derrida, Gadamer increasingly describes this transcendence in *relational* terms as the limiting influence of others.

Gadamer knew little of Levinas, and there is a definite orientation in Gadamer's thought toward the other in *Truth and Method.* Yet it is undoubtedly through his contact with Derrida that he coins another important definition of hermeneutics, which sounds like Levinas: hermeneutics is the admission that the other may be right. "We all must learn," says Gadamer, "that the other person constitutes a primary limitation to our narcissism and our egocentrism. That is a general moral problem" (*GW*, 8:346). Even Gadamer's notion of education (*Bildung*), which he derives from Hegel, reminds us of Levinas's notion of education in *Totality and Infinity*: "Education [*Bildung* or cultivation] means the ability to see things from another's point of view" (*GW*, 8:349).

Gadamer reflected much on the question of transcendence in his last years. For him the very fate of humanity crucially depends on the notion of transcendence, that which lies beyond our grasp or comprehension.[7] Denial of transcendence in any form is detrimental to philosophy and theology alike. Gadamer criticizes both atheistic and Christian thinkers of our century for neglecting or ignoring transcendence. For example, he finds Karl Popper's denial of transcendence "laughable" and also lamentable, because Popper's refusal of this dimension of thought renders his work insufficiently relevant for our time. Gadamer is equally disappointed with theological thinkers one would naturally consider advocates of transcendence, such as Hegel and Bultmann; they, too, can become so caught up in self-reflexivity that they no longer take transcendence seriously (*Lektion des Jahrhunderts*, 83). In both religious thinkers, Christian revelation became fully absorbed into the reflective loop of the human mind and lost its externality.

Yet neither does Gadamer endorse more conservative theological hermeneutics that uphold the status of God's word as the infallibly transcendent source of certain doctrines. While Gadamer confesses his admiration for church-attending Christians, he also fears the narrow-

---

7. Gadamer uses the terms "transcendence" (*Transzendenz*) and "the beyond" (*das Jenseits*) interchangeably.

mindedness and defensive posture effected by institutionalized religion (Zimmermann, "Ignoramus," 207).

Instead Gadamer sees the kernel of all religions in the opening toward transcendence, which informs all human questioning and to which positive religions formulate various answers. In other words, Gadamer is concerned with transcendence as the limit of human knowledge that points to something that is greater and more mysterious than ourselves. When it comes to world religions, this means that we must give up dogmatic pretensions and particular religious doctrines and cults so that we can admit that all human beings are actually looking for the same thing and respect the limits of our own knowledge (Zimmermann, "Ignoramus," 208). This limit applies equally to philosophy and theology. On the one hand, Gadamer states that the natural sciences and philosophy cannot accomplish anything alone, that is, isolated from the religious dimension of human experience. On the other hand, religion itself should admit its limitations by giving up dogmatism and by finding an expression of transcendence that describes what "touches us all" (ibid.).

Gadamer's husk-and-kernel approach to religion seems an ironic replay of Schleiermacher's attempt at religious reduction, the feeling of absolute dependence—ironic in light of Gadamer's own initial rejection of Schleiermacher's hermeneutics. In *Truth and Method*, Gadamer condemns Schleiermacher's hermeneutics as assimilating all real intersubjective differences into an organic whole of pantheism. Gadamer's notion of transcendence looks like a rerun of this concept. I asked Gadamer whether his demand for universal transcendence does not in effect destroy religion rather than affirm it. After all, the world religions cannot simply jettison all positive revelation in favor of a nondescript religious experience because the very notion of such an experience begins with the recorded revelation of the founder of each religion, an insight only he had and then shared with his followers.

Moreover, this comparative reduction of religions to a common experience also overlooks real qualitative differences at the core of the world religions. In the Christian New Testament, for example, the radical equality of human beings follows directly from the good news of Christ's resurrection, which transcends ethnic and gender boundaries, while the inegalitarian Indian caste system seems justified by the doctrine of reincarnation.

Gadamer realizes this problematic tension but insists that he does not see any way to ensure religious dialogue other than to reduce all religions to the lowest common denominator: the experience of transcendence.[8]

---

8. Interview with Jens Zimmermann on hermeneutics and theology, Heidelberg, 26 February 2002.

Transcendence, he concludes elsewhere, "is not simply to believe in God but it is something incomprehensible, that is true even for Hegel . . . for Jaspers . . . and even for Heidegger." In fact, Gadamer agrees with Jaspers that *ignoramus*, the admitting of our nonknowing (*unser Nichtwissen*), is the foundation of transcendence (*Lektion des Jahrhunderts*, 85).

Not unlike Kant and very much like Socrates, Gadamer posits his notion of *ignoramus* as the transcendental barrier of the knowing subject and refuses to allow any positive content for religious experience. Instead transcendence, defined as a sense of the spiritual significance of our limited knowledge, is founded paradoxically on the fact that we cannot really classify the transcendent. Transcendence derives from the admission of our finitude: *ignoramus*—we do not know. "Das wissen wir eben nicht" are the recurring words of Gadamer in his latest conversations on the topic of religion. Gadamer wants to elevate this *ignoramus* to the common denominator of both religion and philosophy. According to Gadamer we should find our bearings (*unseren Halt*) in our admission of ignorance. Transcendence is the absolute limit of our knowledge and allows true conversation to begin.

We remember that for Gadamer, genuine conversation entails radical openness to the other. Conversation is hermeneutical when we let the other speak (*WM*, 308). To let the other speak, however, does not mean to suppress one's own preconceived view in order to be objective (the error of historicism and all scientific method in the humanities); instead it is to risk one's own view by making it the driving motivation of an engagement with the other in the full knowledge that it will have to be revised or given up entirely. This position requires the cessation of positive theology. Dogmatics, after all, is revisable only to a point. It is hard to imagine a Christian theologian entertaining the possibility that the Trinity and Allah are the same thing (or vice versa), yet Gadamer's notion of hermeneutical conversation would require such revision all the way down because for the open-minded, horizons are always moving (ibid., 309).

At the same time, however, Gadamer's notion is more than a mere abstract admission of our finitude that may be played out against the zealous dogmatism of theologians. What sets Gadamer's notion of transcendence apart from mere philosophical speculation is his insistence that it cannot be theoretical but must be genuinely experienced. It must have the power of religious conviction. It is no surprise, then, that Gadamer turns to his own Protestant tradition to describe the feeling of transcendence.[9] The best description he can find for this concept is the

9. The word "feeling" is used here in the same sense as Schleiermacher uses *Gefühl*: not as a fleeting emotion but as a deep sense or awareness that pervades body and spirit alike.

Christian symbol of the cross. Thinking about the crucifixion, whatever it may ultimately mean, presents us with the limit of our knowledge.

Gadamer likens the experience of transcendence to the shock one encounters when contemplating the crucifixion, which confronts us with the radical limitations of our knowledge and with our inability to comprehend—that is, to dominate through certain knowledge by conceptual categorization. "When I think of the cross," Gadamer said, "it is like chills running down one's spine."[10] He believes that the universalization of this experience, a deeply felt belief in the radical limitations of our understanding, is needed to ground the dialogues between differing theologies and between theology and philosophy. Gadamer thinks that philosophy is the better discipline to prepare this interfaith dialogue because it is less beset by dogmatic zeal than are religious communities.

Gadamer answers the objection that his concept of transcendence is ethically and politically useless with the argument that it is, in fact, the only possible common ground for ethics and political action. In thirty years of applying and extending basic hermeneutical concepts on a large number of issues, Gadamer has increasingly emphasized the practical value of philosophical hermeneutics, which he describes, following Aristotle, as phronesis, or wisdom. Gadamer's preoccupation with transcendence as a religious sense of our finitude points to a further refining of phronesis and provides a platform for much future work on hermeneutics and religion. In *Truth and Method*, Aristotle's concept of phronesis serves as a model for hermeneutical understanding. Phronesis is here contrasted with a worker's skill (*techne*), on the one hand, and mere abstract theory, on the other. Phronesis thus describes interpretive knowledge as participation or enactment.

Yet Gadamer has left open the question whether the normative horizon of any particular culture is superior. Whether our larger framework is the golden rule, the Ten Commandments, or other ethical guidelines, concrete moral decisions are only possible as enactment, not as abstract speculation. In short, Gadamer uses Aristotle to advocate ethical wisdom, which is different for every situation, something he calls readiness or alertness of conscience (*GW*, 4:180).

The idea of *ignoramus*, however, introduces Gadamer's notion of transcendence as the hermeneutic whole from which the particular application draws its "guidelines." Hermeneutic wisdom would thus mean to interpret a text or another's communication in the ultimate context of my genuine belief in the limitations of my knowledge based on a beyond that always surpasses my knowledge. Clearly, this "beyond" still

10. Interview with Jens Zimmermann.

arises from human experience and thus still agrees with ethical virtue as enactment. Yet at the same time, Gadamer suggests that his common ground should be normative for everyone (whether a theologian or a philosopher) who engages in ethics.

These two elements taken together, wisdom and a recognition of transcendence, explain Gadamer's conviction that the solutions of our present and future world crises depend on religion. If transcendence is present in our everyday experiences, then to deny its presence and to suggest with the Enlightenment that religion stands in the way of rational discourse is foolishness. Religion has a better handle on the transcendent nature of our being than science, which is still dominated by an epistemological paradigm that rejects the transcendent.

On my reading, Gadamer's position is virtually the same as Caputo's. *Ignoramus* and "radical hermeneutics" share the same passion for transcendence, whose exact content remains unknown. Gadamer, too, has no Secret. Regarding ultimate matters of meaning, that is, concerning the religious stories that lend purpose to our lives, Gadamer's notion of transcendence does not seem far removed from Caputo's bottom line: "I do not know what I love when I love my God."

This rapprochement of Gadamer and Caputo, however, shows clearly that, as with Schleiermacher and Levinas, transcendence is achieved by sacrificing too much. We should welcome, of course, their insistence that religious truth is unlike scientific knowledge and that it requires action rather than mere contemplation. Yet the rejection of any propositional knowledge in the name of religious pluralism and apophasis comes at too high a price. It is highly ironic that the only "other" not allowed difference, uniqueness, and particularity by these two thinkers of respect and dialogue is religion itself. For all their talk of respect of the other, Gadamer and Caputo espouse a doctrine of religious pluralism that reduces religious particularity to sameness. Moreover, we may well wonder why this sameness must consist in the fundamental doctrine of charity. Even Schleiermacher's "feeling of ultimate dependence" seems more plausible. Contrary to Caputo, it matters a great deal to whom I pray (*On Religion*, 130); I also believe that responsibility to my family and community requires conditional hospitality. Opening my arms even to the devil, as noble as this gesture may appear, gives as much reign to Caputo's feared philosopher king as does the Secret-thumping fundamentalist.

Gadamer and Caputo need a good dose of Levinas. Philosophical hermeneutics, whether conservative or radical, focuses too much on ourselves and too little on God. Their denunciation of our human ability to know are well intended, but they remain unwilling to concede the possibility that God himself has shown his face in the incarnation.

Even their well-meant desire for otherness ends up canceling the otherness of religion itself. The only possible answer is a change of focus from one's ability to get it right to the other's ability to have it right, especially when the Other has demonstrated his love by sacrificing his life for those who hate him.

"Religion without religion" and *ignoramus* remain the only alternatives only if knowledge of ultimate meaning is defined in Cartesian rather than incarnational terms. It is puzzling why neither Gadamer nor Caputo allows for revelation in relational categories. Why should our inability to know everything about God have to mean that we cannot have a relation with God and still know who he is—and consequently who we are in relation to him? Why would this, any more than in a human relation, constitute *necessarily* the reduction of otherness to sameness?

It is time to shift the focus from ourselves to the voice of the Other in the incarnation. Only then can we address the basic remaining problem, the interface between ontology and ethical transcendence. Transcendence can be fully present without compromise on account of the incarnation.

Transcendence in the Flesh: The Theological Basis for Ethical Transcendence

Levinas has taught us that transcendence is grounded in personal relation and that this relation is ethical. In his view, the only way out of the prison of egocentricity (of consciousness, intentionality, and transcendental reflection) is the other. Only then is transcendence, and with it a humanism that is human enough, possible. In other words, Levinas has substituted sociological categories for abstract philosophical ones, and in doing so, he has exposed the absolute limit of philosophy: the inability to recognize and respect irreducible, unique otherness. Philosophical reflection from Plato to Heidegger postulates only abstract notions of consciousness and the subject, but it cannot recognize real individuals. Heidegger's flesh-and-bloodless *Dasein* is only one example of this failure. Kant's transcendental unity of apperception is another. Biblically informed theology, however, insists "that each individual person has its unique and irreplaceable value, which is philosophically not justifiable either in pre-Christian thought or in post-Christian idealism" (Balthasar, "Krisis," 274). Levinas has tried to translate this biblical teaching into philosophical language by introducing irreducible individuality or what he calls asymmetry, the anarchy of the other.

I propose that Levinas's ethical approach can reach its full potential within an incarnational framework. I will briefly summarize what I see as the advantages of an incarnational view of self-knowledge: First, the incarnation is the historical statement that the infinite God loves each unique, individual human being, expressed by the fact that the divine "I" dies the substitutionary death for the unconditionally loved thou. Who I am can never be understood from a general "know thyself" of self-reflection but only as the result of the incarnation, which tells me both how much I am worth to God and how far I have strayed from him if the cost to bring me to self-knowledge was the incarnation and the cross. Modern theologians like Dietrich Bonhoeffer and Hans Urs von Balthasar point out that an individual self can only exist because God addresses it as a thou through the total substitution of the Messiah, who is both the wholly other God and another fellow human being. This address, however, is made in radical freedom by God, a freedom that finds its echo or analogy in the freedom of the other who is equally addressed by God.

Second, the incarnation grounds self-knowledge in the Divine but also necessitates self-knowledge in social terms. I can recognize God in encountering the other and in so doing come to recognize what being really is. It is in personal encounter that the answer to the mystery of being actually begins. In the radical freedom or asymmetry of the other, we are confronted with the true reality of being, because we are reminded of the presence of God. The other serves as our memory of God. Each encounter with the other is "anamnesis of God's act in Christ and practical recapitulation of the Christian view of God" (Balthasar, "Krisis," 275).

An incarnational view of relational transcendence puts the ethical demand of the other into the context of the good as a historically embodied act of selfless love and helps us to flesh out the vague notions of goodness and good violence by which Levinas tried to temper the image of the self as taken hostage by the other. If ethical transcendence is rooted in God's self-revelation, the incarnation (which includes the resurrection) is true exteriority rooted not in some abstract notion of God but in the concrete historical act of self-sacrifice, which defines the ethical as the ultimate good.

This historicity is not a compromise of transcendence: in an incarnational account of self-knowledge, the Old Testament language of election is not systematized (as Levinas seems to fear) but made concretely personal and is placed into the eschatological context of the Messiah's death and resurrection. As Balthasar puts it: "Each individual whom one can address humanly [*menschlich*] with 'you' is elevated to the rank of 'You' for God, because God's real You, his 'elect,' his 'only beloved' 'only son,' has died for the human 'you,' bearing its debts, and is therefore to identify with everyone at the final judgment" (*Herrlichkeit*, 3/2/2:411). For Balthasar this personalized account of God's love and its consequent qualification of the I-thou encounter is possible neither in pagan thought nor in the Old Testament context but only in light of the gospel (ibid., 3/2/2:412). Only in the cross does the problem of transcendental reflection, an abstract self and a lack of transcendence, find its final answer.

Third, and finally, the incarnation defines self-knowledge as hermeneutical. The incarnation is itself an interpretation of God, and this interpretation is again given to us in the concrete language and culture of history. Moreover, the interpretation of God's self-interpretation occurs within the Christian community, within the church as the body of Christ. Consequently, self-knowledge unfolds dialogically and hermeneutically in an ongoing personal encounter with the Divine through the church body and its interpretive tradition as it reads and applies the scriptures under the supervision of the Holy Spirit.

In other words, the incarnation provides the real answer to radical hermeneutics and its confusion of Christianity with idealism; in the incarnation, historicity finds its true home. In personal relation to Christ, who addresses our entire existence, self-knowledge unfolds hermeneutically and dynamically. Our self-knowledge is made possible by our relation with Christ.

Again, as Balthasar points out, only God can found the human self in his address in an act of radical freedom because he is in himself already complete as I and thou. On this account, Levinas's ethical transcendence is possible only because there is a social configuration of God at the heart of reality: "If we don't want to fall back into idealism (or collectivist sociology), into materialism and hedonism, or shatter on the absolute limit of the thou (the thou as hell as we find it in Sartre), the Christian way remains the only one that gives the human 'you' infinite value, because God gave it this concrete value in election and death on the cross, which is in turn only possible because the I-Thou-Us relation has itself absolute, divine dignity: in the triune Being of Love" (*Herrlichkeit*, 3/2/2:413).

At its best, the Christian tradition has acknowledged self-knowledge as dependent on communion with the Divine. In fact, we find the hermeneutical circle of self-understanding in Augustine when he prays, "Let me know myself, let me know you." In the Augustinian tradition of the Protestant Reformation, we see the clearest repetition of this interpretive circle in John Calvin's proclamation that "nearly the whole of sacred doctrine consists in these two parts: knowledge of God and of ourselves" (*Institutes*, 1536 ed., 15). Our study of Reformation hermeneutics found this hermeneutical framework also in Calvin's heirs, the English Puritans. The Puritans adopted Calvin's epistemology, his hermeneutic circle of self-knowledge and knowledge of God, and made it the basis for their practical piety.

We find thus in the theological tradition the assurance that self-knowledge is possible, that it depends on divine revelation, that the nature of this revelation is personal, and that self-knowledge is hermeneutical, obtainable only in dialogue with God. These seem to be basic features of theological conceptions of self-knowledge across the wide spectrum of theological traditions.

Yet this assertion of self-knowledge is in no way an invitation to smug self-certainty. None of the major Christian traditions depart from the biblical injunction that we can never completely illuminate the deep regions of our psyche; in this sense, of course, we can never know ourselves fully. It is helpful, then, to define self-knowledge not as psychological depth perception but as knowledge concerning the purpose and meaning of human existence, our *Dasein* as a whole. Self-knowledge, so defined, addresses the questions "What and who am I? What is the purpose of my existence?" Dietrich Bonhoeffer puts this eminently well: "Above the old Greek temple were written the words *gnosi seauton*, know yourself. And the intention was that self-knowledge would grant us self-dominion. And yet everyone knows that in his entire life, he will never know himself. We are and remain unknown to ourselves, known only by God" (*Predigten*, 204).

Incarnational theology thus speaks to Levinas's legitimate concern about sameness as it emerged from our account of the hermeneutical debate between the ethics of deconstruction (radical hermeneutics) and Gadamer's hermeneutic philosophy: If, on the one hand, we admit positive self-knowledge, how can we prevent it from collapsing into egoism, into the oppression of transcendence through interpretive imperialism? If, on the other hand, we posit absolute transcendence as absolute alterity, something that consciousness or knowledge cannot touch or appropriate because it would immediately reduce otherness to sameness, we cannot give it any content.

For incarnational theology, however, this is a false dilemma brought about by the detheologizing of Levinas's ethical impulse in Derrida, Critchley, and Caputo. Levinas's project is certainly concerned with meaning, but with ethical meaning found in personal relation. Levinas's subject is defined by personal transcendence and allows us to recover a theologically grounded understanding of subjectivity and self-knowledge that cuts the Gordian knot of self-asserting knowledge versus the denial of self-knowledge by positing an absolute otherness that entered the dimension of being without compromising its transcendence. The incarnation of the wholly other God in the historical figure of Jesus, the embodiment of otherness in human culture and language without any loss whatsoever of its essential otherness, this personal divine ethical *saying* incarnated in the ontological *said* disrupts both egological and deconstructionist systems alike.

PART 3

RECOVERING THEOLOGICAL HERMENEUTICS

An Incarnational-Trinitarian Approach

I hope to have shown that premodern hermeneutics, despite its shortcomings, acknowledged many of the same issues that thoughtful postmodern criticism of the Enlightenment has raised again for our time: the relational and historical quality of knowledge, the fact that knowledge is inseparably tied to a conception of the self, and perhaps most importantly, that all knowing depends on a worldview and therefore that all knowledge is interpretation based on basic assumptions or beliefs that cannot be reduced to truth as verification according to the scientific model of understanding. On my reading of hermeneutic history, philosophical hermeneutics is more a return to than a departure from premodern hermeneutics. As we have seen in our assessment of Gadamer's work, philosophical hermeneutics marks the return to the premodern position of "faith seeking understanding."

I have not attempted to recover rules for interpretation, either for the scriptures or for texts in general, but rather, following Gadamer's lead, I have tried to outline basic presuppositions for a Christian hermeneutic experience. The question that animates the recovery of theological hermeneutics is "What kind of understanding does faith seek?" In part 1, we examined a distinct reformational premodern framework for interpretation that yielded, among other insights, three main points.

First, adequate knowledge of reality and what it means to be human requires an existential hermeneutical circle of self and God. For Luther, Calvin, and other Reformation theologians, the transcendence of the wholly Other, God, is required to obtain proper knowledge about human nature, purpose, and destiny. The exploration of human nature and culture, however, is also needed because human beings are made in the image of God. The shattering of this image and humans' consequent dysfunctional relation with God and with one another have shaped human history and produced the human condition of grandeur and misery so aptly expressed by Blaise Pascal. Incredible human cultural achievements of grandeur and nobility coexist with equally unconceivable acts of human cruelty and self-destruction. As we have seen, Reformation theology explained human grandeur as a reminder of our godlikeness and human misery as the result of an inherent selfishness and enmity toward God that they called sin—being out of relation with God.

The second important insight for the recovery of *theological* hermeneutics, then, is anthropological: all human endeavors of interpretation are marred by sin and require restoration. Human interpretation is not limited by finitude alone. Neither our inability to have infinite knowledge nor the mediated quality of knowledge is sin. What theological hermeneutics for our time must retain is the "veil" that covers and distorts our view of reality. Premodern theology believed that the loss of communion with God profoundly shaped our conception of human nature and human knowledge: we desire a human nature that is autonomous and then require certain knowledge to install the enthroned ego firmly on its regal seat to rule over a kingdom of human dignity, progress, and world peace, all based on human rationality. As Levinas has pointed out, however, this very effort actually invites inhumanity and destroys real self-knowledge by eliminating the human self altogether and by reducing knowledge to the familiar.

This problem remains, in the final analysis, also the limitation of philosophical hermeneutics, even if we take Gadamer's insistence on self-knowledge in a wider humanistic sense (rather than in a narrow solipsistic one), because Gadamer lacks the ethical transcendence Levinas ds at the basis of human communication and interpretation.

Yet Levinas's welcome insistence on transcendence also fails in one crucial regard: if sin is a reality that not only distorts our interpretations but also effects our fundamental self-centeredness in the fullest sense of that term, Levinas's insistence on radical transcendence evokes the third important point, ethical implementation. Levinas does not really answer the question of how we move from the ethical demand of the other to complying *willingly* with this demand.

As I explained in the chapter on Luther, premodern hermeneutics attached great importance to this question and believed that conversion (i.e., the restitution to a human-divine relation as a radical change in human disposition) and the ongoing work of the Holy Spirit provided the answer to this question. Contrary to Kant, it is not willing the self into conformity to the categorical imperative but rather a willing self categorically disposed toward God that bridges the gap between ethical demand and its fulfillment. Levinas, too, sees the danger of leaving the formulation of the ethical demand and its implementation in the hands of the will and human decision. Ethics should not revert "to the level of decisions made by I know not what compassionate subjectivities" but should be anchored in the absolute of the social, "the *for-the-other* which is probably the very delineation of the human" (*Entre Nous*, 158). This is why Levinas places the ethical demand neither in universal reason nor in the will but in human proximity itself. Yet it is unclear how this proximity overcomes the barrier of implementation: how can this closeness create a truly compassionate heart, a heart, to use Luther's language, that engages the other not out of duty but out of love?

This last part of *Recovering Theological Hermeneutics* is meant to address these questions by outlining a theological hermeneutics that recovers important insights of premodern hermeneutics in light of modern issues and particularly in light of the hermeneutic focus of self-understanding. The previous chapters have served mainly to identify the main issues in the contemporary hermeneutical debate. The following third part is an unapologetically theological vision for hermeneutics. The main concluding argument is that such a hermeneutics must be both Trinitarian and incarnational in order to establish a relational rather than an individual interpreting subject (modeled on the Trinity) and a form of self-knowledge based on divine transcendence yet within limitations that are not merely based on finitude but on the fact that ultimate meaning is a person, Christ the Logos, whose *Gestalt* is at the center of both ethics and interpretation.

8

INCARNATIONAL SUBJECTIVITY

Homo diligit se ipsum perverse et solum quae perversitas not potest dirigi nisi loco suo ponat proximum.
[In a perverse way, man loves himself, only himself. This perversion cannot be corrected unless he puts the neighbor in his place.]

—Martin Luther, *Commentary on Romans*

Introduction

The following outline of an incarnational hermeneutics will draw heavily on the work of Dietrich Bonhoeffer and, to a lesser extent, that of Hans Urs von Balthasar. These thinkers stand out on account of their common emphasis on incarnational thinking—an emphasis that transcends their confessional differences.

The German Lutheran theologian Dietrich Bonhoeffer (1906–45), more than any other modern theologian, translated Luther's interpretive stance into modern theology. Bonhoeffer should be remembered not only for his outstanding Christian witness in a time of a whole nation's surrender to evil but also for his stature as a brilliant thinker who advocated incarnational theology. For him the phenomena of fascism and Nazism were merely indicators of a greater cultural bankruptcy that could not be cured by reviving religion. Advocating a religiousless Christianity, Bonhoeffer refused any starting point for theological and metaphysical

274

reflection other than the incarnation. For him Christ was the center not only of history but also of all thinking about reality.

Differently from Karl Barth, whose theology begins with God's other-worldly transcendence, Bonhoeffer advocated a radically hermeneutical stance for theology. According to Bonhoeffer, theology can never bypass historical development, nor is theological reflection an escape into heavenly realms. Rather, Bonhoeffer, much like Levinas, sought to locate transcendence in immanence, for that was, after all, the divine pattern of the incarnation. Participating in any sense in divine transcendence meant to share God's sufferings in the life of this world. Bonhoeffer hated nothing more than splitting the world into a public sphere of politics and a private enclave of religion. The utter powerlessness of Christianity as a cultural force in his day led Bonhoeffer to recognize, like Levinas, the centrality of ethics and its definition not as moral rules but as a social relation oriented toward otherness. Yet differently from Levinas, Bonhoeffer's reflection on ethics too must begin with the incarnation. His common ethical interest with Levinas and his yet so different angle of analysis make Bonhoeffer a crucial figure for our recovery of theological hermeneutics.

Bonhoeffer's Critique of Idealist Subjectivity

Theological hermeneutics believes that the social self of Trinitarian subjectivity has been embodied in the incarnation, God's self-revelation in the historical person of Jesus. The divine Logos, the union of transcendence and immanence without loss, provides the most human and most hermeneutical model of subjectivity. Bonhoeffer developed this understanding of the human self in his doctoral dissertation, *Sanctorum Communio* (1930).

Bonhoeffer's work provides a wider context for Levinas's ethical philosophy, for it demonstrates that the same problematic of transcendence was being intensely discussed in modern German theology. Bonhoeffer shares Levinas's opinion that philosophy's quest for understanding has traditionally supposed an isolated, independent self. Yet by seeking to establish an autonomous self, the subject actually ends up annihilating the self.

Both thinkers agree that an authentic self depends on transcendence, on exteriority. Like Levinas, Bonhoeffer criticizes materialist concepts of humanity for their failure to recognize the spiritual component of human existence. He also rejects all theories of selfhood that reduce the human subject to a thinking self or consciousness and identifies German idealism, as the main culprit, as particularly guilty of lacking "a concrete concept of personhood" (*SC*, 130).[1] Even theological critics of idealism, like Schleiermacher, who propose a more organic model of selfhood arrive at the same impasse. Instead of otherness and transcendence, Schleiermacher ends up with sameness and immanence. Bonhoeffer concludes that in Schleiermacher, "the Spirit is the one, the eternally identical, the suprapersonal, that which is immanent to humanity; [the Spirit] annihilates the concrete person and so renders any concrete notion of community impossible in favor of an immanent spiritual union [*Geisteinheit*]; one has fallen prey to the danger of seeing community as unity" (ibid., 131).

Much like Levinas, Bonhoeffer also walks the reader through ideas of selfhood from the classical Greek definitions of human subjectivity to the present and finds everywhere impersonal conceptions that resolve the unique subject into totalizing structures. The whole Platonic-Aristotelian construct, for example, is marked by an impersonal ethos that extends to the Aristotelian notion of God as the prime mover. Stoic teaching introduces for the first time an ethical component that defines true humanness as being under an ethical imperative; yet even here the end result emphasizes sameness. obedience to the universal ethical demand unites individuals in a kingdom of reason, "in which every soul conforms to eternal reason and becomes identical to all other souls" (*SC*, 18).

In Bonhoeffer's final analysis, all Western definitions of the human lack transcendence because they define the human spirit as immanent consciousness. Idealism merely brought this definition of human being to its ultimate conclusion: the "I" is person insofar as it is spirit (*Geist*). According to Kant, however, "spirit is the highest formative principle that encompasses the material and overcomes it so that universal and spirit become identical at the expense of individuality. Immanent spirit as highest principle becomes a formal law" (*SC*, 23). Ultimately, all selves are identical, and only on account of this sameness is agreement on the ahistorical, universal truths of reason and interaction with others even possible. Kant does recognize difference, but this difference is socially effected and secondary rather than primordially rooted in personal transcendence. Idealism, from Kant to Hegel, destroys the ethical transcendence of the other because it is driven by overcoming difference in order to establish community and peace on rational principles. The end result, however, is not a truly human community but a collective of sameness (ibid., 24).

1. "Es liegt in den Tiefen der idealistischen Philosophie begründet . . . der zutiefst liegende Mangel eines konkreten Personenbegriffs."

Building on this analysis, Bonhoeffer anticipates Levinas's argument that self-reflection can never lead to a proper definition of personhood. Epistemological categories fail to convey the real existence of subjects radically different from ourselves. This failure is systemic because, in its drive to formulate universal concepts, transcendental analysis always wants to find sameness rather than difference. Bonhoeffer does not deny the possibility of concepts, only that the concept of personhood cannot be constructed along Cartesian lines of self-reflection because the self defined as thought is not the real, factically existing self in the social sphere: "As long as my spirit is the sole dominating power that claims universal validity, as long as all contradiction that might arise in the knowing subject can be seen as objects of knowledge immanent to my consciousness, I am not in the social sphere" (*SC*, 26).

Instead Bonhoeffer calls for a Christian concept of personhood in order to formulate a biblically and sociologically viable notion of the Christian person in community, the church (*SC*, 18). Thus from a theological perspective, Bonhoeffer anticipates and underwrites Levinas's criticism of Western thought as egology. A real concept of subjectivity requires a barrier to thought, and this barrier, given that we are seeking *human* subjectivity, must be ethical. Transcendence as barrier to understanding must be encountered by the whole human being, not, as in idealism, by a consciousness severed from the body.

This does not mean, however, that Bonhoeffer simply dismisses transcendental philosophy any more than Levinas does. Nor does Bonhoeffer devalue a conceptual, cognitive dimension in reflection. What he does reject, however, is a serene world of universal reason populated by abstractly identical clones of selfhood. Such a picture does not correspond to human reality. Instead he advocates, like Kant, a real transcendental barrier but argues, beyond Kant, that this transcendence required for the difference and uniqueness essential for a truly human subjectivity must be ethical—that is, it must be personal. This does not mean that we cannot conceptualize this ethical transcendence; rather we cannot *experience* it as concept, only as living encounter with others in the social sphere.

Like Levinas, Bonhoeffer finds ethical transcendence in the concrete *temporal* encounter with another human being to whom one is responsible. Only from this concrete, nonrepeatable encounter (i.e., it is different every time) can we gain a concrete notion of personhood (*SC*, 29). When we posit transcendence along mental, idealistic lines, we delude ourselves with a transcendence invented by the self: "Idealism has no eye for movement; the movement of the dialectic of spirit was an abstract metaphysical one; that of ethics, by contrast, is concrete; furthermore, idealism has no sympathy for the moment [i.e., the irreducible temporality of the encounter] in which the person is threatened by the absolute [ethical] demand. The idealist ethicist knows what he ought to do, and, what is more, he is basically always able to do it because he ought to be able to do it. Where is there room for the distress of conscience, the infinite fear of decision?" (ibid.).

Incarnational Ethics: No Hostages Required

Bonhoeffer thus mounts principally the same argument as Levinas: human subjectivity must be conceived ethically as an I-thou encounter in which the other remains irreducibly other. To be human is not to be an isolated consciousness; instead the self is founded in mediation, through the ethical responsibility of the other: "Only in experiencing the barrier does the self-knowledge of the ethical person emerge" (SC, 29).

Bonhoeffer calls this the "social ontic-ethical foundation relation of the persons" (soziale ontisch-ethische Grundbeziehung der Personen). This basic relation means that I can only experience the other as irreducibly other although he is also another human being. This ethical transcendence does not negate the realm of consciousness or reflection, but it cannot be objectified by an abstract mental conception of human being; ethical transcendence is experienced only concretely in time and history. This ethical transcendence is experienced uniquely and cannot be universalized from one person to another: "It is a purely ethical transcendence, experienced only by the one standing in decision and cannot be conveyed to one external to it" (SC, 31).

Bonhoeffer's incarnate subjectivity, while very close to Levinas's ethical subject, rests ultimately on Christian rather than Jewish sensibilities. The doctrine of the incarnation allows Bonhoeffer to avoid Levinas's anxieties about preserving transcendence. Bonhoeffer's incarnational subjectivity eschews Levinas's hostage dilemma: if my true human identity depends on the other's ethical call, if I am in this sense hostage to the other, does not the other become the creator of my ethically conceived selfhood? Bonhoeffer knows this problem well from other theologies of transcendence he studied. He believes that to elevate another human being to the creator of the other's ethical person "is an unbearable thought" (SC, 33).

Unlike Levinas's weak gestures toward God's ultimate otherness on this crucial point, Bonhoeffer's approach avoids the hostage scenario by placing the full weight of the ethical call on God. Not only is the identity- and person-forming role of the other independent of his or her status as person, but it is also independent of the other's will: "One human being cannot of its own accord make another into an I, an ethical person conscious of responsibility. God or the Holy Spirit joins the concrete You; *only through God's active working does the other become a You to me from whom my I arises*. In other words, every human being is an image of the divine You" (*Sanctorum Communio*, 54–55; emphasis mine).

Hence for Bonhoeffer, true alterity is not automatic but a gift from God. He rejects Levinas's caution that such positive theological grounding of the self threatens to collapse back into a merely cognitive mental construct and insists that the human being as the ethical image of God in no way negates the concrete reality of the other, as if the other were merely a mimetic quality, loaned by God (*SC*, 33). Bonhoeffer insists that only the "divine You creates the human you and since the human You is created and willed by God, it is a *real, absolute, and holy You*, like the divine You" (*Sanctorum Communio*, 55; emphasis mine). Without bypassing the other's ethical importance, Bonhoeffer nonetheless shifts the weight of this holiness toward God, thus avoiding the problem of burdening humanity with values it cannot bear: "Since however one person's becoming You for an other fundamentally alters nothing about the You as person, that person as I is not holy; what is holy is the You of God, the absolute will, who here becomes visible in the concrete You of social life. The other person is only a 'You' insofar as God brings it about. But God can turn every human being into a You for us. The [ethical] claim of the other rests in God alone; for this very reason, it remains the claim of the other" (ibid.).

Bonhoeffer offers us a richer, more dynamic, and less oppressive model of selfhood as I-thou relation. Along with Levinas and other postmodern thinkers, Bonhoeffer advocates a holistic subject that stands concretely in the social sphere without being swallowed up into a totality. Like Levinas, Bonhoeffer insists on grounding subjectivity in social relations understood as "purely interpersonal and building on the uniqueness and separateness of persons. . . . No unity can ever negate the plurality of persons" (*Sanctorum Communio*, 55). He differs from Levinas, however, in defining otherness or ethical transcendence as a creative act by God and so avoids turning the other into a godlike authority. It is true that Levinas tries to avoid this as well when he rejects suggested formulations that God is somehow mediated through the other. Yet without the incarnation, Levinas cannot develop otherness as God's creative act, for such would compromise God's transcendence.

Law *and* Grace

Bonhoeffer's reformational theology of God's sovereignty, the teaching that ethics is all by God's grace, also helps him avoid Levinas's implicit legalism. Levinas sets up the ethical demand of the other but never explains how we can obey the ethical call. Levinas demands an ethics of neighborly love, but he does not solve the riddle of how we move from this demand to its practical execution. For Kant, as we have seen, our obligations are fulfilled by sheer willpower. And even this Herculean act of willpower still assumes, much like the Stoic view, that rational consent to ethical principles will somehow result in compliance.

Bonhoeffer, by contrast, stands in the long theological tradition that acknowledges Luther's definition of sin as "the will bent in on itself." Even Nietzsche stands in this tradition when he recognizes that "the will is man's kingdom" (*Der Wille ist des Menschen Königreich*), and Dostoyevsky has immortalized the self-preserving quality of the human will in his *Notes from the Underground* when he names ungratefulness and willfulness as the two central human qualities. Even if it were proven, writes the man from the underground, that human action is wholly determined by materialist causes and rationally comprehensible, man would try to commit something unreasonable simply to assert his own will. And if we proceed to explain this behavior on rational principles, man would renounce reason altogether and sooner pretend madness than surrender the privilege of self-assertion (Dostoyevsky 193–94).

While Levinas recognizes this selfishness as reflected in the history of epistemology and advocates the ethical demand of the other as countermeasure, he offers no suggestion on how this is done. At best he suggests that the implementation lies in the realm of ontology and is a matter of institutional justice, politics, and religion. It is again Levinas's distrust of ontology, of the realm of being, that keeps God out of ontology. Bonhoeffer has no such qualms. God himself entered ontology in the incarnation and is constantly active in this realm.

Bonhoeffer understands, of course, that the command to love others is not particular to the Christian religion. He claims, however, that only the historical implementation of divine love in Christ provides the power to enable ethical action in the fullest sense: "The ethical command to love is not specifically Christian and yet the reality of this love is only found in Christ and his community" (*SC*, 108). It is found only there because only in relation with God through Christ is selflessness possible. The Lutheran Bonhoeffer remains faithful to his Reformation heritage: ethics is by grace alone. The ability to heed the ethical command is not a matter of the human will but a matter of divine grace. Bonhoeffer is emphatic in his renunciation of any humanistic ideals of love: "Christian love is not a human possibility. In the first instance, it has nothing to do with the idea of a common humanity, with sympathy, eroticism, or compassion. [Christian love] is possible only through faith in Christ and through the work of the Holy Spirit" (ibid.).

The difference over against Levinas's ethics is that for Bonhoeffer, "I am to surrender my will to God in service to the other, who has the same obligation. The enabling power for this act is the Holy Spirit" (*SC*, 108–9). At the same time, however, Bonhoeffer warns against the tendency to view neighborly love as a means to inaugurate God's kingdom on earth. Real love does not reduce the neighbor to a cog in the kingdom wheel, but perceives the neighbor as uniquely made in God's image. While neighborly love is indeed a means to realize new humanity on earth, a model of the Trinitarian "community," this in no way sidesteps human particularity: "[Christian love] loves *the real neighbor*, not because it approves of his individuality, but because as a human being he addresses the other, that is, because he experiences in the other God's address to himself. Nevertheless, he does not love God through the other person but loves the concrete you; he loves the other by placing himself at the other's service with his entire will" (ibid., 109).

Neighborly love, the fulfillment of the ethical call, is nothing but our "willingness toward the willingness God extends to others" (*SC*, 111). Yet on account of human selfishness, this redirecting of our will toward others is humanly impossible. This love "cannot be forced by human beings but is poured into our hearts by the Holy Spirit" (ibid.). It is God who places on us the ethical command to love our neighbor, and it is God who gives us the power to heed the ethical call.

Trinitarian Subjectivity

In rethinking ethics and human subjectivity, theology has rediscovered the doctrine of the Trinity to establish relational ontology at the heart of reality. Eastern Orthodox theologians have been at the forefront of this development, and mainstream theologians are increasingly incorporating their work in rethinking the individual and community in Trinitarian terms.[2] While Eastern Orthodox theology shares Levinas's concern for an ethical subjectivity, it does not seek this relation prior to ontology but within it. Here the monolithic, autonomous self is not deconstructed from within by showing innumerable cracks in its armor that render it an untenable, inhuman view of the self; instead *ontology itself* is declared to be relational.

Trinitarian theology agrees with Levinas that ancient Greek ontology was essentially monistic in that the being of God and of reality formed

2. See for instance Miroslav Volf's *In Our Likeness: The Church as the Image of the Trinity* (Grand Rapids: Eerdmans, 1998), which draws much on John D. Zizioulas's *Being as Communion*.

"an unbreakable unity" (Zizioulas, *Being as Communion*, 16). This monistic basis was able to create a cosmology of harmony and order, "a world full of interior dynamism and aesthetic plentitude, a world truly 'beautiful' and 'divine.'" While this cosmos of Logos, or rational predictability, enables science and classical ideals of beauty, it has done so at the cost of excluding otherness because "in such a world it is impossible for the unforeseen to happen or for freedom to operate as an absolute and unrestricted claim to existence" (ibid., 30). Here the rational universe exists for its own sake, and humanity is defined in conformity to this impersonal Logos.

In order to amend Greek ontology by breaking its creator-creature unity without falling into the great gulf between God and the world taught by Gnostic philosophical systems, the Greek fathers developed a relational ontology. They realized that "the being of God could be known only through personal relationships and personal love. Being means life, and life means communion" (Zizioulas, *Being as Communion*, 16). This important philosophical change results in a relational ontology in which "the Holy Trinity is a *primordial* ontological concept and not a notion which is added to the divine substance or rather which follows it. The substance of God, 'God,' has no ontological content, no true being, apart from communion. . . . Nothing in existence is conceivable in itself, as an individual, . . . since even God exists thanks to an event of communion. In this manner the ancient world heard for the first time that it is communion which makes beings 'be': nothing exists without it, not even God" (ibid., 18). The Trinitarian ontological formula, "being is communion," defines true being as both communal and free.

The Trinitarian model also differentiates between an ontology of personhood (the self as communion) and an ontology of being and thus offers the deeper ontology Levinas desires. Greek Orthodox theology commends Levinas for his criticism of Heidegger, who is seen as remaining within a sphere concept of being in which the self is reduced to a subject defined by individual consciousness (Zizioulas, *Being as Communion*, 45). Zizioulas follows Levinas in rejecting any totalizing concept because the Trinity itself cannot be reduced to a single horizon of manifestation but appears as the free community of three distinct persons. Moreover, as with Levinas, this Trinitarian ontology defines truth as standing in relation rather than as a cognitive "gnoseological" activity. For Zizioulas "the essential thing about a person lies precisely in his being a revelation of truth, not as 'substance' or 'nature' but as a 'mode of existence'" (ibid., 106).

Trinitarian ontology thus shares Levinas's critique of Heidegger's concept of *ekstasis*. For Heidegger, *ekstasis* meant the revelatory power of being, for which the human being was merely a mouthpiece. Greek theology uses this term to describe the person as revealing truth by its mode of existence in communion. The person, Zizioulas explains, "is the horizon within which the truth of existence is revealed . . . as the unique image of the whole and the 'catholicity' of being." The person is representative of humanity, so that to "destroy a human person is to commit an act of murder against all humanity [which is] a denial of the truth of man's being" (*Being as Communion*, 106).

Yet this correlation does not mean the surrender of otherness: "Truth as communion does not lead to the dissolving of the diversity of beings into one vast ocean of being, but to the affirmation of otherness in and through love." Rather, as in the Trinity, particularity is preserved because, in the mysterious nature of personhood, otherness and communion coincide rather than conflict: "While *ekstasis* signifies that a person is a revelation of truth by the fact of being in communion, *hypostasis* signifies that in and through his communion a person affirms his own identity and his particularity; he 'supports his own nature' (hypo-stasis) in a particular and unique way. . . . So in the context of personhood, *otherness* is compatible with *division*" (*Being as Communion*, 107).

Clearly the Trinitarian conception of the human subject is important for the recovery of theological hermeneutics. There is, however, one significant problem: most presentations of this communal model of subjectivity are not very hermeneutical. They begin in the speculative realm with the doctrine of the Trinity rather than with God's self-revelation in history. Instead of beginning in time and history, speculation begins in the eternal. The danger is that metaphysics begins to shape theology. While much of the Greek Orthodox speculation on the Trinity and personhood is attractive, its tendency to determine human subjectivity primarily through the Trinity rather than through God's self-expression in Christ is in danger of shaping God himself in our own image rather than relying on God's Word in Christ for the constitution of our subjectivity and for the constant disruption of our human misconceptions about what it means to be truly human.

Bonhoeffer warned against constructing subjectivity from a speculative point of view because we then begin to trust human constructs rather than rely on God's word. Bonhoeffer and Trinitarian theology desire the same goal: a self that is neither individualistically nor monistically constructed. Bonhoeffer insists, however, that we arrive at such a collective personhood (*Kollektivperson*) by starting not with the Trinity but with the incarnation. Bonhoeffer insists that the Christian notion of personhood must be thought "historically," and that means that our theological thinking about subjectivity begins not with God in eternity but as fallen human beings addressed by God through his incarnate Word (*SC*, 36–37).

Bonhoeffer roots true humanity, true subjectivity and community, in the Word made flesh: "And so the church in and through Christ is established within the three known basic sociological relations: his death isolates the *individual*, each bears his own guilt and has his conscience; the resurrection justifies and sanctifies the *community of the cross* as *one* in Christ. The new humanity is viewed collectively in the one man Jesus Christ; finally, just as the love of God in our substitute Christ reestablishes the communion between God and humanity, so *human community* has become genuine in love" (*SC*, 100; emphasis in original). Bonhoeffer does not, of course, reject the doctrine of the Trinity, but he refuses to sidestep the incarnation as if it were merely a consequence of the Trinity. This logical order may be true in speculative theology, but it is not what is historically given to us. He believes that it is wrong "to derive the incarnation from an idea about God, such as the idea of the Trinity, for example" (*Berlin*, 342). When we do this, we fall back into the subjectivist paradigm of idealism. We begin to conjure up a world of thought made up of necessary metaphysical speculations, a harmonious totality where each part depends on the other.

Bonhoeffer's construct of the collective individual is more hermeneutical than speculative Trinitarianism because it trusts its own totalizing system more than the word of God. This word comes to us in the church, through the preaching and interpretation of the scriptures with the help of the Holy Spirit. This happens in time and history and requires daily renewed trust in God in the midst of life and its agonizing decisions.

9

SELF-KNOWLEDGE
AND THE INCARNATION

So far I have tried to show that a theologically founded concept of subjectivity as divinely called person-in-community offers the most promising ethical framework for interpretation. A Trinitarian model of personhood grounds the social self ontologically, and an incarnational model of community makes possible the actual existential grounding of self-identity in the incarnate Word of God. The difference with Levinas is decisive: Levinas's ethics is grounded, precariously at best, in the absent God without a face. Bonhoeffer's God, however, has a face. Levinas must cling to the invisible God because this is the only way that the ethical saying can retain its otherness without falling in any way prey to the ontological said. Bonhoeffer, however, is able to draw on the incomprehensible union of saying and said in the incarnation, whose uniqueness is precisely that divine otherness is fully maintained and yet humanity is fully represented. To translate this into Levinasian language, Christ's divinity (the saying) is never in danger of being swallowed up into his humanity (the said).

So far we have talked about subjectivity, but what about knowledge? We have seen that for Levinas knowledge is secondary to ethical "sensibility." To forgo the need for self-preservation, to take bread out of my mouth and give it to the destitute, that is ethics before knowledge. Levinas's fear of the Cartesian *cogito* as self-asserting assimilation of otherness leads to his reduction of hermeneutics (i.e., of interpretation and commentary) to deconstruction. Levinas's caution about knowledge becomes full-blown apophasis in Derrida and his disciple John Caputo, who advocates the rejection of self-knowledge.

In one sense, we should certainly agree with Caputo that we can never know ourselves in a "Capitalized" way, as if we occupied a point of knowledge outside our existence. At the same time, however, incarnational theology insists that we are actually in relation to absolute otherness, through the incarnate Word of God. Since the Logos is incarnated in human flesh, God has a face, and our relation to this person allows us, within all the limitations of personal knowledge, to know something about ourselves. As Caputo might say, not we but God is in possession of the secret, and he is willing to share it with us. Given Bonhoeffer's theological construction of this revelation, self-knowledge is radically hermeneutical and should result in humility and openness rather than in the bigotry and fundamentalism feared by Caputo.

I shall argue in these last paragraphs that the incarnation allows for a chastened concept of self-knowledge that falls prey neither to deconstructionist (a)gnosticism nor to fundamentalist triumphalism. Theological hermeneutics is the fulfillment, so to speak, of philosophical hermeneutics, because it combines Gadamer's desire for self-knowledge with Caputo's desire for its limitations.

We have seen that Gadamer defends himself against accusations of logocentrism by hauling out a theological notion of self-understanding as an infinite and uncertain procedure. What this borrowing lacks, however, is the actual focal point of self-knowledge, namely, the knowledge of God. Here, too, the hermeneutical circle is incarnational and thus relational. Knowledge of God begins as relation with the Trinity through the incarnation of the Son, the Word of God. In knowing God (defined as being in relation), we learn about ourselves. As the following section demonstrates, Gadamer's dictum that all understanding is in the final analysis self-understanding becomes true only when the self first seeks to understand God.

Philosophical and theological hermeneutics do agree, however, on the general nature of self-knowledge. Both theological and philosophical hermeneutics reject the concept of a theoretical knowledge altogether (if theoretical is meant to describe the timeless, ahistorical, and nonparticipatory space of a neutral consciousness). The personal-relational quality of the divine Logos offers the best basis for a rigorously hermeneutical conception of self-knowledge. It provides exactly the kind of hermeneutical limitations deconstructionist ethics wants to uphold: a theological hermeneutics agrees that we can never know ultimate truth and purpose in the Cartesian sense of theoretical verifiability. The personal Logos is the completion for the hermeneutical concept that understanding is possible only in enactment (*im Vollzug*).

As in any interpersonal relationship, we can only "know" the divine Other when we are in relation with him. This is the kind of knowledge John Owen described with the New Testament term "epignosis." The theologian F. F. Bruce explains that "this knowledge is no merely intellectual exercise, no theosophical *gnosis* such as was affected by teachers who threatened to lead the Colossian church astray. . . . True knowledge is founded in practical religion; it is that knowledge which, as the Old Testament wisdom writers affirmed, starts with a proper attitude toward God: 'The fear of the Lord is the beginning of knowledge' (Prov. 1:7)" (*Epistles to the Colossians, to Philemon, and to the Ephesians*, 46).

For theological hermeneutics, relational knowledge and its limitations form the paradigm for hermeneutical understanding. Like God, other human beings are not reducible to cognitive, epistemological content. We cannot know others in comprehending them but rather through their self-revelation to us: "The other human being presents the same episte-mological problem as God himself. Just as I know God's 'I' only through the self-revelation of his love, I can only know the other human person in the same way" (*SC*, 34).

Theological hermeneutics claims that self-knowledge is possible because knowledge of God is possible. This claim to self-knowledge depends on its ability to convincingly develop a hermeneutical view of revelation in which God's self-disclosure is received without compromising its transcendence. The central question, in other words, is Newbigin's earlier concern. Can nature and grace form a continuum without loss of transcendence? Can any hermeneutical conception of knowledge with its claim of correlation between knower and known avoid reducing knowledge of God to self-consciousness? Can difference actually understand difference? I believe this is possible on the basis of the incarnation.

Bonhoeffer's Theological Critique of Self-Knowledge

Dietrich Bonhoeffer dedicated an entire book to the question of how a wholly other God in his transcendent difference can relate to us in his self-disclosure. His second academic treatise, *Act and Being* (1931), aims to formulate a theological concept of knowledge in the wake of Kant and Heidegger. Bonhoeffer wants to determine the relation between "God's being" and the mental act that perceives this being. The basic premise from which he critiques Western possibilities of self-understanding is that the self cannot understand itself out of itself. Like many postmodern critics, Bonhoeffer has identified German idealism as the culmination of this development. The only but decisive difference over against postmod-ern criticisms of idealism is his theological rationale: sin, the breaking of relations with God, is responsible for our love affair with immanent consciousness. Idealism's weakness becomes apparent when we consider the knowledge of God:

> In Kantian idealism, reason is entangled in itself. Here understanding can only mean to understand oneself out of oneself. "I am" thus means "I think." "God is" thus means that the Spirit [*Geist*] returns to itself; it knows itself in the unity of consciousness. In this way the concern for a real belief in God, namely, the claim that God exists outside of the self, appears groundless since reason is only at home with itself. At this point we see clearly that the self cannot transcend itself by itself. It is imprisoned in itself; it sees only itself, even when it sees another, even when it wants to see God. The self understands itself out of itself, but this means precisely that the self fails fundamentally to understand itself, something we can only say when this "I" has been addressed and overcome in its very existence by another; it considers itself free but is imprisoned; it claims authority but has only itself as a vassal: that is what Protestant theology describes as the corruption of reason. This is the [self's] ontic inversion into itself the *cor curvum in se*. (*AS*, 39)

Bonhoeffer rejects the idealist position that "only same can understand same," which dominates transcendental philosophy. This notion effectively eradicates real knowledge of God by assuming that "if God is supposed to approach man, man must be a god of similar kind" (ibid., 47).

Adhering to the premodern conviction that knowledge of self requires knowledge of God, Bonhoeffer criticizes atheistic models of self-knowledge for eradicating transcendence by confining self-knowledge to the first part of Calvin's hermeneutical circle: when the knowledge of God is "incestuous," self-knowledge lacks the necessary exteriority to make it real knowledge rather than self-deception. If understanding is the mind becoming conscious of itself, then interpretation of objects is merely the clarification of what one already implicitly understands.[1] Then the direction of my gaze "remains introspective" and claims to find God in the mental, reflective act of consciousness.

Bonhoeffer insists that real knowledge of God and of ourselves requires radical transcendence, which prevents the reduction of God's being to our mental act. In this important sense, act and being must be different, for in the "genuine transcendental act God remains incomprehensible in the event of knowing [*im Vollzug*] so that the existential god-thinking act occurs within consciousness but is not accessible to the self-reflecting conscious-

---

1. Bonhoeffer here uses the German expression for regaining consciousness after fainting, whose roots are indeed the emergence of consciousness as awakening to self-awareness: "Ich finde Gott in meinem Kommen zu mir selbst vor, ich finde mich, d.h. ich finde Gott" (*AS*, 42).

ness" (*AS*, 44). Knowledge of God, in other words, is an opening toward an exteriority whose transcendence cannot be grasped and reduced to sameness by the reflecting mind. Only this transcendence allows us true self-knowledge through God's address to us, through which we learn of our humanity and identity. Only God, after all, has access to the whole of being within which our existence makes sense.

Like Levinas, Bonhoeffer sees any other model of knowledge as idolatry because it objectifies the other. Our relation with otherness cannot be based on a primordial correlation between interlocutors because then we will understand the other only on our own terms. Grounding interpretation and self-knowledge in sameness inevitably means objectification of the other in my image; Bonhoeffer believes that such hermeneutics of sameness deserve the rebuke given to Goethe's character Faust: "We can only imagine a God whom we can comprehend" (*AS*, 47). That is why God reveals himself to our understanding on his terms in the incarnation.

Kantian and idealist transcendental philosophy and its "egology" have been challenged by atheistic existential philosophy and theology alike. Bonhoeffer appreciates Heidegger's criticism of idealism yet still counts him among proponents of immanence and sameness. He acknowledges that Heidegger takes an important step beyond Husserlian phenomenology by seeking the ontological foundation for our human existence, which remains bracketed in Husserl's approach. Yet this existence leads not to the insurmountable transcendental barrier Bonhoeffer seeks but rather to the serene cosmos of the Greek Logos in which being speaks itself through us. Heidegger's hermeneutics of facticity still strives for meaning (the meaning of being), but, unlike idealism, it does not claim to possess the whole within which individual experiences make sense. In the final analysis, however, Heidegger merely replaces the firmament of universal reason with the house of being, in which being provides the whole against whose fuzzy outlines humans understand themselves: "Man grasps his particular existence in its spiritual and embodied conspicuous care [*Umtastbarkeit*] as an 'existence between' or 'in relation to' something toward which human existence [*Dasein*] points in a way we cannot fully comprehend" (*AS*, 65).

Bonhoeffer also criticizes Heidegger's notion of facticity as running toward death. We know that Heidegger takes this notion from theology but adapts it to his atheistic framework. Departing from Augustine and Luther, he imprisons self-understanding in the atheistic world of being-toward-death within a closed finitude; in this world, human existence has always fallen prey to inauthentic existence in faceless public opinion and discourse (*das Man*) on account of which we are always guilty of inauthenticity.

Bonhoeffer warns against using Heidegger's analysis of existence as an ontological analogy to the theological notions of existence as fallenness and guilt. In Heidegger, after all, we can actually achieve a proper authentic self-understanding by ourselves. Theology, on the contrary, denies such possibility. Theologically, self-understanding is a gift from God and lies beyond human capability (*AS*, 94). Faith is never a state of being we already find ourselves in, something we can discover or attain through conscience's call to authenticity.

Indeed, Heidegger's hermeneutics raises again the central question of hermeneutic universality: in Heidegger's hermeneutics, understanding of existence is posited as a constitutive element of human being (*Dasein*). That, however, raises the question "if and how this element can be compatible with the notion of revelation as transcendence" (*AS*, 94). What theological hermeneutics requires is a hermeneutic ontology that leaves room for divine transcendence. Yet in Heidegger's world, revelation is impossible because atheism seals it off from divine transcendence.

Bonhoeffer insists that Heidegger's contribution to ontology is indeed positive because his ontology posits being as more primordial than the thinking self. Also, Heidegger's world allows for the necessary continuity between being itself and human existence, but this continuity is bought at the expense of transcendence. For even in Heidegger, the ultimate winner is still the reflective self because understanding lies within our grasp. Bonhoeffer claims that even Heidegger's phenomenological method trusts that "we carry within ourselves the possibility to recognize revelation for what it is. Knowledge [*Erkenntnis* = recognition] thus indeed comes to mean, in accordance with its root meaning to re-cognize, to recover the being of being because we already know in principle what being is" (*AS*, 103).

Bonhoeffer concludes that neither Kant nor Heidegger, neither critical idealism nor hermeneutics, has truly understood the limits of human reason. Levinas and Bonhoeffer are united in their judgment that as long as rationality, the Logos, is defined as impersonal totality, true ethical transcendence is impossible. A theological account of self-knowledge and hermeneutics requires ethical transcendence in the ultimate relational otherness of a personal Logos.

In his lectures on Christology, Bonhoeffer clearly contrasted the theological and the Greek concepts of Logos and their significance for interpretation. The Christian Logos is a person rather than an idea. If the incarnation is taken as an idea, it will not challenge the human Logos of rationality but will, even as a challenge, be taken up into its system of thought. Hegel's mastery and tragedy were to have done just this.

If, however, the Logos that challenges human self-understanding comes in a form unfamiliar to it, not as idea but as person, and claims, "I am the truth, I am the death of the human Logos, I am the life of the divine Logos, I am the first and the last," then we can no longer ask how this is possible; instead our intellectual questions encounter the personal transcendental barrier, and we must ask, "*Who* are you?" This, argues Bonhoeffer, is the question about transcendence asked by our dethroned reason. Any possibility of integration of this Logos into our rational structures must fail because the divine personal Logos comes as the end of my human Logos: "He is the Logos, he is the counter word. It all depends on 'being.' The question about the 'who' is the question of transcendence. . . . In the 'who question,' the questioner inquires about the being that limits his being . . . [thus] the question of transcendence is the question of existence" (*Berlin*, 282–83).

It is symptomatic for our egoism that our "who" questions turn out to be objectifying "how" questions. The genuine "who" question is the religious question par excellence. Here we ask about the other, his being, his authority. It "is the question of loving my neighbor. The question of transcendence and existence is the question about my fellow man, it is the question about personhood." Bonhoeffer believes that our constant objectification of others in asking "how" they are is evidence for our being out of communion with God. We naturally treat others the same way we treat ideas, trying to figure them out: "Tell me *how* you are, tell me *how* you think, and I will tell you who you are" (*Berlin*, 283). Our inability to ask the relational and ultimately religious question "who are you," characterizes our human finitude and demonstrates the limits of our critical intellect. In this way, the "existential question is the question of transcendence" (ibid.). Bonhoeffer concludes that "the ultimate question of critical thought is that it *must* pose the question 'who are you' but *cannot* do so" (ibid.). Once again, Bonhoeffer insists on the ethical nature of our knowledge of others and consequently of ourselves: such knowledge depends on self-revelation. In theological terms, true self-understanding depends on the radical transcendence of God because only genuine exteriority, only a question aimed at my entire human existence from the outside, addresses my being objectively. Therefore the question "who am I," or "who is this being called human being" cannot be answered immanently, merely from within our own existence: "[human] existence itself cannot answer the question because human existence cannot step outside of itself, since it remains entirely self-referential, self-reflexive" (ibid., 286). The problem is that we love this self-reflexive prison and cannot stand the logos of difference. We tend to "eliminate the other which confronts us." In a final theological application, Bonhoeffer diagnoses our love for intellectual captivity in self-knowledge as the cause for the general human tendency to preserve the human logos by killing "the Jesus-Christus-Logos which confronts us and puts our existence into question" (ibid.).

Bonhoeffer's critique of the hermeneutical circle and its underlying Logos conception as the basis for self-knowledge already questions the ontological premise of Gadamer's philosophical hermeneutics. Yet Bonhoeffer's analysis results in an even more radical hermeneutics that challenges the very concept of self-knowledge. According to Bonhoeffer, human preoccupation with the idea of self-knowledge, from Greek philosophy to present hermeneutics, is a result of the Fall. In a critique more radical than Caputo's radical hermeneutics, Bonhoeffer insists that our fascination with self-knowledge is an attempt to overcome a deep disunity without our selves.

The Tragic Origin of Self-Knowledge

In his posthumously published *Ethics*, Bonhoeffer explains that the human desire for self-knowledge originates with the Fall. The story of Adam and Eve is really a story of hermeneutical tragedy because humanity gained knowledge of good and evil by breaking communion with God. While this might sound like a benefit, Bonhoeffer interprets the biblical account as indicating a deep rift in human existence. "Man at his origin knows only one thing: God. It is only in the unity of his knowledge of God that he knows of other men, of things and of himself. He knows all things only in God, and God in all things. The knowledge of good and evil shows that he is no longer at one with this origin" (*Ethics*, 21).

For Bonhoeffer, God's pronouncement after the Fall that "man has now become like one of us, knowing good and evil" (Gen. 3:22) is thus tragically true. Humanity broke communion with God in desiring to become an origin on its own terms. The price is high, for now the human being has become god in that the secret of his origin and the secret of the origin of good and evil, deeply shrouded in mystery, is now the burden of human judgment:

> Instead of knowing only the God who is good to him and instead of knowing all things in Him, he now knows himself as the origin of good and evil. Instead of accepting the choice and election of God, man desires to choose, to be the origin of election. And so, in a certain sense, he bears within himself the secret of predestination. Instead of knowing himself solely in the reality of being chosen and loved by God, he must now know himself in the possibility of choosing and of being the origin of good and evil. He has become like God, but against God. Herein lies the serpent's deceit. (*Ethics*, 22)

Humans know good and evil at the cost of estrangement from God. Having become a god against God, we are separated from our true destiny as human beings and so have effectually dehumanized ourselves (ibid., 23).

According to Bonhoeffer, this tragic move radically altered the hermeneutic circle of human self-knowledge by removing the vital element of knowing God. He explains that now "for the first time, man knows himself as something apart from God, outside God, and this means that he now knows himself and no longer God at all; for he can know God only if he knows only God. The knowledge of good and evil thus means a separation from God" (*Ethics*, 22).

This separation changes our humanity from the image of God to the likeness of God. As the image of God, human beings were in complete union with God. After the Fall, in a true albeit disastrous sense of the tempter's promise, *eritis sicut Deus*, human beings have become like God, but against God, by becoming their own creator and judge over good and evil (*Ethics*, 22). As the image of God, humans draw their life entirely from their origin in God—the gift of life is this origin in God. The origin has changed and so the gift (which is God's gift and as such attached to the origin) has changed.

The tragedy is that humans have not actually gained knowledge beyond what they had; knowledge of good and evil is regress, not progress. In arrogating to themselves the knowledge of good and evil, humans become a parody of God. Even the Bible hesitates to talk about God as the origin of both good and evil; these things are veiled in mystery.

The end result is that we live in deep disunion with God, with others, with things, and with ourselves (*Ethics*, 24). The two direct results of this disjointed existence are shame and conscience. Shame, unlike guilt, is our primordial lack of wholeness. This lack is exemplified by the dialectic of disclosure and concealment, which rules our lives: we yearn for both fellowship and solitude—we want to trust others fully and yet always keep secrets in dread of complete self-disclosure; we even lie to ourselves (ibid., 26).

Disunion at the heart of self-knowledge also has important hermeneutical implications for our view of conscience. Besides shame, Bonhoeffer lists conscience as a consequence of knowing good and evil. While shame is the reminder of our disunion with God and others, conscience is "the sign of man's disunion with himself. Conscience is farther from the origin than shame; it presupposes disunion with God and others, and—already self-absorbed—marks only the disunion within himself of the man who is already disunited from his origin. It is the call to the unity of man with himself" (*Ethics*, 28).

Without referring directly to Heidegger, Bonhoeffer provides an excellent critique of Heidegger's conscience as the call of man to himself. We remember that in Heidegger's hermeneutics, interpretation helps us to understand conscience as "the call to the unity of man with himself." Bonhoeffer agrees that this seems evident from the ought nature of this call. Heidegger's conscience, however, is oblivious to the fact that this unity itself presupposes unity with God, so that the call of conscience arises from the original disunity of God and human beings. Conscience does not understand that its call to authenticity, the call to the unity of the human being with himself or herself, is tied to the reversal of knowledge that happened in our attaining knowledge of good and evil. Conscience "derives the relation to God and to men from the relation of man to himself. Conscience pretends to be the voice of God and the standard for the relation to other men" (*Ethics*, 28). Its logic is that the right relation with God must be derived from our right relation with ourselves.

It is fallen conscience's great weakness to put authenticity first and God second. It wants to heal the self before it heals disunion with others and with God: "In conscience man summons himself, who has become evil, back to his proper, better self, to good. This good, which consists in the unity of man with himself, is now to be the origin of all good. It is the good of God, and it is the good for one's neighbour. Bearing within himself the knowledge of good and evil, man has become judge over God and men, just as he is judge over himself" (*Ethics*, 29).

Bonhoeffer's analysis of conscience is crucial for theological hermeneutics because he concludes that hermeneutics' basic goal of self-understanding rests on a fundamental misunderstanding of ontology. While conscience may call us to self-knowledge, this inexorable drive toward self-knowledge is an indication of the rift at our very core caused by our alienation from God: "Self-knowledge is now the measure and the goal of life. This holds true even when man presses out beyond the bounds of his own self. Self-knowledge is man's interminable striving to overcome his disunion with himself by thought; by unceasingly distinguishing himself from himself, he endeavours to achieve unity with himself" (*Ethics*, 29).

Bonhoeffer's theological analysis of conscience points to the limits of Gadamer's position that all understanding is in the final analysis self-understanding. In light of Bonhoeffer's account of self-knowledge, hermeneutic philosophy springs from the desire to interpret reality egoistically rather than transcendently, with ourselves as the focus rather than God and others. Even when we *claim* that we desire knowledge about human nature, we *really* want to know about ourselves, a sign, at least for Bonhoeffer, of our deep disunion with ourselves. For hermeneutics, then, self-knowledge, even when it presses beyond the boundaries of self-examination, will still be self-centered.

Bonhoeffer points to the solution of this hermeneutical problem: "We require being that cannot be captured, controlled, or in any way predicted by us, a real other that, however, encounters us not merely in a historical act of faith but addresses us in the entirety of our human existence and which exists independently of us and our decisions" (*AS*, 103).

Bonhoeffer finds this "real other" in the incarnation: "The nature of God's direct act [of calling and changing us] is not its timelessness" but God's address within time and through culture to us in Christ (*AS*, 95). Even out of this particularity, however, the incarnation addresses our human existence in its entirety. In articulating this insight for our time, theology can only make limited use of philosophical vocabulary and insights. We have already seen the limits of existential hermeneutic philosophy for theological hermeneutics. Heideggerian ontology is problematic because, in Heidegger, I already know myself as fallen and with the potential toward authenticity (albeit in a nontheological sense). When Bultmann adopts this ontological framework for theology, he implies that I find myself always as both fallen and with the potential of understanding God and authentic being in faith.

Neither can psychology help us toward a better self-understanding. Certainly, the experience of faith does not simply bypass psychology; nonetheless, if our ethics and humanity depend on understanding ourselves as addressed by God in Christ, theological hermeneutics cannot ground the correct interpretation of human existence in psychology. In this claim, Bonhoeffer follows again Luther's lead: "According to Luther [we] are impenetrable to ourselves. No one knows his motives, no one knows his sins in their entirety; man is unable to understand himself based on his own psychological experiences [because] they are susceptible to arbitrary interpretations." The only way to achieve a unified self in its entire existence as called or elected by God is by turning from the self to God. This cannot be done, however, through speculative theology or in the Barthian fashion of ahistorical otherness; instead we must turn to the point where otherness and sameness meet in our address by the incarnated Word of God. Bonhoeffer concludes: "Since, however, as we have claimed earlier, self-understanding must proceed from a whole and, second, requires potential re-creation [*Nachschaffen*], we must seek the whole where the human being is created or newly created and this creation happens to him even as it happens in cooperation with him, and where in complete clarity and reality man can know himself; that means, however, the whole picture of man and his existence is established only in God's word" (*AS*, 52). Only God offers an interpretation of human existence from a vantage point of total exteriority, guaranteeing the necessary transcendence that enables his knowledge to be free from our self-affirming, delusional self-interpretations.

Knowing in Community

What sets Bonhoeffer's incarnational concept of self-understanding apart from other approaches, both theological and atheistic ones, is his insistence on the personal and relational quality of truth. Bonhoeffer's central insight is that persons in relation, that is, being in community, are the very basis of true self-understanding. He believes that the self-understanding offered to us in the scriptures is not, as it is so often in evangelical Christianity (and also in Levinas), that of an individual addressed by radical alterity but rather that of a self in communion with others. The model for this is the Trinity and the incarnation. The Trinity presents us with the basic notion of personhood as a self in communion, and in the incarnation (birth, death, and resurrection of Christ), Christ tied himself to the church: "The freedom of God means that God has tied himself to the church as the community in and through which Christ reveals himself as the new humanity, *deuteros anthropos*" (*AS*, 109).

Our self-understanding thus comes about in the shared life of the Christian church, through the word and the sacraments. All theological and nontheological approaches to self-understanding err when they begin with individual consciousness as the foundation of understanding. Both Kantian transcendentalism and Heideggerian phenomenology fail in this regard because man is never an individual, not even an individual "you" addressed by another, but is always in community: "The word of God is addressed to humanity, the gospel to the community of Christians." The interpretation of human existence given in God's self-revelation sees each of us as either being "in Adam," that is, existing as fallen, or "being in Christ" as part of the new humanity (*AS*, 109).

Bonhoeffer offers a hermeneutically rich description of Christian existence as creative *poiesis* (*Nachschaffen*) in which the church as a collective of individuals enacts faith by daily hermeneutic wrestling with God's word. Christ, the incarnate Word of God, is not only the spiritual source of the church's existence but is also the Word preached to it in sermon, baptism, and Eucharist (*SC*, 164–70). Following Luther, Bonhoeffer defines the church as instituted by Christ, shaped by the preaching of the word, and confirmed and strengthened in the Eucharist, which miraculously firms the communal bond between Christ and the partakers. In this way, "the whole edifice [of the church] issues from Christ to Christ; its unifying center and entry point is the Word" (ibid., 169).

This means that the God-world relation and our ontological speculations must begin with God's self-revelation, whose center is the incarnation. This also means that our ontology and notions of participation must be radically hermeneutical within the ecclesial community under the guidance of the Holy Spirit. We cannot follow Bonhoeffer in the rich and detailed interpretation of being in Christian community but must return to our focus on his contribution to hermeneutics and self-knowledge.

The Messiah Has Come: Incarnational Self-Knowledge

Like premodern hermeneuts, Bonhoeffer believes that our accurate engagement with reality depends on accurate self-knowledge or self-understanding. Western philosophy has impeded the natural human desire for self-knowledge by getting wrong both the knowing subject and the quality of knowledge itself. Conceiving the knowing subject as isolated consciousness and knowledge as rational facts or eternal truths of universal reason has created an illusion of self-knowledge in which we invent ourselves by chasing after psychic fantasies.

Even phenomenology, which decenters the self and overcomes subjectivism by having objects appear to consciousness, cannot achieve radical transcendence because the anticipatory structure already posits a correlation between otherness and sameness. Bonhoeffer thus echoes Levinas's (and also Caputo's) claim that the hermeneutical circle does not admit radical otherness. The hermeneutical aporia is that we require radical transcendence for self-understanding but that the dynamics of understanding outlined by hermeneutic philosophy is confined to the realm of a closed ontology and a self-asserting consciousness.

Bonhoeffer addresses these problems by redefining the nature of human existence and the quality of truth. Instead of individualism, he suggests an individuality as person in relation, the social self in community. The ontological model for this is the Trinity. Moreover, truth and meaning cannot be expressed in rationalist terms but only as an ethical address by the divine Logos himself, the second Person of the Godhead as incarnated in Christ. Through Christ, God wills community with human beings. The community is the visible, concrete church, which hears and believes the preaching of the word. The word of this community is preaching and sacrament; its action is believing and loving. The ethical address of radical otherness, the being of revelation, is Christ existing as community in the concrete way of the church. Only then "can we maintain the balance between being and otherness in the concrete existence of a real community—because it is founded in Christ—a community of persons in relation" (*AS*, 111).

Bonhoeffer offers a concrete balance of transcendence and historical reality: True self-understanding is granted to each new member of the community by God, and each person who comes to know the truth through God's gracious act already finds himself or herself in the community of believers, the church. Thus faith encounters a being prior to the act of believing. This exteriority means that God's call and its resulting subjectivity are not dependent on faith, but "on the contrary, faith knows being as independent of its own existence. Everything depends on the fact that faith understands itself not as creating or conditioning but rather as *created* by this new being" (*AS*, 114).

Bonhoeffer helps us to understand Levinas by providing an ethical reason for the fundamentally unethical, that is, egological, structure of Western philosophy. What Levinas calls egology, centered on self, Bonhoeffer calls being in Adam. This is our inauthentic mode of existence, a being in un-truth, torn out of true community with God and fellow human beings, a state in which our will in guilt is inverted, focused on itself. This is the atheistic self-understanding of ourselves as primarily alone: "Because he is alone in the world, 'his world,' our fellow man sinks to the status of a thing (as in Heidegger's *Mitsein*), God to the status of a religious object, and the self becomes its own creator and God" (*AS*, 136).

In this self-understanding, "all knowledge, and even especially the *gnosi seauton* [know yourself], aims at our ultimate self-justification until man, in this terrible burden to be creator and bearer of the world, in the cold sweat of eternal loneliness becomes afraid of himself and tremblingly elevates himself to his own judge—in the voice of conscience" (*AS*, 137). This self-judgment is answered by repentance as the call to authenticity; yet this repentance is a turning of the self to itself. Here again is Heidegger's existential dilemma: I put myself on the defendant's bench, repent of in-authenticity, and admonish myself with appeals to my better self. Yet the cry of conscience merely diverts from the quiet loneliness of "a barren 'for myself' and reverberates echoless in the kingdom we interpret as our own" (ibid.). Heidegger's fundamental ontology is true self-knowledge insofar as it describes our being in fallenness, our being in Adam. Yet even to recognize ourselves as being in this state is beyond human ken because to recognize oneself as "being in Adam" already presupposes a self-understanding as a creature of God. Yet "only in Christ does man understand himself as creator of God; in Adam he was himself creator and God in one" (ibid., 149).

Bonhoeffer challenges the claim of existential philosophy and herme-neutics to be champions of finitude. For him philosophical finitude is not radical enough. Indeed, finitude defined as being without transcendence is not finitude at all but the arrogance to have comprehended finitude. Reducing human existence to existing, to the how (*das Wiesein*), is the paralysis of human existence. In its very claim to the modesty of imma-nence, such an interpretation actually arrogates to itself knowledge of the whole according to which human existence is only readable as the "how" of existing.

The contrary claim of incarnational theology is that the whole is available only in the incarnation. Only in the communion with God can we know ourselves as fallen and forgiven. Here, according to Bonhoeffer, "the circle closes." What Bonhoeffer shares fully with philosophical hermeneutics, however, is that this being in faith is not a theoretical position that can be adopted at will. Truly understanding our finitude as made in God's image, as creature, is only possible for one who exists in faith. Ontologically this means that God is at the same time the very ground of being and its radical transcendence in communion with us.

Authentic human existence is existence addressed by God's self-revelation in Christ. This personal ethical transcendence, which qualifies interpretation, knowledge, truth, and self-understanding, explodes all known metaphysical categories: "The world of being is transcended and qualified by the personal God in Christ as creator, reconciler, and savior." Based on God as the ground of being, the world is for us either in Adam or in Christ: in Adam "as his own, raped, interpreted world of the curse," and in Christ as "the world liberated from the self yet recovered in God as a world of hope and new creation." Knowledge of the self and the world requires knowledge of God, "for in the final analysis, the world is for God, who remains its Lord. A more general determination of being is impossible" (*AS*, 156).

Bonhoeffer defines faith as direct relation with God in community. Here our existence is elevated to full humanity. Faith is irreducible to a reflexive act and is not accessible in its immediacy to consciousness or conscience. Bonhoeffer recovers for theology the notion of *fides directa*, an act of believing trust accomplished by our consciousness but inaccessible to self-transparent reflection because it exists only in the immediate concrete act. This sounds like Caputo's version of radical hermeneutics. For Bonhoeffer, however, an enacted faith orients itself to positive content. The act itself rests on the "objectivity of the revelation event in word and sacrament; clinging to Christ does not have to be self-reflexive but is completely absorbed into the act of believing" (*AS*, 158). Reflection is already outside the immediate encounter, and consciousness is already an act of reflection. This does not mean, of course, that there is no room for reflection. Yet theological reflection must be aware of the egoistical tendencies of consciousness and requires a thorough deconstruction of metaphysical categories.

Bonhoeffer meets deconstruction halfway, so to speak, in suggesting the relational nature of revelation through the *person* of Jesus Christ as the incarnate Word of God. The existential hermeneutical nature of this faith in community requires that we "deconstruct" and rethink our theological categories: "All metaphysical categories of eternity, temporality, being and becoming, life and death, essence and appearance must be measured and reinvented for a Christian ontology through the concepts of being in sin or being in grace" (*AS*, 150).

True selfhood and self-knowledge are possible through faith in Christ because only then is the self's gaze redirected toward radical otherness. In the communal, concrete, lived interpretation of the word, sustained by that very word as participating in a radical transcendence that cannot be sullied by the world of being because he affirms and sanctifies it, ethics finds its fullest expressions. For "to see Christ in word and sacrament means to see the risen crucified One in creation and in one's neighbor in one and the same act. Only here is a future revealed to us that determines the presence by faith" (*AS*, 158). Bonhoeffer follows Paul in insisting that the Christian hermeneutical experience is eschatological. Our being is determined by the future, which has already come and not yet fully come in Christ. In faith "future becomes present" (ibid.).

This stance is fundamentally different from Heideggerian ontology. To illustrate this difference, Bonhoeffer likens Heidegger's position to that of an old man and the Christian faith to the stage of childhood. The child's existence is future oriented (with all the fears and blessings this state of being holds), and only this orientation enables him to live in the present; in other words, the eschatological nature of faith ensures the Christian's full appreciation of the world. The aged man, by contrast, who *wants* to live in the present, falls prey to the past, to himself, death, and guilt. Bonhoeffer argues that "the present can be truly lived only out of the future" (*AS*, 159).

Faith, rightly understood, is therefore not a flight from the present but its fullest appreciation and enjoyment in our full humanity. Humanity does not depend primarily on reason or conscious reflection but on communion with God, the ground of all being. In this posture of prayer, we find the self turned away from itself toward radical transcendence, a transcendence that by definition it cannot comprehend, grasp, or surround with the stifling grasp of self-consciousness—and yet a transcendence whose ultimate declaration of love in self-abnegation fully deserves our trust.

According to Bonhoeffer, this stance is signified by infant baptism, whose rejection in modern theology derives from our disproportionate trust in human consciousness: "The *actus directus* as the sole act given by Christ and directed toward Christ and infant baptism as paradoxical revelation event without the reflecting answer of consciousness . . . is the eschatological beginning for the symphony of life" (*AS*, 160). The baptism of children is the open acknowledgment of our dependence on God rather than our own rationalist obsession with the certainty of salvation. Our true selfhood depends not on intellectual certainty but on trusting in God's work, whose historical self-disclosure, death, and resurrection embeds the life of faith in a greater eschatological framework fully in the present and yet pointing to the future.

Bonhoeffer's theological view of human existence liberates the self from itself for ethics. The difference between Bonhoeffer's incarnational ethical transcendence and that of Levinas and Derrida is illustrated by their divergent views of the messianic. The term "messianic" in the late Derrida is basically a synonym for disruption, the unspeakable, for indeconstructible justice, the breach, and so on. Derrida's concept of the messianic is Levinas's radical transcendence, which can never really arrive, for when it does, it ceases to be transcendence.

Bonhoeffer perceived the same understanding of "messianic" in Karl Barth's early theology. While he appreciated Barth's insistence on radical transcendence and his denial that the wholly other God could ever become the God of our consciousness, Barth's uncompromising stance on transcendence resembles the Derridean concept of the messianic: a God who is always arriving but never dwelling with us (*AS*, 70). The messianic points to the basic problem shared by Levinas, Derrida, Caputo, and Barth. In their desire to guard radical transcendence, they lose history and real humanity with it.

In light of the work of Bonhoeffer, who believes that the Messiah has actually come, the messianic of Derrida appears as a half-hearted attempt to keep the future open toward change and possibility. The central question in dialogue with deconstruction on the messianic is whether the arrival of the Messiah actually destroys transcendence and openness. Bonhoeffer believes the opposite. The revelation of the Secret, to speak with Caputo, nowhere implies that such revelation should cause narrow-mindedness, know-it-all fundamentalism, or even, to speak with Critchley, a disparaging of the ordinary. On the contrary, knowledge cannot be primarily possession of a reflective consciousness but becomes relation in which even the act of trust is *given* rather than achieved. The presence becomes valuable because of a future already and yet not fully come, and as Bonhoeffer points out, appropriation of one's faith is a concrete hermeneutical-communal endeavor. The Secret is not knowledge but a person, the incarnation of God for the sake of a new humanity in freedom and communion.

From this perspective, there is no need to escape into the realm of non-knowing in a show of interpretive humility. Apophasis itself is not exempt from the hermeneutical premise that neutral ground does not exist in interpretation. Most modern versions of apophasis are quite obviously defined as a knee-jerk reaction to knowing as reflection. This is especially apparent when apophasis comes to mean faith in the face of meaninglessness. Faith in meaninglessness, however, is inhuman—no matter how joyfully it may be advertised. The self and knowledge do not become fully human when they are redirected merely to the other, for we do not know who the other is or may be; rather interpretation becomes both more radical and more human only when the other is the very ground and "rationality" of being (the divine Logos) whose incarnation as self-sacrificing revelation of God inaugurates freedom in community. Here, as Bonhoeffer believes, our existence becomes meaningful not in an I-know-it-all clarity but in the adventure of faith:

> In the orientation toward Christ, human existence and the how of existing [*Dasein und Wiesein*] are put aright. The "there" is redeemed from its being raped by the "how" and, in turn, the "how" finds itself again in the God-given there; the echoless cry from a barren world into the solitariness of the self, the protest against violations of any kind has found an unexpected answer and dissolves by and by into the quiet, praying conversation of the child with the father in the Word of Jesus Christ. In looking toward Christ, the tortured knowledge about our split selves [between authentic and inauthentic self] finds joyful conscience and confidence of daring and risk-taking. The slave has been freed. (*AS*, 169)

This is indeed the hermeneutical stance advocated by theological hermeneutics. It is not the stern and all-knowing glare of the scholar father who is always correct and gets on everyone's nerves by correcting all other erroneous opinions; nor is it the skewed perspective of the rebellious youth whose disenchantment with precisely those father figures makes him renounce self-knowledge completely and live for the daily renewal of experience without content. After all, interpretation for interpretation's sake, no matter how much this rebellion is dressed up in terms of ethics and respect of otherness, only aids the disappearance of the human by supporting those who want to destroy the self and self-knowledge.

Instead theological hermeneutics requires the interpretive attitude of the child, who certainly does not know everything but whose filial trust in the father explores, interprets, and revises interpretations, all of which are in the service of understanding and implement the new humanity inaugurated by Christ. This, according to Bonhoeffer, is believing knowing (*Glaubenserkennen*), a hermeneutical act that is irreducible to reflection and that is lived in our daily embodiment of faith (*AS*, 131).

Theology is thus fundamentally hermeneutical, and hermeneutical theology must necessarily challenge cherished notions of fundamentalism, such as absolute timeless truths. The divine Logos is an address by transcendence as person, not as idea: "Christ as the word of God in the sense of address does not mean Christ as timeless truth; rather it is God's concrete address to us in the concrete moment of inbreaking truth. Christ is therefore not timeless, generally accessible truth like an idea but is only perceived as word where he wants to be heard, that is, everything rests in his freedom to reveal himself to me or conceal himself from me" (*Berlin*, 298).

Christ is the Word in address, in interpretation, and in preaching. Thus the Christian life is, paradoxically, one of certainty of being in relation with God and yet one of constant uncertainty in application. The Christian life is one of interpretive adventure, of surprise, and thus of much prayer and agony, but it is also one of joy and confidence, knowing that all is experienced in communion with God. For Bonhoeffer the Christian life is fundamentally hermeneutical. However, to participate in the divine Logos does not mean that one has received a lifetime supply of stock interpretations ready to hand. Instead Bonhoeffer, every bit as much as Gadamer or even Derrida, emphasizes the need for interpretation and decision making.

Bonhoeffer dismisses the view that knowing God's will "takes the form of intuition, which excludes any sort of reflection, a naive grasping of the first thought or feeling that forces itself on the mind," nor is the will of God "a set of rules established from the outset" (*Ethik*, 41). Interpretation is not an unfortunate mistake but the God-ordained way of human living. While theological interpretation, proceeding from its relation with Christ, undergoes the same agony of painstaking work and decision making as ethical philosophy, it is freed from godhood and the burden of ultimate judgment.

Knowing its limitations, theological hermeneutics does not justify itself before God but surrenders this burden to Christ. This is an important point if interpretation is indeed inseparable from application. Every interpretive act is thus an ethical act of responsibility. Like the premoderns, Bonhoeffer ties interpretation and application together. Interpretation of God's word is only in application, and this application is given over to God's judgment: "Only in doing can there be submission to the will of God. In doing God's will, man renounces every right and every justification of his own; he delivers himself humbly into the hands of the merciful judge" (*Ethik*, 46).

We can agree with Gadamer's assessment that the crux of incarnational hermeneutics is the incomprehensibility of the cross. Indeed, human knowledge is radically limited. On a theological account, however, interpretation is not first about us but about God's self-revelation. Ontology and transcendence, sameness and otherness, nature and grace are not two separate kingdoms. In the incarnation, the two have become one. By looking to this self-revelation of God, we gain self-knowledge by losing all pretensions to self-understanding. Self-knowledge is not possessed but given as a gift. Its nature is relational and hence radically hermeneutical. To speak with Caputo, this is what it *really* means to let the other come. Contrary to deconstruction, freedom, unity, peace, and community are found not in apophasis but in the hermeneutical appropriation of God's incarnational address to us in which, mysteriously but truly, difference and sameness reside without compromise.

This, according to Bonhoeffer, "is the new creation, which is already an event in the here and now by faith and whose completion may be glimpsed in the future by faith; this is the vision of him who does not want to look back to himself but only away from himself to the revelation of God. He who looks at Christ, who is born from the narrowness of the world into the vastness of heaven, who becomes what he was and yet had never been, a creature of God, a child" (*AS*, 161).

The Relation of Theological and Philosophical Hermeneutics

What does all of this mean for philosophical hermeneutics? Given the theological claim that the Christian Logos created and upholds reality, the honest answer must be that theological premises provide the best framework for hermeneutics. This becomes especially apparent with the recent ethical turn in philosophy. If ethical transcendence is what we desire in philosophical hermeneutics, then only Christian theology, with its concept of personal ethical transcendence as incarnational and Trinitarian, fulfills the desire for ethics without sacrificing hermeneutics to radical difference.

When philosophical discussion takes ethics seriously, it has begun what Levinas calls good metaphysics, the discussion of ultimate questions of meaning and purpose. The question of ethics is the metaphysical question par excellence, because ethics is the question about our humanity and as such requires views on anthropology and philosophy. Anthropological assumptions, taken in the broadest sense, reflect on who it is that interprets. All the thinkers we have examined agree that we must revise the notion of the self as independent consciousness in favor of an ethical self that originates in the social sphere as an I-you encounter. In line with theological hermeneutics, the current discussion in philosophy and hermeneutics desires ethics, not morality, as the fundamental uniqueness of each human individual.

Without a robust theological framework, however, this desire for ethics runs the risk either of elevating the other to godlike status as creator of one's ethical personhood or of diluting ethics into a completely vacuous welcoming stance toward otherness, whose appeal to trust in the unseen and unknown almost becomes a "fascism of the other." Bonhoeffer has argued convincingly that only an incarnational conception of selfhood and Trinitarian ontology provides a plausible foundation for ethics.

Theological hermeneutics agrees with postmodern ethics that the person exists only in communion with others and that human existence is structured as an I-you relation in which I am called to responsibility.

However, in contrast to Levinas's ethics and also to atheistic or agnostic notions of ethics (Derrida, Critchley, Caputo), theology establishes the ethical address by the other as primordially the call of God. This God who requires the risk of unconditional hospitality, this God who requires our trust even at the risk of having our dearest assumptions radically altered, this God is not the unknown God of Caputo's radical hermeneutics, even though he is ultimately unknowable because he always exceeds our knowledge.

The difference of an incarnational-Trinitarian hermeneutics lies in God's self-revelation through the incarnation. Here the unknown and unseen has indeed become concrete history—the ethical call has become flesh. The uncreated Other, the person in communion par excellence, becomes human subject in real time and history. Otherness is ensured by the uncreated, divine nature of this incarnate Logos: it is the Word that was with God from the beginning (John 1:1). Here the Greek Logos, the rational quality of the cosmos, which still dominates Gadamer's philosophical hermeneutics, gains two important qualities. First, even in its ultimate ethical otherness, the Logos, the living ethical Word, is both divine and human. Hence what undergirds all human understanding is not an impersonal Logos but the divine, personal Logos. In this way, truth and rationality become invested with personal, relational qualities.

Second, the incarnation ensures that our inescapable responsibility toward the other is linked to an ultimate otherness (Levinas's illeity) that deserves our trust on account of its ultimate act of self-negation. So Levinas was correct: selfhood is kenotic—but it is God's, not our, kenosis that grounds subjectivity. True human selfhood comes about in the address through the encounter with this Logos, which grounds ethical responsibility toward others. Bonhoeffer has clearly shown that our concept of selfhood and otherness stands or falls with our understanding of the Divine.

The Levinasian ethical subject is self-denial in proximity, hostage to the other. However, if the other becomes god, then the positive ethical values of service, its ultimate goodness and the negation to kill, seem smuggled in through the theological back door. This may well be the very reason that the few theological traces in Levinas are filtered out by atheistic appropriations of his ethics.

The incarnation, on the other hand, actually establishes Levinas's *imago Dei* concept because now otherness is supported by the ultimate ethical act of self-abnegation: not only has absolute otherness, the divine saying, been fully incarnated in the said without loss, but also the Logos in its absolute freedom has willingly died for his enemies in order to make communion with God possible for all. Paul's letter to the Romans is the locus classicus for ethical subjectivity in the New Testament:

You see, at just the right time, when we were still powerless, Christ died for the ungodly. Very rarely will anyone die for a righteous man, though for a good man someone might possibly dare to die. But God demonstrates his own love for us in this: While we were still sinners, Christ died for us.

Since we have now been justified by his blood, how much more shall we be saved from God's wrath through him! For if, when we were God's enemies, we were reconciled to him through the death of his Son, how much more, having been reconciled, shall we be saved through his life! Not only is this so, but we also rejoice in God through our Lord Jesus Christ, through whom we have now received reconciliation. (Rom. 5:6–11 NIV)

Incarnation is thus not a neat philosophical principle that allows otherness and transcendence to coexist but embodies the quality of love as self-sacrifice that characterizes ethics and should also characterize its embodiment in concrete application as lived truth.

If Christ, as Bonhoeffer has put it, is the center of reality, what does a recovery of theological hermeneutics offer for the important hermeneutical aspect of aesthetics? The entire thrust of my comparison between philosophical and theological hermeneutics has been to show that hermeneutic philosophy advances us a good distance toward theological hermeneutics. Since two important sources for our recovery of theological hermeneutics are Levinas and Gadamer, this recovery would be incomplete without addressing the question of the beautiful. Gadamer insists that self-knowledge requires aesthetics. Indeed, Gadamer's hermeneutical philosophy grounds the phenomenological experience of reality outlined by Heidegger ontologically in the experience of art as an experience of the beautiful. In Gadamer aesthetics defines the kind of knowledge scientific epistemology cannot account for, a self-attesting truth that cannot be measured scientifically (*TM*, 487–88).

If aesthetics is such a central category for hermeneutics, what does theological hermeneutics have to say about it? How does an incarnational theological hermeneutics incorporate aesthetics? While Gadamer makes aesthetics the very benchmark of hermeneutic experience as revelation of being, Levinas, in his effort to uphold radical transcendence, developed a rather negative view of art and texts. They only count as a gateway to the ethical. Our recovery of theological hermeneutics also must respond to his challenge. Does incarnational transcendence also disparage the beautiful? Does not Protestantism's historic iconoclastic tendency attest to this?

10

INCARNATION AND AESTHETICS

If Christ is indeed the incarnate divine Logos, then a theological aesthetics must relate all cultural artifacts to this center. "All our cultural activities are striving toward one last thing, one meaning, one Logos, one God. What avails us our seeking after truth if truth does not exist, when not God but man is the last measure for truth and falsehood?" If cultural self-expression is to aid us in self-knowledge, it must be oriented toward transcendence: "One severs art's vital nerve if one takes away its ultimate reference to meaning, to the Divine" (Bonhoeffer, *Predigten*, 148).

Culture falls under what Bonhoeffer calls the penultimate, that which has full meaning only in light of the ultimate, God. This is not, however, another Platonism for the people, far from it. Transcendence and world are not two separate spheres. Human existence is not doomed to an either-or dilemma: either we deny reality as holistic and retreat into the factical or the transcendent half of this dichotomy, or we try to straddle both spheres and become a being of eternal conflict. Instead theological hermeneutics wants to recover the premodern notion that "there is only one reality and that is the God-reality in the reality of the world which was revealed through Christ. Participating in Christ we are at the same time in God-reality and in world-reality. The reality of Christ contains the reality of the world. The world does not possess a reality independent from God's revelation in Christ" (Bonhoeffer, *Ethics*, 43). This means that all things, the world, nature, the profane, and reason, do not exist in and for themselves but are real only in the divine Logos.

The incarnation places Christianity firmly *in the world*, and a Christian-ity that tries to withdraw from the world "falls prey to the unnatural, the irrational, high spirits leading to carelessness, and arbitrariness" (Bon-hoeffer, *Ethics*, 47). In other words, aesthetics, too, must be seen from an incarnational point of view as part of the divine-oriented reality.

Recovering the Beautiful

Hans Urs von Balthasar (1905–88) is perhaps the best contemporary theological source on aesthetics. Balthasar, a Catholic theologian and a prolific, systematic writer, shares Bonhoeffer's emphasis on the incarna-tion as the center of reality. Balthasar's unique contribution to modern theology is his conviction that theological hermeneutics must include aesthetics as an essential element of human perception. In his massive magnum opus, *Herrlichkeit*, Balthasar develops a theological aesthetics that complements the personal-relational aspect of Bonhoeffer's herme-neutics and allows theological hermeneutics to reflect concretely on the role of culture, art, and texts for fostering true humanity in the image of God. It may be easier for us to realize the importance of the beautiful when we define it with Balthasar as a sense of proportion. Balthasar employs this term in the classical sense as referring not just to visual effects but also to a life lived in harmony with its ultimate goal.

Balthasar bases his view of aesthetics on the *analogia entis*, a theo-logical concept that goes back to Paul's assertion that God's invisible qualities, his "eternal power and divine nature," are discernible in cre-ation itself (Rom. 1:20). Like Gadamer, Balthasar is convinced that form (*Gestalt*) and beauty are the primordial phenomena of appearance. In his view, however, they can have this role only within a created, divinely designed world. For Balthasar, Heidegger's and Gadamer's Greek world of impersonal being presents a distorted vision of reality. He corrects this perspective by placing the beautiful as a hermeneutic foundation within a creationary framework. Only then does the concept of the beautiful allow us to see "the truth of the whole, the truth as the transcendent characteristic of being, which is not an abstract concept but the living tie between God and the world" (*Herrlichkeit*, 1:16). The beautiful is the final frontier and boundary of critical thought because it is the radiance in which the true and the good appear. For Balthasar *Gestalt* and beauty are the primordial phenomena of appearance. He advocates, in other words, a *Gestaltphenomenology*: objects show themselves to us in their *Gestalt* and their beauty.

While Gadamer posits the impersonal Greek Logos as the source of the beautiful, Balthasar ascribes this role to God's incarnation. The incarnation is the model (*Urphänomen*) for how things appear to us because in God's bodily self-disclosure, the object and its transcendent radiance coexist: "Here exist at the same time the gathering of the indifferently disseminated into the service to the one that presents and expresses itself *and* the statement of him who was able to create such a language-body: himself, I say, out of himself, that is, in a superiority, sovereignty out of an interior realm or essence. Here exist at the same time the interiority and its communication, the soul and its body, the free communication within the constraints and intelligibility of language" (*Herrlichkeit*, 1:18). Based on the model of God's incarnation, the original phenomenon of appearance is neither a body without soul or meaning nor an original spirit that seeks out a body to express itself; rather it is a self-revelation that allows us to see the object itself. Only in this way can we overcome naturalism, on the one hand, and Platonism, on the other (ibid., 1:19).

Human beings share this essential characteristic of self-expression. Balthasar follows both Bonhoeffer and Levinas in stating that human culture begins with ethics, begins with the interhuman relation. Yet the human being is not the original phenomenon of appearance; the human is not *Urbild* but *Abbild*, not original but image. We are not "masters of ourselves": neither do we control our existence in total freedom—because we are "thrown" into existence—nor are we free in our communications. All our acts of self-expression are embedded in history and leave traces we cannot alter. We are "not original in being and spirit but copy, not original word but answering word, not freely speaking but expressed meaning, and therefore completely under the demand of the beautiful which we ourselves cannot control" (*Herrlichkeit*, 1:19). In this sense, human existence is in its entirety (body and spirit) a "mirror of God," and human art participates in his glory. Art tries to share in the divine transcendence so evident, if we are willing to see, in creation.

Because of this central importance of the beautiful for our humanity, Balthasar laments the loss of aesthetics in modern culture and particularly in theology. He is convinced that the beautiful is the language of light, the vehicle of God's revelation. Once we have lost the "language of light," once humanity has forgotten that the mystery of being and its ultimate meaning is revealed to us through the beautiful and not primarily through rational deduction, we can no longer discern in being the *Gestalt* (form) of God's beauty of which all creation speaks: "In a world that no longer dares to affirm the beautiful, rational proofs for truth have lost their conclusiveness; syllogisms rattle dutifully like rotating machines or calculating robots, which spit out exactly determined knowledge by the minute without error, but the conclusion has become a mechanism that captivates no one; the conclusion itself is no longer conclusive" (*Herrlichkeit*, 1:17).

Balthasar warns, however, against aestheticism, the separation of art from existence. When beauty is reduced to form and harmony, the power of being is abstracted from form and cannot be replaced. Only when being remains incarnated in art is beauty truthful, a true revelation of being that enables self-knowledge. Only then, too, is aesthetics an expression of ethics. Balthasar's participatory structure enables him to speak even more strongly than Bonhoeffer about art as reflection of the divine. He addresses Levinas's problem concerning art by placing the ethical form (*Gestalt*) of the incarnate Logos, of the being of being itself, at the center of art as the beautiful.

It is crucial not to misunderstand this move as a recovery of Platonism. Despite Balthasar's Neoplatonic vocabulary, Platonism is the very thing he writes against. His solution to Levinas's dilemma of art as unethical is only valid because of its incarnational foundation. We can almost hear Levinas's questions: But is not this a return to sameness? How is this different from Heidegger's being? Have we not simply replaced Heidegger's being with God?

In a way, that is indeed what Balthasar is doing, but the difference is that God is not an idea, not an eternal, impersonal concept, but a person. The Trinity and the incarnation allow Balthasar to recover the beautiful as ethical. As a result, the interpretation of texts and art becomes a legitimate realm for self-knowledge and ethical insights into human existence and yet resists reduction to one's own interpretive framework. With the help of Augustine, Balthasar's incarnational focus also allows him to recover the language of light for hermeneutics.

The Light of the World

In Balthasar's construct, an existential, phenomenological refinement of Augustine's illumination theory, God's light suffuses creation: the earthly only makes sense in light of revelation. This light is not something extrinsic to creation, though its ultimate source is, but something that emanates from creation. Balthasar believes that, for many reasons, we moderns have lost the ability to recognize divine beauty as the ground of our being and that we need to recover this sense. We must "recover an eye for the original form of human existence [*für die Urgestalt Mensch im Dasein*], and driven by the courage to this phenomenon, we must bring to light once again the true, the good, and the beautiful" (*Herrlichkeit*, 1:23).

Again, this is not a recovery of Greek thought, not even early Greek thought, but it is a theological aesthetic, a hermeneutics of the beautiful centered on the Trinity and the incarnation. Balthasar revives the old Thomistic formula *Gratia perficit naturam, non supplet*. Like Bonhoeffer, he sees nature not as supplanted but as fulfilled by divine grace. In other words, while the vision that sees Christ's form in creation is reserved for those made new in Christ, things are not invested with beauty ex nihilo, but rather our eyes have changed and perceive what they could not see before. For indeed, "the becoming human of God fulfills the entire ontology and aesthetics of created being" (*Herrlichkeit*, 1:26). For Balthasar not even the scriptures are the primary speech and self-expression of God. Rather God has expressed himself in "Jesus Christ as the unique one, who is nonetheless interpretable only in the entire context of human history and the entire existing cosmos. He is the word and the picture, the expression and the exegesis of God through the entire human apparatus of historical existence between birth and death with all stages and conditions of life, using both individual and social structures. He *is* what he expresses, namely, God, but he is not whom he expresses, namely, the Father. Incomparable paradox as the origin of Christian and thus of all aesthetics" (ibid., 1:27). The incarnation is the archetype and the pinnacle of God's self-expression in the works of creation. This means that beauty cannot be, as in the Greek conception, impersonal harmony, but beauty is a personal, ethical category.

Ethics as the Foundation of Aesthetics

Like Bonhoeffer and Levinas, Balthasar upholds personal transcendence as the limit of philosophy. Only ethical transcendence, modeled on God's ultimate personal transcendence, both limits and fulfills philosophy's desire for self-knowledge. Even the commerce between God and the soul advocated by Augustine, the hermeneutical circle between knowledge of self and knowledge of God, can easily slide into Platonic, idealistic, or Stoic registers unless personal transcendence is maintained.

Balthasar believes philosophers have customarily rejected this personal transcendence, which invaded Western thought in the form of the Hebraic deity, because they feared for the immanent, the ordinary (*Spiritus Creator*, 273). Yet contrary to their fears, the radical transcendence of a sovereign creator God properly grounds the ordinary and renders the world more profoundly mysterious than the rational cosmos of the Greeks.

Balthasar also concludes that philosophy, tragically still imprisoned in the Greek realm of ideas, cannot understand the importance of the personal. The question, as Levinas has already pointed out, is the question of the human: "Exactly at this point we find the limit of philosophy. . . . In philosophical ethics, questions of interpersonal relations are never approached and dealt with other than on the assumption of identical human nature in all subjects" (*Spiritus Creator*, 273). Balthasar agrees with Levinas that from Plato to Kant, the other is always a version of oneself. The unique and utterly irreplaceable value of each person "cannot be grounded philosophically" but is found only in Christian thought.

This distinctively ethical element in intellectual history is found not in any structure but in the personal transcendence of God: "The distinctively Christian begins and ends with the revelation that the eternal God loves each human being infinitely, which is revealed concretely in the fact that he dies a redemptive death in human form for this beloved 'you.'" Only here do we find personal identity based not on sameness but on otherness: "I cannot know who I am through the motto *gnosi seauton* nor [Augustine's] *noverim me* but only through the effect of Christ's act, which tells me both at once: how valuable I am to God and how far I had been from him" (*Spiritus Creator*, 273).

This human-divine relation is the original meaning of being (*der Ursinn des Seins*). Like Bonhoeffer, Balthasar's transcendence gains its positive ethical quality from a concrete ethical act of universal scope and importance: Christ's death on the cross. The other is an epiphany of Christ, but his otherness is qualified by the same concrete act: "In Christ we encounter the love of God in our neighbor." This address requires one's answer in responsible service to the other. Thus in Balthasar we find, as we did in Bonhoeffer, an immediate reciprocity that cannot lapse into sameness because it is founded on the radical otherness of the incarnate God. In this way, we become to one another a sacramental presence, a reminder of our blindness to God's presence in creation. Interhuman relations are in this sense "an emergency ration of encounters with the divine" (*Spiritus Creator*, 273).

With the incarnation, the true, the good, and the beautiful are no longer concepts but become personal characteristics defined by God's self-revelation in history, which serves, whether we acknowledge it or not, "as the highest and archetypical beautiful" (*Herrlichkeit*, 1:65). Creation and redemption are nothing other than God's self-presentation and self-interpretation in being, in the real world of nature, humanity, and history (ibid., 1:112). To speak with Heidegger, human existence is *ecstatic* not toward an impersonal Logos but toward God.

The Christian structure of knowledge in which art participates is thus similar to and yet radically different from Heidegger's. Self-knowledge is achieved not by grasping an object but by being held in the object's grasp (*Herrlichkeit*, 1:126). Gadamer and Heidegger do indeed speak of artwork as having exactly this effect on us. The proper response is a posture of open-minded listening to be shaped by the text or piece of art rather than shaping it willfully. Only the theological foundation unfolded by Balthasar, however, gives a reason for this trusting stance toward art while providing also an ethical measure by which we can judge its content. This measure is not, however, our human judgment, but the measure found in God's self-revelation (ibid.).

Incarnational Aesthetics

Balthasar claims, in fact, that God's self-revelation anticipated and completed the Greek Logos. The incarnational model of aesthetics thus ratifies Heidegger's and Gadamer's view of art by giving it the necessary ontological traction. The primordial beautiful, God's self-revelation in Christ, dictates the revealing structure of aesthetics. Art and texts have their own integrity, their inviolable wholeness and authority. Heidegger's *aletheia*, his term for the revelatory nature of art, finds its fullest expression in the theology from which it is derived. Like God's self-revelation, the truth of art is an event whose truth lies in its self-presentation ("Der Ursprung des Kunstwerks," 41). Art is not merely an accident hiding the true substance of truth, but it stands forth as truth, a truth that addresses our actual existence in its entirety. Balthasar recognizes that Heidegger's ontology of art owes much to theology. It echoes God's self-revelation in divine freedom, which "like a work of art coincides with the highest necessity" (*Herrlichkeit*, 1:469). Each artwork has its own integrity and unity in which it stands and must be understood. This understanding, as Gadamer insists, is an experience akin to the theological notions of understanding: not a detached theoretical exercise but an existential application. Gadamer's insistence of openness toward the text and its integrity finds its proper home in incarnational theology.

Balthasar's incarnational aesthetics also addresses Levinas's concern that aesthetics arrests the ethical word of life. Levinas pits the pleasure of art against serious ethical responsibility. Art belongs to the realm of ontology, a sphere as necessary for the emergence of the ethical word as it is hostile to its transcendence. Incarnational ontology, however, by fusing immanence and transcendence as divine form avoids Levinas's dualism. For theological hermeneutics, contrary to Levinas, the pleasure of art is not "asymmetrical" to our experience of transcendence. Balthasar rejects Levinas's notion that divine transcendence leads to social-ethical action while art entices us to mere contemplation. His identification of radical transcendence with the divine beautiful allows him to argue, rather, that "the pleasurable enjoyment of art is already just below the threshold of the truly beautiful." That is why Plato spoke of encountering sublime beauty as an overwhelming, shattering experience of unsurpassable majesty that demands something like worship. Without the incarnation as the archetypically beautiful, however, this sense of unreachable majesty so necessary to the experience of the sublimely beautiful leads to melancholy since we can never attain it. Only in the Christian aesthetic, says Balthasar, is the adoring heart taken up into a relation with the beautiful, without, however, collapsing the distinction and distance between transcendence and self (*Herrlichkeit*, 1:309).

Balthasar's theological position on aesthetics, on the realm of art and texts, is reminiscent of Derrida's view that we cannot extricate ourselves from the linguistic-intellectual tradition in which we exist. Balthasar expands this notion: just as we cannot get out of metaphysics, we cannot get out of the divine Logos. The incarnation is, to use Gadamer's terminology, the effective historical phenomenon that directs our experience of art. In reading Goethe, for example, an entire epoch rises up, influencing our understanding and being influenced by us. In the same way, God's created ontological context influences the Christian when he or she "reads" Christ; in this case, however, not only the historical but also the ontological implications of created world and redemptive work determine our reading. Through Christ's *Gestalt*, things are put in proper perspective. Reading texts thus always presupposes an ontological context. So, for example, when Christians read the biblical text, they do not perceive its truths by an irrational leap of faith but rather "see" them with the experiential, spiritual perception common to those who are in communion with God.

The incarnational model redeems aesthetics from irrelevant aestheticism and gives it full existential weight. Aesthetics is, in fact, crucial for an adequate biblical hermeneutics. The scriptures are held together by the contours (or, as Balthasar calls it, the *Gestalt*) of Christ, so that the biblical portrait of the incarnate Logos is its own measure and proportion. If we try to tinker with it and selectively highlight either Christ's historicity or his divine transcendence, we misinterpret and distort Christ's unique existence and destroy the integrity of his portrait. The very figure of Christ lends the text its inherent integrity, and attempting to force our own prejudices on it results in "philological massacres," so that the holistic picture is butchered into stale fragments riddled with unnecessary contradictions (Balthasar, *Herrlichkeit*, 1:453). God reveals himself as he really is, and this authenticity is rooted in his existence and claims. To speak with Luther, Jesus really *is* God's Word, which must be heard in the entirety from incarnation to cross and resurrection (ibid., 1:554). Here the term "recognition" takes its proper meaning without compromising transcendence. Correlation and cohesiveness of the text, its scope, are guaranteed through Christ, whose contours are known to the reader because they suffuse and hold together the biblical text (ibid., 1:405).

Yet Balthasar argues that even the unbeliever will perceive the *Gestalt* of the divine Logos, albeit in darkened and obscured fashion. Thus any reading is in this sense natural theology because "the sensual environment is determined through and through by the central picture and event of Christ, so that in myriad ways his sensual experience puts him in touch with Christ the center." It is the Divine's prerogative of freedom, however, to reveal himself as personal address through these word pictures or to conceal himself (*Herrlichkeit*, 1:405–6). All reality is shaped by God's principal self-revelation, and yet this revelation occurs in a dialectic of concealing and revealing. Throughout history God reveals himself as the incomprehensible God: "The God of Israel, in his revelation certainly understandable and demanding an understanding of faith, proves historically to be the always incomprehensible and thus truly authentic God" (ibid., 1:440).

God is, after all, a person, and the revealing-concealing dynamic also applies to our human relationships. In the incarnation, God's revealedness is fulfilled in concealment. The more God reveals himself, the greater paradoxes become, the more our minds are boggled by the clarity of his love for humanity and yet the incomprehensibility of his nature.

Negative Theology and the Incomprehensibility of God

Within his discussion of aesthetics, Balthasar addresses the very problem John Caputo raised about understanding and self-knowledge in his advocacy of negative theology. While Caputo agrees with Balthasar that religiosity is a fundamental human attribute, religion cannot have ultimately determinable content if it wants to guard transcendence and retain universality. For him God is not an answer but a question (*On Religion*, 117). We cannot have knowledge of God but are left with Caputo's more radical hermeneutics, a *docta ignorantia* that denies positive knowledge for religion and the self. In this way, "holy undecidibility" encourages peace on earth since certain knowledge and institutionalized religion, like all settled interpretations, necessarily lead to violence (ibid., 92–100). Caputo's dilemma, of course, is that his consequent encouragement to enact divine love rather than to think about God's attributes drains all actual content from love. Perhaps this is why crucial questions, such as how the violent action of the cross fits with this general divine love, are not even taken up.

And yet it is the cross that indicates the limits of human understanding. As we have seen, Gadamer, another advocate of learned ignorance, believed that the cross served as a transcendental boundary in the Kantian sense: at the cross, all knowledge ceases; we must finally admit that final meaning and self-understanding are completely inaccessible to the human mind. This demonstrates that at best we can know that we don't know. He called this condition *ignoramus* and tried to make it the basis for a global dialogue that could now include religions because they can give up their pretensions to ultimate meanings.

Both Caputo and Gadamer, however, underestimate the incarnation. Balthasar's concept of the revealed, incomprehensible God shows us a way that preserves transcendence *and* allows self-knowledge. It is indeed true that human art and understanding are arrested by the transcendence of the cross. Here the earthly senses must die with Christ in order to be raised with him (*Herrlichkeit*, 1:475). So far, Gadamer is correct to speak of the cross as a transcendental barrier that resists human understanding; the cross, however, is not merely the contradiction of meaning itself (*Sinnwiderspruch*). On the contrary, the cross is also the very meaning of meaning, because "we can understand [God's] contours insofar as it dissolves the contradiction between God and a godless world. It would be unthinkable and unworthy of our belief to claim that the document that God has given us to read is undecipherable" (ibid., 1:457). The violence of the cross, as the premoderns knew so well, has meaning because it was the death died not only for humanity but for every individual human being. Hence the divine aesthetics of the cross arrest and yet also inform human art and self-knowledge.

Moreover, the drama of redemption presents us with the divine form of beauty, which is Christ. This beauty, however, incorporates also the trauma of violence. Balthasar argues that even human art that wants to be taken seriously must incorporate the demonic if it does not want to become irrelevant aestheticism (*Herrlichkeit*, 1:442–43).

For Balthasar God's concrete self-revelation warrants neither Caputo's and Gadamer's negative theology nor positivistic religious fundamentalism. Instead of a philosophical negative theology in which God remains completely hidden, Balthasar suggests a "revelatory negative theology" in which God truly shows himself in his *Gestalt*, so that even in his incomprehensibleness, he truly appears to us as he is. As a result of the incarnation and the cross, "the incomprehensibleness of God is now no longer a mere absence of knowledge but faith-knowledge determined by God's self-revelation: the overwhelming, shattering incomprehensibility of the fact that God loved us to the extent of giving his only Son for us, that the God of fullness emptied himself not only into his creation but into the modality of sin-determined, God-estranged, and death-bound existence—that is, the concealment that appears as self-disclosure, the comprehendible incomprehensibility of God" (*Herrlichkeit*, 1:443). The incarnation thus directly addresses Caputo's central question: we *do* know what we love when we love our God, and it "blows our minds."

CONCLUSION

Recovering theological hermeneutics cannot mean a simple return to presuppositions of premodern theology, as if centuries of philosophical development had never occurred. While I have defended premodern hermeneutics against its caricatures in hermeneutic philosophy, it remains nonetheless true that its insights must be recovered by working *through* modern and postmodern hermeneutic philosophies rather than by circumventing them. My attempt at doing so was motivated primarily by the desire to examine our interpretive prejudices on two main fronts.

First, theological hermeneutics must realize the full extent of its resources. I hope to have shown that premodern hermeneutics had a fully fledged worldview, an ontology of reading embedded in a hermeneutic circle (knowledge of self and knowledge of God). This hermeneutic circle was not vicious but actually allowed these thinkers to expand interpretive horizons and engage intelligently with philosophical and scientific developments of their time. Our recovery of premodern hermeneutics makes clear that we cannot equate the Puritan and Pietist thinkers of this study with the ahistorical, antihermeneutical ethos represented by much North American Christian fundamentalism.

While such mistaken comparisons by philosophers are understandable in light of their personal experiences with such Christianity, to dismiss theology on the basis of these distorted views of Christian theology commits the ethical and hermeneutical sin par excellence: it does not give the other a fair hearing. It is my hope that the preceding sections on incarnational hermeneutics would convince even deconstructionist theologians like Caputo that, at least for theology, knowing the Secret in no way means the *possession* of truth/Truth. If anything, truth in the

317

relational encounter with God possesses and grasps us, in its revealing and concealing relation.

At the same time, I hope to have shown that caricatures of postmodern thought are equally unhelpful. Philosophers like Heidegger, Gadamer, Levinas, Derrida, Critchley, and Caputo are serious in their concern for ethics and have much to teach theology. Theology must shed any pretensions to timeless, absolute knowledge and will do itself a great favor by abandoning a scientific model of unmediated, naked truth. Instead theology should embrace a hermeneutical model of self-understanding in which truth is not naked but clothed in the self-giving otherness of God, who offers himself in the incarnation for our contemplation and emulation. The incarnation provides what postmodern ethical philosophy seeks: it embodies radical transcendence in history and time with a human face, and it offers a social subjectivity as persons in relation.

Complemented by the doctrine of the Trinity, incarnational theology offers an ontology that places being-in-community at the heart of reality and gives ethical transcendence definite contours in the divine kenotic and redemptive events of cross and resurrection. By becoming human, utter transcendence becomes graspable to human preunderstanding, and yet the extraordinary revealed within these forms transcends them infinitely. Our subjective impressions are always challenged and ever proven wrong by the figure of Christ. No age or culture, no intellectual or poet is privileged in his knowledge of God; this is so, however, not because God is without definite content but because meaning and knowledge radiate from Christ himself rather than originate with us.

Our recovery demonstrated the fundamentally ethical nature of theological interpretation. The central idea that makes ethical transcendence and its communication possible is that in the incarnation, truth is a person rather than a proposition or idea. Theological hermeneutics is conducted on the basis of personal knowledge. It may be a long time until theology can fully embrace the realization that knowledge is interpretation without thinking it has lost something substantial. At the same time, however, philosophical hermeneutics cannot equate the incarnation simply with Kant's transcendental barrier in its denial of self-knowledge.

God's self-revelation is the measure of ethics, of meaning, of truth, and of the beautiful. The incarnation is transcendence in immanence and allows for their conceptual relation by avoiding either total asymmetry or totality. In beginning with the incarnation, hermeneutics becomes truly radical. One of Levinas's penetrating questions to theology was, "Can theological hermeneutics live with uncertainty?" The answer is a qualified yes: uncertainty in the sense that knowledge modeled on the incarnation cannot be predicted or fully comprehended. This is due not so much to our finitude (that is, of course, also a factor) but primarily to God's own otherness. "Complete clarity would please human reason but harm our will. Pride must be broken," writes Balthasar (*Herrlichkeit*, 1:464). Bonhoeffer has shown us how a hermeneutical appropriation of God's self-revelation occurs within the Word structure of the church.

On this incarnational basis alone dare I restate my overall argument: *hermeneutics must be founded on theology* rather than the other way around. *Theology is, however, hermeneutical* in the sense I have outlined here. A theological incarnational hermeneutics addresses three interdependent key points in the current hermeneutical debate: ethical transcendence, subjectivity, and self-knowledge.

Ethical Transcendence

Levinas, we remember, posits a deep rift between ontology and ethics, between being and transcendence. Much of his later work tries to describe the relation between these two spheres. We have also seen that Bonhoeffer called this mode of existence "being in Adam," a deep disunity in human existence. Only the incarnation heals that rift by restoring our communion with God. Being in Christ opens our eyes to an ontology in which transcendence and immanence coexist. In this incarnational ontology, the ethical saying is fully embodied in the structures of language, society, and history without any loss of transcendence. Based on this foundational notion of immanent transcendence, theological hermeneutics can then develop a less traumatic notion of subjectivity than that of Levinas. Selfhood is understood as person in relation, a subjectivity that neither begins with, nor is defined as, solitary, independent consciousness but is brought to life by the call of the other. Here theological hermeneutics is close to the theologically inspired thought of Levinas: the self cannot found itself by itself.

Yet incarnational subjectivity is richer and circumvents the problem of "hostage taking." While the self is formed irrevocably by the call of the other to responsibility, I have argued that this call is possible only as the electing call of God in Christ, by which we gain an identity that is sustained not by us but by concrete hermeneutical appropriation in community through word and sacrament. The origin of subjectivity is ethical in a qualified sense, qualified as love in the concrete act of God's self-abnegation in the incarnation and the cross. Through the embodiment of God's ethical transcendence, history, and time, Levinas's faint "trace of God in the face of the other" gains definite ontological-ethical dimensions: an I-thou reciprocity in which each participant is from the first called to responsibility by Christ, the incarnate transcendence himself. I can therefore serve the other fully without fearing the loss of my own identity because it is not mine (nor the other's but the ultimate Other's, God's) to give.

Subjectivity

Theological hermeneutics also offers a richer subjectivity than Levinas's notion of a substitutionary self. This concept is, as we have seen in Bonhoeffer's appropriation of Luther, a valid principle; it becomes rather unpleasant, however, when combined with the notion of radical hospitality—who is it that demands my allegiance and servitude? Incarnational theology shifts the burden of substitution onto the incarnation and so qualifies otherness as sacrificial love. On this basis, subjectivity is still fully emergent as the call of otherness but in a carefully qualified way that loses none of the transcendence Levinas desires. Only in this context can substitutionary selfhood be a good thing. Here both theologians and philosophers can learn from Bonhoeffer that self-identity is a matter of trust. As Bonhoeffer put it in his prison poem "Who Am I": "Who am I? They mock me, these lonely questions of mine. Whoever I am, you know me, O God, I'm thine" (*Widerstand und Ergebung*, 187).

The essence of theological anthropology is identity as given and held by God and its appropriation in daily life through the power of the Holy Spirit. Based on this subjectivity, self-knowledge is not certain in the Cartesian sense but is based on trust in God's self-disclosure. This is true phronesis: wisdom and application are given by God "according to the wealth of his grace which he has multiplied toward us with all wisdom and understanding [*sophia kai phronesei*]" (Eph. 1:8). Human interpretation is both made possible and humbled by its dependence on God.

Self-Knowledge and Aesthetics

Finally, theological hermeneutics offers a viable concept of self-knowledge through human artifacts. Since the incarnate divine Logos configures reality, we find this model in the daily structures of human knowing. We gain knowledge of the world not in some immediate way but in dependence on texts and contexts. Classical or eminent texts, as Gadamer calls them, the texts and artworks that seem timeless, are not, of course, outside time. Yet even the most radical historicization will not succeed in rendering them completely relative to their time period because they address the great questions of purpose and humanity, of the misery and nobility of humankind, which find fulfillment in the incarnation. We must make room, of course, for cultural preferences and prejudices, but even so, even literary canon formation owes much to common questions of ultimate meaning.

Does this mean that the Christian can get the text right and the non-Christian always staggers around in the dark? Not at all. Aside from human finitude, we have argued that textual interpretation follows the incarnational model of revealing-concealing. This is why Gadamer's philosophical hermeneutics, built as it is on Heideggerian ontology, rings so true. Interpretation remains an infinite task and is begun again by each successive generation, indeed, by each successive reader. Human and cultural uniqueness demands this. Yet the great questions directed to and expressed by these texts cluster around "being human and becoming human." It is, in short, the ethical question. As Helmut Thielicke puts it: "Only if human life is unconditionally sacred and humanity is made the measure of all things are we protected against its being made a thing or a tool and thus consigned to the scrap heap, as machines are when they are no longer of use." The decisive issue is to find a modus of truth that gets at "the real truth of humanity." But even phenomenology, the break with Kant's subject-object split, does not "get at our essential being which is built on freedom and responsibility" (*Being Human, Becoming Human*, 9–10). It is Levinas's accomplishment to have breached this fundamental question and to have invaded philosophy with its ethical demand for radical transcendence to uphold the dignity of the human.

But are we not embarking here on the Levinasian path of aesthetics bashing? Does not art and hence one of the main hermeneutical sources for self-knowledge become reduced to ethics? Even in a broader sense, does tradition become merely an accidental plane for the substance of ethics, a frivolous adornment for stern truth? Are its detractors right to oppose theological hermeneutics as another instantiation of a somber Puritan hermeneutics? On the contrary, both Bonhoeffer and Balthasar have shown that incarnational theology actually establishes aesthetics.

Finally, based on the incarnational model, knowledge and self-knowledge about human affairs occur only in application, as phronesis. What a text means, it always means *pro me*, in application to myself. This self, however, stands as a person in relation within a community and the tradition that sustains it. In this way, the incarnation allows us to ground truth ontologically as that which transcends the subject-object divide. Truth is always subjective and relative to cultural-historical context. If it were not *relative* in this sense, it could never be *relevant* either. Yet Gadamer is correct to protest that this in no way implies relativism. Texts, art, objects reveal themselves as they are, even if such revelation involves revealing and concealing.

Without reiterating every argument we have made in these last chapters, our basic claim should become apparent and plausible, namely, that theological hermeneutics provides the ontology necessary for the interpretive principles of philosophical hermeneutics. In the end, theological hermeneutics provides us with interpretive principles that allow interpretation to be truly ethical and character forming, the very things that both philosophical hermeneutics and radical postmodern hermeneutics strive for. This claim is not meant to be an arrogant triumphalism by any means. Great thinkers like Heidegger, Gadamer, and Levinas have opened up new vistas of thinking on which theological hermeneutics can build. They have done much to enable an intelligent dialogue between theology and philosophy. At the same time, however, theological hermeneutics' central claim of the divine Logos as the ground of being requires for its own integrity to be the measure and center of interpretation. There are not, to give Bonhoeffer the last word, two realms of interpretation or two spheres of human experience: a theological place of comfort for the weak and a philosophical neutral zone for those who dare to think. Heidegger was dead wrong with this assumption. Instead interpretation depends on the claim that God's being encompasses all reality:

> There are, therefore, not two realms [i.e., a realm of grace and a realm of nature], but only the one realm of Christ-reality [*Raum der Christus-wirklichkeit*], in which the reality of God and world are united. . . . Not two competing spheres that coexist and contend with each other about their limits so that questions about these limits would be decisive ones for history; rather all of reality is already drawn into Christ and brought together in him [*in ihm zusammengefasst*] and only from this center and towards this center does history move. (Bonhoeffer, *Ethik*, 43–44)

So does interpretation.

Works Cited

Aland, Kurt, E. Peschke, und M. Schmidt. *Arbeiten zur Geschichte des Pietismus*. 20 vols. Bielefeld, Ger.: Luther Verlag, 1975.

Althaus, Paul. *The Ethics of Martin Luther*. Philadelphia: Fortress Press, 1972.

Augustine. "Anti-Pelagian Writings." In *Nicene and Post-Nicene Fathers of the Christian Church*, edited by Philip Schaff, vol. 5. Grand Rapids: Eerdmans, 1971.

———. *Confessions*. Translated by R. S. Pine-Coffin. New York: Penguin, 1988.

———. *Earlier Writings*. Library of Christian Classics. Edited by John H. S. Burleigh. Philadelphia: Westminster Press, 1991.

———. *Tractates of the Gospel of John*. Washington, DC: Catholic University of America Press, 1988.

Badiou, Alain. *Ethics: An Essay on the Understanding of Evil*. New York: Verso, 2001.

Balthasar, Hans Urs von. *Herrlichkeit: Eine theologische Ästhetik*. 8 vols. Einsiedeln, Switz.: Johannes Verlag, 1961–69.

———. "Krisis: Gott begegnen in der heutigen Welt." In *Spiritus Creator*, Skizzen zur Theologie 3. Einsiedeln, Switz.: Johannes Verlag, 1967.

———. *Spiritus Creator*. Skizzen zur Theologie 3. Einsiedeln, Switz.: Johannes Verlag, 1999.

Barth, Karl. *Göttingen Dogmatics*. Translated by Geoffrey W. Bromiley. Grand Rapids: Eerdmans, 1991.

———. *The Humanity of God*. Atlanta: John Knox Press, 1976.

———. *Der Römerbrief*. Zürich: Theologischer Verlag, 1985.

———. *Theologische Fragen und Antworten*. Zollikon, Switz.: Theologischer Verlag, 1957.

———. *The Theology of Schleiermacher*. Lectures at Göttingen, Winter semester of 1923–24. Grand Rapids: Eerdmans, 1982.

Bates, William. *The Complete Works of William Bates*. Vol. 1. Harrisonburg, VA: Sprinkle Publications, 1990.

Baxter, Richard. *The Practical Works of Richard Baxter*. 4 vols. Ligonier, PA: Soli Deo Gloria, 1992.

Bayly, Lewis. *The Practice of Piety*. Ligonier, PA: Soli Deo Gloria, 1992.

Berlin, Isaiah. *The Magus of the North*. New York: Farrar, Strauss & Giroux, 1993.

Bernstein, Richard. *Beyond Objectivism and Relativism*. Philadelphia: University of Pennsylvania Press, 1991.

———. *Philosophical Profiles*. Philadelphia: University of Pennsylvania Press, 1986.

Birus, Hendrik. "Hermeneutische Wende? Anmerkungen zur Schleiermacher-Interpretation." *Euphorion* 74 (1980): 213–22.

———. "Zwischen den Zeiten: Friedrich Schleiermacher als Klassiker der neuzeitlichen Hermeneutik." In *Hermeneutische Positionen,* edited by Hendrick Birus. Göttingen: Vandenhoek & Ruprecht, 1982.

Bonhoeffer, Dietrich. *Akt und Sein*. DBW 2. Munich: Chr. Kaiser Verlag, 1988.

———. *Berlin: 1932–1933*. DBW 12. Munich: Chr. Kaiser Verlag, 1997.

———. *Ethics*. Translated by Nelville Horton Smith. New York: Touchstone, 1995.

———. *Ethik*. DBW 6. Munich: Chr. Kaiser Verlag, 1998.

———. *Predigten, Auslegungen, Meditationen*. Vol. 1, *1925–1935*. Gütersloh: Chr. Kaiser Verlag, 1984.

———. *Sanctorum Communio*. Translated by Reinhard Krauss and Nancy Lukens. Dietrich Bonhoeffer Works. Volume 1. Minneapolis: Fortress, 1998.

———. *Widerstand und Ergebung*. Gütersloh: Chr. Kaiser Verlag, 1997.

Bouwsma, William J. *John Calvin: A Sixteenth-Century Portrait*. New York: Oxford University Press, 1988.

Brecht, Martin, and Johannes van den Berg. *Der Pietismus vom siebzehnten bis zum frühen achtzehnten Jahrhundert*. 4 vols. Göttingen: Vandenhoeck & Ruprecht, 1993.

Brkic, Pero. *Heidegger und die Theologie*. Mainz: Matthias Grünwald Verlag, 1994.

Brown, Colin. *Jesus in European Protestant Thought, 1778–1860*. Grand Rapids: Baker, 1985.

Bruce, F. F. *The Epistles to the Colossians, to Philemon, and to the Ephesians*. New International Commentary on the New Testament. Grand Rapids: Eerdmans, 1984.

Bruns, Gerald. *Hermeneutics Ancient and Modern*. New Haven, CT: Yale University Press, 1992.

Bunyan, John. "The Holy War." In *The Works of John Bunyan,* vol. 3. Edinburgh: Banner of Truth, 1991.

———. "Pilgrim's Progress." In *The Works of John Bunyan*, vol. 3. Edinburgh: Banner of Truth, 1991.

Calvin, John. *Commentaries on the First Book of Moses Called Genesis*. Edited by Calvin Translation Society. Grand Rapids: Baker, 1989.

———. "The Gospel according to St. John." In *Calvin's Commentaries*, translated by T. H. L. Parker. Grand Rapids: Eerdmans, 1959.

———. *Institutes of the Christian Religion*. Edited by John T. McNeill. Translated by Ford Lewis Battles. Philadelphia: Westminster Press, 1960.

———. *Sermons on Ephesians*. Edinburgh: Banner of Truth, 1994.

Caputo, John D. *Demythologizing Heidegger*. Bloomington: Indiana University Press, 1993.

———. *More Radical Hermeneutics*. Bloomington: Indiana University Press, 2001.

———. *On Religion*. New York: Routledge, 2001.

Caputo, John D., and Mark Dooley, eds. *Questioning God*. Bloomington: Indiana University Press, 2001.

Cassirer, Ernst. *Kant's Life and Thought*. Translated by James Hadin. New Haven, CT: Yale University Press, 1981.

———. *The Question of Jean-Jacques Rousseau*. Translated by Peter Gay. New York: Columbia University Press, 1954.

Charnock, Steven. *The Works of Steven Charnock*. 4 vols. Southampton, UK: Banner of Truth, 1986.

Copleston, Frederick. *Modern Philosophy from the French Enlightenment to Kant*. Vol. 6 of *A History of Philosophy*. New York: Doubleday, 1994.

Cragg, C. R. *From Puritanism to the Age of Reason*. Cambridge: Cambridge University Press, 1966.

Critchley, Simon. *Ethics, Politics, Subjectivity*. New York: Verso, 1999.

———. *The Ethics of Deconstruction*. 2nd ed. West Lafayette, IN: Purdue University Press, 1999.

———. *Very Little—Almost Nothing: Death, Philosophy, Literature*. New York: Routledge, 1997.

Critchley, Simon, and Robert Bernasconi, eds. *The Cambridge Companion to Levinas*. Cambridge: Cambridge University Press, 2002.

Derrida, Jacques. *Of Grammatology*. Baltimore: Johns Hopkins University Press, 1976.

———. *Speech and Phenomena*. Evanston, IL: Northwestern University Press, 1973.

———. "Three Questions to Hans-Georg Gadamer." In *Dialogue and Deconstruction*, edited by Diane P. Michelfelder and Richard Palmer. Albany: State University of New York Press, 1989.

———. *Der ununterbrochene Dialog: Zwischen zwei Unendlichkeiten, das Gedicht*. Translated by Martin Gessmann, Christine Ott, and Felix Wiesler. Frankfurt am Main: Suhrkamp, 2004. An abridged version appeared in *Neue Zürcher Zeitung* 44 (22 February 2003): 69.

Dilthey, Wilhelm. *Gesammelte Schriften.* 13 vols. Stuttgart: Vandenhoeck & Ruprecht, 1964–70.

Dockery, David S. *Biblical Interpretation Then and Now: Contemporary Hermeneutics in the Light of the Early Church.* Grand Rapids: Baker, 1992.

Dostoyevsky, Fyodor. *Sämtliche Romane und Erzählungen.* Vol. 6 of *Der Spieler/ Späte Prosa.* Berlin: Aufbau Verlag, 1994.

Dutt, Carsten. *Hermeneutik, Ästhetik, praktische Philosophie: Hans-Georg Gadamer im Gespräch.* Heidelberg: Universitätsverlag Winger, 1993.

Ebeling, Gerhard. *Evangelische Evangelienauslegung: Eine Untersuchung zu Luthers Hermeneutik.* 3rd ed. Tübingen: Mohr/Siebeck, 1991.

———. *Luther: An Introduction to His Thought.* Philadelphia: Fortress, 1970.

Erasmus, Desiderius. *Enchiridion.* In vol. 1 of *Ausgewählte Schriften* (Latin and German), edited by Werner Welzig. Darmstadt: Wissenschaftliche Buchgesellschaft, 1968.

———. *Vom freien Willen.* Edited by Gerd Hahmann. Stuttgart: Vandenhoek & Ruprecht, 1967.

Fish, Stanley. *Is There a Text in This Class?* Cambridge, MA: Harvard University Press, 1980.

Flacius (Vlacich), Illyricus Matthias. *De Ratione Cognoscendi Sacras Literas: Clavis Scripturae Sacrae Tractatus I.* 1567. Edited by Lutz Geldsetzer. Reprint, Düsseldorf: Stern-Verlag, 1968.

Francke, August Hermann. *August Hermann Francke: Werke in Auswahl.* Edited by Edward Peschke. Berlin: Luther-Verlag, 1969.

———. *Lectiones Praeneticae, oder oeffentliche Ansprachen an die Studiosos Theologiae auf der Universitaet zu Halle in dem so genannten Collegio Praenetico.* Halle, 1726.

———. *Manuductio ad Lectionem Scripturae Sacrae Historicam, Grammaticam . . . et Practicam una cum Additamentis Regulas Hermeneuticas de Affectibus et Ennarationes ac Introductiones Succinctas in Aliquot Epistolas Paulinas Complectentibus.* Halle: Zeitler, 1693.

Frei, Hans. *The Eclipse of the Biblical Narrative.* New Haven, CT: Yale University Press, 1974.

Gadamer, Hans-Georg. *Gesammelte Werke.* 10 vols. Tübingen: Mohr/Siebeck, 1986–.

———. *Hans-Georg Gadamer on Education, Poetry, and History: Applied Hermeneutics.* Edited by Dieter Misgeld and Graeme Nicholson. Translated by Lawrence Schmidt and Monica Reuss. Albany: State University of New York Press, 1992.

———. *Kleine Schriften.* Tübingen: Mohr/Siebeck, 1976.

———. *Lektion des Jahrhunderts: Ein philosophischer Dialog mit Riccardo Dottori.* Hamburg: LIT Verlag, 2002.

————. "The Nature of Things." In *Philosophical Hermeneutics*, edited by David E. Linge. Berkeley: University of California Press, 1976.

————. "On the Origins of Philosophical Hermeneutics." In *Philosophical Apprenticeships*, translated by Robert R. Sullivan. Cambridge, MA: MIT Press, 1985.

————. *Philosophical Hermeneutics*. Edited by David E. Linge. Berkeley: University of California Press, 1976.

————. *Reason in the Age of Science*. Cambridge, MA: MIT Press, 1996.

————. "Reflections on My Philosophical Journey." In *The Philosophy of Hans-Georg Gadamer*, edited by Lewis Edwin Hahn, vol. 24. Library of Living Philosophers. Peru, IL: Open Court, 1997.

————. "Reply to Jacques Derrida." In *Dialogue and Deconstruction*, edited by Diane Michefelder and Richard Palmer. Albany: State University of New York Press, 1994.

————. *Truth and Method*. Translated by Garrett Barden and John Cumming. New York: Continuum, 1994.

Gardner, Sebastian. *Kant and the Critique of Pure Reason*. London: Routledge, 1999.

Garret, Don. *The Cambridge Companion to Spinoza*. Cambridge: Cambridge University Press, 1995.

Graham, Fred W. *The Constructive Revolutionary John Calvin and His Socio-Economic Impact*. Atlanta: John Knox Press, 1978.

Green, Garrett. *Theology, Hermeneutics, and Imagination: The Crisis of Interpretation at the End of Modernity*. Cambridge: Cambridge University Press, 2000.

Grondin, Jean. *Introduction to Philosophical Hermeneutics*. New Haven, CT: Yale University Press, 1991.

————. *Sources of Hermeneutics*. Albany: State University of New York Press, 1995.

Harrisville, Roy, and Walter Sunberg. *The Bible in Modern Culture*. Grand Rapids: Eerdmans, 1995.

Hays, Richard B. *Echoes of Scripture in the Letters of Paul*. New Haven, CT: Yale University Press, 1989.

————. *The Moral Vision of the New Testament*. New York: Harper Collins, 1996.

Heidegger, Martin. *Identität und Differenz*. 1957. Reprint, Stuttgart: Klett-Cotta, 2002.

————. *An Introduction to Metaphysics*. New Haven, CT: Yale University Press, 1987.

————. *Nietzsche II*. Stuttgart: Neske, 1998.

————. *Sein und Zeit*. Tübingen: Max Niemeyer, 1993.

————. "Der Ursprung des Kunstwerks." In *Holzwege*. Frankfurt am Main: Vittorio Klostermann, 1994.

Henry, Matthew: *Matthew Henry's Commentary on the Whole Bible.* Peabody, MA: Hendrickson, 1991.

Hirsch, E. D. *Validity in Interpretation.* New Haven, CT: Yale University Press, 1969.

Howe, John. *The Works of the Rev. John Howe.* London: Soli Deo Gloria, 1990.

Ingraffia, Brian. *Postmodern Theory and Biblical Theology.* Cambridge: Cambridge University Press, 1995.

Jakob, Michael. *Aussichten des Denkens: Gespräche mit Emmanuel Lévinas, Georg Steiner, Jean Starobinski, Cioran, Michel Serres, René Girard, Pierre Klossowksi, André du Bouchet, Paul Virilio.* Munich: Wilhelm Finke Verlag, 1994.

Jeffrey, David Lyle. *People of the Book: Christian Identity and Literary Culture.* Grand Rapids: Eerdmans, 1996.

Kant, Immanuel. *The Critique of Practical Reason.* Edited by Mary J. Gregor. Cambridge: Cambridge University Press, 1997.

———. *Kritik der reinen Vernunft.* Hamburg: Felix Meiner Verlag, 1998.

———. *Religion within the Limits of Reason Alone.* 1793. Reprint, New York: Harper & Row, 1960.

Kearney, Richard. *States of Mind: Dialogues with Contemporary Thinkers.* New York: New York University Press, 1995.

Kisiel, Theodore. *The Genesis of Heidegger's Being and Time.* Berkeley: University of California Press, 1993.

Kistler, Don, ed. *The Puritans on Conversion.* Edinburgh: Soli Deo Gloria, 1996.

Lawrence, Fred. "Gadamer, the Hermeneutic Revolution, and Theology." In *The Cambridge Companion to Gadamer*, edited by Robert J. Dostal. Cambridge: Cambridge University Press, 2002.

Lessing, Gotthold Ephraim. *Die Erziehung des Menschengeschlechts.* Vol. 8 of *Gesammelte Werke.* Munich: Carl Hanser Verlag, 1959.

Levinas, Emmanuel. *Alterity and Transcendence.* New York: Columbia University Press, 1999.

———. *Collected Philosophical Papers.* Pittsburgh: Duquesne University Press, 1987.

———. *Entre Nous.* New York: Columbia University Press, 1998.

———. *Der Humanismus des anderen Menschen.* Hamburg: Felix Meiner, 1989.

———. *Is It Righteous to Be?* Stanford, CA: Stanford University Press, 2001.

———. *Of God Who Comes to Mind.* Stanford, CA: Stanford University Press, 1998.

———. *Otherwise Than Being, or Beyond Essence.* Pittsburgh: Duquesne University Press, 1998.

———. *Outside the Subject.* Stanford, CA: Stanford University Press, 1993.

———. "Philosophy and the Idea of the Infinite." In *To the Other: An Introduction to the Philosophy of Emmanuel Levinas,* by Adriaan Peperzak. West Lafayette, IN: Purdue University Press, 1993.

———. *Proper Names*. Stanford, CA: Stanford University Press, 1976.

———. *Totality and Infinity*. 1969. Reprint, Pittsburgh: Duquesne University Press, 1998.

Lovelace, Richard F. *The American Pietism of Cotton Mather: Origins of American Evangelism*. Grand Rapids: Christian University, 1979.

Luther, Martin. *The Bondage of the Will*. Translated by O. R. Johnston and J. I. Packer. Westwood, NJ: Revell, 1957.

———. *Commentary on Romans*. Translated by J. Theodore Muller. Grand Rapids: Kregel, 1976.

———. *Kommentar zum Galaterbrief*. Calwer Luther Ausgabe 10. Stuttgart: Calwer, 1996.

———. *Luther Deutsch*: *Die Werke Martin Luthers in neuer Auswahl für die Gegenwart*. Band 1. Der neue Glaube. Hrsg. Kurt Aland. Berlin: Evangelische Verlagsanstalt, 1948.

———. *Luthers Werke: Kritische Gesamtausgabe*. Weimar: H. Böhlau, 1883–.

———. *Predigten über die Christusbotschaft*. Calwer Luther Ausgabe 5. Stuttgart: Calwer, 1996.

———. *Predigten über den Weg der Kirche*. Calwer Luther Ausgabe 6. Stuttgart: Calwer, 1996.

———. *Das schöne Confitemini*. Calwer Luther Ausgabe 7. Stuttgart: Calwer, 1996.

———. *Sermon von den guten Werken*. Calwer Luther Ausgabe 3. Stuttgart: Calwer, 1996.

———. "Von Kaufhandlung." In *Von Weltlicher Obrigkeit*. Calwer Luther Ausgabe 4. Stuttgart: Calwer, 1996.

———. *Works*. American ed. Saint Louis: Concordia, 1955–86.

Maier, Gerhard. *Biblical Hermeneutics*. Wheaton, IL: Crossway Books, 1994.

———. *Das Ende der historisch-kritischen Methode*. Wuppertal, Ger.: Brockhaus, 1974.

Milbank, John. *The Word Made Strange*. Oxford: Blackwell, 1998.

Milton, John. *Complete Poems and Major Prose*. Edited by Merritt Y. Hughes. New York: Macmillan, 1957.

Morgan, John. *Godly Learning: Puritan Attitudes towards Reason, Learning, and Education, 1560–1640*. New York: Cambridge University Press, 1986.

Muller, Richard. *Post-Reformation Reformed Dogmatics*. 2 vols. Grand Rapids: Baker, 1987–92.

———. *Post-Reformation Reformed Dogmatics*. Vol. 3, *The Divine Essence and Attributes*. Grand Rapids: Baker, 2003.

Muller, Richard, and John L. Thompson. "The Significance of Precritical Exegesis." In *Biblical Interpretation in the Era of the Reformation*. Grand Rapids: Eerdmans, 1996.

Nash, Ronald. *The Word of God and the Mind of Man: The Crisis of Revealed Truth in Contemporary Theology*. Grand Rapids: Zondervan, 1982.

Newbigin, Lesslie. *Foolishness to the Greeks*. Grand Rapids. Eerdmans, 1986.

Nietzsche, Friedrich. *Die Fröhliche Wissenschaft*. Kritische Studienausgabe. Edited by Giorgio Colli and Mazzino Montiari. München: de Gruyter, 1999.

———. *Werke in drei Bänden*. Gütersloh, Ger.: Mohndruck, 1982.

Owen, John. *Biblical Theology: Or the Nature, Origin, Development, and Study of Theological Truth in Six Books*. Translated by Stephen B. Westcott. Pittsburgh: Soli Deo Gloria, 1994.

———. *The Works of John Owen*. Edited by William Goold. 16 vols. London: Banner of Truth, 1967.

Palmer, R. E. *Hermeneutics: Interpretation Theory in Schleiermacher, Dilthey, Heidegger, and Gadamer*. Evanston, IL: Northwestern University Press, 1969.

Pelikan, Jaroslav. *Luther the Expositor*. Companion volume to *Luther's Works*. Saint Louis: Concordia, 1959.

Perkins, William. "A Golden Chain." In *The Works of William Perkins*, vol. 3. Courtney Reformation Classics. Cambridge: Burlington Press, 1970.

Peschke, Erhard. *August Hermann Francke und die Bibel: Studien zur Entwicklung seiner Hermeneutik*. Pietismus und die Bible. Witten, Ger.: Luther-Verlag, 1970.

Polanyi, Michael, and Harry Prosch. *Meaning*. Chicago: University of Chicago Press, 1977.

Poole, Matthew. *Commentary on the Holy Bible*. Edinburgh: Banner of Truth, 1962.

Ranew, Nathanael. *Solitude Improved by Divine Meditation*. Ligonier, PA: Soli Deo Gloria, 1992.

Reader, Siegfried. "Luther als Ausleger und Übersetzer der Heiligen Schrift." In *Leben und Werk Martin Luthers von 1526 bis 1546*. Göttingen: Vandenhoeck & Ruprecht, 1983.

Robinson, James, and John Cobb, eds. *The New Hermeneutic: Discussions among Continental and American Theologians*. New York: Harper & Row, 1964.

Rorty, Richard. "Do We Need Ethical Principles?" University of British Columbia lecture. Typescript, 1994.

———. "Remarks on Deconstruction and Pragmatism." In *Deconstruction and Pragmatism*. Edited by Chantal Mouffe and Simon Critchley. London: Routledge, 1999.

Rousseau, Jean-Jacques. *Émile, ou de l'Éducation*. Paris: Charpentier, 1848.

Safranski, Rüdiger. *Ein Meister aus Deutschland*. Frankfurt am Main: Fischer, 1997.

Schleiermacher, Friedrich. *The Christian Faith*. Edited by H. R. Mackintosh and J. S. Stewend. New York: Harper & Row, 1963.

———. *Der christliche Glaube*. 2 vols. Berlin: Walter de Gruyter, 1960.

———. *Dialektik*. Edited by Andreas Arndt. 1811. Reprint, Hamburg: Felix Meiner Verlag, 1986.

———. *Hermeneutics: The Handwritten Manuscripts*. Edited by Heinz Kimmerle. Translated by J. Forstman and James Duke. Missoula, MT: Scholars Press, 1977.

———. *Hermeneutics and Criticism and Other Writings*. Edited by Andrew Bowie. Cambridge: Cambridge University Press, 1998.

———. *Schleiermachers Werke*. 4 vols. Edited by Johann Bauer and Otto Braun. Leipzig: Fritz Eckhardt Verlag, 1910.

Scholz, Gunter. *Ethik und Hermeneutik: Schleiermachers Grundlegung der Geisteswissenschaften*. Frankfurt am Main: Suhrkamp, 1995.

Scudder, Henry. *The Christian's Daily Walk*. Montville, NJ: Sprinkle Publications, 1984.

Smith, J. K. *The Fall of Interpretation*. Downers Grove, IL: InterVarsity Press, 1999.

Spener, Philipp Jacob. *Die allgemeine Gottesgelehrtheit aller gläubigen Christen und rechtschaffenden Theologen aus Gottes Wort erwiesen und der sogenannten Theosophiae Horbiospenerianae zur gründlichen Verantwortung gesetzt von Philipp Jacob Spener*. Frankfurt, 1680.

———. *Christliche Verpflegung der Armen*. Frankfurt an der Oder, 1697.

———. *Die evangelischen Lebenspflichten*. 1688. Reprint, Frankfurt am Main, 1707.

———. *Natur und Gnade oder der Unterschied der Wercke, so aus natürlichen Kräfften und aus den Gnaden-würckungen des heiligen Geistes herkommen, und also eines äusserlich erbarn und wahrhafftig christlichen gottseligen Lebens, nach der Regel göttlichen Worts*. Frankfurt am Main, 1705.

———. *Der neue Mensch*. Edited by Hans Georg Feller. Stuttgart: Steinkopf, 1966.

———. *Das nötige und nützliche Lesen der Heiligen Schrifft, mit einigen darzu dienlichen Erinnerungen in einer Vorrede über die Bible vorgestellt*. Frankfurt, 1704.

———. *Pia Desideria*. Translated by Theodore Tappert. Philadelphia: Fortress Press, 1964.

———. *Vom rechtschaffenden Wachstum des Glaubens: Kleine geistliche Schrifften*. Magdeburg, 1741–42.

Steinmetz, David. "The Superiority of Pre-critical Exegesis." In *The Theological Interpretation of Scripture*, edited by Stephen E. Fowl. Malden, MA: Blackwell, 2000.

Swinnock, George. "The Christian Man's Calling." In *The Works of George Swinnock*. Edinburgh: Banner of Truth, 1982.

Taylor, Charles. *Hegel*. New York: Cambridge University Press, 1975.

———. *The Malaise of Modernity*. Concord, ON: Anansi, 1994.

———. *Sources of the Self: The Making of the Modern Identity*. Cambridge, MA: Harvard University Press, 1989.

Thielicke, Helmut. *Being Human, Becoming Human*. New York: Doubleday, 1984.

———. *The Freedom of the Christian Man*. New York: Harper & Row, 1963.

———. *Modern Faith and Thought*. Translated by Geoffrey W. Bromiley. Grand Rapids: Eerdmans, 1990.

Tillich, Paul. *A History of Christian Thought*. Edited by Carl E. Braaten. London: SCM Press, 1968.

Torrance, T. F. *Calvin's Doctrine of Man*. London: Lowe & Brydone, 1952.

van Buren, John. "Martin Heidegger, Martin Luther." In *Reading Heidegger from the Start: Essays in His Earliest Thought*, 159–74. New York: State University of New York Press, 1994.

Vincent, Nathaniel. *The Conversion of a Sinner*. 1669. Reprinted in *The Puritans on Conversion*, edited by Don Kistler. Ligonier, PA: Soli Deo Gloria, 1990.

Westminster Confession of Faith. Glasgow: Free Presbyterian Publications, 1985.

Wright, N. T. *The Climax of the Covenant*. Minneapolis: Fortress, 1993.

———. *Jesus and the Victory of God*. Minneapolis: Fortress, 1996.

———. *The New Testament and the People of God*. Minneapolis: Fortress, 1992.

———. *What Saint Paul Really Said*. Grand Rapids: Eerdmans, 1997.

Yule, George. *The Puritans in Politics*. Abingdon, UK: Sutton Courtney Press, 1981.

Zimmermann, Jens. "Ignoramus: Gadamer's 'Religious Turn.'" *Symposium: Journal of the Canadian Society for Hermeneutics and Postmodern Thought* 6, no. 2 (Fall 2002): 203–17.

Zizioulas, John D. *Being as Communion*. New York: St. Vladimir's Press, 2002.

Zweig, Stefan. *Castello gegen Calvin oder ein Gewissen gegen die Gewalt*. Frankfurt am Main: Fisher, 1936.

NAME INDEX

Subject Index

337